INDIAN PRAIRIE PUBLIC LIBRARY
401 Plainfield Road
Darien, IL 60561

DEC 1 3 2017
4-9-18(2)

D1265873

MICHAEL GRAVES: DESIGN FOR LIFE

MICHAEL GRAVES

DESIGN FOR LIFE

IAN VOLNER

PRINCETON ARCHITECTURAL PRESS   NEW YORK

FOR MICHAEL

Published by Princeton Architectural Press
A MCEVOY GROUP COMPANY

202 Warren Street, Hudson, New York 12534
www.papress.com

© 2018 Princeton Architectural Press.
All rights reserved. Printed and bound in China.
21 20 19 18 4 3 2 1 First edition

No part of this book may be used or reproduced in any manner without
written permission from the publisher, except in the context of reviews.
Every reasonable attempt has been made to identify owners of copyright.
Errors or omissions will be corrected in subsequent editions.

Editor: Sara Stemen Image research: Nolan Boomer
Designer: Benjamin English

Special thanks to: Janet Behning, Nicola Brower, Abby Bussel,
Tom Cho, Barbara Darko, Jenny Florence, Jan Cigliano Hartman,
Susan Hershberg, Lia Hunt, Valerie Kamen, Simone Kaplan-Senchak,
Jennifer Lippert, Kristy Maier, Sara McKay, Eliana Miller,
Wes Seeley, Rob Shaeffer, Paul Wagner, and Joseph Weston of
Princeton Architectural Press —Kevin C. Lippert, publisher

Library of Congress Cataloging-in-Publication Data
NAMES: Volner, Ian, author.
TITLE: Michael Graves : design for life / Ian Volner.
DESCRIPTION: First edition. | New York : Princeton Architectural Press, 2017.
| Includes bibliographical references and index.
IDENTIFIERS: LCCN 2016059450 | ISBN 9781616895631 (alk. paper)
SUBJECTS: LCSH: Graves, Michael, 1934–2015—Criticism and interpretation.
CLASSIFICATION: LCC NA737.G72 V65 2017 | DDC 720.92—dc23
LC record available at https://lccn.loc.gov/2016059450

Contents

PROLOGUE *ix*

NOTE ON SOURCES *xv*

I	The Sea	I
II	The River and the Compass	15
III	The Book and the Doorway	41
IV	The Light	67
V	The Garden and the Machine	81
VI	The Bridge and the Hearth	III
VII	The Tower	143
VIII	The House, the Tomb, and the Teakettle	173
IX	The Sky and the Frame	195

ACKNOWLEDGMENTS 211

SELECTED BIBLIOGRAPHY 213

NOTES 217

INDEX 232

IMAGE CREDITS 240

AND THE SONG
HAD FINISHED:
THIS WAS THE STORY.

— John Ashbery, *The Double Dream of Spring*, 1970

I REQUEST, CAESAR,
BOTH OF YOU AND OF
THOSE WHO MAY
READ THE SAID BOOKS,
THAT IF ANYTHING
IS SET FORTH WITH
TOO LITTLE REGARD FOR
GRAMMATICAL RULE,
IT MAY BE PARDONED.

— Vitruvius, *De Architectura*, I.1.17

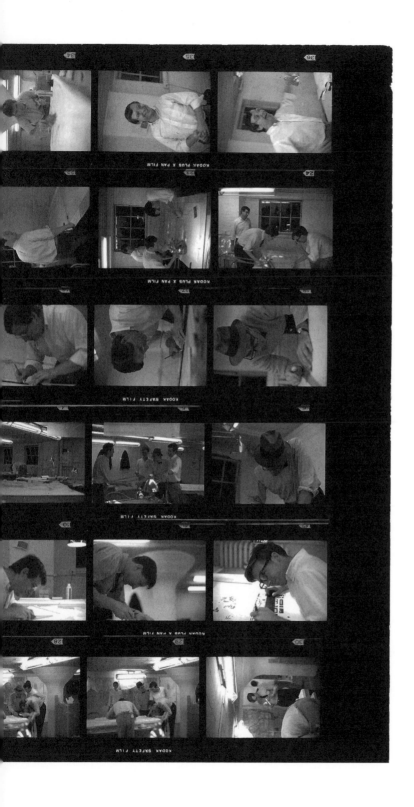

Michael (in wire-frame glasses) and Peter Eisenman (in hat) with colleagues in the basement of the Princeton School of Architecture, circa 1964

Prologue

"Trois rappels à MM. les architectes"
— *Le Corbusier* [1]

FROM THE MOMENT he or she sits down to write, the biographer's goose is pretty well cooked. There is no getting out from under the demands of the genre—the author must attempt to connect the life with the work. This is a dicey methodological proposition in any case, but especially in architecture, a creative endeavor with too many moving parts to be reduced, à la *Citizen Kane*, to some long-lost childhood sled. And yet the present subject lends himself, more so than most architects, to the biographical treatment. Through his intense industry, as well as sometimes extraordinary happenstance, his work and his life entered into something like a cyclic loop, the one perpetually feeding back into the other. What's more, examining the two together befits his particular architectural ethos, which took into its compass the personal and the universal, the monumental and the everyday. If ever a designer's individual history afforded a handy guidebook for understanding both his own designs and the design of his times, it was this one, and the only thing to establish in advance is: Why should this designer, or his times, matter? And why now?

Here's one possible answer. Over and again during the last three and a half years, as I have researched, written, and edited this book, I have been put in mind of Bruno Latour's landmark 1991 anthropological study, *We Have Never Been Modern*.[2] Certainly its operating premise—that continuity is a more informative model of history than repeated disjuncture—has come to seem more and more pertinent. But it is Latour's title that keeps coming back, albeit with a curious twist. In considering the life and afterlife of Michael Graves, his impact not just on the design profession but on the built environment as a whole, I've begun to suspect that, in many of the ways that count, we have never stopped being Postmodern.

No doubt we had thought the moment long since come and gone. Postmodernist architecture—"PoMo" as it is often called, with a slight sneer—burst onto the American scene in the late 1970s amid a flourish of flattened columns and multihued facades.[3] By the end of the following decade, its historical references and pop irreverence had already fallen into disfavor. In 1988 the city of Yonkers took a sledgehammer to architect Walter David Brown's Getty Square colonnade, an unloved pseudoclassi-cal portico built a mere ten years prior. The critic Alastair Gordon, only half joking, claimed the event marked a "Pruitt-Igoe" moment for Postmodernism: the reference was to the infamous St. Louis housing project of that name, whose 1972 demolition had been seen (by another critic, Charles Jencks) as a death knell for the purportedly dull, unadorned severity of midcentury American Modernism.[4]

At least Modernism had enjoyed a good three decades of unchallenged supremacy before the wrecking crews arrived. Postmodernism lasted scarcely half as long before being muscled aside by another "ism." Only months before the Yonkers colonnade came down, New York's Museum of Modern Art debuted its *Deconstructivist Archi-tecture* exhibition. Heralding an abstract and technically daring new approach from a roll call of soon-to-be-familiar names (among them Frank Gehry and Zaha Hadid), the show was godfathered by Philip Johnson, America's premier gadfly-tastemaker and until lately a major advocate of Postmodernist playfulness. The critics panned it, but Johnson's involvement sent a clear signal. For lovers of the nostalgic, the ironic, and the colorful, the lamps were going out all over architecture.

They've stayed that way ever since—or so we've been told. The scholar Jean-Louis Cohen has characterized Postmodernism as a "hesitation within the discourse," a moment when the profession apprehended with a start that much of the social promise of Modernism, its vision of a pristine utopia of glass and steel, had not been borne out.[5] The reaction was less a radical break than a corrective reflex, almost like an immune response. Bubbling up through the academy in the early 1960s, the Postmodernist tendency began as a measured critical attack on the disruptions to the traditional urban fabric wrought by Modernist interventions; practice soon took up the cause, trying to mend that fabric by returning to its traditional constituents. Soon, Postmodernism was everywhere, manifesting in symptoms such as applied ornament, polychromatic surfaces, and familiar typological outlines.

These were already in evidence in what is generally recognized as the ur-Postmodernist project, Robert Venturi's Vanna Venturi House, built for his mother in 1964. An idiosyncratic variant was popularized on the West Coast by Charles Moore, as in his collage-like Moore-Rogger-Hofflander condominium in Los Ange-les of 1975. The architects dubbed the Chicago Seven (Stanley Tigerman foremost among them) would carry the banner for the movement in the Midwest, and Robert A. M. Stern and Jaquelin Robertson (and eventually Philip Johnson) would give it establishment cred in the East. Countless other firms would follow.

But, most importantly, there was Michael Graves. If Getty Square was PoMo's Pruitt-Igoe, Graves's Portland Building of 1982 was perhaps its Seagram Building, the epochal moment of its architectural ascendancy. It thrust the Postmodernist movement to the forefront of the design world, and Graves himself to unprecedented international fame. During the 1980s he was indisputably the most celebrated, the most talked-about, American architect of his generation.

And then—the fever broke. By the early 1990s other architects were vying with Graves for the covers of magazines, for major design awards, and for the idolatry of students at architecture schools everywhere. But what I have come to believe in the course of preparing this biography is this: when the hesitation of Postmodernism subsided and the architectural organism resumed its customary forward movement, its behavior was forever changed. For not only did Michael Graves himself not go away (in many ways his renown, and that of his office, only grew), but the problems and principles that concerned him most have never vanished. Quite the opposite: they remain a crucial part of design culture worldwide and are deeply embedded within practice as a whole, perhaps nowhere more so than in the very places where Graves's influence has been most effectively suppressed.

"Perhaps it's time," wrote the author Jimmy Stamp in 2012, "to reclaim Postmodernism for a generation for whom all of history is only a hyperlink away."[6] Many such sentiments have been floated in recent years, as Postmodernism has come in for a qualified rehabilitation. Several museums, including London's Victoria and Albert Museum in 2011, have staged retrospectives on the topic, and in more commercial quarters there's been a mini revival of sorts, with splashes of 1980s style visible in the booths of the big chair fairs like Milan's Salone del Mobile. In the preservationist community, energies that have long been trained on saving Modernist masterworks are now being directed toward Postmodernist ones presently under threat of redevelopment, including a number by Michael Graves himself. But don't call it a comeback: Gravesian currents have never stopped flowing through architecture, though the channels have often been subterranean.

This has happened before. By the late 1950s Italian Futurism and other marginal movements of the prewar years had been all but written out of the official history of Modernism, their unsavory political associations and aesthetic crotchets considered out of step with the wholesomely corporate-democratic aspirations of the glassy, plainspoken International Style. In the words of the British critic Reyner Banham, those other, discarded Modernisms occupied a "zone of silence"—even though they had been every bit as essential in the evolution of design as more notionally acceptable antecedents such as the Bauhaus.[7] The history of architecture is fairly strewn with such zones of silence, evidence of a recursive process that has subjected successive design movements, from 1900s Beaux Arts to 1920s Art Deco to 1960s Brutalism, to a variety of institutional forgetting. Postmodernism has undergone only the latest of these serial sublimations.

And yet step outside and take a walk in almost any major American city, in particular in those neighborhoods the real estate agents like to call "emerging" or "transitional." There you will see urban infill apartment housing, block upon block of it, much of it clad in brick with quasi-historical touches: cornices, windows with dip grooves, maybe a little flashing over the crown—all of it done in a good-faith effort to play nicely with the nineteenth-century neighbors. Even where the newer building stock is a little splashier—faced in shiny composite panels with strip windows—you'll find things like datum lines that match perfectly with the row houses on either side, or surface patterning on the facade meant to give it some of the textural quality of older masonry buildings. This has been the lingua franca of real estate development in cities, to say nothing of suburbs, all across the country for decades, and it is unmistakably Postmodernist in inspiration.

Admittedly, in the more rarefied reaches of high design, such gestures are held in low esteem. But look closer. However irregular their forms, however bracingly innovative the technology and materials they use, contemporary designers will unfailingly avow (especially to any journalist within shouting distance) that their buildings are "contextual," blending in ways subtle and overt with their urban surrounds. This might be regarded as merely a rhetorical holdover of Postmodernism—but that is a shade too cynical. The design process of even the most progressive architects working today includes careful and serious consideration of the existing urban fabric, a sensitivity that has become a practical necessity, given a preservation-minded bureaucratic climate that is itself a product of the same forces that gave rise to Postmodernism.

Of course, even if they admitted to Postmodern precedents, contemporary designers wouldn't necessarily credit Graves. Nor would they have to: Postmodernism had many fathers, and not a few mothers, and its latter-day reverberations can't be wholly ascribed to any one of them. But in addition to a few specific features of Postmodernism that can be confidently attributed to his influence, there is a broader narrative connecting the 1980s to the 2010s, and it centers on the person of Michael Graves himself.

The word *starchitect*, that lamentable portmanteau, has come into general use to describe the architectural headliners, Hadid and Gehry foremost among them, whose inventive hypermodernism displaced Postmodernism in the years following the MoMA "Decon" show. Celebrity culture in architecture certainly predates the term: Johnson, Eero Saarinen, and Edward Durell Stone were just a few of the architects featured on the cover of *Time* before 1981, and Frank Lloyd Wright was once a guest on the 1950s panel show *What's My Line*. And obviously the advent of the internet, and the concomitant obsession with celebrity of all kinds, has hastened the rise of marquee names. But the 1980s marked a key juncture.

This was, after all, the first decade in which growth in the American service sector far outstripped manufacturing.[8] As the US economy shifted rapidly to a postindustrial basis—under the influence of a president who was himself a media celebrity—there emerged a new media landscape, one that prepared the way for the digital age to come. Postmodernist architecture during its heyday was a creature of this bigger, more riotous media landscape, and above it all there stood but one figure.

Michael Graves's fame not only made Postmodernism a normative mode of practice in the United States; it made him, for good and ill, the progenitor of the twenty-first-century global starchitect. That Graves achieved this status was ultimately as much a function of his product designs as his architecture (although there's a crucial reciprocity between the two). But besides the fact that industrial design remains very much within the purview of today's design stars, their architectural activity really only picks up where Graves's product work left off. Commissioned by cities all over the world shopping around for an urban-scale collector's item, starchitects' museums and condo towers are as indelibly branded to them as Graves's teakettles and toasters were to him: for many architects—and not just star ones—buildings have *become* products. Only lately have practitioners begun to grapple with this hypercommodified condition. It was known to Graves long ago, and much can be learned by his example.

Add to that the enduring legacy of his forty years as a teacher at Princeton University, the monument he left nearby in the form of his beloved Warehouse, and the ongoing work of his namesake firm, and one begins to see how much Michael Graves is still with us. Since well before his death in March 2015, Graves and his contribution to design had become specters (though there are countless others) haunting the profession. His story is the half-neglected story of design in the last half century, and each of his projects is a signpost along the way, reminding us of architecture's twists and turns, its dashed hopes and surprising successes.

That his work is so riven—to borrow the famous phrase from Venturi's foundational Postmodernist treatise—with complexity and contradiction is indeed a reflection of the man who created it. And for that reason he, and the life he lived, are of the utmost consequence to anyone who wants to know why the world today looks the way it does.

Ian Volner

Harlem
January 2017

xiii

Note on Sources

I FIRST MET MICHAEL GRAVES in 2009, while I was briefly employed in a Manhattan public relations office that was representing his firm. I wasn't working on the account myself, but I insisted on tagging along to a meeting in Princeton, and being an architectural historian by training I couldn't resist bending Michael's ear for several minutes afterward. It wasn't until four years later that I found myself back in Princeton at the suggestion of my agent, conducting a series of interviews with Michael in furtherance of a collaborative book project of undetermined form, imagined as either an oral history or a memoir.

In the succeeding months, it evolved into the latter, and after nearly a year and a half we began the formal process of organizing Michael's life into a first-person narrative, with me acting as amanuensis. By then we had accumulated more than thirty hours of material, recorded (and most of it simultaneously transcribed) during a series of five meetings at his office in Princeton, each lasting upward of five hours. These were augmented, as the text took shape, by edits and additions from Michael's own hand, as well as those of his firm partners, some of whom were shown the proposal drafts for review. These sources are referred to in the notes as MGMD (Michael Graves monograph documents).

Sadly, only weeks after Princeton Architectural Press accepted the proposal, and before several more planned interviews could take place, Michael passed away. Determined to bring his story before the public, the publisher, Michael's office, his family, and I resolved in the fall of 2015 to turn the project into a critical biography. This meant expanding its scope dramatically, interviewing dozens of former clients, students, and colleagues, as well as carrying out extensive archival research and consulting scores of scholarly articles. This I did over the following year while continuing my primary activity as a journalist and critic of architecture, in the course of which I was able to visit many of Michael's buildings and the buildings that inspired him most, as well as to meet more and more people eager to share their own memories of the late designer.

Still, the anecdotes and insights garnered during my one-on-one sessions with Michael remain central to this text. In some instances, especially as relates to his early childhood, there are no living persons to verify his version of events, and in cases of doubt the appropriate qualifiers appear. Michael was as prone as anyone to failures of memory—and was known to occasionally embellish the record—but whenever documentary or third-party evidence has differed from his account, the latter has naturally given way to the former.

Given the amount of uncertainty surrounding any individual's life, and the often-conflicting perspectives on it of friends, family, and fellow professionals, there is still room to cavil over this or that attribution or assessment. Such are the pleasures of history. Many of these knotty points are taken up in the footnotes, and in the acknowledgments and bibliography one can find a few of the more valuable sources that brought a level of detail that Michael sometimes either did not or could not contribute.

All in all, the biographer must be reckoned very lucky who has the opportunity to meet his or her subject while living, to become acquainted firsthand with the subject's character and outlook, and to bring these to life in writing. When the subject in question is Michael Graves, the biographer—and, it is hoped, the reader—will feel luckier still.

I

THE SEA

ON THE MORNING OF Monday, February 24, 2003, Michael Graves awoke in his home in Princeton, New Jersey, with what felt like a nasty flu. He'd been feeling poorly for several days, but that was hardly uncommon.[1]

At sixty-nine, Michael maintained a travel schedule that would have worn out a man half his age; sickness, in his case mostly sinus infections, came with the territory. The heady days of the 1980s and early '90s, when the office phone seemed to ring off the hook at all hours, were behind him. But that only seemed to strengthen his resolve, and with his powerful work ethic he was always on the lookout for new opportunities, constantly traipsing around the globe in search of clients.

At symposia, in interviews, and at dinner parties in city after city, people would turn to him and ask, "Which of your buildings is your favorite?" His answer was the same every time: "The next one."[2]

There always seemed to be a next one, despite the changing times. In 1997 the completion of the Guggenheim Museum in Bilbao, Spain, by Michael's old friend and competitor Frank Gehry had caused a sensation even greater than Michael's own Portland Building had fifteen years before, proving that the high-flown schemes of the late-1980s Deconstructivists (the name, mercifully, had already fallen into disuse) could be made real. The folksy monumentality of the PoMo that Michael had helped champion, already in eclipse, would now be in full rout.

Which left some to wonder why Michael didn't change too. "He could have done anything he wanted," said Peter Eisenman, Michael's best friend of more than five decades. Eisenman shared with him a bond that had survived sometimes profound professional differences. "We always used to talk about sports," he recalled, and their regular outings to college football games helped sustain an alliance that seemed, in other ways, rather improbable.[3]

Michael, with his lifelong virtuoso ability as a draftsman, was an architect of the eye, a devotee of the image; Eisenman was and remains an architect of the idea, sworn to a lofty conception of design as an autonomous discipline on par with art or literature. Eisenman's theoretical absorptions had been a major influence on Philip Johnson in the run-up to the theory-infused *Deconstructivist Architecture* exhibition at MoMA in 1988, and in the fifteen years since, he had watched with growing consternation as his old comrade Michael had drifted further and further from the architectural avant-garde.[4] Up until the late 1970s, Eisenman and Michael had plied more or less the same waters, both of them members (along with colleagues Richard Meier, John Hejduk, and Charles Gwathmey) of the famed ultra-Modernist group the New York Five—until Michael had abruptly cast off the Modernist mantle for a Postmodernist one. Why, Eisenman thought, did Michael not now reverse course? Or at least alter it?

What had seemed, twenty years before, a thrilling change of direction—"the equivalent for architecture culture," quipped the critic Paul Goldberger, "of Bob Dylan going electric"—Michael's turn to color, classicism, and kitsch now looked out of season.[5] In 2001 Herbert Muschamp, Goldberger's successor at the *New York Times*, wrote that "Postmodernism's pseudo-history has been driven back to the wealthy suburbs whence it came," and few design watchers seemed to lament its passing.[6] In the age of the starchitect, Michael was cast as a PoMo revanchist, a pandering populist, a Luddite with a retrograde commitment to the art of drawing. His work was ridiculed as too jokey, too thin, too repetitive.

Yet the Graves name still held considerable commercial, if not critical, cachet, and his firm was still securing major commissions, even if it required a little more campaigning to do so. A surprise burst of positive media attention had come the firm's way at the turn of the millennium, thanks to its design for the scaffolding of the Washington Monument during its late-1990s renovation. It seemed, at first, a modest enough proposition—maintenance infrastructure is not typically the stuff of tourist snapshots—but Michael Graves & Associates' luminescent blue envelope, with its rectangular patterns echoing the masonry of the tall obelisk behind it, proved such a hit with the public that a movement was launched to keep it in place indefinitely. Among the scaffold's admirers was its near neighbor, First Lady Hillary Clinton, who invited Michael to several White House dinners. Chelsea, he later remarked, seemed to hate public settings, and when he reached out to shake her hand, he could sense her anxiety in her nervous, shaky grip.[7]

Thanks to the Clintons' support, the scaffolding was kept up for the city's millennium celebrations, where it was seen in innumerable news clips of the New Year's Eve fireworks lighting up the National Mall. The exposure helped garner Michael a National Medal of Arts in 1999 and brought a few big new commissions into the office from New York, Texas, and Washington, DC. But architecture was hardly the fastest-growing part of the practice.

The scaffolding initiative had been sponsored by the Minneapolis-based Target Corporation, the country's third-largest discount retailer, and that collaboration led to a Graves-designed product line for the company that became a major commercial success upon its introduction in 1999. In the early years following the launch, the chain's locations maintained a separate shop-within-a-shop, a dedicated twenty-four-foot aisle, exclusively for Graves's designs—toasters and alarm clocks, coffeepots and teakettles, all from the Michael Graves Design Group, its signature blue branding sticking out amid the store's red signage. Even more than his buildings, the Target homewares made Michael (in a pun that journalists never tired of repeating) "a household name," and in the winter of 2003 he and his client were laying plans to make their growing family of products even bigger.[8]

With all this, not to mention a crowded schedule of lectures in the United States and abroad, Michael could not let a flu get in the way of his busy day—least of all when his personal life was no less demanding than his career.

The two, he found, often became entangled. Michael had been happily unmarried for more than twenty years, and the bachelor's life suited him, but in the late 1990s he had begun dating one woman to whom he'd grown particularly close. In 1998 she introduced him to the comedian Jerry Seinfeld, whose television comedy was then in its final season and who was looking for someone to design his new Manhattan apartment. Actor and architect met and spoke at length, and the latter was impressed—especially given Seinfeld's famously snide on-air persona—by his candor and modesty as he walked casually into the shabby, unfurnished old space. "What do you think, Michael?" asked Seinfeld. "Coat of paint?"[9]

Michael was certain he'd gotten the job, but he was more than slightly taken aback when, before any contract had been signed, his then-girlfriend stepped in to demand a fee for having made what had seemed like a casual introduction. The relationship ended shortly thereafter—but it was a loss that seemed to rankle Michael less than the loss of the Seinfeld commission. After he mentioned it to a mutual acquaintance (he later claimed), word of the imminent project reached his old friend and fellow New York Five alum Charles Gwathmey, who swooped in and snatched it.

Not long thereafter, Michael was introduced to a Florida-based, Chinese-born architect named Lynn Min, who was consulting on a project for a Chinese developer that Michael was being considered for. The two became romantically involved, and Michael began making frequent trips to Boca Raton, spending more and more time with Min and using the visits to meet with prospective clients in the area. In the end, however, he found that the demands of his practice were calling him elsewhere and decided it was best to end the relationship—only to find that Min was pregnant. A few months later, in August 2002, Michael Sebastian Graves was born in a Florida hospital, four decades after the birth of Michael's older son, Adam.

IT WAS A STRESSFUL TIME, if a happy and productive one, and instead of dashing off to work that chilly February morning, Michael might just as soon have remained in the comfort of his very comfortable home—though even that, his sanctuary for three decades, was part of the fraught intermingling of his personal and professional activity.

The Warehouse, so called for the building's original purpose when it was built in the 1920s, had transformed into an all-purpose receptacle for Michael's shifting artistic tastes and architectural ambitions. Shaping and expanding the interior consumed much of his energies and not a little of his resources, with every trip abroad presenting a new opportunity to snap up something for the living room or upstairs study. The habitual belt-tightening of his early life, together with his native shrewdness, kept him from giving in altogether to his voluptuary instincts, and his foreign travels were always for work, never pleasure. Yet the life of the Lord of the Warehouse did not come cheap, least of all when combined with all the other impedimenta of his existence: alimony was no longer a consideration, his two divorces being long in the past, but he had grandchildren by his daughter Sarah in Calgary, Canada, to spoil with presents, and his young son in Miami to support. Although his teaching days at Princeton had ended several years earlier, he would still wine and dine visiting professors at the Warehouse, to which an invitation remained much coveted.

All this—plus the expenses of running a firm with simultaneous ongoing projects around the globe—made for a staggering volume of overhead. Michael continued working as hard as he did because he loved it, but he also worked because he felt he had to. And so, instead of staying in bed, he ignored the throb in his temples and the aches in his joints. He got in his car and made the three-minute drive to his office, just as he did every Monday morning.

He carried with him a bottle of Bactrim, a low-level antibiotic hastily prescribed the week prior by his local doctor. Feeling another sinus infection coming on and looking ahead to a difficult week of foreign travel starting on Valentine's Day, Michael had persuaded his physician to grant him a last-minute appointment.[10] The examination, he later claimed, had been cursory at best, and the prescription written only grudgingly. It may be wondered how many of the pills he had actually taken: according to one account, the bottle he brought back with him to Princeton might not have been an antibiotic at all but a decongestant prescribed simultaneously, which he had mistaken for a second bottle of Bactrim. Michael was not, on the whole, known for assiduous self-care, and for all of his sports fandom he engaged in no athletic activity more strenuous than golf (though he was fiercely competitive when playing it, to the point, occasionally, of cheating).

The four days in transit between the doctor's visit and the return to work in Princeton on Monday had done nothing to bolster his health. The first stop had been Frankfurt, Germany, for the Ambiente fair—the furniture and product show at the Messe Frankfurt trade hall—where Michael met with his collaborators at Target to discuss upcoming product deadlines. On the plane over the Atlantic and in the endless meetings that followed, he felt the illness intensifying, leaving him weary and muddle-headed. By February 18, when the Frankfurt fair was over, it was off to Geneva, Switzerland, where Michael toured a construction site for three hours in the freezing cold. Once he'd finished there, as often happened, his client wanted to take him out for a long evening of dinner and drinks. Keen to stay in his good graces, Michael obliged.

Come Saturday, he was back in the United States—but not in New Jersey. He had gone to New York to give a pair of lectures on Sunday, had managed to get through both, and then had endured another evening among friends and colleagues, the kind of evening not uncommon in the social run of the New York design world. Michael could hold his own in any such company, but though he was no teetotaler he rarely ever drank to excess. (Growing up in his father's house had cured him of *that*.) He was out late but got back to Princeton in time to get a good night's sleep before the working week began.

The office was a fifteen-minute walk from campus, in two converted houses on either side of Nassau Street. On the north side were the offices of Michael Graves Design Group, the portion of the practice expressly devoted to consumer products, while to the south, in a pair of conjoined colonials, were the offices of Michael Graves & Associates, responsible for the firm's buildings and interiors. The two structures together sheltered some hundred-plus designers, all busily turning out proposals and models and drawings and prototypes. Preferring to stay somewhat aloof from the moil but close enough to keep an eye on the proceedings, Michael kept his personal studio and library suite on one side of the south building.

Sitting down at his desk, he started to work. Ever since childhood, pen and paper had been his constant companions; drawing, the simple action of translating those forms and colors that inhabited his head into images on the page, was to him an almost irresistible impulse, part of what drove him to keep designing and building according to his own lights, his own idea of a possible architecture. But on this particular Monday, he could draw nothing. For perhaps the first time in his life, he told his colleagues he was leaving early, and around noon he drove back home again to the Warehouse.

Here, in the cozy warren of well-lit rooms packed with Biedermeier chairs and ancient Greek potsherds in built-in niches, Michael thought he would finally be able to relax. Yet the Warehouse afforded him no refuge that day. He lay down in bed and only felt worse, the pulse in his head and the pang in his limbs making it impossible to sleep. By early evening, a neighbor stopped by to check on him. Alarmed by what she saw, she notified Michael's colleagues, promised to take care of his dog, Sara (he'd kept a series of Labradors for years), and called an ambulance.

At the University Medical Center of Princeton, Michael was put into a hospital bed. And there, as he recalled many years later, "it really started."[11]

WHAT EXACTLY WAS HAPPENING in Michael Graves's body at this point remains something of a medical mystery. Bacterial meningitis seems a probable candidate, though he never tested positive for it despite several diagnostic lumbar punctures. Myelitis, a viral or occasionally fungal disorder with similar effects, is the likelier culprit, but—while theories abound—no variety or vector has ever been definitively identified. As a matter of epidemiological record, Michael's illness remains essentially idiopathic, a one-off disease afflicting practically no one in history except for Michael Graves.

The most one can say is that somehow, whether by exhaustion or by sheer fluke, Michael's bodily defenses had become dangerously compromised, and the sinus infection he had been battling for days managed to do what almost every infection, from the common cold to the Spanish flu, longs to do: jump the ramparts of the human immune system and spread uncontrollably through the body. In Michael's case, it made directly for his spinal column, ravaging the cells of the central nervous system. Many similar disorders also affect the brain, causing swelling that can induce coma and leave patients with serious cognitive impairments. But Michael's brain, remarkably, was largely unaffected by the progress of the disease.

In the future that would make all the difference. But for now it only meant that for those first twenty-four hours in the hospital, Michael was fully, appallingly conscious, not knowing what was happening to him except that it was agonizing. The center of the pain, as he remembered it, crept along the length of his spine, spreading down his upper back until it rested at about chest level and hovered there. Any kind of movement was nearly impossible. He was able, at one point, to drag himself to the bathroom—only to find when he got there that he couldn't urinate. He lay back down again, and again the pain spread and intensified: a lashing, incisive pain that seemed to drive down on every fiber of his body at once.

A nurse came in during the night. The only words he could manage were, "What *is* this?"

"It's nerve pain," she said, unhelpfully, and gave him morphine.

She gave him more morphine, and then still more; it did nothing. He remained awake and in incredible suffering. Hours passed.

Of what followed on that first night, Michael did not remember much—except for this. It was the middle of the night and two colleagues had arrived, sitting at his bedside, watching him. He recalled a sensation, an image: that he was holding on to the mainsail of a ship, an old sailing ship caught in some terrible storm out at sea. He was gripping the mast and draped out in the gale like a flag, battered by the wind. Why that image should come to mind he couldn't think; he'd spent almost no time at sea in his life. But he knew that he had to hold on to that slender wooden shaft with all his strength or else die.

For a time, he started to favor the latter option—he just wanted it to be over. Again and again he recalled crying out, "I don't want to hold on anymore!" until by the end he was screaming it. Or at least he *felt* he was screaming it: his longtime senior partner, Karen Nichols, who was there with his lawyer, Susan Howard, sat with him the whole night, and could not recall him crying out anything coherent, except to complain that his feet and legs were deathly cold.

Somehow, in the early morning hours, the storm died down and Michael fell asleep.

When he awoke, he found that the pain had subsided enough for him to speak and think at least halfway clearly. He hadn't managed to get back to the bathroom and was aware, however dimly, that he should probably do so. Susan Howard called in a urologist, and when he came in he told Michael he was going to have to put in a catheter. "But don't worry," he said. "You won't feel a thing."

Something about the urologist's particular choice of words struck Michael as suspicious. "Do you mean," he asked, in a small voice, "that *one* does not feel it, or that *I* won't feel it?"

The doctor flashed a sad, sympathetic half smile. "I mean that *you* won't, Michael."

His meaning was clear enough. For any normal patient, having a catheter inserted is an uncomfortable experience, to put it mildly. Michael wouldn't feel it because he could no longer feel anything below his rib cage.

Overnight, his entire body had changed. The void of feeling that had swept over the lower half of him made it feel like he was adrift—perhaps on the same sea where he'd borne out the storm—with only his head and arms bobbing above the waves. It was maddening, he recalled, feeling he *should* have some sensation in his feet, his legs, somewhere, and expecting every moment for it to come back. It did not.

Nor was that all. Even into his sedentary middle age, Michael had remained in good enough shape to fit into the fashionable clothes that were among his favorite extravagances. But that morning in the hospital in Princeton, he looked down the length of the bed in disbelief: his stomach had swelled grotesquely, as though he'd put on weight in his sleep. A doctor later explained that the muscles in his abdomen had lost all their strength, leaving his midsection to simply spill out. Even if he were starving to death, he would still bulge at the belly.

And then there was the fact that he wasn't able to move. He had the use of his arms and hands, and could turn his head, but that was all he could manage. He couldn't even roll over in bed, obliging the hospital staff to do it for him—mostly in order to prevent bedsores, which can be fatal (and which he, of course, would no longer be able to feel). Unable to shift his weight, Michael found he had forgotten how to sleep, only dozing lightly when he was too exhausted to keep his eyes open any longer.

But worse than all that had happened was all he didn't know. No one had any convincing medical explanation for what was going on—only that he'd had an infection and that it had spread to the rest of his body. None of the doctors could tell him when he was likely to be back on his feet and in the office again. He was frightened, naturally, but mostly the situation was too surreal, too immense, for him to even be certain how he felt.

On the advice of an infectious disease specialist summoned by a firm associate, the Princeton hospital staff made the prudent decision to move Michael to New York-Presbyterian hospital in Manhattan, where he would have access to superior care, including another specialist who was reckoned among the country's preeminent neurologists. Matters did not, however, improve in Manhattan: there Michael was kept for another six weeks, subjected to an unremitting regimen of tests and scans, shuttled from room to dreary room through the corridors of New York-Presbyterian. Shortly after he was admitted, it was discovered that the specialist he had hoped to consult was leaving that very day for an extended vacation. Michael's pain had ebbed, but even after a host of other doctors descended upon him, no one could solve the underlying mystery of what had happened or what could be done about it.

All Michael could do in the interim was lie flat on his back, brooding and surveying the dismal scene around him. Boredom and anxiety preyed on him—until finally, stretched out miserably on a gurney, waiting for yet another test, Michael decided to occupy himself by doing what he had always done, what he had done for generations of Princeton students in his graduate studio course. He began to criticize the architecture.

The review was scathing. Everything around him was unwieldy and alien—the boxy, off-beige seating; the awkward wheelchair; the bedside table he couldn't reach. It was an odd moment to be contemplating aesthetics, and his mind remained clouded with pain. But Michael Graves was still Michael Graves, and as much as he hated *how* he was, he hated *where* he was nearly as much.

I can't die here, he thought to himself. *It's too ugly.*[12]

STABILIZED, AND HOPING FOR some measure of improvement, Michael was transferred again, this time to the Kessler Institute, a rehabilitation hospital in West Orange, New Jersey, made famous by the actor Christopher Reeve, who underwent extensive treatment there following his own paralysis. Kessler's course of therapy promised to help Michael adapt to, if not to overcome, his paralysis, and his old golf gloves were quickly repurposed to help him lift the hand weights the staff said would improve his upper-body strength. Soon the steady stream of visitors that had been coming to Manhattan diverted back across the Hudson: his friends Peter Eisenman, Richard Meier, and Charles Gwathmey; Target executive Ron Johnson; his daughter, Sarah Stelfox.

Michael was always careful in how he presented himself, and even those closest to him had access only to those parts of himself he chose to reveal: Eisenman never knew that his football buddy was, like him, a lifelong liberal Democrat; Meier was no less serious than Michael about painting, and even shared a studio with him in the 1950s, but they scarcely ever talked about art.[13] To most of his well-wishers at Kessler, Michael presented an image of only slightly thwarted good cheer, refusing to credit the idea that his present immobility would last. "He was upset and concerned," recalled Stelfox, "but composed. He seemed to always put a good face on things."[14]

But to one friend—one perhaps better able to stomach a darker view—Michael showed a different turn of mind. "Michael was in a state of rage," said Fran Lebowitz. The notoriously caustic New York writer had been one of Michael's closest intimates for twenty-five years, and there was little he could have hidden from her even if he'd wanted to. He may have made a show of "Christian optimism" to others, as Lebowitz put it. "But he wasn't showing it to me."[15]

His frustration was kept well hidden, as his frustrations long had been, under a pile of work. The illness that had rendered walking impossible had not affected the sharpness of his mind, and with the pain now under control a new routine had been put in place at Michael Graves & Associates. Almost every day, one of his six senior partners would appear at the door of his room at Kessler, accompanied by other staff members bearing paint samples or renderings of a new project and usually cradling under one arm a contraband lunch of a quality not obtainable in the facility's cafeteria. Surrounded by notes from former colleagues and clients ("I'm sitting in your building thinking of you—Michael Eisner"), the associates would show Michael what the team in the office was ginning up, keeping the chief abreast of all the latest developments. Hedging against a full recovery, the team began to talk about other ways of getting Michael into Manhattan for client meetings.[16]

And Michael began to talk to his associates—and, perhaps more importantly, to a visiting reporter from the *New York Times*—about the shabby, careless, and otherwise subpar quality of design visible everywhere in the health-care space. Michael, the paper strongly implied, could do something about it because he could still draw: so long as he had that, he could still create. He retained the one skill that even his

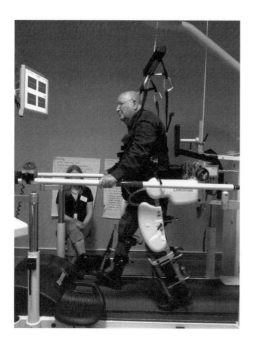

On the treadmill
in rehab, 2013

most determined critics had always admired, one that had always given him the greatest pleasure.

His ex-girlfriend Kitty Hawks, daughter of the film director Howard Hawks and herself a trained designer, came to visit Michael at Kessler and was relieved to find him sketching away, as always. "Once I knew he could still draw," she said, "I knew he'd manage. He'd survive."[17]

SURVIVE, YES; BUT as Lebowitz saw, coming to terms with his affliction would take a great deal more time and at least a little more understanding of what the affliction really was. Despite some halting progress at Kessler, there was no breakthrough—until another old friend, the architect Elizabeth Plater-Zyberk, paid a call in July 2003, five months after Michael's harrowing first night in Princeton.[18]

Plater-Zyberk, whose New Urbanist practice had helped spread Gravesian Post-modernism into the realm of town planning, hadn't arrived expecting to play medical adviser. But as they chatted, Michael mentioned that a sense of numbness had lately begun to steal over his arms and hands—only in the early mornings, usually tapering off by afternoon. He wasn't overly concerned: his symptoms, he had been assured, were confined to his lower body and unlikely to spread further. But Plater-Zyberk was not convinced. "He was languishing" at Kessler, she felt, and she immediately arranged for him to confer with Dr. Barth Green, a personal friend and the director of the Miami Project to Cure Paralysis at Jackson Memorial Medical Center.[19] Green requested an MRI of Michael's spinal cord as soon as possible.

The test meant getting to leave Kessler, and that, for Michael, was reason enough to agree to it. Having carried his rehabilitation as far as they could, the doctors in West Orange gave him leave to have the test done and discharged him from their care until further notice: he was headed back to his beloved Warehouse, to all the treasures and comforts so laboriously attained and enhanced over the years. The actual MRI proved a bit of a trial—the staff at the testing center was not equipped to help Michael either onto or off of the table, and the image quality proved so poor that a second test had to be carried out in Manhattan the following week—but that was merely an afterthought. Michael was headed home, as soon as his home could made ready for him.

The call from Green came only a few days later. The second MRI painted a grisly picture: Michael's spinal column "looked like it was covered with barnacles, like the bottom of a sunken ship," the doctor reported, and surgery was urgently needed to "clean those barnacles off." Green visited Michael to urge him to come to Miami the instant he was able, and a surgery was scheduled for late August.

And yet, just as he had done when the illness had first struck, Michael attempted to duck this latest diagnosis. Finally beginning to claw his way back to some kind of normalcy, he simply couldn't bear to give it up to return once more to the barren, colorless world of the unwell. In any case, he'd already agreed to travel to Target headquarters in Minneapolis for a series of meetings, and he was looking forward to the trip: it would be a chance to return Ron Johnson's kindness in coming to visit him at Kessler and to sustain what had been for both of them a very productive and lucrative partnership. The surgery could wait an extra day or two.

In a magnanimous gesture, Target provided one of its company planes to spirit the Graves team to Minnesota. The small aircraft was not ideally suited to Michael's new wheelchair, but it felt good to be airborne for the first time in months, a return to the architect's usual jet-setting ways. Arriving in Minneapolis, the group checked into a hotel, and a nurse whom Michael had brought along for the trip helped him into bed for a brief nap before the meetings began. A couple of hours later, he awoke.

The mild numbness he had described to Plater-Zyberk had completely overtaken his arms and hands. In a flash, the fever was back, and with it the pain and the delirium. The staff contacted Dr. Green, who arranged for a trusted colleague in Minneapolis to visit Michael at the hotel; no sooner had the colleague arrived than he again called Green, informing him that the situation was dire. Michael was rushed back to the airport and flown directly to Miami. Semiconscious during the flight, he recalled almost nothing until the plane touched down around midnight and was met on the tarmac by an ambulance, standing at the ready to take him to Jackson Memorial.

For the second time in a year, his life was at stake, and all that went with it: his newborn son and grandchildren, his hard-won place in the profession, and his still-contentious place in the canon—his "competition with architecture," as he'd once called it, begun so long ago. Yet as he was being prepped for surgery, he had only one question for the doctor: "Will I come out of this with my hands? Will I still be able to draw?" he asked.

"You got it," said Green.

The first order of business was to stabilize the patient. Michael's spinal column had filled with fluid, and a shunt had to be installed to drain it away. Up to that point, as Green later explained, the architect had been "drowning, neurologically."[20] Stress tests, scans, and blood work followed—more poking and prodding—and the constant drip of morphine to blunt the ever-present pain.

Finally Michael was ready. The surgeon's confidence notwithstanding, his task would not be an easy one: "The virus was ascending up his spinal cord," Green later recalled. "We released some of the adhesions and blockages....The infection had risen up to his neck, threatening to go to his brain."[21] The damage already inflicted to the lowermost portion of Michael's spine, which had been the cause of his initial paralysis, could not be reversed, but the newly affected areas were still mid-infection, and the doctor concentrated his efforts there. For nearly twelve hours, Green operated.

Michael stayed on in Miami for weeks following the procedure, remaining under the care of Green and his staff as he retraced the steps toward recuperation already undertaken at Kessler. There would be more hospitalizations over the ensuing months: minor crises, occasional setbacks. But now, having seen the images of his tattered-rope spinal column, Michael knew precisely what he was up against, and although the intelligence was in no way comforting, at least he was no longer left wondering about it. And at Jackson Memorial, in addition to all the family and colleagues who had followed him first to Manhattan, then to New Jersey, and now down to Florida, there was one more close at hand who bucked up Michael's spirits: Michael Sebastian, who lived with his mother, Lynn Min, only a short drive from the hospital. "I think that boy was a source of pure happiness to him," said Fran Lebowitz. "It really kept him going. Being together, that was the only time Michael really seemed like his old self."[22]

There was even one glimmer of hope on the medical horizon, albeit a dim one. During Michael's stay in Miami, he and Green had become friends, and the doctor tipped his patient off to a promising new avenue of research then being conducted in the field of stem cell therapy. If the right variety of embryonic nerve cells could be identified and then grafted onto Michael's spinal column, there might be a way to regenerate the ruined tissue, restoring part or all of his mobility. Sadly, politics intervened. "We didn't know Bush was going to be elected for a second term," said Michael, his partisan sympathies duly reinforced.[23]

In fairness to the GOP, it does not now seem likely that stem cells would have cured Michael's paralysis within his lifetime. Nerve damage of the kind he had sustained remains all but irremediable, and the only question left to most people in that state is: What now? Dr. Green had been as good as his word, and Michael still had the use of his hands. What was he going to do with them?

FOR MONTHS FOLLOWING his illness, Michael dreamed almost nightly about walking. In one instance he imagined he was seated before a television watching a baseball game, when suddenly a commercial spot came on for a science fiction movie. "There was a superwoman with a twenty-fourth-century gun. She looked at me. I was walking. And she said, 'The amphibian walks!'"[24]

The biting humor is typical. Depending on what happened to be striking it at any given moment, the substance of Michael Graves's temperament could give the appearance of being either extraordinary pliable or hopelessly obdurate. His rare capacity for resilience could quickly shade into a self-defeating stubbornness—but it could as easily go the other way, and it did so in the case of his illness. His anger at his condition, still very real, didn't so much undercut his determination to survive as reinforce it: he was optimistic not in spite of his frustration but because of it. A chip on the shoulder, it would seem, can be a powerful asset.

Michael had his share of chips already, and he simply added his illness to the list. As his friend and former associate Caroline Constant put it, "People who have insecurities either fold into themselves or fold outward—and he went outward."[25] In the twelve years that remained to him following the surgery, Michael came to recognize the permanence of his condition without ever becoming truly acclimated to it. He would rebuild his practice, though he would always maintain that he might have done more had he not been stuck in a wheelchair. Alternating between bitterness and resolve, he used both to propel himself clear of the one thing that might have robbed him of the desire to keep moving, to keep working: resignation.

Single, and with his children either too young or otherwise unable to look after him, Michael would find his independent streak put to the test. He had good friends, and plenty of them, yet his inner circle had been subject to an unusually high degree of attrition over time; charming and warm when he chose to be, he could also exhibit considerable remove, and he never minded going his own way. This had been his modus operandi for much of his career, but now it left him in the lurch—at times quite literally. Early in his treatment, he was being hoisted into his wheelchair by a device known as a Hoyer lift, a large fabric sling suspended from a metal crane. A nurse's aide was in the middle of operating it when another member of the hospital staff came into the room, announcing that it was time for their break. With that, they left him there, dangling in midair.[26]

"Empathy," Michael would say, "is the magic word." It was a quality he found in short supply in his new life. He had begun to notice the deficit in his first hospital room, and now he could see it everywhere, in the frustrated sighs of people trying to pass his wheelchair in narrow corridors, in the uncomprehending stares of old acquaintances seeing him for the first time in his altered state. The irony, of course, is that he had been—especially following his rapid rise to success in the 1980s—an exceptionally breezy personality himself, flitting from relationship to relationship almost as easily as he did from country to country. All that would have to change. He would have to rely on others as never before.

At the same time, he would have to learn, or relearn, to return that empathy in kind through his work. In the last decade and change of his life, Michael would dedicate himself and his office to a vision of architecture as public service, and to design in the service of human life. It was to be his last, and perhaps most lasting, contribution to his profession—the more remarkable given his reputation as a notorious aesthete, a man who "drew like an angel," as the critic Martin Filler once put it, but who was presumed to be unconcerned with the social dimension of architecture.[27] It was a presumption that Michael himself had done much to fuel over the years, as his formalist commitments often came at the expense of the functional, and his knack for merchandising made him seem anything but politically *engagé*.

Nevertheless, Michael was always socially minded, after a fashion, always cognizant of design's empathic power. Part of what had prompted his transformation as an architect in the late 1970s was a feeling that architecture was failing to connect emotionally with the very people it purported to serve. Even his soft-hued vision of the world—the cerulean blue that filled his paintings and graced the handle of his iconic Alessi teakettle—grew from a deeply ingrained feeling that to be humane was a fundamental artistic duty. He had, after all, known adversity all his life, known the landscape of disability long before he was disabled. He'd grown up there.

II

THE RIVER AND THE COMPASS

At some point in the not-too-distant past, some misguided occupant redid the tiny house on the corner of Indianola Avenue and Kessler Boulevard in an unfortunate faux-masonry veneer. But it used to be like all the houses around it, a little wooden rambler in no particular style—a somewhat vulgarized American Craftsman perhaps—built in the 1920s, around the time when the surrounding municipality of Broad Ripple Village was annexed to the then fast-growing city of Indianapolis.

Thomas Browning Graves, Bud to his family, bought this house shortly after 1940, moving there from a home of equally unarresting aspect in nearby Forest

From left:
Tom, Bud,
and Michael,
circa 1937

Hills.[1] He brought with him his wife, Erma Lowe Sanderson Graves; their first son, also named Thomas, born in 1932; and their secondborn, Michael, who had arrived July 9, 1934.

Michael Edward Graves was named for his paternal grandfather, known as Max. At the time of Michael's birth, Max was living not far away from his new grandson, on Washington Boulevard in the upscale division of Meridian-Kessler. The house

MAX GRAVES HOME AT 4820 WASHINGTON BOULEVARD.

The Max Graves residence, designed by J. L. Holmes in 1924

there, in which Michael's father, Bud, had spent a portion of his adolescence, was of markedly different character from the little rambler in Broad Ripple Village where Michael grew up: the Max Graves residence had been built expressly for him and his family, a decorously trimmed suburban villa that made the pages of the *Indianapolis Star* when it was completed in 1924. "In the south living room the furniture is upholstered in taupe and gold mohair, with taupe carpeting," reported the paper.[2] No such accoutrements were to be found in Michael's boyhood home on Indianola.

The course of the Graves family fortunes was not something on which the architect often dwelled in later life. Occasionally, on visits to the area with his daughter, Sarah, Michael would point out the car window in the general direction of Meridian-Kessler and grumble vaguely about how his grandfather Max "had one of those nice houses on one of those 'big house' streets." He would go on in a similarly oblique vein to say that Max "drank his money away" and then trail off.[3]

It is likely, given what would appear a familial penchant for taciturnity, that Michael himself did not know precisely how his family's material circumstances had come about. And yet those circumstances, and an acute self-consciousness about them, were to be crucial factors in his life in design.

BEFORE THOMAS SMITH (T. S.) Graves—the family patriarch and Michael's great-grandfather—came to Indianapolis in the early 1870s from his native Kentucky, the city had not seemed destined for commercial greatness. The site on the banks of the White River had been selected for the state capital fifty years prior because of its central location, but the waterway was soon discovered to be too shallow for steamships, at least one of which ran aground there.[4]

But in the years following the Civil War, things changed rapidly. No fewer than eight railway lines eventually converged at the city's Union Station, the first such common passenger hub in the world. On a long, sloping line connecting St. Louis to

The only extant photo of the old Indianapolis stockyards— not the yards themselves but the adjacent railroad entrance —in 1912

New York by way of Columbus and Pittsburgh, Indianapolis was a perfect stopover point for agricultural goods heading east, and it was upon this strategic point that T. S. Graves shortly constructed a sizable business empire.

Cattle, pigs, and other livestock arrived in Indianapolis at the Union Stockyards in the southwest corner of the city, there to be divvied up among the various meatpacking concerns for slaughter on site or transport elsewhere. And between the farmers or railroads shipping the animals and the companies acquiring them, there was the livestock agent: passing through the pens, he would appraise the livestock on behalf of the buyers and either bid in auctions or bargain directly with sellers for the best price. In return the agent received a commission, modest in itself but accruing to a tidy sum. Beginning with mules, T. S. launched himself in the commission-agent trade in Indianapolis, and within a few years of his arrival had risen to the position of partner in the firm of M. Sells & Company.

He had had either the very good luck or the very good sense to fall in love with Miss Emma Sells, his employer's daughter, and married her in the same year he assumed his partnership. When his father-in-law died some twenty-five years later, T. S. took on a partner of his own, founding the company of Graves, Nave & Company in 1903. Not just a local figure, T. S. soon wielded considerable influence over government policy and business practices across the state and the country, serving as president of the National Livestock Exchange from 1908 to 1910. The picture of success in the booming American Midwest during the Gilded Age, he was a Mason, a member of the Indianapolis Chamber of Commerce, an active parishioner of his church, and the owner of a library that was, by the reckoning of at least one contemporary, "one of the finest and most complete in the city." The same observer also pointed out that he was "an enthusiastic motorist."[5]

The marriage to Emma produced two sons—Edward, born in 1877, and Max, born three years later. To them Thomas bequeathed his Kentuckian taste for horses, as well as a sense of themselves as being perhaps a cut above the common herd, even if their fortune was born of hogs and sheep. By the standards of the time and place, the Graves clan had good claim to something not unlike aristocracy: T. S. was related to the celebrated frontiersman Daniel Boone and was a cousin on his mother's side to the famed Confederate outlaws Frank and Jesse James.[6] In his later years, the patriarch wintered in South Florida, just as the area around Miami was first becoming fashionable. His house there was a stone's throw from the estate of three-time Democratic presidential candidate William Jennings Bryan, with whom he visited on occasion, coming back to Indianapolis with tales of the Great Commoner "dressed in workman's clothes, with his trousers in boot tops... assisting a number of negroes in cleaning off the land." T. S.'s return from these annual pilgrimages was noted in the social pages of the *Indianapolis Star*.[7]

By that time, however, the Graveses had already had their first brush with misfortune, in rather dramatic fashion. On the afternoon of March 13, 1894, Emma Sells Graves was cleaning the family home on North New Jersey Street; she was using gasoline, a common detergent in those days, and the canister somehow exploded. A young relative who happened to be visiting suddenly found himself surrounded by flames, and Emma ran to save him, her clothes catching alight in the process. She then ran into the street, where a deliveryman who was bringing a carpet to the house wrapped it around her in an effort to smother the fire. It was too late. Emma died the next morning after a brief hospitalization.[8]

It is not known whether Max, Edward, or their father was home to witness Emma's awful death, but the family was obviously devastated. T. S. did not remarry for ten years—and then to a woman who was also, oddly, named Emma, with whom he had no children.[9] Almost forty years later, Edward Graves, by then a successful executive in Chicago, shot and killed himself at the age of fifty-five in his home library. "Relatives and friends," his obituary read, "could give no reason for the act."[10]

As for Max, who remained in Indianapolis to head up his father's firm, things did not proceed altogether well following T. S.'s death in 1922. At least in family lore, much of his difficulty was attributable to alcohol, although events beyond Max's direct control were to compound his frustrations.

Michael's grandfather Max (center), great grandfather T. S. (right), and great great grandfather Michael Sells (left). The architect's father would be the last Graves in the Indy stockyard.

Three Generations at Yards.

Scarcely two weeks after his father died, Max was named in a lawsuit by a former business associate, who claimed that the Indianapolis Livestock Exchange—on which Max had inherited a seat—was operating as an illegal trust. The plaintiff, who had been pushed out of the organization the year prior, sought $12,000 in damages (nearly $200,000 in today's money), claiming that Max and his colleagues had conspired for years to fix livestock prices in order to benefit their private enterprises, to the exclusion of would-be competitors. There is no record that the case ever went to trial, the implication being that it was settled privately out of court for a large sum.[11]

After this period Graves, Nave & Company showed signs of a general slackening. George Nave lived to the age of ninety-one, devoting increasing time to hobby farming while leaving the business largely in Max's hands. The latter remained a member of the Indianapolis Livestock Exchange and continued to run the business, following Nave's death, as the Graves Commission Company. But for Max there was to be no National Livestock Exchange presidency, no fraternizing with presidential candidates. The firm remained in the same aging office near the stockyard where it had been for decades. Neither the company nor its owner attracted much attention from the press.

Part of this slackening was no doubt the result of Max's drinking. But part of it was likely the fact that his father had, almost undoubtedly, been operating the business as part of a trust—and now it was over.

The American livestock industry in the early twentieth century was rife with semi-licit monopolies, informal cartels designed to keep things profitable among the tight-knit, familial business elite that ran the nation's stockyards.[12] T. S. had been present at the creation of the modern livestock business in Indianapolis: he had married into the business, and he had been a founding member of the Indianapolis Livestock Exchange. He didn't have to participate in anything so elaborate as a conspiracy—just a series of well-placed gentlemen's agreements, father-in-law to son-in-law, neighbor to neighbor. The National Livestock Exchange itself had been accused, during T. S.'s tenure as president, of price collusion.[13]

The Graveses' wealth and social position up to the 1920s was likely the product of some form of trust, and it was just Max's luck that the law of the land happened to catch up with the family in his lifetime rather than his father's. New antitrust legislation governing the livestock trade had been enacted just two years prior to the lawsuit, and in an atmosphere of increasing litigation the Indianapolis Livestock Exchange could no longer play fast and loose with the rules.[14] The good times were at an end.

In any case, Max was busy with other concerns. After twenty-two years of marriage and the birth of their children, Thomas and Margaret, Max left his wife, Bessie, for a woman many years his junior.[15] The divorce was extraordinarily messy: Bessie remarried, to her own in-law—the father of Margaret's husband, to whom Max was obliged to make a large land transfer by way of settlement.[16] Only a few years later, Max divorced his second wife and married yet again, further depleting his resources. The rest of Max's time and money were given over to buying, trading, and riding horses—he was an active member of the local saddle club—and, of course, to drinking.

By the end there was little left for Max to pass on to his son, Bud—certainly not the fine house he'd built for himself on Washington Avenue, with its taupe-on-taupe interior, which is presumed lost in one or the other of the divorces. Still less was left for Bud's children. Max did give young Michael and his brother, Tom, a pony once, whom they named Tony the Pony, but despite the fact that Broad Ripple Village was only a few minutes away from Meridian-Kessler, the boys saw little of their paternal grandfather.[17] Max died in 1946, when his namesake was twelve years old.

THE TRAJECTORY OF the Graveses of Indianapolis does not adhere to the typical legends of class in the United States—neither the relentless upward march nor the slightly less common rags-to-riches-to-rags-in-three-generations narrative. Theirs was a story of a different sort: sliding from upper-middle-class privilege to lower-middle-class striving, it was a change in station subtle enough to go almost unnoticed but sharp enough to sting if anyone thought about it. No one could have thought about it as much as Michael's father, Bud, who witnessed it firsthand. But he made sure everyone else felt his pain.

The fine homes, the automobiles, the horses—all were gone. As in other cities, activity at the Indianapolis stockyards was in decline. The Depression was in its fifth year by the time of Michael's birth, and with improvements in refrigeration on the

Erma Lowe
Sanderson
Graves, 1931

MRS. THOMAS B. GRAVES.

one hand and the expansion of national highway networks on the other, the transportation of live animals by rail was becoming less and less economical. Livestock agents like Bud were by that time required to travel far from the city, out into the countryside around Indianapolis, to negotiate directly with farmers. Max had usually worn suits and ties; Michael never remembered his father in anything but work clothes.

The bitterness that Bud felt at his reduced state was unmistakable. "My father was certainly a bigot," Michael said, "and certainly an alcoholic."[18] In addition to his time on the road, Bud would disappear on long drinking sprees, sometimes for weeks on end. Michael recalled an episode where he and his brother, Tom, sensing that their father was about to embark on a bender, hid his shoes. Bud reacted at first with laughter, but his joviality quickly curdled into rage, and he began shouting at the boys and storming around the house. Michael's mother, Erma, finally insisted that Michael and his brother give the shoes back. As soon as he'd put them on, Bud left and did not return for several days.[19]

During these absences Erma was usually oblivious to her husband's whereabouts—though during one such episode, driving through Broad Ripple Village with young Michael, she pointed to a house near the end of the street. "That's where your father is," she said.[20]

The plain suggestion was that he was with another woman. This would not seem out of character. For while the boys were hiding their father's shoes, their father was hiding something far more serious from them: a previous marriage that had ended in divorce sometime in the late 1920s.[21] Michael never knew about his father's first wife. It is possible that Erma didn't, either.

If she did, she chose to remain silent about it, and this too would seem in character. Erma Lowe Graves was a formidable figure, unshakable in her convictions and

Michael around age twelve. The toy car he kept for decades, later giving it to the children of one of his associates.

unshaken by the sometimes rocky course of her married life. She was descended from one of the first families to settle the area around Greensburg, just south and east of Indianapolis, her family of modest means but sounder reputation than the mercurial Graveses. In marrying into the enterprising Indianapolis tribe and moving to the big city, Erma might have entertained visions of a grander life, but the failure of those hopes never left her outwardly disillusioned. Remaining married to Bud for forty-two years, she was committed to her husband despite his obvious failings, and committed to her children despite having given up a career in nursing for which she'd gone to both college and hospital school.[22] She was the whole world of Michael's early childhood.[23]

Erma performed all the usual parental offices: packing the school lunches, arranging the doctor's visits, paying the piano teacher.[24] But she was also the standard-bearer for morals in the family, and for morale. Keeping at bay her husband's wrath, she single-handedly spared Michael from inheriting the full catalog of his father's resentments. She had a seemingly bottomless reserve of fortitude and perhaps only one true vice: a slender, handsome woman in her youth, she was possessed of a well-deserved vanity.

When Michael was eleven, his mother, doubtless with an eye toward her wayward husband, decided to have elective surgery to remove a varicose vein in her thigh. No one was ever sure what happened. During the procedure, the doctor cut the wrong artery, or perhaps the wrong nerve, or else allowed the incision to become infected. The doctors decided that her leg would have to be removed below the knee. In keeping with her stoic, midwestern mind-set, Erma never thought to sue the hospital, accepting the blow in silence.[25]

Everything that she did for her children in the years that followed she did not only alone but on one leg. Though she wore a prosthetic limb most of the time, she found it stiff and uncomfortable, and routinely padded it with multiple socks that could quickly become sweaty and dirty. Walking was painful, and fast movement of any kind impossible. She did not greet misfortune gladly—she always acted, Michael said, "as if somebody owed her something"—but neither did she surrender to her husband's corrosive self-pity.[26] Undaunted in the face of her disability, she made it a part of her child-rearing ethic.

Among Michael's earliest memories was a long trip to St. Louis by train, pressed up against the window, watching the flat expanses of Indiana, Illinois, and Missouri roll by. They had traversed the Midwest and crossed the Mississippi to reach the manufacturer of Erma's preferred prosthesis: she wanted to have a new one fitted and to pick it straight off the line. When they arrived, Erma brought Michael along with her into the warehouse—a bizarrely artificial trophy room, with thousands of plastic arms, legs, and other body parts massed on the walls and hanging from the ceiling. It might sound like a macabre spectacle to which to expose one's child, but it did not seem so to Erma. For her this was simply another necessity of her condition, and if young Michael didn't like it, he had best keep his thoughts to himself. Such were her hard-edged lessons in empathy.

There were others. Not long after the operation, Erma attempted to hire someone to help her around the house and placed an ad in the local paper. When the applicant arrived, Michael opened the door and ushered the would-be aide into the modest one-floor house on Indianola. Immediately visible down the length of the hallway, lying in her bedroom, was Erma, still convalescing from the operation and with her amputated leg in full view. A shriek went up from the visitor: "They didn't tell me there was a *sick person* here!" Michael remembered her saying. "I'm not going to be in a house with *sick people*!" And she ran out.[27]

Erma was shattered; Michael was furious. He wanted his mother to be a happy warrior, to remain the cheerful soul she had been. But attitudes toward the disabled in the 1940s and '50s were not, in the main, so accepting as they are today, and the expectation that others would view her with either pity or disgust soured Erma's humor. She was, in her rough way, unashamed of her condition, but her strength sometimes emerged as meanness directed at anyone she didn't know—at sales clerks and waitresses especially. Awful scenes at department stores were a recurring feature of Michael's youth.

Still, Erma's pragmatic, no-nonsense brand of compassion, born of her disability and the reactions of a hostile world, would be key in shaping Michael's future path. His mother had, after all, been a nurse, and beneath her sometimes brusque exterior remained a desire to ease others' pain. The variation on the Golden Rule that she presented to her children was an unsentimental, all-American imperative: *be of use.* It was a lesson Michael internalized early.

HE ALSO, JUST AS EARLY, ran afoul of it. For there was only one thing, from as early as he or anyone who knew him in Broad Ripple Village could recall, that Michael was absolutely certain he wanted to do. It was by no means something that seemed likely, in itself, to satisfy his mother's strict, utilitarian standard. But it was something he felt compelled to do: he wanted to draw.

Sitting by the window, Erma would look out in muted bemusement as the eight-, nine-, or ten-year-old Michael wandered through the front and back yards and along the sidewalk, drawing everything in sight. Indianola Avenue was lined with tall maples and oaks; overhead the power lines stretched from post to post, bowing deeply in between, and the houses, seen obliquely, produced a muddle of overlaid figures trooping one after another as far as the banks of the White River. Michael took it down as best he could with the pencils and loose-leaf paper his mother allowed him to keep. She could tell he had promise, but the situation was not to her liking. Tom excelled at math and science; why couldn't Michael be more like his older brother?[28]

Besides the notebooks, the only real indulgence of Michael's artistic talent that Erma ever permitted was during a single summer when he was a child, when she signed him up for a painting class at the Indianapolis Museum of Art. It lasted one afternoon, and its sole product was a painting of a papier-mâché tiger that Michael had seen in the museum's collection.[29] Years later Ada Louise Huxtable—the *New York Times*'s first architecture critic (and still the most powerful one in its history)—asked him about his "artistic education," and he mentioned briefly this one-day intensive seminar in Indianapolis. Huxtable, apparently deeming this a sufficient pedigree, went on to claim in print that Michael Graves was "a painter before he was an architect."[30] No copy of the painting exists to vouch for Michael's early academic bona fides.

The tiger, however, was all Erma was prepared to tolerate. One day, not long thereafter, she made her feelings plain to her younger son.

"I'm tired of you telling all my friends that you're going to be an artist," he remembered her saying. "Unless you're as good as Picasso, you'll starve. What you should do is find a life's work that uses art, but that's a real *profession*."

"Like what?" Michael asked.

"I don't know. Like engineering, or architecture."

Unfamiliar with either trade, Michael asked first what engineers do. Erma explained in a hazy way the process of preparing schematic drawings, resolving the technical problems of construction, figuring out how to make buildings stand up, and so forth.

It sounded complicated. "All right then," said Michael. "I'll be an architect."

"But," Erma pointed out, "I haven't told you what an architect *does* yet."

Michael said he didn't need to know; he just knew he didn't want to be an engineer. If he was not to be an artist, he would settle for being an architect.

And that was that.[31]

THERE WAS AT LEAST one other way in which Erma's disability was formative in Michael's development as a designer, however accidentally. On the eve of his mother's amputation, he went to see her in the hospital. He entered her room to discover a huge dome—a horrible glass vault, used to freeze the leg in preparation for severing it—covering one half of her body. Michael remembered being terrified, not understanding what had happened, who was to blame, or what was going to happen next.

Then and there, his mother pulled him close. "You've got to make me a promise," she whispered. "You will never have cosmetic surgery."[32] This might seem an extraordinary promise to extract from an eleven-year-old boy, in particular one already trembling in fear and confusion. Then again, Erma was no ordinary mother. Michael nodded his assent.

It was, in any event, an easy enough promise to make: What likelihood could the boy possibly foresee of ever *wanting* to have cosmetic surgery? But even at that tender age, there were already the first faint signs of a condition that would affect Michael for his entire life and shape the way that he—literally and figuratively—viewed the world.

It usually begins in early childhood, so was likely evident by the date of Erma's amputation. Every now and again, when he looked at objects in the far distance, young Michael's left eye could be seen to drift slightly, modulating toward the corner farthest from his nose. The problem tends to intensify with age, such that by the time Michael was in his late teens—having never had, as he swore he would not, the surgery that might have corrected it—he had developed a pronounced case of lazy eye. Constant exotropic strabismus, the technical name for the disorder, is one of a number of classifications related to amblyopia, a failure of the eye to communicate with the brain due to neurological factors, resulting in the eye's physical decentering. The underlying cause of Michael's was never known, since he never considered an operation on it. He might have pursued a number of alternative therapies, such as wearing an eye patch over his healthy eye to force the skewed one to align properly. He did not.[33]

The consequences of this decision for Michael's way of seeing are difficult to tease out, if only because vision is among the more subjective topics in medicine: one can only see the way one sees, and Michael never had anything with which to contrast his own experience. But some aspects of life with exotropia can be described with certainty.

Michael's high school graduation photo. His eye defect is clearly visible.

In the normally sighted individual, the world appears monoptically, both eyes being trained on a given object to form a single image. The exotropic viewer, on the other hand, may experience double vision: the object appearing side by side, the strong and the weak eye viewing it independently. But this is rare, at least in those who carry their lazy eye into adulthood. After a certain phase in cognitive development, the brain simply corrects the problem, creating a synthetic image that combines the two discrete perceptions of each eye, with an emphasis on the fully operable one. But it is a unified image very different from that seen by the orthoscopic majority. The image fused together by the brain is flattened, the object's position relative to those around it being less than perfectly gauged. The downside, as one can imagine, is a general diminution in depth perception, which—even with the corrective lenses that Michael wore to help improve the nearsightedness of the weaker eye—can make it difficult to play sports, to estimate distances, or even (in extreme cases) to tell the difference between a picture of a thing and the thing itself.

The upside, however, is that it can make for great art.[34] If the flattened landscape of exotropia sounds a little like a Cubist painting, that is no coincidence: Pablo Picasso, Erma's model of the financially successful artist, shared with her son an abnormally aligned eye that seems to have played a major part in the early phase of his career. And Picasso wasn't alone. According to recent research, Rembrandt van Rijn, Marc Chagall, Frank Stella, Alexander Calder, and Edward Hopper are only a few of the startlingly high proportion of prominent artists who exhibited some degree of strabismus. Obviously, merely having the condition is no guarantor of artistic ability. But since the strabismus-affected individual already views his or her environment in something very much like two dimensions, it is that much easier to translate three-dimensional phenomena onto the flat expanse of the canvas: even if the artwork doesn't betray an explicitly Cubistic quality, there's one less cognitive leap to overcome. For this reason, art teachers frequently advise their pupils to cover one eye while trying to draw a subject.

One might also speculate as to another explanation, more difficult to pin down, for why art history is so filled with cockeyed geniuses. In the exotropic experience, there may be a degree of difference that lends those artists' work (to recall the Russian theorist Viktor Shklovsky) a quality of *estrangement*. Their perceptive mechanism forever at odds with that of the rest of humankind, lazy-eyed artists reproduce the world in compellingly unfamiliar fashion, creating something that feels *like* the world as we know it, yet somehow not, as in the world of dreams.

MICHAEL WAS ALWAYS AWARE, at least in the abstract, that his eye played some role in his creative process. "I'm the only artist and architect I know," he would joke, "who sees the world from a skewed perspective."[35]

Not the only one, evidently. But the only one *he knew*. The consciousness of his condition as a demarcation of difference—of both seeing and being seen differently from those around him—was another element of the condition for Michael, and this too may be symptomatic of strabismus. Almost as important as its perceptive implications are its psychosocial effects. The awareness that others were looking at him strangely, fixated upon that odd eye, never left Michael; years later he would sit in business meetings and watch as a new client first noticed his peculiar gaze and then sat puzzled for the remainder of the session, trying to figure out precisely what Michael was looking at. It gave him, at key moments, the advantage of inscrutability.[36]

That might not have felt like such a fine thing to an adolescent. Current studies show that the conviction among their peers that children with strabismus are "weird" or "shifty" can lead to isolation and feelings of low self-worth, with ongoing symptoms of social anxiety lasting well into adulthood.[37] This too may contribute to the artistic impulse: What is an artist, if not a perpetual outsider? Feeling oneself to be different, one becomes so. Jean-Paul Sartre, perhaps the most famous intellectual walleye of the twentieth century, might never have become his aloof, confounding self without the aloof, confounding expression that made him seem so from the start. But Michael was not exchanging witticisms with Simone de Beauvoir and the rest at the Café de Flore.

Mike—as he was then universally known—was in Indianapolis in the 1940s: a skinny kid with thick glasses, spiky hair, and a comical, moonlike countenance, charmingly out of sync with the world yet wishing deeply to be as much like everyone else as he could.

Downtown
Indianapolis
and the Soldiers
and Sailors
Monument
(Bruno Schmitz,
1901), seen
at midcentury

IT WAS NOT a place and a time that offered much nourishment to an aspiring young architect. Beyond the determined indifference of his mother and father to what might be deemed "high culture," Indy was a town of almost unbroken social homogeneity and religiosity, where the local taste rarely exceeded in complexity the local delicacy, the sugar cream pie (ingredients: flour, sugar, butter, vanilla, and cream). Even in 1944, in the middle of the Second World War, the city went solidly for Franklin D. Roosevelt's Republican opponent, Thomas Dewey.

"I wasn't exposed to much of anything as a kid that might have made me want to be an artist or an architect," Michael later said, although there were buildings of note in the city.[38] Indianapolis had a library designed by the great early twentieth-century American architect Paul Philippe Cret, a stately affair with a columned porch in front and a triangular pediment above. Cret (pronounced "cray") was an exponent of a rather harsh, reduced form of classicism, his Beaux Arts training hardened by a distinctly American sobriety. Unhappily for him, the approach proved popular with the German architect Albert Speer in the 1930s, who drew on Cret's work for his buildings for the Nazi regime.[39]

The city also had a World War Memorial, a heavy, high-shouldered building, tomblike and mysterious, and Michael spent much of his childhood pining to get inside of it. He never did—it was never open to the public—and the fascination may have resurfaced in his later attraction to the work of the eighteenth-century French-man Claude-Nicolas Ledoux, which the memorial resembled slightly in its blocky simplicity and exaggerated proportions.[40]

The memorial and library were part of a monumental corridor in the middle of downtown Indianapolis that resembled, on a smaller scale and with slightly less formal organization, the National Mall in Washington, DC. This was no coincidence: the city was first designed by an associate of Pierre L'Enfant, the man who drew up the original scheme for the country's new capital in the 1780s. Like Washington, Indianapolis is laid out on a radial plan, with diagonal streets converging on a large circle in the center of town, which punctuates the southern end of the corridor that includes the World War Memorial and library. And in the very middle of that circle is an obelisk—a looming pseudo-Egyptian tower, not dissimilar from the Washington Monument—surrounded by decorative sculptural groups and encircled by staircases. Dedicated to the dead of the Spanish-American War, it is known as the Soldiers and Sailors Monument.

Visitors were permitted to walk to the top of the obelisk, climbing 284 feet to take in a sweeping view of the whole of Indianapolis stretching out in perfect flatness in all directions. Here at a glance was the entire *terra cognita* of the first eighteen years of Michael's life: to the north, Broad Ripple Village and its adjacent suburbs, Graves territory since the days of his great-grandfather T. S.; below, Downtown, a conventional business district with a few fine specimens of American vernacular buildings (but nothing particularly stirring to Mike); and in the far southwest, the stockyards, much diminished from their early-century peak but still very much in operation.

There, intriguingly, was a piece of architecture that *had* stuck in the mind of the young designer. Every now and again, when Bud was in a more accommodating and less dissolute mood, he'd take his younger son to the stockyards with him. High above the pens, there was a second floor, a series of elevated catwalks crisscrossing the airy void. The slaughterhouse owners would come out from the city to negotiate purchases with Mike's father; standing in their suits and ties, they would remain well above the muck, looking down at the livestock below, with Michael standing alongside them. The catwalks were just simple planks of wood, but the future architect never forgot the feeling of that gridded system suspended in air. Everything, it seemed to him, had a grandeur to it, a feeling of importance—the light streaming down from above, the solemn businessmen, and his father below, jumping athletically from aisle to aisle.

Decades later, when Michael first saw the famous *Imaginary Prison* drawings by the eighteenth-century draftsman Giovanni Battista Piranesi, his first thought was: "I've *been* here."[41] The interweaving wooden structures, the game they played between transparency and opacity, the sense of an ordered system interposing itself on the abstraction of space: the boy could not have articulated it at the time, but the stockyards were his first encounter with that mysterious sensation—that electrification of the subconscious—that certain places and forms would always induce in him. Years later he returned to Indianapolis and went looking for the building, only to find it had been torn down.[42] No photographs survive to show what, exactly, Michael Graves's first authentic architectural experience was like.

His father's business was the occasion for another encounter, equally unintentional, that would presage a rather different aspect of Michael's architectural development. As he related decades later to his colleague Peter Waldman, Bud once took him into town to show him the office where he and all the Graveses past had sorted out their receipts and shipping orders. His father gestured up to the old building, trying to point out the window next to which he kept his own desk. He couldn't find it: all the floors were too alike. The moment stayed with Michael long after. "Architecture," he told Waldman, "is responsible for making a place so that a father can tell his son where he works."[43] For Michael, understanding a building would always be as important as how it made him feel.

The stockyards and an old office building were as likely places as any to find inspiration in 1940s Indianapolis—though there was one bit of culture that Erma did enforce upon her son, much to his displeasure. As a teenager, Mike was

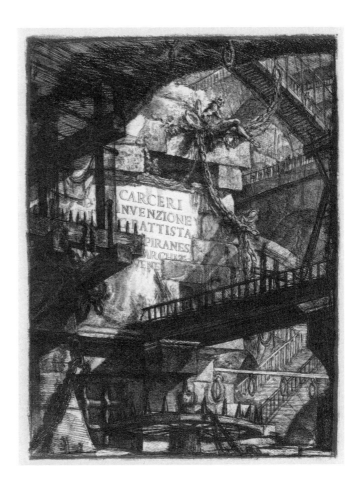

Piranesi's
"Carceri
d'Invenzione,"
frontispiece to
the second
edition, 1760

frog-marched by his mother into a ballroom dancing class. He was expected to take the bus downtown every week, head directly to Mrs. Gates's Dancing School, and then take the same bus directly home afterward. The entire excursion—home, bus, class, bus, home—took about two hours, after which time his mother expected to see him walking through the front door on Indianola. But Mike and his childhood friend Rick Williams had other plans.

Regularly, week after week, they would hop on the bus at the prescribed time—but instead of getting off at the dance school, they continued on to the Soldiers and Sailors Monument, dashed to the top of the obelisk, took in the view for as long as they dared, and then clambered back down as fast as they could, grabbing the bus home. Erma was none the wiser: their timing was perfect, and Michael feigned just the right quality of put-upon, post-foxtrot annoyance. Their cover was blown only when Mrs. Gates called Erma to find out if Mike was sick, since he hadn't been to class for some time. His attendance record thereafter was stellar.[44]

Little did Mike imagine that one day the Washington Monument scaffold—a system, in essence, for getting up an obelisk—would be one of his best-known creations.

INTRIGUED AS MIKE WAS by the stockyard catwalks, his interest in his father's (and his grandfather's, and his great-grandfather's) line of work weighed in at exactly nil. With the provisional blessing of his mother, he had already decided upon being an architect. Even had he not done so, he was hard set against any career involving sheep and cows.

It hadn't been expected that he would take that path: his older brother Tom was next in line to take over the trade. But it soon became apparent that Erma and Bud's firstborn—a brilliant if slightly remote boy, whom Michael remembered once angrily shunning his mother's embrace for no particular reason—was destined for other things. Bud was incensed.[45]

Their father's sulks didn't always spill over into visible anger—only when such things as the continuation of the family legacy seemed at risk. Escape was his preferred strategy. On a few occasions, driving Mike back from one of those visits to the pens, Thomas would stop the car partway back to Broad Ripple Village, not far from a small bar.

"I'm going to go see a man about a horse," he would tell Mike.

It seemed a plausible story—his father was, after all, a livestock agent. It took a number of such visits, and many hours spent alone in the car, before Mike realized what his father was up to and that there was no horse trading going on in the bar.

Even had Tom or Michael been inclined to enter the family business, the business was not quite the family's anymore. The Graves Commission Company was now the Shannon Graves Commission Company, one of Bud's partners having assumed greater authority in light of his chronic absenteeism. The company office was still the same as it had been in T. S. and Max's day: Michael recalled it as being "like the old West," a stuffy, saloon-like atmosphere, filled with wood paneling and spittoons. Perhaps sensing that this way of life belonged to a fading past, Bud did not waste too much breath trying to badger his younger son into the livestock profession.

But Mike found other ways to twit his easily irritated father. In his midteens, he befriended a classmate at Broad Ripple High School who was a member of a local Episcopalian church, St. Paul's. The friend persuaded Michael and a group of six or so other boys to accompany him one Thursday night to a service officiated by a young priest there, perhaps only ten years older than the boys themselves. The group took to him right away. The cleric's youth, but also his maturity, his kindness and quiet seriousness, all seemed to inspire confidence and loyalty in the high schoolers. "Especially me," recalled Michael, who saw in the priest a model of manhood not available back home. "It was the fact that he was a grown-up. I didn't consider my father capable of being in charge of his own life."

The young priest invited Mike and the boys to come on Sundays and attend services as altar boys. "They told me what I had to do," Michael said, "where I had to kneel and stand and how to move the Bible from one side of the altar to the other. And I adored doing that." Every week, Mike got up at dawn (which he *didn't* adore), dressed in his vestment, a long gown secured with countless buttons, and walked over to St. Paul's. His mother knew where he was going; his father, as per norm, was not even aware that Mike was out of the house on Sunday mornings.

One evening at dinner, his mother said, "Mike, why don't you tell your father what you're doing at the church?"

"What church?" asked Bud.

"St. Paul's," Mike said.

"What's St. Paul's?"

"It's the Episcopal church over on North Meridian."

His father looked stricken. "You're not a member of St. Paul's. You were baptized as I was baptized, as a Presbyterian."

Bud wanted to know everything: What was it Mike was doing there, and why, and with whom? Mike said he was going because he liked it. As Michael recalled, Bud claimed not to know what Episcopalianism was, or what Communion was. And when he told his father that the services at St. Paul's were conducted by a priest, "the word," Michael said, "made his hair stand up."

His father began shouting and pounding the table in rage. "Is this one of those *cults*?" Bud demanded. "I mean, do you have to break a *glass*?"

It is, needless to say, absurd that one of the oldest denominations of American Christianity—the one to which nearly all of the country's Founding Fathers belonged—should incite in Michael's father such a bout of ill-informed paranoia. It is the more absurd given Bud's conspicuously irreligious deportment, not to mention the fact that the Graveses' ancestors back in Lexington, Kentucky, had been Baptists, not Presbyterians.[46] But none of that mattered to Bud.

Provincialism of a most orthodox variety was the order of the day, not just in the Graves household, but for many of their neighbors. Few people traveled, fewer still studied back East at the older American universities. The Graveses once did— Bud's poor uncle Edward, before his self-inflicted death, had been a graduate of Cornell—but that was in the past.[47] There was no getting too big for your britches in Bud Graves's house. In truth, Michael's father knew perfectly well what an

Episcopalian was, and what it represented: ivy-covered walls, people who spoke foreign languages. From there it was only a short step to barefaced treason and losing China to the Reds.

As oppressive as the atmosphere at home may have been, it did not as yet engender in Michael the express desire to escape. Where could he escape to? Some of his friends and classmates might have had it better than he, others worse, but whatever their separate struggles, getting out was never a major topic of discussion in the locker-lined hallways of Broad Ripple High School. With a few notable exceptions, very few of its graduates did. Fifteen years separated Michael from his best-known co-alumnus, the talk show host David Letterman.

Looking back, Michael said of his school that it was a place where "you had to play three sports a year, or you were considered a nerd."[48] Given his poor eyesight, he was seriously handicapped from the start, and well into his teens he was an object of fun on the playground: a meager boy with one eye that seemed to wander off at will and a broad, sleepy smile. Michael always felt himself to be a step behind, and it bothered him. But he had already learned from Erma Graves how to bear up under pressure.

Broad Ripple High did make it slightly easier in one respect, affording Mike an educational opportunity extremely rare in the 1940s Midwest—or, for that matter, in any school anywhere, even today: a course in construction and architecture. It seems almost inexplicable that a middle-class suburban high school, even one of reasonably good repute, should include such a course as part of the general curriculum. Design classes at the pre-undergraduate level, in those days and later, have tended to be the stuff of more progressive (and more posh) institutions on the order of Michigan's Cranbrook School, which could draw on the resources of an actual undergraduate program nearby. Doubtless Broad Ripple established its architectural program not in a spirit of liberal arts–ish creativity but more in the way of vocational training, to provide a solid, practical skill that might prepare a young man for a life spent delineating oil derricks.

Mike, with his parentally sanctioned career already settled upon, took the course in the first semester of his sophomore year, and his progress was astonishing. His native ability for drawing, which had yet to be directed into any particular channel, was quickly honed into a talent for architectural draftsmanship. Before the year was out, he'd learned how to prepare vertical elevations to represent buildings' facades, how to create perspective renderings to picture them as they might appear in the real world, and how to make basic plans, shading in the poche to indicate the thickness and shape of the walls. When he'd finished the course, he was ready for more, and once again Broad Ripple came through: an instructor was found to work with him one-on-one for months, drawing building after building. Other classes of young people would come in for the first-semester course, and there would be Mike, sitting in a corner, sketching the floor plan of a house.

If the architecture course gave Mike a little relief from the prevailing dullness of his milieu, it was also the only bright spot in an academic career that did not show any immediate promise of leading to a tenure-track position at Princeton. Math, science, literature (he was an appalling speller until the day he died)—Mike's failures were not confined to the athletic field, and this was a source of still more tension in the home. Feeling himself in competition with his brother, Michael said he was forever coming in second place for Erma's approval. "He was in the so-called honor society, which I wasn't," Michael said of Tom, "and he also got a letter in track in his sophomore year, which is unheard of."[49] Even six decades later, with both his mother and brother long dead, Michael's envy was as fresh as though he and Tom were only then turning in their report cards, knowing already what Erma would say.

MIKE DID, EVENTUALLY, join the football team, and earned his varsity letter. He tried wrestling and track. But his greatest success, besides at the drafting table, was in a very different field of endeavor.

"We called him François," recalled his friend Lois Hickman (now surnamed Rothert).

The zesty Gallic moniker stemmed from Mike's putative success as a ladies' man. Rothert had known Mike (or François, or "Mox," as she also called him) since grade school and had dated him briefly in junior high. "He gave me his Boy Scout ring," she remembered.

A token of his affection—but not, as she found out, his constancy. "I kept it on my finger with a pound of adhesive tape," Rothert continued. "Then what happened: in the eighth-grade Indiana basketball tournament, everybody went to the sectionals, and Mike Graves went to a ball game and ran into a girl from the county school named Eleanor Hackemeyer. A vamp!" Shortly thereafter, Rothert said, "he asked for his Boy Scout ring back."[50]

Even after that, Mike still had the effrontery to try to kiss Rothert on a streetcar back to Broad Ripple Village following a midnight showing of *Frankenstein* on New Year's Eve. His louche tendencies became legend, but did nothing to affect a friendship that would last for decades and grow to include Rothert's subsequent boyfriend, whom she began dating a short while thereafter, fellow classmate Jay Hanselmann.

Hanselmann was the quarterback for the football team; periodically Mike was put in at center, where he would routinely forget the snap signal. In addition to his superior athletic prowess, Hanselmann was also a far more successful student, getting straight As to Mike's mingled Bs and Cs. He took the same architecture course shortly after Mike, who confessed one day in class to Hanselmann that this—this mapping out of buildings silently in the corner—was what Mike wanted to do for a living. Hanselmann explained that if that was really what he wanted, he had better start working on his grades. Mike replied that the only reason he had bad grades was because he was inattentive. He promised to straighten up.

Not long thereafter, Erma came into her younger son's room and saw Mike engaged in an unfamiliar activity. "What are you doing?" she asked.

"I'm studying!" he replied.[51]

In an effort to catch up, Mike took summer classes. His grades improved, at least somewhat, and he began to assume an air of somewhat greater seriousness.

Even François, it seemed, was ready to hang up his beret.

"I MET HER at a high school party," Michael remembered. Broad Ripple Village had, in a manner more common to American universities, its own fraternities and sororities, and Mike was in one of the former—"a very big deal," he would claim.[52]

The fraternities usually gathered one night out of the week at the family home of one member or the other. Following one such get-together during his junior year, Mike and his brothers went to one of the houses where a sorority meeting was being held (they always made sure to know where those meetings were taking place), and there Mike was "fixed up," as he claimed, with Gail Devine, a petite, attractive young woman one year behind him in school.

They had much in common, especially in the context of down-to-earth Broad Ripple Village, where both stood out for their creative ambitions—he an aspiring architect, she an aspiring artist. Their backgrounds were likewise comparable, both from bluish-collar families. Gail's father had owned a gas station before quitting to join local engine manufacturer Allis-Chalmers as a jet mechanic. "He was a good guy," Michael remembered, "and her mother was a sweetheart."[53]

The two would go on double dates with Jay and Lois, out for Cokes in the afternoon or movies in the evening. Reserved but sweet-natured, possessed of an unmistakable warmth, Gail made an excellent counterweight to Mike's playful space-cadet act, buttressing his efforts to become more grounded and mature. That her family life was somewhat more stable than his must have seemed an added perk, as did a nurturing quality that Erma was not always able to provide in sufficient quantity.

Whatever François's reputation, this was still Indianapolis in the years just after World War II, and Mike and his high school sweetheart were usually under the watchful eye of one or both sets of parents, to say nothing of their own quaking consciences. "Scared to death," Michael said, the two quickly began to look forward to marriage, as all their friends did, as the conventional next step, the only acceptable form for an adult relationship to take.[54]

Michael always maintained that the idea of starting a family was not, for him, a means to flee from his own, but only "what you did." Things in the Graves home had in actuality taken a surprising turn for the better toward the end of Michael's high school years: Bud and Erma moved out of the Indianola house and into a slightly more ample one on College Avenue, and Bud entered Alcoholics Anonymous, giving up drinking for life. By that point, however, enough damage had been done. The years of neglect, punctuated by instances of genuine cruelty, meant that Michael was effectively estranged from his father for life—though not untouched by his father's persistent angst, in ways that would become clear only later.

JUST BEFORE MIKE GRADUATED from Broad Ripple High School in 1952, he received word of a competition for high-school-age artists and designers sponsored by Purdue University in nearby West Lafayette, Indiana. The contest was aimed at rising seniors who aspired to careers in engineering—precisely the group Broad Ripple's architecture course was meant to nurture. Most of the prizes were to be awarded to schematic drawings and technical documents—the kinds of things that interested Mike least when he first heard from Erma what an engineer does. But there was one prize category that was more of a free-for-all, a miscellaneous brief that invited applicants to draw whatever building they liked. Opting for this more artistic challenge, Mike created a rendering of the Parthenon, the most famed Greek temple of them all, built in Athens in the fifth century BCE. He copied his drawing from a photograph in a library book.

Why he chose that particular subject is anyone's guess. Perhaps it reminded him of the stern grandeur of the World War Memorial downtown; perhaps he had heard it mentioned, or heard mentioned its great patron, the Athenian ruler Pericles, in one of those high school history lectures he had felt it prudent to pay attention to. Perhaps he'd accidentally chanced upon it while flipping through the book. Despite having acquired a facility as a draftsman almost unheard of for a person his age, Mike had not up to this period received anything approximating an education in the history of architecture. He did not know, except for what little the book he copied from could have told him, how important the Parthenon was to the whole development of building design, from Vitruvius to Le Corbusier. He did not yet even know who Le Corbusier was, much less Vitruvius.

Mike won the competition and received as a prize a mechanical drawing set—a full suite of compass, protractor, and other handy tools that he had been making do without all through his early years of drawing and drafting. "For a kid like me," he said years later, "it seemed like a very big deal."[55] It convinced him that he was on the right track. If Erma still looked somewhat askance, it also convinced Gail, who never once questioned Michael's pursuit of architecture through all the years that followed. Together they decided that Michael should attend architecture school at the University of Cincinnati and that Gail would follow him there the year after, once she too had graduated. With the recent improvement in his GPA, Michael applied and was accepted.[56]

IT IS UNFORTUNATE that the Parthenon drawing has not survived, nor the painting of the papier-mâché tiger. What little of Michael's juvenilia still exists comprises several sheaves of childhood drawings—most of them of popular cartoon characters, with a particular focus (remarkably, in light of his subsequent career) on Mickey

From a sheaf of Michael's childhood drawings: a picture of things to come. Drawn on the back of a piece of Graves Commission Co. stationery—the letterhead is visible in the background.

Mouse. Together with a few letters to his brother, the ribbon from Purdue, and random ephemera from later decades, these were consigned to a box squirreled away on the Warehouse compound and forgotten until well after Michael's death. The lack of sentimentality was symptomatic: to Michael, the past was the past. It was not a place he revisited often.

In the annals of architectural upbringings, such willed oblivion is almost de rigueur. Beginning in 1917, Charles-Édouard Jeanneret-Gris "carefully applied the eraser," as the scholar J. K. Birksted put it, "to his first thirty formative years"—leaving behind a small town in Switzerland, taking French citizenship, and rechristening himself Le Corbusier.[57] A similar transformation was effected by Aachen-born Maria Ludwig Michael Mies, who adopted his mother's maiden name with a false Dutch nobiliary particle and passed himself off in cosmopolitan Berlin as Ludwig Mies van der Rohe.

It has not always been thus. Closer to Michael—both geographically and culturally—Frank Lloyd Wright never turned against his midwestern roots, elevating the lush landscape of his native Wisconsin to a romantic ideal. But this too constituted a form of erasure. Casting himself as a plainsman philosopher-king, Wright rewrote a personal story that had long seemed, to him at least, dangerously prosaic. His middle name at birth was Lincoln, not Lloyd; he dropped the former and its association with his Eastern-born father, taking on the latter for its connection to his mother's Welsh family and their more appealing, pseudo-Druidical heritage.[58] Looking at Wright through the lens of Sigmund Freud, the historian Vincent Scully once wrote that the architect had disposed of his paternity to "sally forth as an Oedipus unrivaled, conqueror of the city."[59] In Michael's case, however, psychobiography of this kind is not so easily applied. The child and the man share their customary relation, but the bond between them was snapped much later, and in a different spirit than it had been with Wright, Mies, or Le Corbusier.

Even as he readied himself for college, Michael displayed none of the markings of a young man on the make, eager to re-create himself anew as far from home as he could get. The miracle of Michael's growing up is that he never hated his childhood, never hated Indianapolis, and for a long time after leaving continued to assume that he would one day return there to stay. He never even hated his father; or if he had hated him, he'd given it up long before settling into his twilight years in Princeton.

In part, young Mike Graves never shared his father's anger, because young Mike Graves never knew that life could be very different than it was. That would only come later, as he got out of Indianapolis and out into the world—though when he did, he too would be prey to a gnawing class anxiety not so dissimilar from Bud's. There were things, Michael would feel, that had been unfairly denied him, things that Bud had regarded with spite because he—or, more accurately, Max—had lost them. A sense of refinement, the grandeur of the past, the world of culture and the arts: Michael would try to reclaim these through the power of his exceptional eye, even if the beauty of the result was sometimes marred by the all-too-visible effort.

But he would always remain Erma's son more than Bud's. Michael was never ruled by his jealousies (although it was sometimes a close call). And because he loved his mother and wanted her to be proud of him, and because he did not hate his father and wanted to prove there was nothing to be afraid of in that bigger world—because of this, and a durable fondness for the quiet suburban streets of Broad Ripple Village and the even-keeled, unassuming people who lived there—there was always a little bit of Indianapolis in whatever Michael Graves did as a designer. He was always playing to the hometown crowd.

"In the end," said his old friend Peter Eisenman, "Michael just wanted to be the captain of the Broad Ripple High School football team."[60]

III

THE BOOK AND THE DOORWAY

Not all the graduates of Broad Ripple High School in that spring of 1952 would be headed straight to college the next fall—not even all of those who had applied and been accepted. Under the rules of the nation's Selective Service System, some college-bound men would be exempt from the ongoing military draft. But others, fully 40 percent that year, would be headed to Korea, where the United States and its allies were engaged in a protracted stalemate after nearly two years of war.[1]

Qualifying for an educational deferment meant placing in a certain percentile on a specially devised aptitude test, and even with the recent improvement in his grades Michael was no shoo-in. As it happened, he never had to be: he reported to his nearest processing station, received his physical examination, and shortly thereafter was informed that he'd been deemed 4-f—physically unfit for combat by reason of poor vision. Once again, and not for the last time, Michael's life was changed by his bad eye.[2]

Spared the rigors of army life (which were not likely to have suited him), Michael made ready to leave for Cincinnati. He would spend his first year alone and the subsequent years with Gail, living in rather straightened circumstances, leaving almost everything behind in Indianapolis save for their friendships with Jay and Lois and a few others. For Michael, the departure was to be permanent, though he hardly imagined it so at the time.

It was not, as escapes go, a particularly daring one. A scant one hundred miles separates Indianola Avenue from the Clifton Heights neighborhood where he now settled, and there was and remains a great deal in common between the metropolis on the White River and the other on the Ohio. At midcentury, Cincinnati was only slightly larger and slightly older than Indianapolis, more industrial but no less sober- and business-minded, and if it seemed to Michael and Gail a touch more exciting than their hometown, it was largely because of the busy cultural life centered on the city's big, bustling college.

Not that Michael would have much spare time to enjoy it. The University of Cincinnati's architecture program was a demanding one: fashioned, at the time, after a cooperative model, it entailed a part-time apprenticeship that saw students attending classes for two months, then working in a professional design studio for two, repeating the pattern until graduation. This gave them practical experience, but it meant long hours, and it extended the typical term of study by half.[3] For six years, the young couple would live out a provisional adulthood, Michael trotting off to the office many mornings while Gail studied at home—though not, at least for the first two years, in the *same* home.[4] After her matriculation, the couple maintained separate apartments, enacting a kind of pantomime of the American domestic dream.

The office to which Michael headed those mornings was itself a bit of midcentury Americana, a species of architectural practice that has almost entirely died out in the decades since. Many years later, a late-life encomium to the architect Carl Strauss appeared in the *Cincinnati Enquirer*: "Week after week, you can find his name in the Sunday paper, somewhere deep in tiny type, buried in the bowels of classified advertising under 'Houses for Sale.'"[5] A staple of the local development scene for fifty-five years—"Cincinnati's best-known architect," as the paper called him—Strauss ran a studio that was small but never wanted for work, designed upward of one hundred houses for the city's great and only slightly less great, and occupied a comfortable niche that seemed perfectly suited to his refined, aristocratic bearing. He was among the last of his breed: a true gentleman-architect.

"He looked like Alan Ladd," Michael recalled.[6] Strauss's matinee-idol looks were complemented by a taste for the finer things, for clothes and furniture, and having attained his municipal celebrity shortly after the war he apparently saw little reason to overexert himself. Michael would recall how, if a building was under construction, Strauss would stop by the worksite in the morning, then drop into the office around noon to answer letters and make phone calls. He would look over the drafting boards of his young associates—seven of them at the firm's height in the 1950s and early '60s—and then, at around the four o'clock hour, would take his hat from beside the door and bid them all adieu, as he stepped out to attend the theater or a social function.

His firm specialized in houses of what has been called the "good-life Modernism" variety—a soft, domesticated amalgam of styles, familiar from a thousand midcentury women's magazines and once devastatingly summed up by the critic Peter Blake as "the holy trinity of fieldstone, flagstone and the kidney shape."[7] High-end counterparts to the period's middle-class ranch house, Strauss's homes featured elegantly glassed-in living rooms in steel frames faced in wood siding, with upper-level dining rooms that cantilevered out over the lower floors to command views of the surrounding landscape. The designs were always accomplished, if rarely daring, and although Strauss's kindness and personal charm won him the affection of his newest assistant, Michael was not much impressed by his employer's ability as a designer. And not without reason: Strauss himself was not responsible for some of the office's finest work.

That role fell to his most senior associate, a man named Ray Roush. More than anyone else during Michael's years in Cincinnati, it was Roush who taught him how to be an architect.

FOURTEEN YEARS MICHAEL'S SENIOR, Raymond E. Roush Jr. was also a product of the University of Cincinnati, a native Ohioan raised in nearby Manchester. During the Second World War he'd worked at the Supreme Headquarters Allied Expeditionary Force as a model maker, mapping in exquisite detail the terrain of the continent over which British and American troops were about to advance. After VE Day, he'd remained in Europe to tour the continent he'd just helped conquer, winding up with a year in Paris at the École des Beaux Arts.[8] His personal exposure to the latest developments in European architecture, combined with his well-honed sense of

Ray Roush's Breuer-esque house in suburban Cincinnati, built in 1951

precision, made him a perfect foil to the older, airier Strauss. It also made him, for Michael, the ideal architectural role model.

"Ray was enamored of Marcel Breuer, and he built himself a Breuer house," remembered Michael. "That was the first piece of modern architecture I knew—I lived in it, slept in it. My world was so tied to Ray Roush."[9] Not only the first Modernist building Michael had seen up close, but the first architect's house he'd ever been in, Roush's home in Anderson Township, just southeast of the city, was a summa on his design thinking: a flowing sequence of indoor and outdoor spaces sheltered under a flat wooden roof, with exposed brick, wooden panels, and brass fixtures within. The Hungarian-born Breuer had started his career at the German Bauhaus school before moving to the States and modulating toward a more personal (and arguably more personable) style, and Roush's design nodded toward Breuer's binuclear floor plan, with the public and private spaces separated by a central corridor.[10]

Roush's range of experience, and his devotion to his work, outstripped anything Michael had known. Jayne Merkel, a Cincinnatian herself and years later the architecture critic of the *Cincinnati Enquirer*, recalled Roush as a retiring, unprepossessing man with a "hippieish" streak, happy to live in his wooded retreat and focus on work while leaving the glad-handing to Strauss.[11] One of the partners' shared projects was a house for a local industrialist, C. Lawson Reed Jr.—an adventurous patron of Cincinnati architecture, who had seen Mies's original Barcelona Pavilion in 1929—and Roush would return every five years or so to see that the Reed residence was kept up to his personal standards.[12] Roush had little patience for mediocrity, and almost instantly he recognized that Michael was anything but mediocre. "He knew," Merkel said, "that he had this talent."[13]

But there was more to the burgeoning friendship than just mutual professional admiration. Roush and his wife, Lucille, had no children—"just cats," Michael recalled.[14] Ever since the episode with the Episcopal priest back in Broad Ripple Village, Michael had been casting around for a father figure. The reclusive designer soon took on that role for his young protégé.

Roush imparted to Michael all he knew, far more than the rudimentary skills his high school had given him. "He taught me everything about detailing a building," Michael recalled, "how to keep the rain out, how to lay foundations."[15] In the small, two-room office of Carl A. Strauss & Associates, Michael learned how the actual business of architecture was conducted, how a project moved from inception to completion. All this Roush spelled out for him, both at work and during long evenings they'd spend together with Lucille, Gail, and the cats.

And Roush did more. Always anxious to stay current on the newest products of Modernism in America, he and Lucille would drive for hours to cities around the central United States, and soon Gail and Michael were accompanying them. One such stop was Columbus, Indiana, a sleepy town that had lately begun to emerge as an unlikely hub of modern design after a local benefactor, J. Irwin Miller, volunteered to pay the architects' fees for any building going up in town, provided the designer was approved by him. The itinerary of the foursome from Cincinnati included buildings by Eliel Saarinen and Saarinen's son Eero, and landscapes by Dan Kiley, all major figures and all completely unknown to Michael. The trip was a memorable one for Gail too.

"One of the buildings they wanted to see was the Miller House," she recalled—the residence the younger Saarinen had created for the city's modern Augustus. "We got there and it was just finished, with all the new furnishings inside, but no one was living there yet. We walked around, peeking in windows, taking photos, and either Michael or Ray tried a door and found it unlocked. So we sneaked inside, snapping photos frantically."[16]

Decades later, Michael met one of the Millers and related the story of his youthful archi-trespassing. The family member was not amused.

That journey was one of many. Together Roush and Michael drove to Chicago to see the newest masterwork from the only architect Roush admired even more than Breuer—Mies. The German designer had been living in the States since just before the war and in 1952 had just finished another piece of his first major American commission, the campus plan for the Illinois Institute of Technology (IIT). A stark, bare box of brick and steel faced with glass doors, the Robert F. Carr Memorial Chapel of St. Savior was fast becoming a pilgrimage site for architecture fans from around the country, and Roush and Michael were among the first to pay their respects.

The Robert F. Carr Memorial Chapel, 1952, the centerpiece of Mies's campus design for the Illinois Institute of Technology

As the two visitors entered and looked around, they saw before them at the end of the unadorned interior a narrow, square tube of brilliant chrome, about three-quarters of an inch thick, that separated the altar from the main space. The beauty of that one exquisite element—all the symbolic weight it carried in such a simple detail—sent Roush into raptures.

But Michael was flummoxed. *Why,* he thought, *am I supposed to get all excited about this piece of metal?*

In the hushed, dimly lit interior of the Carr Chapel, Roush and Michael fell into their first, and practically only, serious argument.[17]

DESIGN TOURISM PROVED habit forming, and Michael was soon making trips both with and without Roush. Cincinnati had few Modernist buildings of its own, but the city turned out to be excellently situated for excursions to other towns that did.

He recalled going with a University of Cincinnati classmate to Detroit to meet Eero Saarinen in person. It had been, Michael was to say, a "spur-of-the-moment" decision, and they were dropping in unannounced—bad planning, it turned out, since after they'd driven for hours, the Finnish-born master greeted them cordially and instantly passed them off to a junior associate. They enjoyed their visit, however, and got a good look around courtesy of the studio hand, a young Argentine whose name Michael instantly forgot. It took many years for him to realize that his tour guide that afternoon was Cesar Pelli, in later life a major architect (and frequent competitor of Michael's).

On still another excursion, Michael returned with Gail to Chicago to get a gander at more buildings there. Gail enjoyed looking at architecture, but this was not truly her passion, and, sensing this, Michael promised that one day of their visit would be her day, to do whatever she wanted.

"I thought a bit," Gail recalled, "and said I'd like to drive north of Chicago and stop at some beach along the way—a day walking along the beach."

The next afternoon the couple duly headed up the coast of Lake Michigan, and when Gail spied what looked like a perfect spot she suggested they pull over. Michael said he thought they could do better and kept driving. Again and again, Gail kept pointing out plausible bits of beach, and again and again Michael kept urging them onward. Finally, far in the distance, Gail made out the outline of a looming brick tower.

They hadn't gone to the beach. They had gone to Frank Lloyd Wright's Johnson Wax Headquarters in Racine, Wisconsin.

"Needless to say," Gail said, "I did not get out of the car when we got there."[18]

THANKS TO RAY ROUSH, Michael had caught the architecture bug, and the case had advanced far beyond the stage of sketching buildings out of books. But there was still a notable disconnect, a gap, between Michael and all the new buildings he was coming to know.

The moment in front of the steel bar in the Mies chapel was not unique. Wright's distinctive style, his long horizontal volumes and original ornament, seemed somehow too "personal" to Michael, too much like an exercise in novelty; the same was so for the younger Saarinen's idiosyncratic, expressionistic gestures. As Roush had learned, Mies's somber reductivism left Michael cold, and even the warmer Breuer, whom Michael had come to know so well through Roush's Breuer-esque house, didn't strike him as a designer he himself wanted to emulate. The irony was that Michael, given the ease with which he could draw almost anything, could "do" Mies or Breuer without any prompting. Much of his work in Carl Strauss's office consisted of just that, aping the masters in accord with Roush and Strauss's in-house flavor of Modernism. But Michael didn't particularly *want* to do Breuer, or Mies. Well on his way to becoming a modern architect, he hadn't yet found a modern architecture of his own.[19]

In the United States in the 1950s there were only so many options to choose from. As Michael put it, "All the people who were doing Modernist architecture"—people like Mies and his fellow German émigré Walter Gropius—"were gods."[20] Like the pioneers of the Old West, the pioneers of Modern design (so dubbed by the scholar Nikolaus Pevsner, in his groundbreaking 1936 book of that title) were shrouded in a mystique so compelling that, for many architects, it blotted out not only any pre-Modern forms of architecture but any future alternative. The architects and theorists Peter and Alison Smithson would refer to a period of "heroic" Modernism in Europe beginning in the 1920s, and on these shores that heroism was taken quite literally, an article of faith for a generation of American designers.[21]

Many of Michael's professors at Cincinnati had been products of Harvard, where they had studied under Gropius; most had since fallen under the spell of Mies, seduced as Roush was by the clarity and logic of his perfectly rectilinear structures, exemplified by the chapel at IIT. Beginning with the campus there, Mies had set himself up as the heir to the midwestern skyscraper tradition that included figures like Daniel Burnham and Louis Sullivan, and Mies's native-born acolytes had coalesced into a new "Chicago School" whose influence extended well beyond the Midwest. "My work," Mies would say, "has so much influence because of its reasonableness," and this unfailingly reasonable branch of Modernism, with its symmetrical forms, hard-edged materiality, and monumental plazas, had flourished in America following the Second World War, a foundational component in the stylistic amalgam commonly known as the International Style.[22]

All across the country, the International Style was cropping up in office towers, public buildings, and apartment complexes. Its postwar ascendancy was the product of manifold circumstances: the mechanization of the national economy, government policy, mass demand for housing, the vagaries of changing tastes. But alongside these was an almost spiritual element, a rejection of the colonnaded, marble-hewn past as being in some way tainted: "The abandonment of classical architecture," the historian David Watkin would write, was predicated in part "on the assumption that it was irrevocably associated with Nazism."[23] Paul Philippe Cret, no less than Albert Speer, was now politically suspect, and the old must make way for the new. With the triumph of Modernism not yet a decade old, the consequences of this ideological condition for the American city were already beginning to be felt. But they were only imperfectly understood, and hardly more so by the young Indianan still trying to grasp what Modernism was.

And so Michael proceeded, for the time being at least, more or less on faith alone, following the Modernists who were as yet the only architects whose work he truly knew. "There was no criticism of them," Michael would say. "All the younger architects just said, 'This is what we're supposed to do.'"[24]

In late March 1955 an item appeared in the *Indianapolis Star*, announcing "a late summer wedding...being planned by Gail Devine and Michael E. Graves."[25]

After four years as a couple, the two were married in Broad Ripple Village, and when they returned to Cincinnati, they began living together for the first time in the Swifton Village Apartments in the Bond Hill neighborhood. It was a singularly drab Modernist complex, inhabited mostly by students—or rather uninhabited by them. The newlyweds had few neighbors due to the new building's high vacancy rate, which drove it to bankruptcy shortly after they moved out. (It was promptly snapped up by a developer from New York and given to his son to manage, the first real job held by a twenty-five-year-old Donald Trump.)[26] Poor enough that they couldn't afford to buy a couch or a dining room table, the couple made their own from parts they bought from the lumberyard, the first Graves furniture ever designed.

Alone at last, Michael and Gail were in a sense the most intimate of strangers: a longtime couple who had not yet figured out what life together would really mean and whose marriage had been to some degree another instance of doing what they were "supposed to do." But they were then, and for a long time after, very happy. Looking back, Michael said, "She was marvelous."[27]

Michael and
Gail on their
wedding day,
March 27, 1955

As IN HIGH SCHOOL, Michael and Gail joined a fraternity and sorority, respectively, and for the remainder of their time at the University of Cincinnati enjoyed a fairly typical college experience. Michael's increased devotion to his studies, begun in high school, had continued in his undergraduate years: for his first project, he stayed up all night to produce a proposal for a new kiosk at the college gate, rendering it in watercolor (his first time working in that medium) and coming away with an A-plus.

After that, he claimed, his grades were never lower—except once. Facing a surveying exam the same day that a sketching problem was due, his roommate persuaded Michael to complete his drawings for him, in return for which the roommate promised to teach Michael all he needed to know to ace the hated technical test. This *Strangers on a Train* approach backfired—Michael's hastily drawn sketches earned his roommate an A-plus, but Michael failed the exam.[28]

The real action, however, was still happening in the half of each year spent in Carl Strauss's office. Helped along by Roush, Michael continued to make great strides, taking on increasing responsibilities. In early 1958, while Roush was hard at work on a house for a local doctor, Donald Jacobs, in the Western Hills division, Michael had his first chance to add something of his own. As Jayne Merkel relates:

> The entry procession, across the footbridge, wasn't quite right. There was an empty place to the left of the front door. So Graves made a tall stele-like abstract sculpture to fill it. The two architects [Roush and Michael] stayed up all night one night completing it and placing it in the space while their wives slept in the car.[29]

Strauss and
Roush's Jacobs
house, featuring
Michael's court-
yard sculpture

The sculpture, long since removed by subsequent occupants, was a most intrigu-ing objet d'art: a tower in concrete standing about five feet high, it comprised five individual boxes with alternating apertures stacked one atop the other, suggesting perhaps some of the rectilinear formal logic of the house itself—a signpost for visi-tors, advising them of what was inside.[30] It betrayed the fairly clear influence of the Japanese designer and sculptor Isamu Noguchi, as well as that of the artist Henry Moore, both of them very much the sort of artists Roush approved of. Michael's skills as a copyist were put to good use elsewhere in the house as well: empty areas on the living room and bedroom walls were filled with colorful paintings (both of which still exist) in the then-current Abstract Expressionist style. Michael could "do" Jackson Pollock and Willem de Kooning too.

The painters of the New York School were among the first artists whom Michael consciously imitated (other than his early efforts at aping Walt Disney). Early on, his personal take on Ab Ex was careful and controlled, his canvases almost pixelated in closely matched swatches of red and orange. Derivative as they were, these abstract works showed little of the painterly impasto or the depth of Pollock's sprawling masterworks; then again, the texture of the real thing was mostly unknown to Michael at the time, as very few such paintings could be seen around Cincinnati. Never much of a museumgoer, Michael derived most of his early knowledge of art from books and magazines, which would remain his preferred means of looking at and learning about art for most of his life.[31]

Along with the Jacobs house paintings, another artifact of Michael's college years survives, at least partially. His undergraduate thesis at the University of Cincinnati was a design project, conventional enough for its time, though with a provocative tweak. After six years at the school, Michael had been thoroughly inculcated in Miesian Modernism. But rather than simply rehearse that position in his thesis, he took an unexpected detour, developing a proposal that was simple enough yet spiked with some rather original thinking. In it, he dared to incorporate two things somewhat outside his training.

The first was social responsibility. The title of the thesis was "The Amenable Shelter." Subtitled "A Shelter to Expand with the Physical and Economic Growth of the Inhabitant," it proposed the use of prefabricated hut-like homes, each comprising a pitched pyramidal roof hoisted atop thick pillars, which could be assembled easily on a simple six-square plan around courtyard voids [**PLATE 1**]. The approach, Michael contended, would allow families to construct new units as circumstances required, at low cost and without sacrificing communal outdoor spaces. A community of such homes would have the added advantage of appearing not as a hodgepodge of accretions but as a consistent landscape. Michael wrote (with characteristic poor spelling), "Pre-designed buildings give unity to whole communities. There is only chaous [sic] without unity." The whole idea ran very much against the Miesian grain, as the elder architect never much cared for prefabrication, and most of his followers were actively uninterested in such reformist do-goodism as experimental housing for the poor.

The other, no less extraordinary facet of "The Amenable Shelter" was its reliance on something toward which Modernists of almost all descriptions were profoundly ambivalent—history. By way of precedent, in order to demonstrate the feasibility and urban cohesion of his scheme, the documents that accompanied Michael's models of the Amenable Shelter included photographs of an unusual housing type, the *trulli* houses of Alberobello, Italy, some distance south of the ancient city of Bari in the Itria Valley.[32] "'The important thing is how little the differences are,'" reads one of Michael's captions: the quotation marks suggest a scholarly source, but the stilted grammar (and the fairly scant research in the accompanying text) reveal it as Michael's own interpretation of the elegant pragmatism of these primitive precursors to his modular scheme.

Dating to at least the fifteenth century, but with roots in the Apulia region stretching back to prehistoric times, the *trullo* is a type of yurt composed of locally available stone, chipped into flat, irregular bricks and piled into a round drum at the base that tapers into a conical top. In Alberobello, hundreds of gray-and-white *trulli* stand one beside the other, an entire city of rocky cairns like the hive of some ancient inhuman species. The houses were little known in the United States until the publication, in 1964, of *Architecture without Architects*, a book by the famously eccentric theorist Bernard Rudofsky based on an exhibition he curated at the Museum of Modern Art in New York. The show and the book, which included photos and text captions on the *trulli*, were daring, offbeat explorations of the building traditions of pretechnological societies, indigenous communities, even the animal world. A former woman's footwear designer and occasional nudist, Rudofsky was throwing a tiny monkey wrench into the grand works of Modernism and its hegemonic, technocratic stranglehold on architecture.

But that was several years in the future. Michael's art-historical education at the University of Cincinnati was ample, but not so wide-ranging that the *trulli* were likely to have come up in the classroom. Roush would seem a probable vector of introduction, given his time spent abroad; it is also possible that Michael first saw them in a fashion spread in *Harper's Bazaar* that appeared in 1955, since he acquired his thesis images from the photographer Louise Dahl-Wolfe, who had shot the magazine editorial with the model Evelyn Tripp.[33] But however the houses came to Michael's attention, his use of them seems more than just a convenient device for explaining his Amenable Shelter concept. It betokens an early interest, anticipating Rudofsky's, in some ill-defined otherness, beyond the conventions of the Modernism he'd been taught. At the time, of course, the subject might simply have struck Michael as a pleasantly irreverent digression, capping six years of survey exams and Miesian steel with a scholarly idyll among the weird hillside houses, none of which he had any reason to believe he would ever actually see.

MICHAEL FINISHED UP at the university as a trained architect, a married man, and a Democrat. "Before that time I hadn't paid any attention," he said, but the incipient civil rights struggle and the "hippieish" Ray Roush made him take notice.[34]

His horizons expanding rapidly, he began to look ahead to the next step, which for the first time was not a thing laid out in advance by someone else's expectations. When he had entered school, Cincinnati seemed as if it would be education enough; Michael was shocked when his friend and fellow classmate Robert Frasca picked up and left for the University of Michigan, looking for a more progressive undergraduate program. Michael's original plan had been to earn his bachelor's degree and then take up work in a practice in Indianapolis immediately upon graduation. But now he was thinking bigger.

Postgraduate education was by no means compulsory for American architects at midcentury. Architecture graduate schools were mostly reserved for those who wanted a career in academia or who wanted to establish their own offices, and their students were either wealthy, trained at Eastern colleges, trained overseas, or some combination of the above. Michael was none of these things.

Carl Strauss, however, had attended Harvard's Graduate School of Design (GSD), and it helped give him the edge he needed to build a practice of his own rather than work in someone else's office. Michael was determined to do the same, and so, packing once more into the car with Roush and Lucille, the seasoned architecture tourists set out for what would be Michael and Gail's first journey beyond the Appalachian Range, heading East for interviews at a couple of big-name schools.

"We went to Harvard and Yale together, and I watched [Roush] on a jury," Michael recalled. "We went to Penn together. We didn't go to Princeton."[35] Following in Strauss's footsteps, his top choice was GSD—not because the program particularly suited his architectural tastes, which hadn't yet really developed. "It was the draw of big names," Gail recalled.[36]

Accepted into the program, Michael enrolled, and in the fall of 1958 he and Gail made ready to move to Massachusetts. They had acquired a car of their own, a sporty Austin-Healey barely big enough for two people sitting side by side, much less the furniture and clothes they had acquired to fill up their Swifton Village apartment. "Ray and his wife pulled a trailer filled with our furniture, and we drove in tandem to Cambridge," Gail recalled. When they arrived at their new home at 82 Charles Street in Boston (Cambridge itself was far beyond their means), Roush and Lucille helped them unpack and put the furniture in place, in accord as always with Roush's sense of interior decor.

After that, Gail remembered, "we all drove north for some camping and relaxation," and then they said goodbye.

OWING TO HIS six-year-long spell as an undergraduate, Michael was allowed by GSD to compress the usually eight-term master of architecture program into a single year. His longer-than-usual college experience also meant that Michael was older than most of the new students at GSD, save for those who had not failed their fitness exams and had been conscripted into the military. Many of the students in his own year were products of Cambridge itself, having gone through Harvard's own undergraduate program, and several shared a scrap of advice with their new classmate, a message that distilled (at least in Michael's memory) to a simple warning:

"This is bullshit."

In his adult career, Michael never bore Cincinnati any ill will, even coming back decades later to design a building for his alma mater. He felt nothing but gratitude for Carl Strauss and an immense affection for Ray Roush. But for GSD, and for Harvard in general, he carried a flame of contempt so bright and so assiduously maintained over the years that it must have been a source of authentic pleasure.[37]

At the University of Cincinnati, though some of his teachers had been products of GSD, theirs had been a different GSD—back when Walter Gropius was at the helm. Gropius had helped develop a curriculum based on the collaborative ideal that he had first advanced in Germany after the First World War, during his days as director of the famous Bauhaus in Dessau. Ground zero for the Modern movement in Central Europe and beyond, the incubator that hatched not just designers such as Breuer and Mies but painters such as Paul Klee and Wassily Kandinsky, the Bauhaus's inventive pedagogical system had been the model for GSD when it was established in 1936 as a union of the formerly discrete schools of architecture, landscape architecture, and city planning. The following year, Gropius himself—along with his friend Breuer—was brought in to head up the architecture side, working under the leadership of founding dean Joseph Hudnut.[38]

But Hudnut, Breuer, and Gropius were all long gone by the time Michael arrived in Cambridge. Dean Josep Lluís Sert was now in charge. Barcelonan by birth, living in exile in the United States since the end of the Spanish Civil War, Sert was a true believer in a specific genre of architectural Modernism, and he imposed his preferences upon faculty and students alike with a force that belied his remarkably short stature. Behind his back, Michael and his friends referred to him as "the Teeny-Weeny Deany."[39]

Within the limited menu of Modernism then available in the United States, there were still a few selections on offer. Miesian Modernism Michael had already learned at the University of Cincinnati; thanks to Roush, he could also bring in a bit of Breuer to add a homey touch. At Harvard, on the other hand, all this was in poor taste. As his classmates told him, "You better do Corb."[40]

Michael had seen enough of Le Corbusier's work in college to know what that meant. Favoring white exteriors with occasional washes of color within and asymmetrical massing of pure geometries in artful juxtapositions, Le Corbusier's was a looser, more self-consciously poetic approach than that of either the stringent Mies or the humbly antimonumental Breuer. Unafraid of a certain quantum of symbolic resonance, Corb's definition of architecture as "the masterful, correct, and magnificent *play* of volumes brought together in *light*" wasn't quite in tune with the more functionally inclined Gropius, either.[41] Sert's importation of the Corbusian strain signaled a changing of the guard at GSD.

Le Corbusier's
Villa Stein in
Garches, France,
1927

Sert had been following in the master's footsteps since the very beginning, having set up the Spanish chapter of the Congrès internationaux d'architecture moderne (CIAM), the worldwide organization devoted to spreading Corb's vision of Modernism and his radical proposals for reinventing the urban landscape. In his "Five Points of Architecture," Le Corbusier called for rooftop terraces; Sert responded with a Barcelona apartment building that had just that.[42] Le Corbusier called for a "Radiant City" of ultratall towers set in wide-open parkland; Sert would go on to create campus buildings for Boston University along roughly those lines.[43] Le Corbusier saw Modernist architecture as engaged in millenarian combat for the soul of modern society, which the architect claimed was faced with a choice between "architecture or revolution": either humankind would accept the serenity and simplicity of his own abstract, technological forms or civilization itself would perish.[44] Sert saw himself as a foot soldier in this struggle.

This is not to diminish Sert's skill as an architect. "One of the strongest proponents of the Mediterranean mentality," as the eminent historian Sigfried Giedion called him, Sert was in many ways a superlative designer. His own country home on Long Island included an astonishingly beautiful lofted living room with a herringbone brick floor—"a town square in Catalonia," as the artist Saul Steinberg once described it.[45] He had been a champion of the Republican cause in his home country and a fearless opponent of fascism everywhere—despite the pro–Francisco Franco sympathies of his famous painter uncle Josep Maria Sert.[46] But Sert could also be philosophically straightjacketed, and he could be a bully.

A mutual antagonism between him and the new midwestern transplant took hold early. In his first semester, as Michael recalled, students were tasked with designing a museum; for the interior sections, Michael drew wooden walls with a texture indistinguishable from maple, while in his bird's-eye plan of the building's front ter-race he rendered a brick patio in such minute detail that every individual brick was outlined. He had done it, in truth, because he *could*—a bit of shameless, if harmless, showboating. If Sert liked bricks, Michael would give him bricks.

At the end-of-term charrette, when the students presented their work, Sert made his way around to Michael's station. Before he launched into his critique, the dean leaned in to examine the drawings Michael had so carefully prepared, and without saying a word he started scratching them vigorously with his forefinger. "He was thinking it was some film I'd put down," Michael remembered. Sert believed the detail was fake, a decal applied to the paper.[47] Far from impressing him, Michael's facility had merely aroused Sert's suspicion, and suspicion swiftly escalated into hostility.

Sert's more unfettered, free-form design thinking meant Michael's GSD projects didn't have to be quite so rigid and symmetrical as they had been at the University of Cincinnati or in Strauss's office. But so far as Michael was concerned, the basic approach to architectural teaching was unchanged, a matter of looking to this or that Modernist pioneer and copying his work wholesale. Michael had begun to grow restless. His thesis on the *trulli* houses had marked a brief foray into the architecture of the past; with another year of schooling ahead of him at Harvard, he began to look back again.

He was in the wrong place to do it. Michael recalled how once, early in his first semester in Cambridge, he had been sitting with a book open to an image of the Palais Garnier, the Paris opera house completed in 1875 and known to the world by the name of its architect, Charles Garnier. The building, its extravagant front foyer graced by a richly ornamented, delicately contoured grand staircase, was a high point of Second Empire design, an impressive if slightly gaudy instance of the French Beaux Arts style. Sert walked into the room and approached him.

"What are you looking at?" he asked.

Michael showed him.

"You won't need *that* here," Sert said, and snapped the book closed.[48] Art history belonged to the art historians; GSD students were to keep their heads down and deal with the real, the here and now. Although architectural history had been reinserted into the curriculum following Gropius's departure, the professor who taught the most celebrated course was Sigfried Giedion, a dyed-in-the-wool Modernist and former secretary general of CIAM. As in his influential book *Space, Time, and Architecture* (1941), Giedion's lectures propagated an occasionally fanciful teleology that reduced much of human history into a centuries-long march toward the ultimate triumph of Le Corbusier, Gropius, and the Bauhaus. His mythmaking, and his reductivism, did not endear him to many students, who referred to his magnum opus as "Spare Time and Architecture." Michael, given his advanced placement in the program, was exposed to but little of Giedion's thinking, and appeared to have absorbed even less.[49]

In his second semester, Michael took a studio with the dean himself. At the time, Sert was becoming interested in new techniques in concrete construction; a decade later, he'd deploy an inventive semitubular system for the roof of his Fundació Joan Miró, the museum in Barcelona built and named in honor of the painter who had been Sert's friend since the early 1930s. To acquaint his students with the process of mixing and molding in cement and aggregate, the dean sent Michael and a couple of other students down to the school workshop, charging them with making some concrete and pouring it into inverted forms like those Sert would later use for his museum.

"I thought, my god," Michael said, "I've been on construction sites all my life, for six years. I don't want to do this."[50] Finding that some of his colleagues felt the same, Michael proceeded to lead a small mutiny. The group demanded another, less menial assignment, and though their insubordination must have galled him, Sert finally conceded. They could design a house, he told them, provided that it too used inverted concrete shells. They accepted.

But Michael's budding interest in the history of art wormed in, and once again he and Sert were at loggerheads. In conceiving his house, Michael did exactly as he knew Sert would want him to, devising an asymmetrical plan, as in a Le Corbusier house, and giving the exterior walls a slight sculptural wave in deference to Sert's repeated exhortations to "animate the facade! Animate the facade!" But Michael added one tiny detail that spoiled the whole effect.

On a long wall in one of the perspective drawings of the house's interior, he pasted a photo of a painting that he'd cut out of a magazine. (He might as easily have drawn a sketch of it, but he'd learned that that would avail him nothing with the dean.) The painting, Michael recalled, was the work of Nicolas Poussin, the early nineteenth-century French artist who had forged the bridge between the baroque and the classical in French art. The piece was one of his enchantingly enigmatic landscapes: tunic-bedecked shepherds and tall cypresses under a cobalt-blue sky. It was not, in other words, anything like the work of Joan Miró, Alexander Calder, or the other contemporary artists Sert favored.

Michael remembered watching Sert as he first espied the painting in the interior and then abruptly launched into a stream of richly accented invective. "I've spent my entire life getting rid of *that shit*," Sert exclaimed, "and you bring this into my school willy-nilly!"

But the student pleaded his innocence. "*I* didn't do it," Michael told him. "The painting is in the collection of my client."

As Michael related, the Fictional Client Defense only fanned the flames of Sert's anger. He threatened to flunk Michael for the course and was dissuaded only when a sympathetic faculty member, the Polish-born architect Jerzy Soltan, persuaded him to fail the student for the project but pass him for the semester as a whole.

It might be said that the same mooncalf kid who had run up the Soldiers and Sailors Monument was still just playing hooky from dance class. Michael's quarrel with the tempestuous Sert was largely a function of personality, not of principle; the accuracy and artistic flair that the student from Indianapolis could bring to the most difficult of sketching problems simply meant that he was often bored. He had no real allegiance to anything outside the Modernist current, only curiosity.

His Poussin moment notwithstanding, Michael was generally more inclined toward modern artists than Renaissance ones. In addition to Abstract Expressionism, he was increasingly exposed at GSD to those artists whose work was generally smiled upon by the CIAM axis: Miró, Picasso (who had created his famous *Guernica* for Sert's Spanish Pavilion at the 1937 Paris Expo), and Le Corbusier himself, who for his entire career maintained an active sideline as a painter. More than anyone else— and more than Michael would sometimes, in later life, care to admit—Le Corbusier was exerting an outsize influence on him, as both an artist and an architect.

Le Corbusier's artistic proclivities were on display both in his buildings' colorful interiors and in his "free plans," which were practically abstract paintings themselves, juxtaposing curved walls with straight. "The plan is the generator" was Corb's oft-repeated phrase: the *parti*, the fundamental idea behind each project, always found its initial and most important expression in Corb's floor layouts, and Michael learned to craft his designs in the same fashion.[51] It was during these years that Michael began to affect a pair of round, black spectacles, identical to the ones that were a Le Corbusier trademark. And just as he was adopting the Swiss designer's signature look, Michael took his signature, too, changing his autograph to more closely resemble Corb's. If Michael was not quite a card-carrying Corbusian by the time he left Harvard, he was awfully close, whatever his misgivings about Modernist buildings and education in America.

"A house is a machine for living in," another one of the Swiss genius's most quoted lines, did not sit so easily with Michael.[52] Enchanted though he was by the beauty of Le Corbusier's machinelike forms, he was never partial to mechanical thinking. What he did not quite recognize, or was only beginning to, was that he was not the only one who harbored such reservations.

In September 1959, only months after Michael's semester *en enfer* with Sert, Le Corbusier's CIAM officially disbanded during the organization's ninth congress in

Otterlo, the Netherlands, the pressures that had pulled it apart representing the first stirrings of dissent within the Modernist ranks. An international group of loosely affiliated designers later known as Team X, who had first come together under the CIAM umbrella, had begun to openly criticize the conformism, bureaucratization, and cultural tone-deafness of mainstream Modernism. Charged with reviving Modernism's three-decade-old bastion, its members deliberately dismembered it: at the final meeting, several held aloft a cemetery cross and wreath bearing the legend "C.I.A.M."[53]

They were part of a going trend. In England the Independent Group—whose membership overlapped with Team X's—had been advocating since as early as 1952 for a more dynamic, pop culture–infused attitude in art and design—less all-white-walls-and-pure-geometries and more color, light, and futuristic technology. Even in the United States, at least one figure at the fringe of the profession, Philadelphia-based Louis Kahn, had spent years quietly advancing an architecture more primal, more expressive, and more protean than anything in the pale and repetitive cities of glass and stucco from Le Corbusier's prewar imaginings.

In point of fact, Corb had been changing too. His Notre Dame du Haut in Ronchamp, France, completed in 1955, showed that the old arch-Modernist would not be confined artistically within one of his own white boxes. The building's boatlike form jutted dramatically out of a hill, and the nave twinkled and gleamed in the light of narrow, irregularly cut windows. It was not a break from Le Corbusier's previous work, which had always had a music and a depth of its own. But it was an evolution.

These developments were beginning to penetrate even the cosseted precincts of Harvard Yard. Jerzy Soltan, whom Michael remembered as his second-semester savior (and who would advise him on his GSD thesis portfolio), had worked in Corb's studio but was by that time a Team X fellow traveler.[54] Magazines like *Architectural Forum* were filled with images of Modernism in transition. None of the emerging alternatives necessarily appealed to Michael any more than what had preceded them, and for the time being he remained, architecturally speaking, a man without a country. But change was afoot, and he was not alone.

WHEN THE WEATHER was fair, the GSD architecture crowd would go over to old Cardullo's deli for sandwiches and bring them down to the banks of the Charles River. On one such sunny day in the spring of 1959, Michael was introduced to Peter Eisenman, a young designer of about his age working at Walter Gropius's Cambridge-based firm, The Architects' Collaborative (TAC).

They saw each other around the riverside once or twice thereafter. "Peter would always bring a construction problem because he couldn't do working drawings," recalled Michael.[55] The latter was wrapping up his studies and working part-time in the office of a local architect, Carl Koch.[56] "Sert's office, TAC, Koch," Eisenman remembered, "this sort of coterie of Harvard-based offices—we thought we were at the sort of high point of the world." The clubbiness of it all began to grate, and Eisenman shortly thereafter decamped to New York to finish his master's degree at Columbia, and then went to Cambridge, England, for his doctorate.[57]

The lunchtime companions hadn't spoken much at all, and neither took much notice of the other. Nearly sixty years later, Eisenman didn't even remember their first meeting until his memory was forcibly jogged—partly by concern that their mutual friend Richard Meier might claim that *he* had been the first to meet Michael.

"We didn't become friends or anything," Eisenman said. "But we knew who each other were."[58]

ALTHOUGH IT WOULDN'T actually begin for years yet, that was the nearest thing to a lasting friendship that Michael formed at Cambridge. He remained closer to Roush than to any of his GSD classmates or teachers, not feeling much in common with any of them. And that feeling, at bottom, was the root cause of much of his durable contempt for Harvard.

"I was kind of the hayseed in the class," as he put it.[59]

When he'd arrived, he was the only one of his contemporaries who knew, thanks to Roush, how to design a building in toto, and that gave him a leg up on the competition. But his practical aptitude only served to highlight his lack of cultural polish; almost all of his colleagues had traveled to Europe, and most had been educated at schools of grander and much older vintage than the University of Cincinnati.

They were Bud Graves's dreaded Episcopalians—even the ones who weren't. Few had any idea what a livestock agent was, or what it was like to miss the snap signal in front of a hundred jeering Hoosiers. Most of them, too, were more willing to conform to Sert's architectural dictates, or at least more easily cowed by his imperiousness. (One student to whom Michael did form a brief attachment, Lo-Yi Chan, described an incident where a young student presented a project to the dean. When Sert objected to his design, the man fainted.)[60] Few of his fellow graduates that year went on to start their own practices. Most of them, perhaps, simply didn't have that much to prove.

But Michael did. "I wasn't in competition with my brother at that point," he would say, "or with my parents, to get out of the nest. I was in competition with architecture."[61]

He had begun to feel this way back at the University of Cincinnati, and the fear that he was out of his depth in Cambridge, surrounded by others so different from himself, added fuel to the fire. His overdrawn renderings, his historical allusions, even the refusal to mix cement: it wasn't all schoolboy truancy. He felt he had to be better, do more.

Gail, meanwhile, did not weather so well the abrupt shift in social climate, at least in Michael's view. As he recalled:

> Early on, after the start of the first term, we were invited to a clambake on the beach. Marblehead, maybe. And she didn't want to go. Only Harvard people were there, and they were too highfalutin for her. Lo-Yi Chan had us to dinner one night, and she said, "Now this isn't so bad. Just regular folks." But then she'd hear me say that the guy sitting next to me was the heir to the Welch's Grape Juice fortune....And to see him wearing white pants, blue blazer, loafers, no socks, shirt open to the waist—she couldn't understand it. Her life being wrapped up in people like that? It really meant we didn't see anybody in my class except the Chans.

What Michael perceived as his wife's shyness may not have been quite the culture shock he supposed: Gail would prove, in time, that she could more than keep pace with the Ivy League set and come to embrace it. But next to Michael's own burning drive to succeed, her more subdued response to their new surroundings might have appeared to him like retreat.

BY EARLY SUMMER—having barely avoided that failing grade from Sert—Michael had earned his master's. Once again, he and Gail had to decide what to do next without a formal road map to show them the way.

Staying on with Koch or with one of the other Cambridge firms would have meant becoming a Cambridge architect, possibly for life—a proposition that held as little allure for Michael as it had for Eisenman. Though Indianapolis still beckoned, Michael might have been considered a little young to start his own office just yet. There was some gravitational pull from one direction: New York. A little seasoning at a big firm in the Big Apple would be just the thing.

"I expected I would work there for about five years," Michael said. After that, "I'd go back to Indiana."[62]

He secured a position in the Manhattan office of the designer George Nelson. From the unlikeliest of beginnings (as a college student at Yale, he had run into the architecture school to get out of a rainstorm), the fifty-one-year-old Nelson had risen to become one of American Modernism's foremost hierophants, an early admirer of Mies and a brilliant polemicist who made his case for simplicity and precision though his products, his buildings, and his writing.[63] "Good design," he once averred, "like good painting, cooking, architecture, or whatever you like, is a manifestation of the capacity of the human spirit to transcend its limitations."[64]

Nelson's output, and his fame, were more focused on his chairs and tables than on his houses and high-rises; given Michael's education as an architect, the new office might have seemed an odd fit. But Michael was already very much interested in industrial design, and long had been. On the fabled trip to Racine with Gail, though he was unsure what to make of the Johnson Wax building's decorative and spatial quirks, he was instantly drawn to Wright's stylish desks with their built-in wastepaper baskets and en suite chairs. Corb had designed furniture, as did Mies; the whole Modernist mind-set in which Michael had been reared had always put interiors and products on at least equal footing with any category of design, and Nelson was of the same persuasion. With his stature in the profession enhanced by his years as an editor of *Architectural Forum*, Nelson could give Michael the ins and outs of the trade from every angle. He was a good person to know, and a better one to impress, if Michael could.

He did. He and Nelson never grew close—with his fingers in so many creative pies, Nelson "had his own life," as Michael would say—but maintaining the same level of industry he had kept up in school, Michael made his presence felt, helping turn out an array of products and doing some residential work alongside the firm's primary architectural partner, Gordon Chadwick.[65] Occasionally some of Nelson's illustrious design-world connections would blow through the office, and the boss would introduce them to the new recruit from GSD. Michael recalled in particular "a very shy little guy," Charles Eames, though the two did no more than shake hands.[66]

AS WITH LE CORBUSIER in Cambridge, so with Nelson in New York. The enlargement of Michael's design outlook was still proceeding somewhat below the surface, the young designer groping his way half-blind toward what he really wanted from architecture. His job, at any rate, was sufficiently demanding that it pushed aside any consideration of the bigger picture. It even pushed aside New York.

Gail had been wary about moving to the city, especially the prospect of living in an older building, so the two took up a lease in the Washington Square Village apartments, one of the enormous new housing complexes near New York University.[67] It was a tiny place, humbly appointed with some of the self-made furnishings they'd trucked from Cincinnati and Boston to Manhattan—despite the income from Nelson's studio, they were still living on scratch. Right smack in the middle of Greenwich Village, in the early days of the folk boom, with the newly opened Cafe Wha? just around the corner and Willem de Kooning and Frank O'Hara drinking at the San Remo only a few blocks away, Michael managed to miss out on the city's midcentury golden age. Even had he and Gail known it was going on, they couldn't have afforded to participate.

They did like the Village. "We'd go out in the morning, get the *Times*, get donuts," Michael recalled. Gail was continuing to work on her art, putting some of her skills to use as an illustrator at a department store. On the way to work they'd take a "short *passegiata*," as Michael called it, strolling through Washington Square and stopping occasionally to listen to the performers around the park fountain.[68] They didn't have any children yet, and they didn't have terribly many good friends—though that was shortly to change.

Early in 1960 a coworker from Nelson's office invited Michael to join him for drinks with another friend then working in the studio of Marcel Breuer (who was now based in New York, following his departure from Harvard). That evening, Michael was introduced to a tall, slender, serious-seeming young architect—twenty-six just as he was, bespectacled just as he was, but with a forehead that sloped away precipitously, giving him a hawklike aspect altogether different from Michael's googly-eyed ingenuousness.

What Michael did not know, and would not learn for some time, was that Richard Meier was the second cousin of Peter Eisenman—the TAC associate from Boston with the bad drawings. Meier and Eisenman had grown up together in Maplewood, New Jersey, both sons of upper-middle-class Jewish parents, and had set off for college together at Cornell. More soft-spoken and outwardly less energetic than his cousin, Meier had an understated manner that masked an appetite more capacious than Michael's for wine, women, and song. It didn't take long for the unmarried Meier to conscript his new friend into some of his after-hours escapades.

What Meier and Michael shared from the start was intense ambition, and an equally intense enthusiasm for art. Michael had kept up with his drawing and painting clear through Harvard, and, looking to expand his repertoire, he proposed that Richard and he should be creative stablemates. "At that time I had been doing small paintings at home," Meier remembered. "Michael had, I guess, been painting, so he said: Why don't we find a studio space where we can work together and share the space? So that summer we rented space in what was then the Tanager Gallery, on [East] Tenth Street, and started working together."[69]

Meier's abstract paintings at the time were large canvases, jets of color in layer upon layer; Michael's, as Meier recalled them, were "very somber, dark brown and dark blue palette knife paintings" **[PLATE 2]**. The two would go into the studio together, work side by side, and then go out for drinks afterward. They did not, despite being in what was then a teeming gallery district, take in much contemporary art together, nor did they spend a great deal of time discussing what kind of art they wanted to make. As Meier put it, Michael "didn't grow up with a knowledge of art....He had a certain disdain for a lot of artists," younger ones especially.[70] The disdain extended to one of Meier's other new friends, the artist Frank Stella, whose work Meier very much admired. In late summer Michael would show his work as part of an open studio, but while he'd hoped to lure the celebrity architect Edward Durell Stone (who had lately graced the cover of *Time*), he didn't seem to much care about the artists of the inchoate Pop movement, such as Alex Katz and Tom Wesselmann, who were then in the orbit of Tanager.[71]

"I don't think Michael had the same respect for art at that time that I did," Meier said, and the vague sense that their tastes differed on this point meant they largely avoided the subject.[72] On architecture, however, they found they were more compatible. That summer of 1960, the two submitted a joint entry in the competition to design a Franklin Delano Roosevelt memorial in Washington, DC. As much as either of them could remember in later years, their proposal comprised four large pillars of glass to be poured into place on site, like concrete—suggestive of some of Meier's later fascination with glass, paired perhaps with Michael's training in Miesian symmetry. According to Michael, they used Nelson's office, and some of Nelson's money, to prepare their scheme, and the competition entry was ultimately credited as the "George Nelson scheme," much to their annoyance. Not that it made any difference: "We got last place," Michael recalled.[73] As it transpired, none of the winning projects was realized, and the capital remained without a memorial to FDR until the late 1990s.

To the young designers, the setback didn't feel like a very big one. Looking back, Meier said, "We had a good time." Undaunted, spirits still high in spite of all the hard work at Breuer's office and at Nelson's, the two found a little time that summer to kick up their heels. One night they had dinner together, followed by drinks, and then shared a taxi back home. Arriving at the latter's apartment, Meier lifted himself tipsily out of the cab and announced as he looked back through the open car door: "Frank Lloyd Wright? *Frank Lloyd Wright?* He ain't seen *nothin'* yet!"[74]

Surpassing the grand old man of American architecture wasn't such a bad goal. Hitting the mark, though, would take more than martini-primed bluster.

But by then Michael could back up his own bravado. A friend from the University of Cincinnati, an artist and designer named Ted Musho, had lately been in touch from a more colorful clime—from Rome, where he was living for the year. He had won a fellowship from the American Academy in Rome, the study and research center for American artists and scholars in the Eternal City, and he encouraged Michael to apply.[75]

The fellowship had been on Michael's mind for some time. Nelson had been a winner back in 1932, and his time abroad had been decisive in his joining the Modernist cause.[76] Everyone at GSD would have been aware of it, though few might have seriously considered applying. In December 1959, before the disappointment of the FDR competition, Michael had adequate faith in his accomplishments to think it was worth a try. He had a full portfolio of work from his Harvard days, more from Nelson's office, and most crucially he had the backing of Nelson himself, who liked his chances and wrote a flattering recommendation to the Academy jury on Michael's behalf.

Not that Michael was confident he would win. The lingering doubt as to his own suitability—not for the art of architecture, but for the profession—was still with him. His written essay, though remarkably free of copy errors, was a pallid retread of first-generation Modernist buzzwords, to the effect that he wanted to understand the "space value" of old European cathedrals.[77] Worse, he was up against applicants from all over the country with more experience outside the country (where he had never been) and more knowledge of foreign languages (of which he had none). The breadth of his architectural purview had grown steadily under the tutelage of Roush, Strauss, Nelson, and (in spite of himself) Sert, and with a pencil in his hand Michael could speak fluent Corb and flawless Mies. But did he really *understand* the architectural language he was using? He felt himself, at least in retrospect, more suited to a deanship at some school and a reasonably quiet practice of his own, somewhere in Indiana or Ohio.

The judges felt differently. They selected him as a finalist for the Rome Prize (as the fellowship is known), no small honor in itself. The jurors in 1960 included some of the most prominent names in American architecture: Edward Durell Stone, later to become Michael's Tanager invitee; Edward Larrabee Barnes, a model-handsome former student of Gropius's; and Nathaniel Owings, one of the founding members, though not quite the most famous, of the Modernist megapractice Skidmore Owings & Merrill (SOM).[78]

SOM, dubbed by Frank Lloyd Wright "the Three Blind Mies," had only just finished work on the Pepsi-Cola Building, overseen by their star principal, Gordon Bunshaft, and it was here that the finalists were summoned to be interviewed in person by the jury.[79] In the lobby outside the office where the interview was to be held, Michael sat with the four other finalists—the men in narrow ties, the women in patterned dresses—staring anxiously out the enormous windows looking onto the avenue. Casting a glance across the room, Michael saw one of the women holding a copy of *Golf Digest*. She was reading it upside down.[80]

At last he was brought into the room where the older architects waited to quiz him on his work. "They said, 'When you get to Rome, you've got do this or that,'" he remembered. "They asked me questions. They had already looked at my brochure and ranked me, but I didn't know where I was ranked." It was nerve-racking, and though they seemed to approve of his Harvard work (more so, indeed, than Sert had), he came out no more confident than before—though not necessarily less.

Michael had, on the whole, very little to lose. His ongoing competition with architecture notwithstanding, if he had returned to Indianapolis at that time, he would have done so trailing clouds of Eastern glory. He could have continued painting and drawing, had a family, grown a practice that would have given him at least the stature that Strauss had had, the creative satisfaction that Roush had had, and he could always have said of the Eastern scene that he had been there and done that.

But that is not what happened. By the time of his summer revels with Richard Meier, Michael truly had something to celebrate. The Harvard hayseed had made good. The mechanical drawing set awarded by Purdue University paled in comparison.

THAT SPRING MICHAEL PENNED a letter. He was not of an epistolary habit, and what little correspondence he did engage in he rarely ever saved. This was plainly a capital-O Occasion. "Dear Dean Sert," it began:

> I'm writing this letter to inform you of the very good news I have recently received. The American Academy in Rome has awarded me a Rome Prize Fellowship for 1960. The Grant entitles me to a year of study at the Academy with the possibility of renewal for a second year.
>
> In a sense this is your award as well as mine, for I'm sure it wouldn't have been possible without your most excellent turotrage [sic].
>
> When I first arrived at Harvard last year I was addicted to a formalistic-axial-symmetry in my work. But if you'll remember you quickly shook me out of my "precious" rut. (I must admit, at the time, I thought you shook a bit severely.) After being with you in your studio last year I am enjoying Architecture and its possibilities more than ever. "Variety", and what it can mean, was my lesson from you.
>
> I will keep in contact with you while we are in Rome and try to let you know of any "progress" I might make.
>
> Sincerely yours,
> Michael Graves[81]

It is perfectly gracious, of course. But the scare quotes and the parenthetical give it away, and the self-satisfied smile is nearly audible. Michael never did send another letter to the Teeny-Weeny Deany.

IV

THE LIGHT

AFTER SOME EIGHT DAYS at sea aboard the SS *Cristoforo Colombo*, Michael and Gail arrived in the late afternoon of September 30, 1960, in Naples, where they were met dockside by Ted Musho and a small delegation from the American Academy.[1] Piling into a car, the group drove north the 140 miles to Rome, a fairly bumpy ride in the early 1960s, passing through a dozen-odd small towns as the sun set over the low hills and coastal plains of the Mezzogiorno: Aversa, Cassino, Frosinone, Colleferro.

Shortly after nightfall they entered the region of Lazio, and at around eleven o'clock at night they reached the Academy, high on the Janiculum hill in Trastevere, the sprawling district of Rome on the west bank of the Tiber River. The Academy rustled up some food, gave Michael a peek at the space that would be his studio, and showed the couple to their room. No sooner had they set down their bags than a friend of Musho's showed up with another car. "I'll give you Rome in an hour," Musho announced, and in the middle of the night they struck out for a moonlight tour.[2]

Down the Janiculum, through the medieval maze of Trastevere, they made their way into the lush urban undergrowth of Rome. The year 1960 was a momentous one for the city: the Olympics had wrapped up there only a few weeks earlier, and a number of fine modern structures had been built to accommodate them. Pier Luigi Nervi, Italy's great engineer-poet, had designed two concrete sports palaces, their coffered domes vaulting unsupported over the bleachers and arena floors; in one of them, Cassius Clay had lately boxed his way to a gold medal for the United States. The architects Luigi Moretti and Adalberto Libera had teamed up to create a new Olympic Village, curving rows of apartments separated by irregular courtyards in a pattern that felt equal parts organic and rational. Even the city's ancient buildings had been enlisted in the effort: the Baths of Caracalla hosted the games' gymnastics contests.

Michael and Gail took it all in through the car window. The Colosseum in those days was covered in a thin grime of automotive exhaust, and the center of the Piazza

Venezia was doubling as a parking lot, with ranks of Fiat 500s cluttering up the view. Italy was entering the new decade with an antic buoyancy born of newfound affluence, and in its new design-obsessed consumer culture, everything modern and American was the rage.[3] *Tu vuò fà l'americano*, as the song had it.

Yet it was the city's agelessness, its centuries-old ruins and crumbling monuments, that caught the attention of the young stranger from the Midwest. The group headed first to the Vatican, driving as close as they dared to the steps of Saint Peter's Basilica. "It was like nothing I'd ever seen before," said Michael. "The ellipse of the piazza, and all those figures on top of all those columns—I thought I'd died and gone to heaven." They took a moment to catch their breath and then cut eastward, past the dark fulcrum of the Castel Sant'Angelo, over the river to the Campus Martius.[4]

They drove past the Spanish Steps; through the Piazza Barberini; and past the Trevi Fountain, designed in 1735 and frolicked in only a few months before by Anita Ekberg in *La dolce vita*. They turned south to the Piazza Navona, then looped back toward the Pantheon and east toward the Via del Corso, where riderless horses once raced during the Roman carnival. Hopelessly turned around by the winding, narrow streets, Musho steered them toward the Forum, and when they reached the foot of Capitoline Hill, they left the car and mounted the steps. At the top of the Campidoglio, in the middle of Michelangelo's famous plaza, the group stopped and stared. It was a festival night, and there were candles on the corners of the three exquisite buildings flanking the piazza, streaking the scene in bolts of light and shadow.

As they turned to descend once more the gently sloping stair, one of their hosts explained that the width of the ramp had been fashioned by Michelangelo so that the city's *cavaliere* and other distinguished visitors could go up it on horseback. Something about that fact—the specificity of it, the way it revealed the fine grain of history, visible in built form if only one knew where to look—caught Michael's imagination.

"I wanted to make sure I knew things like that," he said. "That they would influence my architecture. That I knew what the *meaning* was."[5]

It had taken them well more than an hour. Exhausted, the Graveses returned to the Academy at last and went to sleep.

"NO OTHER CITY offers such a field for study or an atmosphere so replete with the best precedents," declared the founders of the American Academy in Rome.[6] It was true in 1894, when they said it, and it was still true in 1960. By some reckoning it may yet be true today.

The Academy had begun life as the pet project of a group of prominent American architects and artists who had collaborated on the famed World's Columbian Exposition in 1893. The massive "White City" erected on Chicago's South Side had brought

Studio
number nine
at the American
Academy in
Rome during
Michael's resi-
dency. One
of his abstract
canvases is
visible on the
wall.

French-inspired Beaux Arts architecture to America on a grander scale than ever before, touching off a vogue for decorative neoclassicism that its creators—designers such as Daniel Burnham and John Wellborn Root—were eager to sustain. To do so they envisioned a vehicle that could put talented young Americans in touch with the culture of antiquity, right in the very capital of the ancient world.

The program they had in mind was modeled on that of other national acade-mies that had sprouted up in the Eternal City—most especially the French Acad-emy, which had produced some of the most noted practitioners of the Beaux Arts. Modest at the start, the American Academy in Rome struggled in its early years and was saved from insolvency only by a generous benefactor: Charles Follen McKim, a fellow White City architect and a partner in the celebrated firm of McKim, Mead & White. McKim's patronage extended to designing the first permanent home for the organization. Aligned northeastward toward the city, McKim's Academy was an idealized Renaissance palazzo, a cousin to his stately buildings for Columbia Uni-versity in Manhattan but here centered on an elegant cortile and shady portico, with a rambling hillside garden at the rear and a grand carriage entry in front embraced by terraced pavilions.

Michael's studio, number nine, was above one of these, on the building's northern side. The space had direct access to the adjoining rooftop so that he could walk straight out the huge picture window into the open air, sitting alone or with a companion and taking in spectacular views that stretched clear across the city as far as the Villa Medici, home of the French Academy, miles away on the Pincio.[7] Any visitors making their way to the American Academy he could hear coming as they crunched along the gravel path, and he could dash down the staircase just outside his studio door to greet them as they arrived in the high-ceilinged forecourt, decorated in first-century *spolia* and engraved plaques with the names of Academy benefactors including Rockefeller, Vanderbilt, and Carnegie. It was a privileged perch, and the best part was that Michael had very little to do except to enjoy it.

Fellows at the Academy weren't expected to produce anything in particular during their stay. No final exam would be administered, no more portfolios would have to be submitted to a panel of stone-faced worthies. Michael had even won an additional fellowship to round out the stipend provided to most of the incoming academicians. What he and Gail made of their time in Europe would be entirely up to them.

There were, however, certain codes and rituals that were more or less obligatory. "Within the first week I was in Rome," Michael recalled, "the director of the Academy asked us to dress properly, to remember that we were representatives of the US."[8] For the men, shirts and ties would be standard; this was easy enough for Michael, who at the time rarely wore anything else. Beyond that, a certain level of individual activity, and of collective participation, ensured that one remained in the good stead of the administration (and thereby increased one's likelihood of being asked to stay on for a second year). Group dinners were a central event, and all thirty-odd fellows, working in every kind of scholarly and artistic field, were expected to show up on a near-nightly basis to sit around the long tables in the dining room or in the central courtyard, sharing with their peers whatever exciting new research or boldly avant-garde creative project they were embarked upon at the moment.

For a person who, at twenty-six, had already earned a Harvard degree and held down demanding jobs at two highly successful design firms, attending a string of splendid Italian dinner parties must have seemed a very attractive proposition. But it wasn't as clear-cut as that.

Within the first few days of his arrival, Michael began to get the measure of his new colleagues. In the year he arrived, he was sharing the palazzo on the hill with an outstanding clutch of talent from across the intellectual spectrum. There was John C. Eaton, a composer who would go on to help develop some of the earliest electronic synthesizers. There was John La Montaine, another composer and pianist who had won the Pulitzer Prize for music the year before. There was Richard Brilliant, a historian of art who had just earned his PhD from Yale on Roman painting and sculpture, his dissertation a tour de force of formal analysis that explained how figures in classical art communicated to their audiences by way of gesture. And there was R. Ross Holloway, another classicist who'd gone from summa cum laude at Amherst to a PhD at Princeton—his thesis had been titled "The Elder Turtles of Aegina."[9] To the uninitiated, such as Michael was, the name alone could cause a shudder of incomprehension.

Michael didn't know what the Turtles of Aegina were, any more than he knew about Pompeian second-style illusionism or how to compose microtonal music. Fortunately, he *knew* that he didn't know. "I realized that these people knew what they were talking about," he recalled, "that these were very, very smart people, talking about minute conditions of their investigations and so on."[10] At Harvard, when he beheld the worldliness and sophistication of Sert's other students, he reacted by showing off: he could outdraw them, and he could prove it. But drawing wouldn't save him at the dinner table at the American Academy. He would have to adopt a different, more cunning strategy.

In those first nights, he laid out a new plan. "I sat there," he said, "and I thought, 'Boy you've got to be smart enough, Michael, to be quiet and not say a thing. Don't reveal what you don't know yet.' And I didn't reveal it. I just listened. For an entire year."[11]

HE LISTENED, AND HE LOOKED. To satisfy the expectation that he do something with his time other than take lunch on the terrace, he began once again to do as he'd done in Broad Ripple Village: he went into the street, and he started to draw.

He began, necessarily, at a degree of remove from the city. Michael did not yet speak Italian (and only ever acquired an elementary command of it), and life at the Academy tended to be somewhat cloistral, with most of the other fellows spending hour after hour lost in books or working in their studios.[12] His colleagues could point him toward major monuments, and the rest he could piece together with guidebooks, but once he made his way beyond the Academy's tall iron gates, he was essentially on his own.

In the shade of a portico, on a crowded sidewalk, or in the corner of a teeming piazza, Michael would sit down, still in shirt and tie, and begin to draw [**PLATES 3–5**]. He might have kept up with the watercolors he had first experimented with at the University of Cincinnati, but opted against it; he did continue the paintings he had begun in his shared Manhattan studio with Richard Meier, and he might have done those outdoors if he chose. ("Corot for his entire life wore a tie to paint," Michael would point out, and Corot did most of his work *en plein air*.) But what paintings he completed he did in the privacy of studio number nine, and they were never his primary focus during his time in Rome. For his safaris into the city, his weapons of choice were pen, pencil, and, for the first time, a camera—a clunky old Kodachrome.

Originally using spiral-bound sketch pads forty by twenty-eight inches, Michael laid down thick washes of ink to create suitably monumental images of the monumental edifices scattered about the city. His style drew on at least one major source: before coming to Rome (and at much greater length after his arrival), he had received some exposure to the *Carceri* and other architectural etchings of Giovanni Battista Piranesi. The effect that the Italian achieved with his engravings—the aggressive, high-contrast chiaroscuro that gave his Roman landmarks and cave-like interiors their feeling of amplitude and drama—Michael was able to re-create, to a limited extent, without the complex apparatus Piranesi used to produce his prints.[13]

He went everywhere. In front of the Arcibasilica di San Giovanni in Laterano, Michael got down the architect Alessandro Galilei's solid, palatial facade, capped by the heroic figures of Christ and the Apostles. Just down the hill from the Academy, he executed a perfect sketch of Donato Bramante's Tempietto of 1502, a tiny rotunda built as a tomb in the courtyard of San Pietro in Montorio; he portrayed it as though semitransparent, showing the full ring of the main colonnade with the balustrade above and the drum of the false clerestory topped by the domed roof. Just up the road, he produced an elevation of the Fontana dell'Acqua Paola, part of the enormous waterworks erected by Pope Paul V in the early seventeenth century to provide water to the city—he included the full inscription on the architrave, though for whatever reason he omitted the portals from which the water jetted. He drew the spindly, winnowing tower of Sant'Ivo alla Sapienza, just off the Corso, and the dome of Santa Maria del Loreto. He drew anything and everything that struck his fancy as he trudged in all weather along the hard paving stones of Rome, long before the city's metro system was large enough to make it of much use.

More than anyplace else, Michael came again and again to the Forum. In the early 1960s, preservationist measures were not so highly developed as they would become: arches, temples, and stoas that today can only be seen from a safe distance could be walked into and touched. Going wherever he pleased through the deep valley in the heart of Rome, Michael sketched it all. He sat at the base of the Colosseum on its southwestern side, capturing the bold diagonal cut where the original facade shears away to reveal the ruin within; he drew the Forum's triumphal arches, his lines wavering nervously as though sensing the full weight of the years upon them; and he pictured, in all its half-wrecked gigantism, the Basilica of Maxentius, the last great testament to the old Roman constructive genius before the city fell, in 312 CE, to the Emperor Constantine and his Christian legions from the East.

WHEN HE RETURNED from these marches through the ancient world, Michael's routine at the Academy was always the same. He would play a quick game of pool and then head into the Academy library, remaining there until it was time to join the other fellows for dinner. As he put it at the time—in a reference to the popular American television show—he would use his stay in Rome to finally "get smart."[14]

There's no reliable account as to what he was reading during those long sojourns through the vaulted reading rooms of the Academy. Its holdings on architecture, however, were immense and included volumes (most of them in English translation) that he would cite repeatedly in the years to come. Musty old editions of the great Renaissance theorists Sebastiano Serlio, Leon Battista Alberti, and Giacomo Barozzi da Vignola were all at his fingertips; from these he would learn the nature of the classical orders, the differences between the unadorned Doric, spool-like Ionic, and vegetative Corinthian capitals that topped the columns of the porticos he was seeing all over Rome. He could read Marcus Vitruvius Pollio, the first-century BCE architect and engineer whose *Ten Books on Architecture* described Roman building practices as they were carried out in the time of Julius Caesar, explaining the proper way to lay out everything from the plumbing system of a private villa to the plan of an entire town. And he could find some of the foundational scholarship that established the history of art and architecture as formal academic disciplines: the writing of Johann Joachim Winckelmann and Giovanni Morelli, who spelled out for the first time the fundamentals of connoisseurship, how to date and categorize sculptures and buildings by way of stylistic hallmarks, and how—above all—a work of art can be subjected to visual dissection, revealing the sometimes-hidden messages of its creator.

In the hours between billiards and pasta, Michael slowly taught himself the history that had been withheld from him at Harvard and at Cincinnati. But the real revelation was still to come.

"IT MAY PERHAPS yeeld some little encouragement," wrote Thomas Coryat, "to many noble and generose yong Gallants…to travell into forraine countries, and inrich themselves partly with the observations, and partly with the languages of outlandish regions, the principall meanes (in my poore opinion) to grace and adorne those courtly Gentlemen."[15]

In 1611 Coryat, an English courtier and writer, published a record of his peregrinations through Europe under the title *Coryat's Crudities*. It was among the first, arguably *the* first, full account of what would come to be known as the Grand Tour, that traditional Continental jaunt of aristocrats, dandies, artists, and poets in search of inspiration and adventure abroad.

Coryat's chronicle helped touch off a phenomenon. Not just from England, but from France, Germany, and points beyond, the well-moneyed and the well-bred began migrating south and eastward in journeys that could last months or years, adding a final gloss to their education with visits to cathedrals, cemeteries, and scenic sites of sea, lake, and mountain. The itinerary differed depending upon the traveler's whims and country of origin, but by the mid-1700s its basic contours were fairly well established: the Low Countries, Paris, the Alps, northern Italy, and on to the Mediterranean—the cradle of Greco-Roman civilization, the common heritage of Western Europe a millennium and more after the collapse of the Roman Empire.[16]

Well into the twentieth century, this circuit was common practice. Le Corbusier had done a version of it between 1907 and 1911, straying as far as Turkey and the Balkans; Louis Kahn had done the same. Yet two successive world wars had somewhat broken the cultural habit, and the increasing popularity of foreign travel among the postwar middle class—particularly among Americans—tended to stress tourism at the expense of grandeur. No more did patrician treasure hunters scrounge at leisure amid the ruins of Pompeii, pulled along by their *cicerones*, picking out ancient amphorae to adorn their mantels back home.

The American Academy, however, had been an outgrowth of that tradition, and many of its fellows still used Rome as a staging ground for expeditions throughout Europe. Michael and Gail determined to do the same. Only more so. "We did our own Grand Tour," Michael said.[17]

Michael's discoveries in the library were a prime motivating factor: many of the figures whose work he'd encountered there (Winckelmann in particular) had been formed intellectually during their time in Greece and southern Italy. Gail, more game to see the glories of Europe than the towers of Racine, was placed in charge of sorting through the foreign-language travel guides and working out their general route; Michael chimed in with particular sites he wanted to visit and helped gather funds to get them there. His major moneymaking scheme—the reason many of his Rome drawings are lost to us—was to sell them, freshly inked, to passersby for a cool fifty bucks apiece.

Before beginning in earnest, they started with a brief initial excursion in late January 1961, not planned by themselves: a group trip in company with a few of their colleagues, escorted by one of the senior fellows who sometimes took up temporary positions at the Academy. The trip leader was Max Abramovitz, architectural partner to Wallace K. Harrison, the court favorite of the Rockefeller family. He guided the party up the boot of Italy, stopping in San Gimignano, a town rich in Gothic and Romanesque buildings, before continuing on to Bologna. (Though not usually remembered as the most accomplished designer, Abramovitz proved to have excellent taste in restaurants, taking the group to Pappagallo's, one of the oldest and most extraordinary eating establishments in a town famous for its food.) The rest of the trip, spanning about a week, packed in a full sweep of northern Italy's most beautiful cities: Padua (Giotto's frescoes were a highlight), Vicenza (loaded with Palladian villas), Verona, Bergamo, Milan, Viterbo, and more.[18]

It was a short trip, and rather rushed. Thereafter, Michael and Gail would break their makeshift Grand Tour into several segments of a couple of weeks or months, taking their time in each town and each country before resuming their residency in Rome. To help stretch their meager funds, they would stay in campsites for twenty-five cents a night, driving as far as three hundred miles in a single day before pitching their tent in the evening and staying as long as they pleased, while hewing to the outline of Gail's itinerary. For the first of their solo expeditions, in April of that year, they bought a black Volkswagen Beetle and headed south, to the area around Bari and Brindisi. Their objective was Alberobello.

Gail wrote her mother a postcard the day after their arrival: "Alberobello yesterday and the countryside was very beautiful. Saw fields of red poppies growing wild. The Trulli houses (Mike's thesis at U.C.) were everywhere you looked." In her diary she was more frank, confessing that the town had turned out to be more "commercialized" than they'd hoped.

But the *trulli* did not disappoint. Seen in person, the distinctive details that marked each hut were easier to make out: the pinnacles at the top of each dome were not extraneous decorations but markers, unique signatures identifying the builders who made them. Some huts were short, some tall; some domes were painted with symbols, some not; some doorways had a straight lintel and others an arch. What was more, seen in a long file down the steep hills or in small groups of two and three in front of a piazza, the *trulli* formed coherent ensembles, their varying features giving them an almost human quality, like a family gathered together for a festive occasion. Individually they were remarkable, but en masse they formed an ever-changing but unified streetscape, a thousand variations on a theme coming together to create a sense of community [PLATE 7].

They caught the ferry from Brindisi and went to Greece, driving all over the country. They saw Athens and the Acropolis. Michael got his first glimpse of the Parthenon he had drawn as a high school student.

From Greece they headed to Turkey. They had been told that exchange rates for Turkish currency were more favorable on the black market on the Greek side of the border, but while Michael was negotiating for lira a group of women surrounded Gail as she stood by the VW.

"One woman was holding a baby about ten months old," Gail remembered. "They indicated that I should take the baby, and the woman put the baby in the back seat on top of our tent and blankets." Shaking her head, frantically trying to wave the women off, Gail hurriedly removed the infant from the vehicle and returned it to its mother. Apparently shocked at her ungracious refusal of the proffered gift, the women instead asked if they could take some of Gail and Michael's belongings from the car as recompense. The Americans sped off as fast as they could.[19]

After Turkey, the Balkans. "We were warned not to go to Yugoslavia because the roads were terrible and sometimes impassable, but we decided to try," Gail recalled. The advisory was spot on: the Byzantine churches and monasteries they were looking for were hopelessly out of reach. Instead, said Gail, "We decided to stick to the coast and drive through the country that way."[20]

In Greece they had begun to notice a faint hostility coming their way from some of the locals, and it sharpened measurably in Yugoslavia. Slowly they pieced together the reason: in lands only fifteen years earlier occupied by the Nazis, here they were driving a German-made car. As a countermeasure, they put signs in the front and back windows reading "USA." It helped—somewhat.

"The car was stoned once as we passed through mountains in Yugoslavia," said Gail. "We also had a very unpleasant stop by military with guns pointed at us. They made Michael get out of the car and clean off the headlights again and again."[21]

Their final night, in the Croatian coastal town of Split, turned into a fiasco. Situated right on the edge of the sea, their campsite was struck hard by a gale-force rainstorm during the night that almost destroyed the couple's tent. "It was off season," said Gail, "but there were bungalows at the campsite and a caretaker. Even though we begged to be allowed in one of the bungalows he refused to open the door." They slept in the car instead. By the time they woke up, the caretaker—repenting, presumably, the impolitic treatment he'd shown the smartly dressed and potentially well-connected young people from the West—did the only decent thing: "He begged us not to complain to the authorities," said Gail.[22] After a month on the road, she and Michael hurried back to Italy, happy to return to their home away from home.

THEY STAYED PUT for a few months and then continued on their Grand Tour. In early September they set out for southern France. They saw the fortified town of Carcassonne and the scenic ruins at Arles, as well as a few spots of more niche interest: Le Corbusier's Unité d'habitation, the 1952 apartment complex in Marseille that was the closest realization of the master's urban vision. Michael captured its chunky, lumbering pilotis and sculptural details in heavily applied pencil, making it appear less like a building and more like a layering of abstract, irregular geometries jockeying for space on the page [PLATE 8].

Making their way westward, they headed for Spain. In Barcelona, Michael sketched the still-incomplete Sagrada Familia and Casa Batlló of Antoni Gaudí, giving the latter a seasick, frenzied expression that recalled the contemporary landscape-cum-portraits of Willem de Kooning. Michael's eye for painterly forms and contrast was equally visible in his Kodachrome photos in Italy, which sometimes focused on surfaces and details to a degree that was almost abstract. As time wore on, however, he took fewer and fewer pictures, relying on his hand alone to capture all that he and Gail were seeing. "You only really remember things," Michael would often say, "when you draw them."[23]

From Catalonia, the couple drove across the Iberian peninsula, trying to make it all the way north to Santiago de Compostela, but the roads were washed out because of heavy late-summer rains. Back they went to Rome for another five months of dinners and library visits.

THE "THIRD TRIP WAS our last 'big' one," recalled Gail. Leaving Rome the first week of May 1962, they covered an enormous swath of Central Europe: St. Gallen, Einsiedeln, Zurich, and Basel in Switzerland; Colmar and Strasbourg in France. Someone broke into their car in Paris. In danger of running out of money, they had to skip Austria.

They crossed the channel into England and hit London, Oxford, Bath, Stonehenge, and Salisbury Cathedral. By June 11 they were in Brussels: "Weather so miserable we decided to cut Amsterdam and head for Cologne," Gail wrote in her diary, but they got to Germany only to be foiled again—"Our guidebooks are so old that we wasted much time seeking churches, chateaus, etc., only to find them in ruins after the war." They did manage to take in Speyer Cathedral, Schoenberg Church, and the pilgrimage church of Marienkapelle in Würzburg, Germany. "By accident we drove through the tip of Austria and then back into Germany."

After nearly two months and thousands of miles, they turned the VW southward again, heading back to Rome, their Grand Tour complete.

LOOKING BACK DECADES LATER, Michael would say that when he arrived in Europe, he "was not somebody who was wholly, how shall I say it, conversant with the idea of urbanity." Indianapolis, he said, "was no place." (Indian-no-place, he sometimes called it.)[24] Cambridge and New York had given him some taste of the world beyond Broad Ripple Village and Cincinnati, but in his own view, it was Rome that made him the designer, and the individual, he became.[25]

Those who knew him before and after sensed the change Europe made in him. "His time in Rome," Richard Meier would speculate, had "some kind of profound influence on everything that happened after." ("He started using Italian phrases,"

Meier added. "He never did *that* before.")[26] Lois Rothert remembered the talented boy from Indy as one whose "grasp of architecture only went to some level." When she saw him again afterward, he wasn't just drawing buildings, but talking about them; the difference, she said, was "those two years in Rome."[27] "That was when my mom said he changed and buckled down and became more focused," recalled Sarah Stelfox, Michael and Gail's daughter. "She noticed a new push to succeed."[28]

It is at this juncture that any thought of returning to Indianapolis receded permanently from Michael's mind. His expectations had been raised as much by the glamour of the experience—how you gonna keep 'em down on the farm once they've seen Saint Peter's?—as by the caliber of his colleagues. At the Academy, unlike at Harvard, he met people of origins no less humble than his own who had excelled in their chosen fields. "We were there," said Richard Brilliant, himself the son of a Jewish immigrant, "because we were smart." Another art historian at the Academy, the Bronx-born Donald Posner, was the first in his family to receive a college degree, not from Harvard or Yale, but from Queens College.

With examples like these before him, returning to the Midwest would have mortified Michael's already vulnerable pride. But as throughout his life, the chemistry between his personal and his creative aspirations formed an unusual compound. His deep-felt need to compete with others was now seconded by a nascent conception of how he might get ahead in that other, larger competition—his "competition with architecture."

What revealed itself to him in Italy, both in what he was seeing and what he was reading, was not the "space value" he'd claimed to be in search of when he'd applied. It was what had been missing in the architecture of Modernism as he'd received it: the capacity to communicate. Mies's chaste spatial and structural phenomenology had always registered to him as obtuse; Le Corbusier, though infinitely more adaptable, clung to a geometric order just slightly too Platonic to enunciate explicit ideas or narratives. In contrast, one could look at the facade of the Arcibasilica di San Giovanni in Laterano and, armed with a little history, apprehend not just its functional hierarchy—how to enter it, how the inside is divided into nave and side aisles—but its spiritual hierarchy as well, the centrality of Christ and the nature of the Holy Trinity. The imperative that Michael first felt on the steps of the Capitoline on his first night in Rome, to "know what the meaning was," was becoming the guiding principle of his thinking, an architectural idea not divorced from, but inextricably part of, the architectural image that his eye and hand could readily fabricate, thanks to his outstanding visual acuity.

Much trial and error would be necessary before he found a way to realize, to his own satisfaction, his sought-after sense of meaning. But the goal was now in sight, and it would be the animating objective of his career from here on—whatever the consequences. In time, this dream would crowd out not just any thought of Indianapolis (too small a sphere by far to accommodate it) but many other prospects, other paths, that would periodically run parallel with its pursuit, pushing Michael always onward toward an architecture that "speaks of its accessibility," in Peter Eisenman's words, even if that meant eschewing architecture's power "to speak of its own 'sacred realm.'"[29]

From Gail's Diary:

March 17, 1961. Climbed to top of the Pantheon. [A classicist from Bryn Mawr, T. Robert S.] Broughton took a group from the Academy. He obtained permission for us to climb to the top, go out on the exterior of the dome and at end [sic] crawl up on hands and knees to peek over the edge and down into the interior [**PLATE 6**].[30]

For both Michael and Gail, the greatest pleasure of their time in Rome was always Rome itself. Having secured their second year there, the two finally felt comfortable joining in the conversation at the Academy's nightly dinners, and they might happily never have left, spending every evening of their lives chatting away in the late southern twilight and every afternoon basking on the terrace with the whole of Rome at their feet. "Nothing was more interesting than the city," Michael would say. "I can't stress that enough."[31]

His drawings had changed during his time there. He had become good friends with another academician, the painter Lennart Anderson, who had advised him that by doing his drawings in such a large format and by resting his paper flat on the sidewalk, Michael was unable to look at the buildings as he drew them and was missing their proper proportions and perspective; Michael switched to smaller sketchpads.[32] Anderson also had a pronounced disregard for Abstract Expressionism or for any artists, even figurative ones, whose canvases were too loosely constructed. Looking at one painting cluttered with thousands of stray lines, he turned to Michael and said, "Well, I'm sure *one* of 'em's right."[33]

Anderson's critique chimed with other visual stimuli that had by then floated into Michael's ken: the wall drawings at Pompeii, the deftly composed still lives of Giorgio Morandi, and still more of the work of Picasso and his Cubist compatriots Georges Braque and Juan Gris, all of them less inclined toward pure abstraction than their latter-day American counterparts. Though evidently familiar with most of their work by the time he left Rome, he would not begin to register much of their influence for a while, though there was a slight reduction in the "hairy," labored quality of his streetside drawings.

Besides his artistic busking, Michael found other means to support his Grand Touring. In the summer of 1961, he picked up some work in the Rome offices of Walter Gropius's TAC. The project he spent most of his time on was student housing for the University of Baghdad, part of Gropius's master plan for the school's campus. Michael's only memorable encounter with the august founder of the Bauhaus was a sternly issued proviso that Michael not make the men's and women's dormitories "so close together that they could put a board over from one roof to the other and sleep together." "Ve don't vant to be responsible for any babies," Gropius said.[34]

More memorable was the afternoon when he was working in the office and two men stopped in: the British architectural historian and theorist Colin Rowe and his prize pupil at Cambridge, Peter Eisenman. "Michael remembered seeing us in our white shirts, white shorts, and long white socks, like people out of the 1920s, dancing into the Graves purview," Eisenman recalled. Michael recognized him from their acquaintance back in Cambridge, said hello, and they went out for drinks. It was their second meeting, but it proved as inconclusive as the first, and the two lost touch immediately afterward.[35]

By the time of Michael and Gail's last sweep through the Continent in the spring of 1962 they were already looking ahead to their return to the United States. A position had recently been made available at Princeton University School of Architecture, and one of Michael's colleagues at the Academy was a Princeton English professor on sabbatical. He encouraged Michael to apply, writing him a letter of recommendation and advising him that the current faculty of the school could make use of someone of Michael's youth and energy. "They're all tired," he said. "You might give them a lift."[36]

Michael had received an offer from George Nelson to rejoin his firm as a junior partner, but it would have meant working in conjunction with Gordon Chadwick, whom Michael did not care for. The pull of New York was still powerful, but Princeton responded to his application with an attractive offer and wooed him further by making the case that he could easily commute to the city from New Jersey whenever he pleased, becoming a Princeton professor but a New York architect. Convinced, he took them up on the offer, accepting a position as a lecturer on a limited-term contract beginning in the fall semester of 1962.

1 A model
of Michael's
"Amenable Shelter"
proposal, pre-
pared for his
undergraduate
thesis, 1958

2 An early
Graves abstraction,
circa 1960

3 Michael drawing on the streets of Rome, 1962

4 Among the most accomplished sketches of his Rome years, Michael's drawing of Bramante's Tempietto of 1502

5 The Basilica of Maxentius, completed in 312 CE, sketched by Michael in 1960. Visitors can just barely get this close today, as fencing surrounds the site.

6 "Nothing mattered as much as the city...." Rome from the top of the Pantheon, photographed by Michael, March 1961

7 One of Michael's photos of the *trulli* houses, taken April 1961

8 Le Corbusier's
1952 Unité
d'habitation in
Marseilles,
as rendered by
Michael in
September 1961

9 One of Michael's early presentation sketches for the Jersey Corridor proposal. The casual diagram with its simple declaratory text is unmistakably Corbusian.

sun, space, green

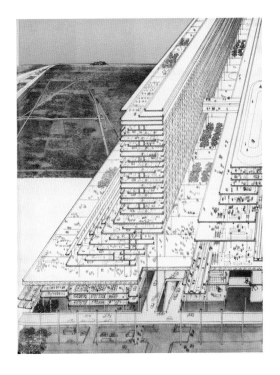

10 The final Jersey Corridor scheme, sketched by Anthony Vidler, 1965

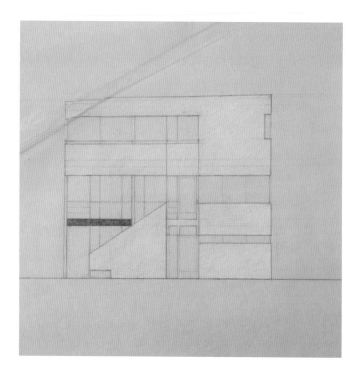

11 The first "layer": the approach to Hanselmann

12 Elevation of the Hanselmann House, 1967, on what would become Michael's signature yellow trace paper

13 A river—in the form of a blue banister—runs through Hanselmann's third floor, one level above the entrance.

14 Inside Hanselmann, Michael's mural, the house's visual centerpiece and narrative master key

15 Benacerraf House, south facade. Note the cloudlike cutaway on the terrace, also suggestive of the treeline beyond.

16 Alexander House, 1971

17 Snyderman
House, 1972

18 Snyderman's
second-floor
landing, a riot
of overlapping
frames

19 One of
the series of
murals Michael
produced for
Gwathmey's
Transammonia
offices, featuring
the repeated
cornice motif

20 Claghorn
House, 1974

21 Schulman,
garden facade

22 Interior
living room of
Schulman,
with fireplace
as built

23 Monumental image: the dramatically classicized Crooks fireplace drawing

24 Yellow trace elevation of the Crooks House main facade

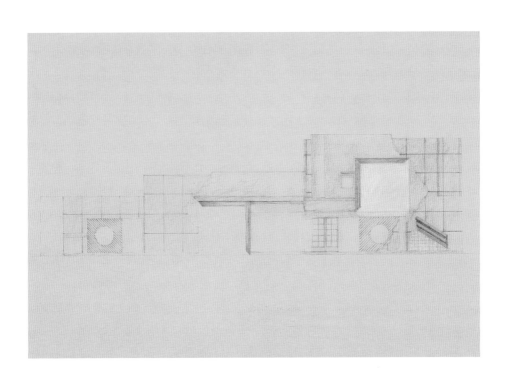

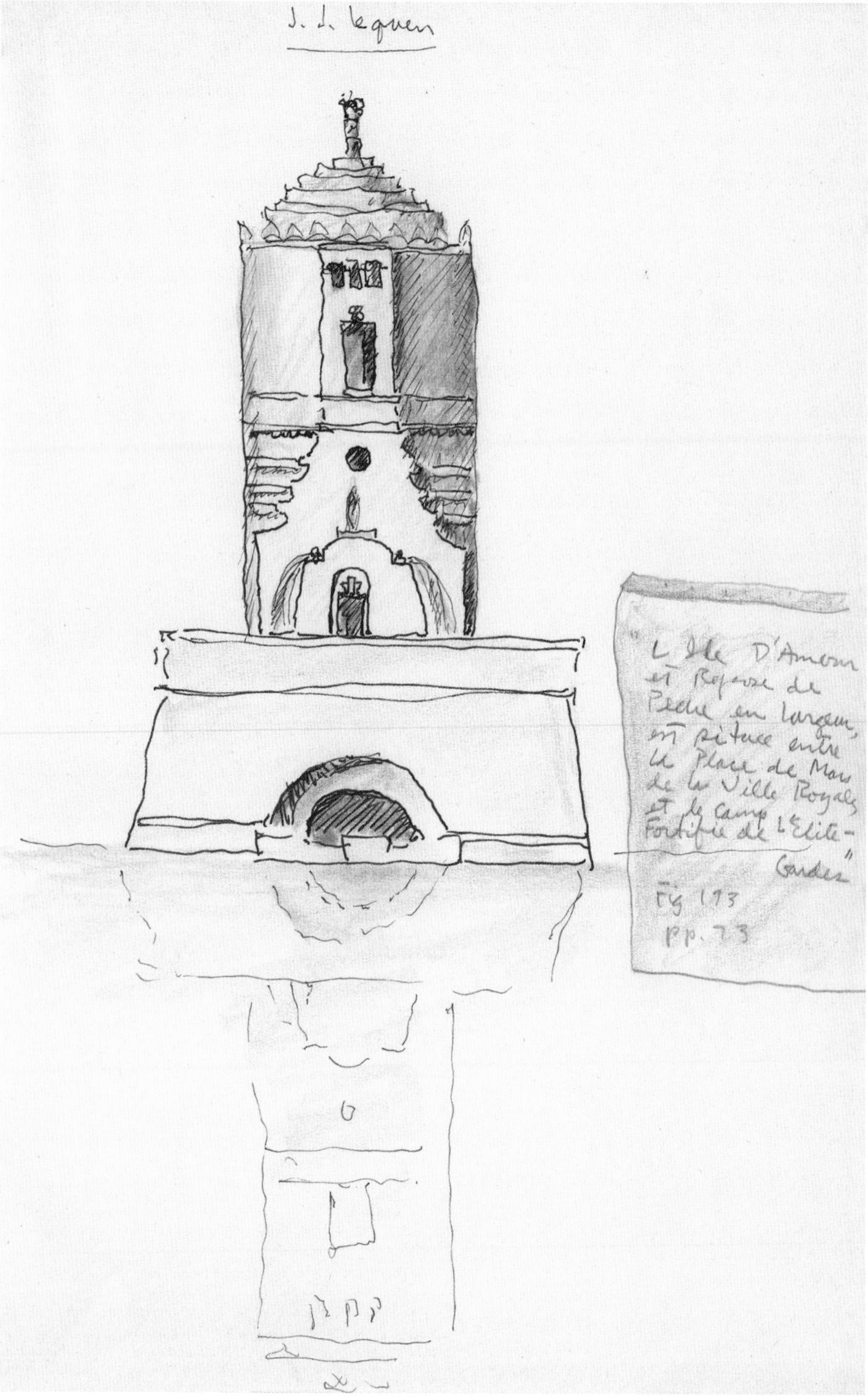
J. J. Lequeu
"L'Ile D'Amour
et Repose de
Peche en largeur,
est situee entre
la Place de Mars
de la Ville Royale,
et le camp
Fortifie de L'Elite-
Gardes"
Fig 173
pp. 73

25 A "referential sketch": an imaginary temple by the eighteenth-century visionary Jean-Jacques Lequeu, from Michael's 1977 maroon sketchbook

26 Plocek House, 1977, as completed in 1982

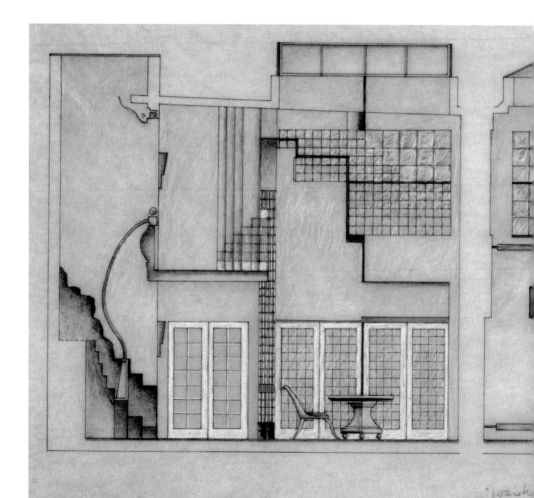

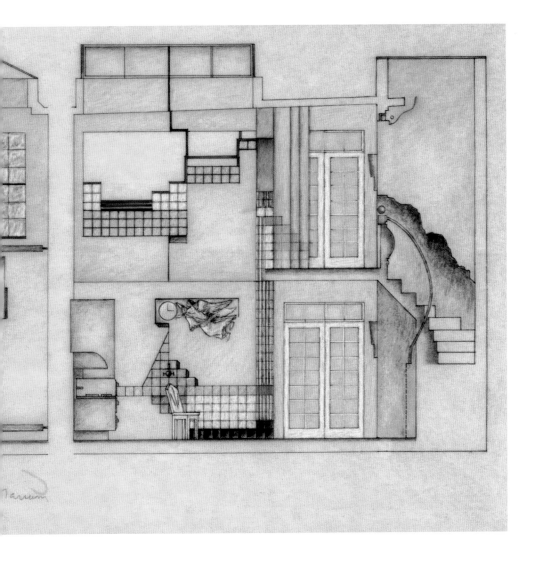

28 Fargo-Moorhead Bridge, south elevation

29 The cover
for a special
1979 edition of
*Architectural
Digest* on the
Roma Interrotta
exhibition.
The illustration
was created
by Michael;
all twelve con-
tributors were
featured in
its central panel.

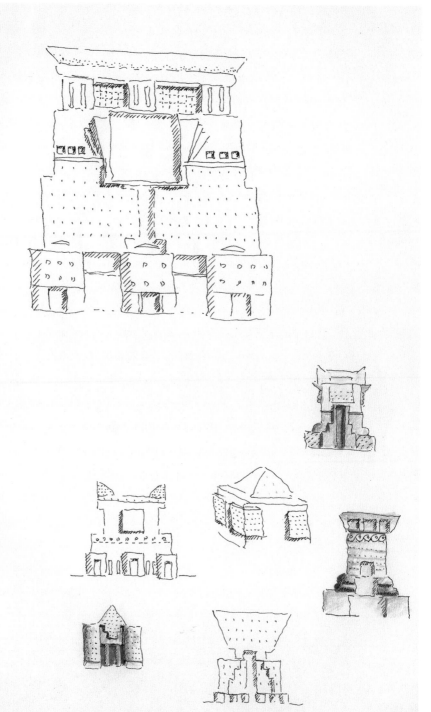

30 "A Case
for Figurative
Architecture":
Michael's
sketches for
the Portland
Building
referenced the
human body
and classical
motifs in
countless
configurations.

31 Portland
as it appeared
after the instal-
lation of the
"Portlandia"
statue in 1985

32 Michael
Graves Architect's
Los Angeles
showroom for
furniture brand
Sunar

33 Dressing
table for Memphis
—a building
for the boudoir

34 From an early 1980s volume of the maroon sketch-books, some early versions of the Alessi teakettle, with both squared and rounded handles

35 The Alessi 9093 in its final form. The wings of the bird were swept back, recalls firm associate Donald Strum, to "receive the fingertips."

36 Stage set for the Joffrey Ballet, commissioned for a 1982 performance by the choreographer Laura Dean, for which Michael also designed the costumes. In foreground, the easel—a recurring feature of his artwork since the mid-1970s.

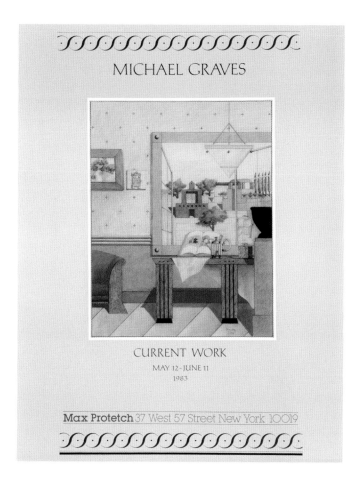

37 A poster for one of Michael's shows at Max Protetch. The outline of his Sunar chair is visible at left; on the table sits one of the original Alessi "Coffee Tea Piazza" coffeepots. (The image had originally been used as a cover design for *Architectural Review* in 1981.)

38 Interior courtyard of the San Juan Capistrano Public Library, 1982

39 Diane
von Furstenberg's
Fifth Avenue
storefront, 1984,
recently spared
destruction by
local preserva-
tionists

40 The "Winter" fireplace from Michael's living room for Charles Jencks in London, 1984. Jencks had originally commissioned a suite of themed rooms from other architects, including Rem Koolhaas; only Michael's was completed.

41 Humana's lobby: forty-five thousand square feet of marble under forty-foot-high ceilings

42 Humana Building, 1985, seen from the plaza of Mies's 1969 American Life Building with Harrison & Abramowitz's 1972 National City Tower at left

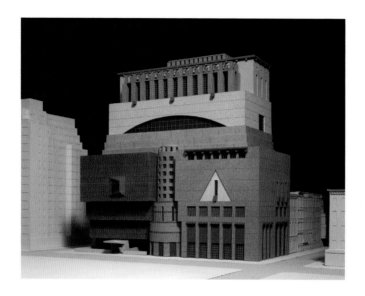

43 Model of
the original
Whitney scheme
from Michael
Graves Architect

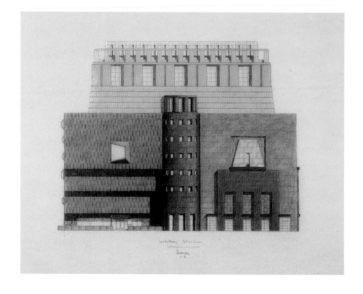

44 The second,
more moderate
Whitney proposal

45 Third time
not a charm:
the final, much-
reduced Whitney
proposal

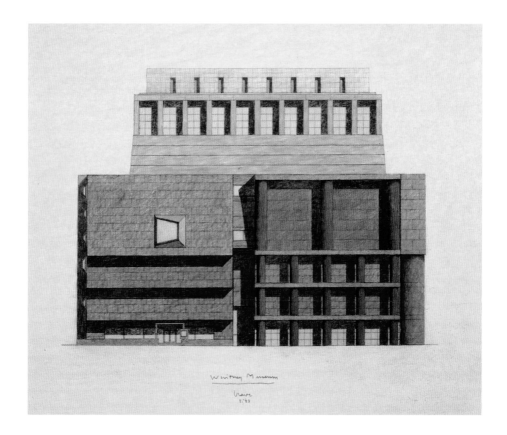

46 The model
for the Dolphin
and Swan Resort,
Orlando, 1987

47 The interior
of the Swan,
opened in 1990

48 Engineer-
ing Research
Center, College
of Engineering,
University of
Cincinnati, 1990

49 The Fukuoka
Hyatt Regency
Hotel and Office
Building, Fukuoka,
Japan, 1990

Denver

South

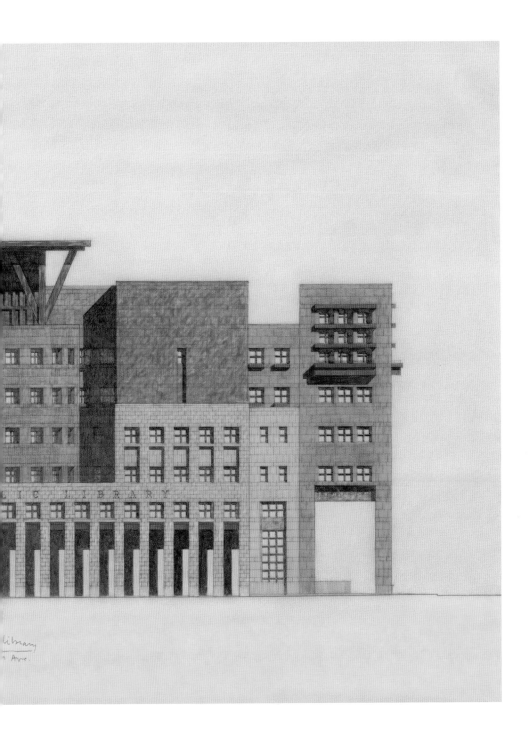

50 Denver Public Library,
1991, south elevation

51 Southwest corner of Denver Public Library —the alternative entrance is in the base of the "Pencil."

52 Michael's sketches
for the Target teakettle

53 Michael's sketch
of the Target toaster,
one of the original
products included in
the 1998 rollout

54 The Target toaster
in its final form

55 The Washington
Monument scaffold
by night

56 St. Coletta
of Greater
Washington,
2006, a school
and physical
therapy center
for special
needs children

57 Drive Medical
shower head, 2005

58 Stryker
Patient Chair,
the Michael
Graves Design
Group's
stand-assist
chair

59 The Stryker
Prime TC Transport
Chair, released
in 2013 and the
product of intensive
real-world research
by the firm

60 Michael's
drawing for
an ideal hospital
room, 2009,
featuring
elements of
the Stryker
collection

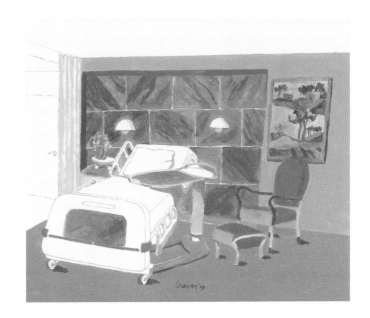

61 Michael's upstairs study at the Warehouse. After his disability, it was mostly a repository for furniture and artifacts.

62 The Warehouse dining room in its final iteration

63 Wounded
Warriors house,
one of two
completed by
the firm in
Fort Belvoir,
Virginia, 2011

64 Digital
aerial rendering
of Michael
Graves College
in Wenzhou,
China

65 The Painting, also called by Michael *Archaic Landscape*. He produced countless similar canvases in the last years of his life.

66 Michael in his home studio at the Warehouse in 2011

V

THE GARDEN AND THE MACHINE

Obligated under Michael's contract to spend their first year in Princeton, he and Gail installed themselves in an unassuming faculty-housing block on the shore of Lake Carnegie, a stone's throw from campus.[1] It was in some ways a return to the kind of life they had led in Cincinnati, a little more picturesque but no less humdrum, and after the excitement of their time in Europe it required some readjustment. That might have been so wherever they'd gone. But they hadn't gone just anywhere.

It had been nearly half a century since F. Scott Fitzgerald described Princeton University as "the pleasantest country club in America,"[2] and at the time of Michael's arrival Princeton remained perhaps the most insular of the Ivies: close as it was to New York, it was an ivory tower within an ivory tower, an academic citadel in a small town girded by miles of bucolic farmland. Notwithstanding the progressive mood of Kennedy-era America, Princeton in the early 1960s was still a place of nearly pristine conservatism, an attitude that touched almost every department in the school. Its first-ever female graduate student had enrolled only the year prior to Michael's arrival.[3]

And no program was sleepier than architecture. "Stagnant!" Peter Eisenman called it. "No one had been hired there for seventeen years."[4] Few promising design students bothered applying there—Michael hadn't. The director who recruited him, Robert McLaughlin, was typically rated an affable and capable administrator, though one without a clear vision of what the school, or architecture in general, ought to be. Instead, the dominant presence on the faculty was that of Jean Labatut. The French-born and French-trained Labatut had been in his post since 1928, and his engaged, energetic teaching style made him a favorite among his students (who nicknamed him "Labby"). But his Modernist convictions were grounded more in his own highly refined intuition than in any rigorous theory. "He was very much a rationalist about design," recalled Robert Hillier, who studied with Labatut in the 1950s and early '60s. "He didn't really have any direct influences."[5] If Cincinnati had preached the gospel according to Mies and Harvard the gospel according to Corb, Labatut's Princeton was a church with no evangel.

It didn't even have a chapel. When Michael began teaching, the school did not yet have its own building, sharing a suite of spaces with the Department of Art and Archaeology in and around the Princeton Art Museum. This kind of arrangement wasn't unusual—Yale's architecture school had had a similar one for decades—but the late nineteenth- and early twentieth-century buildings in which Princeton's architecture students studied were woefully inadequate. In 1962 the university began work on a new stand-alone facility for the school: designed by the alumnus-led Fisher, Nes, Campbell and Partners, the structure was a charmless midcentury assemblage of glass and brick, but it would add new drawing rooms, offices, preceptor rooms, and more. Dedicated in October 1963, the building was already under construction by the time Michael joined the faculty, and there was a sense that with its completion a different kind of school might emerge.

This sense of optimism, despite the program's many flaws, was the appeal of Princeton—and Michael wasn't the only one who felt it. "I thought if I wanted to go somewhere and do something," said Peter Eisenman, "I wanted to do it in a place that's a void."[6] Entirely unaware of what his not-quite-friend from Cambridge and Rome was planning, Eisenman had gone seeking a job at Princeton in the summer of 1962 and had joined the faculty the following year. Each was a little surprised to see the other. "There he was again," Eisenman recalled. "Third time we'd crossed paths."

But this encounter was different. Thrown together into the relative backwater of Princeton, bursting with energy and ideas, the two young architects formed a bond that would become the most significant of either of their careers. "We became instant buddies," said Eisenman.[7] It had only taken them four years.

PERPETUALLY BOW-TIED, usually clutching a pipe, Eisenman cultivated the image of the tweedy young academic, though the impression was slightly undercut by his puckish, gap-toothed smile. In those early Princeton days, he and Michael spent most working hours and not a few off-hours in each other's company, with and without their wives. Dinners and cocktails, trips into New York for lectures—and, of course, football games—all became standard fare. Occasionally they even talked about architecture.

Besides being the only young faculty "for miles," as Eisenman noted, there was a concurrence in their progress as architects that would not have been the case had the two met for the first time a mere four or five years later. Both had lived abroad, both had worked for major design firms in the States, and neither much wanted to work in someone else's studio again. The theoretical side of architecture was already

Peter Eisenman
and Michael at
Princeton, 1965

emerging as Eisenman's demesne, and given Michael's historical and artistic preoc-
cupations, the two found themselves similarly at odds with the plodding, unimagi-
native atmosphere that hung about the American design scene at the time.

What Rome had been to Michael, Rowe was to Eisenman.[8] The forty-two-year-
old Colin Rowe—whom Michael had met in passing at the TAC office, when Eisenman brought his professor there—was a product of London's Warburg Institute and
had become a fly in the academic ointment on two continents, having moved from
Cambridge to Cornell the same year Michael came to Princeton. A specialist in the
work of the Italian Renaissance architect Andrea Palladio, Rowe had built his reputation discovering links between cultural and architectural developments that spanned
centuries, upending prevailing thinking on architectural history and unearthing
hidden truths about how Modernist architecture had come into being—and how it
might yet be practiced. Recognizing, as he wrote in 1956, that "the *idea* of modern
architecture is a subject of some confusion" (his emphasis), Rowe saw that within
and around the movement's fissures there had grown a smothering orthodoxy, a
moralistic regard for formal purity that "threatens to become injurious to [Modern-
ism's] whole idealization of the future."[9] Rowe's tutelage had instilled in Eisenman a
conviction that Modernism needed to be saved from itself.

Rowe's Modernist revisionism differed from Team X's. The latter called for an
architecture of deeper and more complex feeling, while Rowe gestured toward an
architecture of deeper and more complex thinking; Team X represented the heart,

Rowe, the head. ("He was, in a way, my enemy," Team X leader Peter Smithson would later say of Rowe.)[10] But together, they were part of the same tectonic shift in global architecture. Alone in New Jersey, Michael and Eisenman saw that they were poised to make Princeton a part of the same movement.

They couldn't be sure how they were going to do it; if pressed, they would have had to admit they didn't really know what their new architecture would look like. They agreed that Mies's Modernism, and the proliferation in American cities of the immaculate glass boxes of the International Style, had unfairly sidelined the true and more vibrant Modernism of Le Corbusier—which could yet be reinvented, if only one applied the right intellectual tools. What those tools were, however, and how they should be wielded, they couldn't say. Still, nearly from the moment he arrived, Michael felt he was in the right place to figure it out. "I liked it," he recalled. "I liked the university and what we could do there—what Peter and I could do there—in remaking it."[11]

TEACHING, THEY KNEW, would have to play into their remaking. They had to prove their chops in the classroom if either was to be put in line for a tenured position. Their teaching methods evolved in tandem, as did their commitment to teaching as an integral part of the architect's craft; unlike many of their most prominent contemporaries, neither Michael nor Eisenman ever put aside pedagogy for practice. It became another part of their friendship, this shared feeling that they were scholar-architects, working both sides of the professional fence.

Michael's professorial duties in his first semester were confined to advising graduate thesis candidates, but thereafter they expanded into regular studio courses. In the spring of 1963 he began teaching undergraduate design students. The class—Architecture 204, a GSD-ish, Bauhausian studio—was oversubscribed, and Michael recalled being asked to invite one of his "fancy friends from New York" to teach with him.[12] Michael selected Richard Meier, Eisenman's cousin, with whom he had rekindled his Manhattan friendship following his return from abroad. Meier would stay at Michael and Gail's house while in Princeton; periodically Michael would stay over at Meier's New York apartment, sleeping on a spare mattress on the floor. Once, while Meier was out, Michael remembered sneaking over to look at whatever he had up on his drafting boards, and then retracing Meier's work with his own revisions. Meier accepted them. "Richard was easily influenced," said Michael.[13]

Meier never really got hooked on teaching—not the way Michael did. In his first undergraduate studio course, and in all the studios that followed for the next thirty-eight years, Michael typically taught between fifteen and twenty students, tasking them with the same kind of speculative projects he had carried out under

Sert but never exerting so heavy a hand. Julie Hanselmann Davies, a student of Michael's in later years, spoke of his "singular delight in teaching and being with young people"; he was as happy, perhaps happier, to sit with struggling pupils, poring over their drawings and making minute suggestions, as he was to do anything else in his professional life as an architect.[14] Eisenman remembered him as "one of best teachers I know, an encyclopedic memory for what he needed to teach, to draw, to show the diagrams of the buildings he was talking about. He'd just sit there with a roll of paper and give them the design."[15]

Pedagogically, Michael's studios were less innovative for what they did than what they did not do: they did not, by and large, foist his own architectural prejudices onto his students, as Sert had done. That first semester, one of his students was Peter Waldman, a future associate and friend, who recalled one assignment for which—instead of the tidy boards of his peers—he strung up some of his crumpled sketches, calling it an experiment in texture. Far from chastising Waldman for breaking form, Michael praised his inventiveness and hung his project up beside the rest.[16] Another, later pupil, Steven Harris, characterized Michael as "an extraordinary critic, particularly with work very different from his own"; Michael could be unsparing on a jury, but rarely on the grounds that the work failed to conform to his own tastes.[17] Especially at the outset of his academic career, when those tastes were still in flux, the Princeton studios were as much a space for him to train his own eye as they were an opportunity to train the eyes of his students. It remained so for as long as he taught, another reason he kept at it despite the distractions of his practice.

"I wanted them to be self-critical," Michael would say of his students. "There will be a day I won't be there to criticize their plans, nor will their colleagues."[18] To back up their critical capacity and to ground their architectural training in a larger body of knowledge, Michael would speak to his students about and encourage them to read the work of theorists and art historians—figures like the humanist cultural philosopher Ernst Cassirer; the scientifically minded art historian Ernst Gombrich; and, in time, Colin Rowe—trying to equip his pupils with the kind of intellectual firepower his own schooling had left out. (When Rowe was briefly a visiting critic at Princeton, Michael assisted him in a graduate design studio and later wrote, "I learned as much or probably more than the students.")[19] Those thinkers, and their ways of seeing and speaking, became part of deskside chats, as well as conversations over lunch and parties and wherever students and faculty mingled around Princeton.

None of this signaled as such the kind of new direction that Michael and Eisenman were seeking for architecture. The basic outline of design training at Princeton remained—and still remains, everywhere—much the same as it was in the days of the Beaux Arts, with students slaving away on design charrettes (the term comes from the French word for the wheelbarrow in which students' work was carried) and finishing their models and drawings just in time for a jury that, in Michael's studio, might include Meier, Eisenman, and other visitors from New York. Michael had found his niche in the academy, though the more intellectually ambitious and more uniquely Gravesian side of his teaching career would not get underway for some years.

His niche as an architect was slower to take shape. But there was progress, however halting: within months of his arrival in Princeton, Michael secured his first independent commission, a house in town for a professor and his wife. Michael had not officially launched his practice, but after his first year in Princeton he and Gail moved into a converted carriage house in Hopewell, New Jersey, about seven miles away, where a spare room acted as his "so-called office," as he termed it. It was there that he prepared the working drawings for the project.[20]

Michael described the house design as "really a box, plus walls that went out," the suggestion being that these projecting wings served no real programmatic or structural purpose.[21] If so, the proposal may have been an opening bid in Michael's search for meaning: a Modernist box, but with disengaged surfaces that did nothing save announce the building's presence, the walls operating almost as poetic representations of themselves. (Such a description smacks of the work of Michael's future colleague John Hejduk.) We can't be certain, however, as the house was never built, and none of the drawings can be located in the Graves archive. "The university came to the couple," Michael recalled, "and said, 'Somebody is leaving, and there's a house available right now.'" The clients took the empty house rather than have the new one constructed.

After that, there was nothing. This lack of work is not in any sense unusual: in architecture years, a thirty-year-old is still a babe in arms, and most designers cannot hope to see their first realized project until they've crossed the meridian of forty. There was a special urgency for Michael, however, as pressure closed in from several sides.

On the one hand, while he struggled, his friend Richard Meier already had not one but two buildings under his belt. The first had been designed back in 1961, a vacation residence on the seaside at Fire Island, New York, for the illustrator Saul Lambert. A simple wooden rectangle constructed in the space of barely two weeks, it was a chic if unoriginal exercise in hardware-store Mies—but whatever it was, it was a commission. Only two years later, Carolyn and Jerome Meier, Richard's parents, hired their son to build them a new house in Essex Fells, New Jersey, steps from his childhood home. This, too, Meier designed in a limited vocabulary of planar volumes, offset by a single rounded turret that added a little Corbusian plasticity to the ensemble.

Richard Meier's
Lambert House,
Fire Island,
New York, 1962

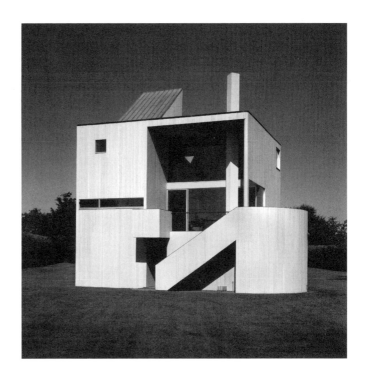

Charles Gwathmey's
house and studio
for his parents,
Amagansett,
New York, 1965

Another acquaintance of Michael's, four years his junior, was also fast out of the gate. Charles Gwathmey (Charlie to his friends) was a Yale graduate and a young associate in the office of Edward Larrabee Barnes. "A muscle man," as Michael recalled him, Gwathmey was an avid weight lifter, as well as a bon vivant to rival even the lusty Meier. On a green apron of land next to the sea in Amagansett, Long Island, Gwathmey had built a house for his parents, just as Meier had for his, and it was remarkable: almost more Corb than Corb. The house's careful arrangement of curved and flat surfaces created what the architect called a "perceptual dynamic of corner versus facade," like a piece of sculpture meant to be viewed in the round.[22]

Michael had met Gwathmey and knew about the house. He also knew that Gwathmey was the son of the painter Robert Gwathmey, whose collage-like images of the rural South had made him a favorite among left-leaning art lovers since the 1930s. Gwathmey's parents had the taste and the means to support their son's career, just as Meier's parents had—Michael would refer to Meier's project in Essex Fells as "a rich man's house." Michael had no so such parental support. Quite the opposite.[23]

Though he avoided discussing it himself, Michael was all too mindful of Erma's ongoing skepticism regarding his creative proclivities. Despite Harvard, despite the Rome Prize, despite the job at Princeton, his mother did not, by most accounts, view her son as having yet gotten himself a real job.[24] In the years since both of her sons had left Indianapolis, Erma's eldest had been forging ahead in the business world, while Michael was—to Erma's mind—still drawing pictures of houses. When times were especially tough, it was Tom, not Erma, who helped keep Michael afloat as an architect. "He supported me," Michael said, sometimes with cash.[25]

Michael's accepting his brother's generosity could only have confirmed Erma's feeling that he had not made himself of use. But Michael wasn't in a position to refuse charity. By 1964 he and Gail had still another reason to worry about their balance at the bank: the birth of their daughter, Sarah. Michael had always had it in mind to be a father—the delay, which had lasted for five years of marriage, turned out to be the result of a minor medical issue. Now that parenthood was upon them, the couple would be even harder pressed for funds.

Michael's starting salary at Princeton was $7,000 a year—more than he'd made at Nelson's office, but far from lavish. He received a modest promotion to assistant professor in 1963, with a marginal increase in pay, but it put only a small dent in the couple's penury.[26] Gail had taken to making Michael's clothes for him, including a brown velvet Nehru jacket that went as low as his knees. The Beatles look "was very fashionable," Michael noted, "but then, to wear that coat in Princeton was something else! I wasn't in New York. So I didn't wear it very much."[27] In later years, fine clothes (along with cars, and furniture, and much else) would be among Michael's major indulgences, but for now they were off the table. So was New York, for the most part, which was not becoming the base of operations he thought it would be when he first came to Princeton.

"WHO IS THIS PERSON 'Eisenman Graves'?"

The question, put to a colleague while strolling near Cannon Green, came from Professor Arthur Szathmary, a distinguished—if occasionally befuddled—Princeton philosopher who'd been at the university for decades.[28] His conflation of the two upstarts at the architecture school could be forgiven, of course, in view of how quickly Michael and Eisenman had made themselves an indivisible and unavoidable presence on campus.

Not content with the support of Dean McLaughlin, the duo had established personal ties with Princeton University president Robert F. Goheen. Appointed in 1957 at the astonishing age of thirty-seven, Goheen had set himself up as a one-man task force to drag his dowdy institution into the twentieth century. He recognized an intellectual ally in the persons of Eisenman and Graves.

"He got us a hundred thousand from Ford," recalled Eisenman. "It was a lot of money in 1964."[29] Indeed, it was almost $800,000 in 2017 terms—and with it Eisenman and Michael expanded into para-academic activities, using Princeton as a home base. Principally they created an innovative subprogram, somewhere between a working group and a debate society, composed of various architect friends from New York and beyond. They called it CASE: the Conference of Architects for the Study of the Environment.

"The group served as an answer," wrote the historian Suzanne Frank, "to the complaint from England that architecture in the US was uncritical and lacked a forum for ideas."[30] CASE was founded on the notion that Modernism had reached a critical impasse—the same impetus behind Team X—but CASE's muse was Colin Rowe, an active participant in its early meetings in Princeton as well as from his new perch in Ithaca, New York. Richard Meier was also on board, along with John Hejduk, then a professor at New York's Cooper Union. Other participants joined up from the University of Pennsylvania and MIT, as did the British critic and historian Kenneth Frampton, who began teaching at Princeton in 1965.

The organization's diverse initiatives are difficult to summarize, as its core and peripheral members engaged over the life of the group in an array of panels and symposia, public programs, teach-ins, exhibitions, and the distribution of published materials—though not, as Eisenman had originally hoped, a magazine. CASE was, in a sense, everything and nothing; by 1968 Eisenman would declare it "a rather ugly child, ill-formed and without direction."[31] Despite Michael's serving at numerous levels on its committees and subcommittees, CASE was always too nebulous an entity (and too dominated from the start by the entrepreneurial Eisenman) to further his personal interests and talents.

CASE did, however, have a lasting impact on the direction of American architecture. And in at least two particulars, it had a lasting impact on Michael.

The first stemmed from a speculative project developed by Michael and Eisenman, working with a circle of associates in the basement of the new Princeton School of Architecture. Intended as a response to CASE's focus on city planning, it was entitled the Jersey Corridor Project, a vision for a new kind of metropolis twenty miles long and only a mile wide between Philadelphia and New York [**PLATES 9 AND 10**]. In plan, it comprised "two parallel strips," as the critic Karrie Jacobs would describe it, "running like a ribbon through an otherwise pristine natural landscape": on the one side stood housing and commercial accommodations, on the other, industrial plants, and in between them, a long band of parkland and recreational facilities.[32] Most important was what flowed beneath the twin ranks of buildings: freeways, railways, and other transit infrastructure. Embedded within the mass of the city, these allowed residents direct access to their homes, thereby mitigating the suburban sprawl that resulted from conventional highways, which (in the young architects' view) was at the root of America's growing social disarray.

Caroline Constant was a young architect whose husband was studying at Princeton, and in 1965 she found herself pulled into the preparatory work for the Jersey Corridor scheme. "They couldn't read Corb because he hadn't been translated into English yet," she recalled. Acting as factotum, she helped Eisenman and Michael fill out their grasp of urban theory with the requisite Modernist bibliography.[33] The "linear city" concept had long been in the bloodstream of architecture, with roots stretching back to nineteenth-century Spain, and as the Princeton duo readied themselves to present their idea to their fellow CASE members, they drew on a large body of scholarship and enlisted the help of others, including Constant and a young Englishman, Anthony Vidler, who completed many of the final drawings himself.

It was a visionary, blue-sky idea, one that practically out-CIAMed CIAM, and it seems strangely at variance with CASE's supposedly critical mission. Unsurprisingly, its technocratic grandeur did not earn it a warm reception at the group's second major symposium at MIT in 1966. By then, however, the project had already yielded a tangible benefit to its creators.

Arthur Drexler, director of the Department of Architecture and Design at New York's Museum of Modern Art, had paid a call on the cellar dwellers at Princeton during the Jersey Corridor's development and liked what he saw. "He said he didn't know young architects were working on urban projects like this," recalled Eisenman.[34] The Jersey Corridor was already slated to appear in a show organized under the auspices of the Architectural League of New York (curated by a young Yale-trained architect, Robert A. M. Stern), but Drexler, excited by the proposal's scope and scale, took up Eisenman's suggestion to stage something bigger, a full exhibition at MoMA featuring similarly outsize proposals for reinventing the city. Eisenman, as ever, would take the lead in developing the show, bringing in teams (many of them CASE connected) from other universities to complement a new plan from the Princeton contingent, which naturally would include Michael.

In an additional stroke of good fortune, *LIFE* magazine ran a banner issue in December 1965 under the portentous headline "The U.S. City: Its Greatness Is at Stake."[35] In an impressive full two-page spread, there was the Jersey Corridor, along-side stories on renewal schemes in Chicago and New York (and the odd advertisement for Armour-brand hot dogs). If CASE had done nothing else for Michael, it would at least have put his work in the pages of one of the nation's most popular weeklies and given him a berth in the most important museum for the promotion of new architecture in America.

THE JERSEY CORRIDOR PROJECT and the 1967 MoMA *New City* show represented a high point in the attempt to salvage modern design not through retreat but through advance, at least as it touched Michael's career. That the suggested means of doing so were rather improbable (not to say megalomaniacal) was not lost on those involved in the effort. As Caroline Constant put it, when she first signed on for the Jersey Corridor project, "I thought all of them"—Michael, Vidler, Eisenman—"were brilliant. And then I thought they were maybe full of shit."[36]

The second major consequence of Michael's involvement with CASE was completely contradictory to the results of the Jersey Corridor project. For while a brash Modernist plan got Michael into MoMA, it was the borderline anti-Modernism of some of CASE's contributors that got into Michael.

Among the attendees at the CASE inaugural summit in Princeton in November 1964 was Robert Venturi, an architect and University of Pennsylvania professor who had worked for Louis Kahn and had been at the American Academy in Rome just four years ahead of Michael. During the proceedings, Venturi acted as the resident wet towel: as MIT's Stanford Anderson recalled, at the end of the three-day session everyone else was looking forward to the next meeting, while the Philadelphian "rhetorically enquired whether participation would lead to architectural commissions, and then demurred."[37] Thereafter, Venturi distanced himself from CASE, skeptical as to how the "forum for ideas" could have any relevance to architecture as it was then being practiced or to the American city as it was being built—or, as the case often was, demolished.

Doubts about Modernist theory and planning formed the keynote of another major speech at the first CASE confab, delivered by Vincent Scully. The Yale academic had almost single-handedly discovered the history of American architecture as an object of serious research, and though an avid proponent of Modernist design, he voiced misgivings about some of the movement's foundational assumptions, regretting "the general devaluation of the past" and pleading for an emphasis on the "anti-Utopian" and "past-present continuity."[38] Only a year prior, Scully had decried the destruction of New York's Penn Station and its replacement with a lame Modernist successor. Here he paraded the banner of the newborn preservationist movement before a group of practicing modern architects.

A mounting sense of caution came from another quarter as well: Colin Rowe. "Complaining of the messianic complex of architects," Anderson recalled, Rowe suggested that designers do not, as a rule, possess all the answers. The presumption of historical innocence that had always shielded Modernism—the belief that because it was not of the past, its buildings were an antidote to the ills of the past, Nazism among them—could no longer, in Rowe's view, be taken for granted. While at Cambridge, Rowe had imbibed the writings of the philosopher Karl Popper, and his message to CASE echoed the Austrian-born thinker's antiauthoritarian sentiments. "The public," Rowe said, "should offer opposition."[39]

No one at that first CASE meeting seems to have judged any of this chatter to be terribly transgressive. No gauntlets had been thrown, no dies cast. What was important was that they, and Michael, had heard it.

IN THE SAME YEAR that Sarah was born, Gail and Michael moved again, this time to an apartment at 10 Bank Street, just across the road from campus.[40] In 1967 they were joined there by another occupant: their son, Adam. Gail had embraced life in Princeton to an extent that she had not done in Cambridge, making friends of her own in addition to those, like Eisenman's wife, Elizabeth, who had entered their circle through Michael's work.

To all appearances, the Graves household was a fairly stable one. Michael flourished under his wife's care—visibly, becoming quite heavy for a period in the mid- to late 1960s.[41] Still, looking back, he was to maintain that Gail's being "shy" remained a point of difference between them. This tends to downplay Michael's own capacity for diffidence, and if any distance had grown between them following the arrival of their children, the cause was more likely Michael's compulsive attention to his work, which became more and more pronounced. His new studio was directly opposite the Bank Street apartment, and in the small hours of the morning Gail could look out the window and see him still at the drafting table.

He had formally launched his practice, Michael Graves Architect, after receiving his official registration in 1964, and was ramping up work on competitions and speculative projects such as the Princeton portion of the *New City* show—another far-fetched megastructural proposal, this time for the waterfront of Upper Manhattan. The exhibition was well received, a feather in the cap of the whole Princeton team, but there was no money in it, and it attracted no clients. Michael was working just to find work—submitting competition entries, some in collaboration with Eisenman, for commissions in California; Washington, DC; and elsewhere, and the hunt consumed time that otherwise might have gone to his personal relationships.[42] He remained, as he had for years, in sporadic touch with Ray Roush and a couple of his old Broad Ripple Village friends, but his Princeton associates were his only regular company.

In that arena, the MoMA show ultimately had a perverse effect. Robert McLaughlin had retired in 1965, replaced by a new dean (the first to hold the title), Robert Geddes, a more forceful character and more in line with Goheen's new direction for the university. Geddes and Eisenman had squabbled over the membership of the Princeton *New City* team: Geddes felt he should appoint it, while Eisenman felt that the choice had been entrusted to him by Arthur Drexler. "He wants us, not you," Eisenman told Geddes. Eisenman got his way. After that, Eisenman recalled, "I can count the number of days I had at Princeton."[43]

By the time the MoMA show opened in January 1967, the Princeton School of Architecture had declined to offer Eisenman a tenured position. It offered it to someone else instead—Michael. Dean Geddes, in looking back, was to say that it had mostly been a bureaucratic snafu, and a regrettable one, only one tenured position being available that year.[44] Regardless, the disappointment was a bitter one for Eisenman, since (as he recounted decades later) he had largely written Michael's tenure application for him. He expected the friend for whom he'd done so much to step up and object, if not reject the offer out of hand. It was not to be. As Eisenman described it:

> I said hey, you gotta go tell 'em! And he didn't. We lived with that as a datum for our being friends, and I think a lot of Michael's anxiety came from that early moral misstep he knew he had taken. I tried as much as possible to stay out of the way of reminding him, but there was this debt.

Eisenman Graves was dead.

Or so it seemed. In the end, Eisenman did not suffer unduly as a result of his peremptory dismissal from Princeton. Almost immediately he founded what he described at the time as "a halfway house, between academe and the profession."[45]

Known as the Institute for Architecture and Urban Studies (IAUS), it was a successor outfit of sorts to CASE, but of far greater reach and, in due course, influence. Eisenman was also underway with a small residential commission—in Princeton, no less, bringing him back within Michael's orbit and allowing their friendship, though strained, to carry on. Michael kept up with the goings-on at the IAUS and preserved his nominal affiliation with the now semi-orphaned CASE; the latter would bear fruit for him a third and final time in the form of another small MoMA function, though that would not come until 1969.

So far as the two friends were concerned, it seemed that karmic justice had been done. Eisenman had been denied a lifetime academic sinecure, but Michael still had no work as an architect. In his office, Michael painted a large, de Kooning–esque mural that fit snugly into the steep gable of the annex space, creating a rather grand focal point for what was otherwise a most ungrand workspace. In it, with so little in the way of architecture work to do, Michael had time to continue painting—not just the aggressive brushwork and "all-over" canvases of his Abstract Expressionist years, but increasingly more Cubist-inspired paintings, the patches of color bigger, juxtaposed collage-style, the palette lightening from brooding reds and oranges into pellucid blues and whites, closer to the creamy look of Morandi. The Italian artist, along with the Cubists Juan Gris and Pablo Picasso, were occupying more of Michael's thoughts; a young student named Peter Carl, later an associate in the studio, recalled his first conversation with Michael as being about "rotated squares in Cubism."[46]

Art seemed always on his mind. Books on Édouard Vuillard, Renaissance altarpieces, medieval diptychs, Henri Matisse—he riffled through them all, dog-eared them, marked pages with slips of paper. But what did all these murky historical ponderings have to do with architecture, or making architecture more "meaningful"? Michael couldn't prove that it did, since he hadn't built anything. Until, remarkably, he did.

ALL THROUGH THE YEARS they'd spent in Cincinnati, Cambridge, New York, and Rome, among the few Indianapolis acquaintances with whom Gail and Michael had stayed in contact were their old friends Lois Hickman and Jay Hanselmann. Now married to each other, they too had gotten out, having left Broad Ripple Village for Los Angeles. Unlike Gail and Michael, they had then gone back, at least part of the way, returning to Indiana and settling in Fort Wayne, where Jay had taken a job with the Lincoln National Life Insurance Company. Michael had kept his former girlfriend and former football teammate abreast of his progress, telling them tales first of Roush and then of Rome, later of Eisenman and Princeton. The Hanselmanns had always thought that if they had the chance, they would ask him to design a house for them, and their return to Indiana afforded just such an opportunity. They had acquired an undeveloped one-acre property to the southwest of Fort Wayne, and they asked Michael if he thought he could put together a tentative proposal.

Michael first requested that the family write up a program—"not what we wanted, but the way we lived," Lois recalled.[47] Jay was a classical music fanatic; Lois was a weaver; their daughters, Jennifer and Julie, were taking ballet lessons. The family on *The Brady Bunch* had a patio, and nine-year-old Julie asked for one too (even spelling it right, to her enduring pride).[48] Michael worked up a scheme that included a studio for Lois, space for Jay's hi-fi, a practice room for the girls, and not just one patio but several outdoor areas. The family had a budget of exactly $40,000, no more. It would have to cover materials, permits, the contractors, and the architect's fee.

On a visit to Princeton, Jay and Lois Hanselmann were treated to a lengthy presentation of Michael's initial plan, complete with a slide show that brought together Le Corbusier, Picasso, Rome, and all the inklings and insights he'd been storing up for years. His design took as its starting point two touchstones of his Grand Tour: Athens and Alberobello.

"His first presentation was of two separate small buildings," Lois recalled, "one for Mama and Papa and the other for the kids." Using Le Corbusier's crisp, white geometries and strip windows, Michael created a *trulli* village for the twentieth century, the two disengaged buildings related to each other in form but distinct as befit their respective inhabitants. The smaller, foregrounded building would also act as a gatehouse—a processional entrée to the main structure behind it, echoing the *propylaea* of the Acropolis that stood before the Parthenon. Both of these historical precedents Michael cited to defend his multibuilding scheme—to no avail, as Jay and Lois were anxious to keep costs low and to keep themselves and their four children (the girls had a pair of brothers) under the same roof.[49]

Over the next year, Michael set up a small satellite office to work up the final construction documents, spending a few days at a time in Fort Wayne while the Hanselmanns put the project out to bid with local contractors. They were alarmed to find that the lowest estimate came in $8,000 above their stated maximum. Walking into Michael's studio, Lois gave him the bad news.

"We just don't have the money," she remembered telling him.

Michael, who rarely ever raised his voice (least of all at his friends), resorted to actual shouting: *"Lois,"* he begged, *"be resourceful!"*

His combativeness paid off. Lois got resourceful. Discussing the matter at length with Jay, she decided that the couple would act as their own general contractors, building the house by themselves with the help of a few subcontractors. The do-it-yourself method would, they estimated, run them $39,000, within a hairbreadth of their price ceiling but feasible if all went well. Neither husband nor wife had any experience whatsoever in building a house, but they forged ahead, heedless of pitfalls.

They started with an actual pitfall, a large ditch that prevented the backhoe from entering the site. "The first thing Jay and I had to do was put in these two twenty-foot, thirty-six-inch-diameter culverts," Lois remembered, channeling and covering the gap. "We rolled them in, and they were perfect." The date was October 6, 1969, Lois's thirty-fifth birthday.

What ensued was a seemingly interminable cavalcade of harrowing near misses, lucky breaks, and heart-wrenching setbacks. Building a house on one's own while raising four children was not perhaps a thing that any two sane people, however "resourceful," should seriously have contemplated. But that is what the Hanselmanns had bitten off, and for nearly two years, that is what they chewed. As Lois later admitted, "We were pretty dumb."

"It was Murphy's Law," she continued. The Teamsters went on strike, and Jay and Lois had to drive to Wisconsin to pick up the windows. Before they had a chance to install them, a subcontractor insisted on putting in the siding first, allowing rainwater to seep in. They hired a subcontractor to hang the Sheetrock, only to have him quit on the spot, refusing to work without proper scaffolding; they had to hang it themselves. They hired still another subcontractor to pour the concrete; he didn't like the steel joists, and he quit as well. And then there were the floors. The house was to have oak flooring on the first and second levels, and Jay laid it down expertly around the columns of Michael's open plan, with Lois crawling along behind him to apply the varnish. ("When I put my jeans in the washer," she remembered, "they came out with the knees bent.") Everything looked perfect—until they turned the heat on.

"All the boards shrank," said Lois. Jay had to start all over, sanding down the planks and refitting them as best he could.[50]

The children, meanwhile, thought all of this was a grand adventure. "My mom put all of us to work," said Julie. She and her siblings were charged with putting the flags in during the surveying, sweeping up the site at the end of the workday, and doing whatever other odd jobs could keep them busy while their parents continued to build.[51] From time to time, Michael would come by and stay at the Hanselmanns' temporary home nearby; on one visit, he brought along his daughter, Sarah, who promptly got stuck in a tree and had to be helped down by her father. The episode lowered her stock in the eyes of the very self-sufficient Hanselmann children but raised their already lofty esteem for Michael, the "exotic" and "cosmopolitan" easterner in their midst, whom their parents claimed, dubiously, was really a simple midwesterner like them.

Even in the most difficult moments, Lois said, "I was never mad at Michael," saving her spleen for the inept hired hands who came and went.[52] When it was all over, they awoke from their nightmare to find themselves at last in their dream house, a dream as much Michael's as their own.

With the multibuilding arrangement jettisoned, the house does not read—at least at first—as anything laden with meaning or reference, presenting instead a flat white front in the conventional Corbusian manner, albeit interrupted by horizontal bands of varying configurations and by a projecting stair and bridge leading to a second-floor entrance [**PLATES 11 AND 12**]. Only as one begins moving inward, channeled along that very prominent gangway, does the logic of the house begin to disclose itself.

As Julie Hanselmann Davies wrote years later, the house unfolds over several layers, as though one were presented not with a building but with a succession of paintings—or as if one were looking at a single, highly involuted painting, like a work of Cubist collage, peeling it back one stratum at a time.[53] After that initial impression of stair and facade, the next layer in the sequence opens up as the visitor enters the house on the second floor, alighting directly in the Hanselmanns' living room. Dead ahead is a twenty-foot-long mural, painted by Michael himself, a riot of color and swirling shapes that makes literal the building's dedication to artistic collage: occupying the whole rear wall of the room, it represents a terminus of the linear procession. It is not, however, the last of the house's highly composed visual moments, which appear again at intervals—both upstairs in the parents' bedroom and study as well as downstairs around the children's rooms and play space.

Many of the subtler details of the design, its jumbled asymmetries and irregular windows, could be considered simply for effect. Recollecting Sert's teaching ("animate the facade!"), Michael's painterly tactics were sometimes deployed here for no better purpose than to keep things interesting. But the liberties he took with Le Corbusier went further than that.

Above all there is the use of color. Corb advocated polychromy in architecture for its "psychological and physiological effects," as the scholar Barbara Klinkhammer observed.[54] Michael plainly recognized color's power to alter the mood of a space, but atmospherics are not the primary aim of the Hanselmann painting program. Progressing through the house's successive strata, Julie Hanselmann Davies described how color added narrative to each one in turn:

The blue spandrel on the entry facade is a reference to the stream that flows through the site. The same blue is repeated on the top floor, as a gently curved shelf parallels the stream and recalls its path [**PLATE 13**]. The soffit of the upstairs skylight is painted a bright yellow, warming the light and recalling the sun. The powder room on the main floor is painted a vivid green, a tongue-in-cheek reference to a bush, behind which one could find a private moment. The closet behind the master bed is a painted haystack.[55]

Most dramatically, there is Michael's mural [**PLATE 14**]. The attentive viewer could pick out a tablecloth, trees, a garden, the head of the family cat, and the angles and curves of the house itself encrypted in the loose, painterly composition.

False windows, windows between rooms, a window frame on the rooftop terrace looking out to the landscape—the house is freighted with references to its own condition, its own uses and organization, engaging its inhabitants in an ongoing dialogue that changes with every point of view, every framed encounter. Michael had always complained that much of Modernist design didn't speak to him. Here was a Modernism that was trying to speak.

This, Michael's first commission, was an attempt to reinvigorate Le Corbusier's pure, abstract language of "masses brought together in light" using the formal techniques of art—of Cubist painting specifically—to furnish a narrative about the house, about the site, and about the family who lived there. Whether it said what it meant to, or whether anyone understood it, would be a question that would preoccupy Michael for years to come. But for all of its intricacies and aspirations, and whatever its failings, real or perceived, for the family that occupied it the house was an extraordinary place to live. The Hanselmanns divorced some years later and have long since moved away, but Lois still returns on occasion to visit. "Living there was the most amazing time in my life," she said. "I cry every time I go back."[56]

OVER THE NEARLY TWO YEARS between the Hanselmann commission's beginnings and its groundbreaking in Fort Wayne, much had happened to transform Michael's practice in Princeton. New work, new opportunities, and new responsibilities at the university had taken him from a sole practitioner to the proprietor of a tiny but bustling office, as well as the rising star—absent the now-departed Eisenman—of the School of Architecture faculty.

Having granted him his tenured position, Dean Geddes had become an active partisan on Michael's behalf. As early as 1966, he'd recommended Michael for a proposed master plan of the town of Oyster Bay, New York, on the North Shore of Long Island. "I spent a lot of time, made presentations," recalled Michael; his efforts came to nothing, and the project was shelved.[57] Geddes had also been instrumental in helping Michael get a small commission for a nature and science museum in New Jersey's Watchung Mountains. The client, apparently objecting to Michael's elaborate color scheme and artfully arranged windows, "drew a red line" through the plan (as Caroline Constant recalled), and when the project was finally completed years later, it bore little resemblance to the intended design.[58] Nonetheless, Geddes allowed Michael to exhibit his original scheme in a small exhibition at the school.[59]

Also in 1966 the Newark Museum asked Geddes to recommend three architects for the institution's planned expansion, and Michael's name was at the top of the list. Museum director Sam Miller and the trustees gave him the nod, and he spent the next year and change working up a multicomponent scheme that featured an amphitheater, passerelle galleries surrounding outdoor sculpture gardens, and more. By 1968 the city of Newark was wracked by riots and a major donor had died, leaving the institution in no position to move forward with construction. Still, Michael's proposal was included in a MoMA show on new museums, his second appearance there in as many years, and the Newark Museum—and Miller—would go on to become one of Michael's most loyal and longest-running clients. The firm would design a number of small renovations, one major addition, and several more master plans over the next forty-plus years.

Meanwhile, there was more built work. Paul Benacerraf, a Princeton philosopher of mathematics who had been at the university since 1960, owned a gracious Tudor-style house not far from campus, part of a row of nearly identical homes on Broadmead Street. He had become acquainted with Kenneth Frampton, who had taken up a full-time post at Princeton after his initial introduction to the school via CASE. During what Frampton called "a casual conversation," the architectural historian happened to hear that the philosopher was considering building an addition. "Why don't you think of Michael Graves?" asked Frampton, thus bringing about Michael's second residential commission.[60]

The Hanselmanns' grindingly slow construction process meant that the Benacerraf House was the first to be completed, wrapping up work in 1969. Completely invisible from the street, the extension springs from the rear facade, occupying a good portion of the backyard. Taking up the basic stylistic trappings of Hanselmann, it is still more vexed in composition, more eager to express its narrative content, and while ostensibly an homage to Le Corbusier's villas of the 1920s—their Mediterranean airiness implausibly relocated to central New Jersey—the project exhibits an ever more willful symbolism, seeping further into its disparate formal elements.

Most of its area consists of a series of outdoor terraces, wrapping around and perched atop a glazed volume that shelters expanded living spaces for the family. But both that and the outdoor spaces themselves are secondary to the disengaged elements that spin around them: a giant L-shaped steel bar, painted bright yellow; a beam on the southern facade, painted bright green; and a retaining edge, a thick blue column turned on its side. All reference elements of sun, garden, and sky, in an effort to fuse house and environment. Its most theatrical gesture is a ripple in the upper portion of an unglazed faux window above the southern-facing terrace: acting in part as a sunshade, its wavy outline deliberately mimics the shape of clouds or trees [**PLATE 15**]. Still in line with Cubist aesthetics, and still basically Corbusian in character, it is a moment of deliberate humor, representational rather than abstract and best appreciated when viewing the house straight on from the outside.

Michael's most promising unrealized commission of the late 1960s was for a client who signified, and not just in Michael's view, the absolute last word in establishment credibility: the Rockefeller family. How precisely this opportunity came to him is not entirely clear, though by general consensus the likeliest vector was a figure many years Michael's senior—and later a major player in his career—the Zelig-like architect and impresario Philip Johnson.[61] Johnson was aware of Michael as a bright young entity on the Princeton staff, and through his long-standing relationship with the Rockefellers (on whose behalf he had designed a Manhattan guest residence in 1950) he would have known that they were contemplating an additional house on their compound in Pocantico Hills, New York. Nelson Rockefeller's son Steven was a Princeton alumnus, and Michael may have seemed a logical recommendation, especially given the Rockefellers' extensive patronage of new American architecture.

Their faith in Michael did not last long. His design for the Rockefeller house tuned the tactics of his previous two houses to an even higher volume, amplifying them to the scale of the much larger house (and its much bigger budget). A gaping open portal on the facade telegraphed an internal entry court, curved surfaces mimicked the slope of the hillside site, and a raised canopy and sculpted balustrades signaled the presence of an enormous rooftop deck. The scheme was a very busy one, indeed—too busy for the Rockefellers, who were not sold on Michael's claims that all these features served as communicative motifs. They pulled the plug on the project.

There wasn't much opportunity to mourn it, or much reason to. Between ongoing projects, prospective projects, and teaching, Michael already had his hands full, to the point that he now required other hands. For his earliest competition proposals he'd collaborated with Eisenman, but that was out of the question now; in any case, what he wanted was not a design partner but people who could attend to the technical nitty-gritty that had never been his forte. And so he began to assemble a small band of associates, mostly culled from the ranks of favored graduate students, many of whom would cycle in and out of the office in the following years as their academic and professional careers (and, occasionally, their personal relationships with Michael) evolved.

Among the first were Peter Waldman and Peter Carl; in the ensuing years, they would be followed by Bruce Abbey, Caroline Constant, Robert Carey White, and others. The mood around the office was freewheeling, congenial: "He'd get a pound or two of spaghetti and some white clam sauce," recalled Waldman, and the young designers would eat together and talk about art, architecture, and theory, a re-creation of Michael's Rome days around the tables at the American Academy.[62] During these early years, his associates' influence on Michael was every bit as important as his influence on them; Peter Carl, in particular, would expose Michael to the writings of philosophers like Gaston Bachelard and the architecture historian Joseph Rykwert.[63] They were not just employees but colleagues—though he did at least make a token effort to pay them, along with the rent on the little studio on Nassau Street. Already, Michael could see that if he wanted to keep building, he would have to be not just a good architect but a savvy businessman.

As RAPIDLY AS HIS PRACTICE had been changing, the alteration in Michael's personal affairs had been even more precipitous. Among the closest friends Gail had made in Princeton was Lucy James, a former dancer and widowed mother of two daughters nearly the same age as the Graves children. The women were a study in contrasts: Gail, medium in stature, maintained the self-effacing sincerity of her Broad Ripple Village days, though seasoned now by travel and culture; Lucy was tall, and by all accounts much earthier and more assertive in her opinions. Born in Virginia to a wealthy doctor, she was employed following her husband's death as a social worker, managing a low-income housing development near the university known as Princeton Community Village.

In view of the strains in Michael and Gail's marriage, a reemergence of the adolescent romantic whom his friends had called "François" was perhaps only a matter of time. The negative example of his father's boozy indiscretions might have afforded some conditioned restraint, but that had largely worn off by this point, and although it was—in Michael's account, anyway—Lucy who pursued him, the history of the male Graveses demonstrates a definite susceptibility.

Whatever the case, Michael found himself drawn to her, and his marriage to Gail swiftly unraveled. That it unraveled as quickly as it did was in part because, as was immediately apparent, Michael and Lucy's was no fleeting passion: they had fallen in love. "We were very much alike verbally," recalled Michael. "We liked humor and playing jokes on each other."[64] Feeling a kinship that he hadn't known he'd missed, Michael was, as he put it, "hooked."[65] He moved in with Lucy, divorcing Gail in 1969.

The year is worth noting. Michael and Gail were a long way from the Midwest of the early 1950s. The world around them had changed, and they had changed too. Michael was now on the rise professionally, and Lucy's openness and energy resonated with his growing self-confidence; here, he thought, was a partner for his new life as a major East Coast architect. But the changes were not Michael's alone. Following the divorce, Gail left Princeton, taking Sarah and Adam with her and moving them to Cambridge, where she had lived a decade before. She might have been intimidated by it then, but she wasn't any longer. She chose it, Sarah recalled, "because she loved it."[66]

In declaring, as he sometimes did, that Gail was a shade too impassive, a shade too self-contained—in short, a shade too Broad Ripple—Michael perhaps revealed more about his own desires and anxieties than he did about his wife's. Gail, meanwhile, had come into her own, and she demonstrated both her good nature and her newfound sense of empowerment in how she handled the separation.

"They had, to my mind, a very amicable breakup," said Sarah. "I never heard either say anything bad about the other."[67]

LUCY AND MICHAEL MARRIED three years later, but the course of their relationship never ran smooth. "Lucy was everything negative [where] Gail was positive in terms of my career," recalled Michael. As with his previous relationship, Michael's assessment was slightly biased; doubtless Lucy wanted to see Michael succeed, and in fact would later introduce him through a family connection to an important client, the Claghorns. But Lucy was never prepared (or not so prepared as Gail had once been) to simply play the supportive helpmeet, her own independent streak rivaling Michael's.[68] Still, regarding his work as an architect, Michael felt that Lucy "could take it or leave it—what it meant to her was that she didn't get to see me, and I was with pretty girls all the time," primarily his students and young associates.[69] Lucy's jealousies came with the package, another facet of the extroverted and voluble personality that had attracted Michael in the first place.

The difficulty, even the friction, was part of the appeal, and when Lucy and Michael were together the relationship seemed to work almost in spite of itself. Once the Hanselmann House was rendered livable, the couple came and stayed there with Michael's clients and old friends, and their hosts looked favorably upon his new partner. "Lucy was great," recalled Julie Hanselmann Davies. "They were great together."[70]

Michael had been returning to Indiana with some frequency, thanks to another commission that had come his way courtesy of the Hanselmanns. Not long into their time in Fort Wayne, Jay and Lois had made the acquaintance of prominent local doctor Sanford Snyderman and his wife, Joy. The latter couple had recently purchased a hilly forty-acre site near suburban Ellisville, and on a visit to the Hanselmanns' newly completed home, Joy posed what seemed an innocent enough question: "Do you think Michael could talk to me about who should design the house?" she asked Lois.

Lois said yes—an answer she had occasion to regret. "I feel partially responsible for what happened to them," she said.[71]

Problem plagued as Michael's last project in Fort Wayne had been, this one was worse. Once again the clients decided to serve as general contractor, and though the

Snydermans did less of the heavy lifting themselves, their progress was every bit as star-crossed. "Everyone who worked on it blames someone else for the problems," Sandy Snyderman claimed years later, while the local architect who oversaw the work, Matt Kelty, contended that the detail and sophistication of Michael's design was simply "beyond the ability of most home contractors to carry out," at least in central Indiana. ("The roofing material was put down by a carpet contractor," he added.)[72] In fairness, the design might have stumped even more experienced builders than those of Fort Wayne. It was the apotheosis of the earliest stage in Michael's career as an architect.

Since Benacerraf, Michael had continued to expand the lexicon of his architectural idiolect, in the hope (as it seemed) that the introduction of still more color and more recognizable forms would allow his audience readier access to the plotlines threading through the work. In a professional office back in Princeton, Gunwyn Ventures, hatches and stairways and banisters proliferated with reckless abandon, producing a fraught visual system tied together once again by a huge mural, this time wrapped halfway around an undulating wall. For a medical office in downtown Fort Wayne, he placed multiple freestanding doorjambs over the waiting room entry, each a different size and hue, as if to proclaim the varying scales and colors within. (It was, in fact, Dr. Snyderman's office, completed before the travails of the house.) Two uncompleted houses—Mezzo and Keeley—played on the same themes, while a third (completed) one in Princeton—Alexander House, a Benacerraf-like extension [PLATE 16]—showed Michael, arguably for the first time, referencing an existing work of architecture, with a raised steel square that clearly mimicked the window on the upper story of the adjacent 1930s colonial.

Snyderman outdid all these. Though not so spacious as the Rockefeller project would have been, it was roomier than most of Michael's early residential commissions—five thousand square feet in all, nearly twice the size of Hanselmann. Like the previous Fort Wayne house, the new one was at first envisaged not as a single structure but as a group, three in all, connected along a slender walkway. This scheme was abandoned in favor of a single two-story building, but one whose larger scale allowed for a plan more wrought than any that had preceded it. It was as though Le Corbusier's simple columnar grid were being incessantly attacked by forces pushing at it from inside and out.

"An overlay of several *different* oppositions," as the scholar Alan Colquhoun would write (his emphasis), the house was not merely a three-dimensional collage but an architectural kaleidoscope.[73] Instead of offering discrete pictorial impressions following one after the next, as Hanselmann had done, Snyderman confronted the visitor with an array of images piled up in thick profusion. On its completion, *Progressive Architecture*'s Suzanne Stephens wrote of the house that it was "attempting

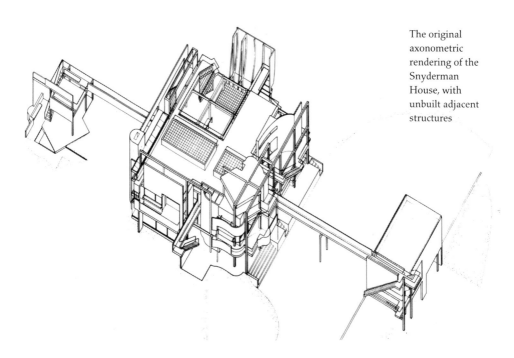

The original
axonometric
rendering of the
Snyderman
House, with
unbuilt adjacent
structures

to do more than create gradual transitions from one domain to another."[74] Between interior and exterior, first floor and second, and from room to room, Michael staged a continuous and revolving scenography, with the forms of the landscape repeatedly intruding on the house and the house's forms extending beyond the white frame that surrounded it, becoming a part of the landscape [PLATE 17]. Polychromy reappeared as a guiding element, but this time the solid walls of color almost entirely concealed the glass windows, and their tones had drifted from emphatic primaries into soft pastels: faded pinks and washed-out blues [PLATE 18]. The effect is less reminiscent of early Modernist architecture of the 1920s than of one of Jean-Baptiste-Camille Corot's landscape paintings of the 1820s.

These departures and others signaled a change in mood. For while the house represented the apogee of Michael's neo-Modernist thinking, it also bespoke a sense of frustration—almost rising to the level of violence—directed at its own language. The vocabulary was still Le Corbusier's, and the syntax was still Cubist, but every inch of wall space was now being wrung for potential signification. What seemed all too assured in the giant Rockefeller scheme here appeared beset by nervous energy. Visiting the house in 1980 and looking at it in the context of Michael's subsequent work, the critic Martin Filler diagnosed the condition perfectly. As he put it, "This is an early Michael Graves building with a later Michael Graves building trapped inside it, fighting to emerge."[75]

WHEN, AS SOMETIMES HAPPENED during a summer storm in Fort Wayne, the Hanselmann family found themselves dashing to put buckets under the assorted drips coming from their ceiling, Lois, with characteristic wit, would lighten the mood by paraphrasing a quote usually attributed to Frank Lloyd Wright: "If the roof doesn't leak," she'd say, "the architect hasn't been creative enough."[76]

By the time the Snyderman House was finally finished in 1977, its owners discovered that they too had many leaks to contend with. But they did not greet the situation with half so much good humor. In Lois's view, her friend Sandy "developed a hatred for Michael"; Joy was more measured in her criticism, saying of the design only that "it should never have had a flat roof, not in this climate."[77]

The Snydermans spent nineteen years in the house, and though it had its pleasures (one family reunion featured a multistory water-gun battle) it was, at the best of times, a trial. "It was hot in summer, cold in winter. The stucco cracked," recalled the couple's son, Sanford Jr. "Something was always wrong with it."[78] When the family finally moved out, they sold it to a local developer, who planned to demolish it to make way for a subdivision; local preservationist groups sent up a distress signal, and the local government stepped in to save it. It was all for naught: after being repeatedly vandalized, the Snyderman House was destroyed by fire in 2002, in what the authorities suspect—but have never confirmed—was an act of arson.

Notwithstanding its sorry fate and the justifiable gripes of its owners, the Snyderman House was far from a failure: at least until it was built, it was a resounding success. In the architectural ambit that Michael inhabited when the project was moving forward, the mere fact that he was building it was a badge of honor. John Hejduk had been pursuing similar themes in his own work but had built almost nothing, while dozens of the field's most prominent figures seemed destined to spend their lives spinning their theoretical fancies in permanent academic seclusion. The 1970s produced more than its share of "paper architects"—the combined products of a bumpy economy and the cerebral mood of the field—and in this group Michael stood out as one of the few who had shown, on a limited basis, that brains and building were not incompatible.

It was this distinction that prepared the way for the next major development in his career. And while Michael could thank his clients for setting the stage, the one who lifted the curtain was Peter Eisenman.

Even after Eisenman started the IAUS, his neglected stepchild CASE still limped on, divided into regional groups that assembled episodically to discuss recent work. With the support of Arthur Drexler, two CASE meetings, numbered seven and eight, were held at MoMA in 1969 and 1971, both of them presentations highlighting the work of CASE's East Coast membership: Eisenman, Michael, Gwathmey, Meier, and Hejduk.

"The marginal figure," Eisenman later averred, "was John Hejduk—because he was John Hejduk."[79] Born of Czech parents in 1929, Hejduk cut an odd figure on the national architecture scene: an enormously tall man with wild, thinning hair, a mien of the absent-minded professor, and a voice that came directly from the streets of New York. In addition to having no built work to speak of, Hejduk was the most senior of the five—fully a decade older than Gwathmey—and in his longtime position at Cooper Union, and before that at the University of Texas at Austin, he'd had ample opportunity to elaborate his "mystical ideas about architecture," as one observer called them.[80] He was at once one of architecture's best-known characters and one of its most elusive. "Everybody seemed to know John," said Michael, who could never quite recall how they met.[81]

For the latter of the two CASE MoMA meetings, Eisenman also persuaded Anthony Vidler, the New Haven–based architect Allan Greenberg, and a host of others to attend as critics. The designers hung up their work and then engaged in a daylong colloquy in the museum's trustees' room. Michael could remember little of the event—"I have no idea what they said," he claimed—and though Eisenman called the discussion a lively and engaging one, it received no substantive attention from the architectural public.[82] This was the third providential outcome of Michael's CASE association, though at first it seemed to be a dead end. A pamphlet was considered but never appeared.

Another year and more would go by before Eisenman's estimable abilities as an architecture tout once again brought the five together. Living at the time on the Upper West Side (having also divorced his first wife), Eisenman would sometimes take the Seventy-Ninth Street bus across town to the Madison Avenue bookshop of art publisher George Wittenborn—another in Eisenman's wide circle of well-placed acquaintances. Arriving in the store on a certain Saturday in 1972, he approached the proprietor with an idea.

"I've got a good book for you," Eisenman told him.

"What is it?" asked Wittenborn.

"Well, we had this meeting…" Eisenman began, and went on to explain the daringly avant-garde work that he and his four fellow travelers were doing. Then he announced his suggested title: *Cardboard Architects*.[83]

It was one of Eisenman's pet phrases at the time. Wittenborn liked it well enough and printed up a flier; as soon as the other four friends caught wind of it, they declared themselves adamantly opposed to the title.

They consented to another. *Five Architects* was published in 1972, in a tiny hardbound edition of "about fifty," as Eisenman recalled.[84] It featured two projects from each of the included designers—Hanselmann and Benacerraf being Michael's—as well as essays written to accompany the photos of Eisenman's, Michael's, and Meier's

The Five—minus one, plus one—eating ice cream, ca. 1972. Left to right: John Hejduk, Robert Siegel (sitting in for partner Charles Gwathmey), Richard Meier, Michael, and Peter Eisenman

buildings. Eisenman's essay was a lengthy exegesis on his theory of "deep structure," as derived from the linguist Noam Chomsky; Meier's a more measured account of his progress; while Michael's was a brief appreciation from the critic William La Riche. More pertinent, however, were the contributions of Colin Rowe and Kenneth Frampton, who were responsible for the introduction and opening essay, respectively, and neither of whom seemed to much endorse the whole undertaking. "It is indisputably bourgeois," Rowe wrote of the Five's work, "and it is all of it belligerently secondhand."[85]

In hindsight, it's hard to resist the sense that *Five Architects* was unpardonably flimsy in pretext: a group of white men making white buildings, their sole raison d'être being Eisenman's knack for public relations. The Five's most effective defense against these accusations is that, for the most part, they felt the same way themselves. "The group that admits it wasn't," in the words of the critic Paul Davies, the Five were bound together less by their shared enthusiasms—their fascination with Le Corbusier, their belief in design as high intellectual art—than by the constellation of differences that allowed each to admire something in the others that he himself lacked.[86] "Each of the Five Architects could have had his own separate show, a little exhibition with a little catalogue," Michael once said. "Can you imagine a show of John's work? It would have been wonderful."[87]

But there was strength in numbers. As representatives of a hypothetical trend, however specious, the Five were able to attain a visibility they might never have found separately. In early 1973 they were invited to participate in the XV Triennale di Milano, with Meier and Peter Carl accompanying Michael to present their work (plus an original Graves mural) alongside that of other international exhibitors. Here Michael met for the first time two future friends and collaborators: the show's curator, Aldo Rossi, and another participant, the Luxembourger Léon Krier, whose booth was right beside the Five's. Krier recalled looking over into the neighboring stall and seeing a slender man in glasses with longish hair, sitting on the floor. "It was Michael," said Krier. "He was drawing."[88]

Of more immediate import was the appearance of a special section in the May issue of *Architectural Forum*, the flagship publication of the American design press. "It was a little bit hatched by Eisenman and me," said Robert A. M. Stern: together with the architect Charles Moore, original CASE attendee Jaquelin Robertson, and like-minded colleagues Allan Greenberg and Romaldo Giurgola, Stern produced a multi-part rebuttal to *Five Architects* under the heading "Five on Five."[89] Earnest and in places quite stinging in its criticism, the article nonetheless was prepared and pub-lished with the full connivance of the original Five. "It was all staged," said Eisenman, the article merely a bigger and more theatrical platform for a debate already under-way in American architecture.[90]

What had begun as a fault line at CASE 1 had widened, by the time of *Five Archi-tects*, into a chasm. The belligerents did not yet have official names, but they soon would: in May 1974 a conversation at UCLA took place between what was termed for the first time the "Whites" and the "Grays," two inimical affinities divided over the legacy and the future of the Modern movement in the United States.[91] As they had since the days of their Princeton insurgency, Michael and Eisenman argued for staying the Modernist course while pushing the principles of the pioneers to their formal and conceptual limits. This (along with the fact that most of their buildings were, of course, white) made them emblematic of the White faction, and for the first time since those early Princeton days, it meant that they, along with Meier, Gwath-mey, and Hejduk, were on the defensive.

Against them were the Grays, the party of dissent. Represented by what came to be called the "Yale-Philadelphia axis"—anchored by Vincent Scully in New Haven and Robert Venturi at the University of Pennsylvania—the Grays were far less credulous of Modernist pieties and far more appreciative of the patterns of pre-twentieth-century urban life. Their architectural scripture was Venturi's *Complex-ity and Contradiction in Architecture*, a radical revaluation of architectural values that had been steadily gaining adherents since its publication in 1966. In the intro-duction to the book's first edition, Scully took Modernism to task for sins of both commission and omission, citing "its utter lack of irony, its splinterish disdain for the popular culture but shaky grasp on any other, its incapacity to deal with monumental scale, its lip-service to technology, and its preoccupation with a rather prissily puristic aesthetic."[92]

Venturi himself was more concise. Describing his pragmatic, pluralistic outlook, he wrote: "I prefer 'both-and' to 'either-or,' black and white, and sometimes gray, to black or white."[93] The color choice stuck, and the Grays were picking up speed.

Although both blocs were born of the same simmering discontent with the mid-century mainstream, the Grays' quarrel with Modernism was of a heavier caliber than that of the loyal opposition that had gone before. Stern, Robertson, and the rest used "Five on Five" as an opportunity to denounce their opposite numbers for "machismo" and "puritanical cultural attitudes," calling the buildings in the book "a depressing and disjointed assortment of parts."[94] Though they reserved a token regard for Le Corbusier himself, their attack was aimed squarely at the moral chauvinism, austere form making, and indifference to history that had marked Modernist thinking for decades. The Five were merely a convenient proxy.

None of them afforded so serviceable a target as Michael. "Subscribes too much to a formal vocabulary," wrote Giurgola.[95] "Graves' dependence on Le Corbusier can be unintentionally ironic," wrote Stern.[96] "Imagine my orange and black apoplexy," said Moore, "on reading a deadpan announcement…that 'the organization of the Hanselmann design of Michael Graves is intended to recall, more than anything else, the procession from the profane to the sacred spaces of the Athenian Acropolis.'"[97] Why, Moore wondered, was such "puffing up" necessary? If the processional narrative was truly present, why enlist an essayist to point it out?

Most cutting perhaps was Jaquelin Robertson's assessment:

> Both [Graves] houses are crawling inside and out with a sort of nasty modern ivy in the way of railings, metal trellises, unexplained pipes, exposed beams, inexplicable and obtuse tubes—most to no apparent real or architectural purpose.…The "language" has become so mannered as to defeat its purpose.[98]

These were the very devices Michael had inserted into his designs to make their meaning more, not less, legible. What didn't Robertson understand?

To the other four, this going-over in the design press was all in good collegial fun; they could give as good as they could take, and usually did. (Eisenman even launched a partnership with Robertson years later.) But it was not so easy for Michael. "A bit shy and self-conscious," as his former student and longtime Columbia professor Mary McLeod would describe him, Michael was far touchier than his fellows.[99] "We called him Michelangelo," said Peter Waldman. "His sensitivities were right on the skin, his enthusiasms and disappointments."[100] The sudden burst of sharp-tongued critical attention was difficult to bear, and not long after the appearance of "Five on Five," Michael had a private conversation with Charles Moore.

"I score very high on the reading of architecture," Michael remembered Moore telling him. Then he pointed to Michael's work. "Here I don't."[101]

Michael let it sink in. *If Moore doesn't understand,* he recalled thinking, *then the layman won't know.* It was the beginning of a crisis of architectural conscience that would define the next several years of his life.

The attention attracted by *Five Architects* was not universally negative, and "Five on Five" served the purpose that the conspirators behind it had intended, raising the profiles of all concerned. One morning in November 1973, Eisenman was reading the *New York Times*—the sports page, naturally—when one of his sons gasped from across the breakfast table.

"Daddy!" he shouted. "There's your picture in the paper!"[102]

All five of their pictures were there, in fact, lined up on the left side of the page in alphabetical order, with Benacerraf featured prominently at top right. The article was among the first by a twenty-three-year-old Paul Goldberger, the publication's future architecture critic, and though circumspect in its praise, the mere fact of its appearing in America's paper of record was validation enough.[103] All publicity, as Eisenman knew, was good publicity. The New York Five, as they came to be known, were now national news.[104]

VI

THE BRIDGE AND THE HEARTH

FROM AS FAR AWAY as the West Coast—among the freeways and factories of central Los Angeles, where he's spent most of his career—the architect Eric Owen Moss watched the steady ascent in the media and in academic discourse of the New York Five, and Michael in particular. Moss and Michael were never more than passing acquaintances, and in their practices (to say nothing of their backgrounds) the two couldn't have been more different. A native Angelino, committed to a cryptic and intellectually probing California Modernism, Moss was several degrees removed from the Gray-White debate and its central figures. And yet, speaking of the years immediately following the arrival of *Five Architects*, Moss formulated a judgment of Michael as apt as anyone who knew him better.

"Graves," Moss said, "was most interesting when he wasn't sure what he was doing."[1]

It is tempting to attach every circumstance of Michael's life, his every strength and failing, to the work for which he became best known. Surely such causal links do exist. But what the next period in Michael's career demonstrates is that his practice might yet have gone in almost any direction, taken any turn. More than just a disavowal of an overly deterministic methodology (or old-fashioned fatalism), this sense of contingency and possibility comes with seeing just how wildly diverse Michael's practice was during the 1970s.

It would be a decade of rapid-fire improvisation. Flying in the face of Mies's admonition that "one does not invent a new architecture every Monday morning," every new project from Michael's office seemed to take a different tack, to explore a different architectural *parti*, and any one of these might have opened into an avenue toward a new architecture. That Michael developed as he did should not preclude speculation as to what other kinds of buildings he might have built, and what American architecture might have been, had he emerged from this personal and professional interregnum in a different form, or if had he found a way to somehow prolong this time when—in so many ways—he wasn't sure what he was doing.

"It was the stupidest thing I ever did," said Michael.[2]

On a Sunday morning in 1970, he was out for a walk in Princeton in the company of one of Lucy's two daughters. Since his divorce he had been living near the university, establishing himself as the somewhat overcommitted paterfamilias to two households, with periodic visits to Adam and Sarah in Massachusetts balanced by stepfatherly duties in New Jersey. In performance of the latter, he was strolling with his stepdaughter down a quiet street not far from their own when he spotted a "For Sale" sign, unaccountably sticking out of a small mound of rocks and broken cement.

Looking beyond it, between two neighboring houses, he saw what he later described as "a real oddity."[3] In the middle of the block, there was a building he had never noticed before, occupying a site that ordinarily would have been divvied among the backyards of the homes surrounding it. The lot was flyswatter-shaped, with a narrow handle connecting it to the street, and the sole building on it had been constructed back in the 1920s by Italian masons who were in Princeton erecting the stony spires of the neo-Gothic campus. In a canny bit of opportunism, the craftsmen had built the structure in their spare time for the purposes of commercial storage, charging well-to-do professors for the privilege of leaving their furniture there. It contained forty-four rooms, none of them more than ten feet long; it had neither electricity nor water; and the only source of heating was an open fire that the owner kept in a small office toward the back. "Zoning would never allow it to be built today," Michael said, and probably no halfway decent homeowners' association would allow it to be resold as a residential property, either.[4] He was immediately taken with it, and the asking price was a steal at $35,000—not that it much mattered. A sale was already pending, the buyer a local developer who planned to convert it into rental apartments.

Lo and behold, the deal fell through. The developer could not secure the necessary permits, and no sooner had the building gone back on the market than Michael procured a mortgage and grabbed it. He and Lucy immediately put her house up for sale, sold it, and made ready to move into what Michael had already begun to call the Warehouse, planning to take up residence there just as soon as it was fit for human habitation. "I was buying a ruin," he said, and he was ready to begin the long process of rehabilitating it, piece by junk-strewn piece.[5]

Princeton felt otherwise. The borough government chose this precise moment to institute a "sewer moratorium" prohibiting all construction in the area until a major new upgrade to the community's water and drainage systems could be completed. Lucy and Michael were obliged to move into the housing project that Lucy helped manage.

Thus, by the time they were properly married, Michael and Lucy were living in a provisional shelter. They had a mortgage hanging over their heads, her two children to look after, and his two children in Cambridge to consider, with the ever-present distractions of his practice and a mounting record of mutual suspicions (some of them well founded) leading to a veritable crescendo of marital discord. Something had to give; by and by, it would.

There were good times as well as bad. Michael and Lucy would stay at Richard Meier's house in East Hampton, New York, stopping by Robert A. M. Stern's place nearby.[6] On one of their visits to the Hanselmanns in Fort Wayne, just as the house was being completed, Lucy helped sketch out the pattern for Michael's mural.[7] The couple would host dinners for Michael's students, and those who were there remember Lucy as cutting a singularly stylish figure in the sometimes drab, scholastic setting.

Things had, meanwhile, become more interesting around Princeton. Caroline Constant, who had worked on the Jersey Corridor almost a decade earlier, came back to study with Michael in 1973; the year before, Mary McLeod had enrolled as well. In a profession where women were only beginning to make inroads, the addition of these two—both of whom would go on to major academic careers—was a mark of the program's progressivism. With additions to the faculty such as Kenneth Frampton, Anthony Vidler, Alan Chimacoff, and Diana Agrest, as well as a revolving cast of prominent guest lecturers, Princeton was finally catching up with its peer institutions.

Into this new ferment, Michael tossed two more intellectual ingredients. In 1973 he introduced an assignment in his studio course that was to become a staple of his teaching repertoire, the first assignment he gave to every incoming studio class for the remainder of his life as a teacher.[8] This was the Asplund Problem: seemingly straightforward, easy enough for a first-year student, it was nonetheless a clever bit of pedagogical sleight of hand.

The Swedish architect Gunnar Asplund had died in 1940, and his work was little known outside Scandinavia, save for a handful of lyrical, low-key projects completed just prior to his death—early iterations of the Nordic Modernist style that would take hold across the region (and gain a following around the world) after the war. But this was not the period in Asplund's career that had caught Michael's fancy. He'd been introduced to the semiforgotten architect by a Swedish visiting professor, Sven Silow, who'd been in Princeton the year that Michael arrived there, and his interest had grown under the influence of Colin Rowe, who shared it.[9] For Michael, what was most compelling about Asplund was not his later portfolio but his earlier, non-Modernist buildings.

Typical of these, if slightly more restrained than some, is the Villa Snellman, built in the genteel Djursholm district north of Stockholm for a wealthy private client in 1918. Deceptively plain in appearance, the building seems at first an only slightly

Villa Snellman,
1918, by Gunnar
Asplund. Drawing
created by Peter
Carl for Michael's
students

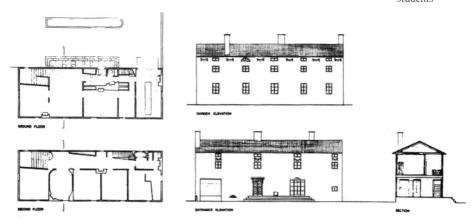

more polished take on an old Swedish farmhouse, an oblong box topped by a pitched roof and symmetrical windows. On closer inspection, however, it boasts a few puzzling anomalies. The main door sits not at the center of the house but just to the left, atop a raised terrace that it shares with a large French window giving onto the main parlor. Above the latter is an almost abnormally small decorative emblem, a sort of double volute, mirrored in a number of equally small swags set above the second-story windows. These windows are themselves very small and are topped by even smaller ones in the attic story.

This was the house Michael presented to his students, along with the following instructions:

> A guest house is to be built as an addition to the existing villa. You are asked to design the guest house which will provide the following spaces: living, bedroom, kitchen with a small eating area, and toilet. The guest house must be physically connected to the existing villa at either the first or second level or both.[10]

With this simple brief, Michael punctured a minute hole in the fabric of architectural training in America.

"A vehicle," as Peter Carl later wrote, for "opening a challenge to the limitations of 'form' and 'space,'" the Asplund Problem dared students to consider aspects of the building art that had been off-limits to young architects for decades (and entirely *verboten* at Sert's GSD).[11] Confronting them with a pre-Modernist building, one whose distinguishing features were located entirely on its facade, it tasked them with creating an extension to that building that would, perforce, respond to the way the facade was organized. It thereby upended the received order of the Modernist design process: instead of beginning with the plan—always "the generator," according to Le Corbusier—students would have to begin with the elevation; instead of focusing on making an autonomous architectural object, they would have to be sensitive to the historical character of an older building. While they were at it, they would have to think about Asplund, an architect who fell outside the accepted canon of pioneers and who, as Villa Snellman demonstrated, was sufficiently uncouth as to continue using the classical ornamentation of the nineteenth century well into the twentieth.

That wasn't all they would have to think of. In an essay he would write in 1975 (with a key assist from Caroline Constant), Michael said of the Villa Snellman that it "can be seen as a wall in a layered system of increasing degrees of privacy": the twinned exterior doors, for example, one transparent and the other solid, bespeak twinned impulses for shelter and for exposure. The building's symmetry, its tall first-floor windows, and the detailing above them make reference to "body image," to the shapes of the human form and the human face, inspiriting it with an air of welcome —of empathy, even.[12] Snellman, in Michael's eyes, was teeming with meaning, and he wanted his students to see it.

To ensure they did, he made a couple of telling changes to the house in the drawings—executed by Carl—that he gave to the class. He lopped off the house's real-life service wing, replacing it with a garage, and shifted it ninety degrees from its oblique relation to the street. Instead of an early twentieth-century house in Sweden that you approach from the side, Michael's students found themselves face to meta-phoric face with a house approached dead-on, which looked for all the world like it could be in any American suburb.

IF THIS CLASSROOM DEVIATION from the Modernist norm sounds suspiciously Grayish, it should be borne in mind that although Michael had read Robert Venturi's *Complexity and Contradiction in Architecture* (1966)—as well as its follow-up, *Learning from Las Vegas* (1972), written with Venturi's wife, Denise Scott Brown, and Steven Izenour and published the same year as *Five Architects*—he was not much invested in the philosophical literature that preoccupied the Yale-Philadelphia axis. Semiotics, structuralism, and the other hothouse theories that informed their readings of the city were slow to reach Michael, and even when they did, he was more concerned with their application to art history, which was where he made his other signal contribution to Princeton's academic culture.

In the 1974–75 academic year, Michael began teaching an undergraduate seminar, denoted in the SOA bulletin as Architecture 402, "Visual Studies in Architecture."[13] It was arranged as a series of lectures and classroom conversations that explored the history of architecture not chronologically, nor through types and forms, but through images and encounters, the subjective miscellany of architecture as its makers make it and its users live it. While the reading list neglected the touchstones of the Grays—neither Charles Sanders Peirce's work on signs nor Roland Barthes's on pop culture was on it—it did highlight, in keeping with its experiential premise, the phenomenology of the French thinker Maurice Merleau-Ponty.[14]

Most important, however, were the formal analytics of those scholars, Ernst Gombrich and Ernst Cassirer especially, whom Michael had likely first happened upon in the American Academy in Rome's library. With their ideas as a baseline, the content of 402 changed from year to year as Michael's thinking changed, each new lecture receiving an evocative title ("The Plan," "Fragments," "Replica").[15] In them, Michael would deliver highly nuanced close readings, not just of buildings, but of paintings and sculpture, showing his pupils how architecture existed in a visual continuum with art—how, for instance, Le Corbusier's Villa Stein could undergo the same interpretive treatment as a painting by Sandro Botticelli.

"It was meant for seniors," Michael said of the class. "It got to be so popular that all the grad students wanted to take it, too."[16]

The lectures were a hit because they were informative, but they were also fun, and often very funny. One was devoted to questions of exteriority, interiority, and how movement between the two could be expressed in buildings: it was called "A Little of the Old In and Out," the name a quote from the novel (and film) *A Clockwork Orange*. Jokes and pop-culture references grew to be regular features of the class, a bait and switch to hold students' attention as Michael inducted them into an understanding of art, design, and history—an understanding that, as he'd long felt, was necessary for the making of an architecture that was more than vapid gestures. "The lectures were history and theory lessons," remembered a former student, John DaSilva, "but they were also lessons in the practical application of history and theory."[17] In the class, Michael would show his students how to connect the dots between art and architecture just as he'd begun to do in his practice, explaining how the hinged diptychs of the fifteenth century created a spatial narrative of difference and change; how the symbolic drama of entering or exiting a space could be seen in an open door in an Henri Matisse painting; how the maps of Rome by Giovanni Battista Piranesi and Giambattista Nolli articulated the continuities and disjunctures between public and private, past and present.

"One way or the other, most students had me," said Michael.[18] Between 402 and the Asplund Problem, he had become a leading light of the department, a star performer in what had turned into a star-studded school. And because he was building—and because he was a member of the New York Five—Michael exuded a glamour that his more bookish colleagues did not. In the view of Robert A. M. Stern, "He dominated that school. He was the new Labatut."[19]

As had been the case since he'd come to Princeton, Michael's teaching was running a few steps ahead of his evolution as an architect. It wasn't just that his built projects had been restricted to private homes and small offices. Even as he traveled throughout the United States, lecturing and sitting on university juries with his friends in the New York Five—three of them anyway; Hejduk rarely left Manhattan—Michael felt more and more that he, rather than Hejduk, was odd man out.

"Richard would get on stage," Michael recalled, "and he'd say, 'The entry is here, here's the dining room.' I was determined not to do that. I wanted to have something more to say about my work."[20] Michael was beginning to feel ill at ease with the underlying assumptions of his own practice, and of the whole White enterprise.

In 1974 the dawning apprehension that there would have to be a change—that an architecture of meaning might not be attainable within the neo-Modernist idiom of his fellow Fivers—broke into Michael's work in the unlikeliest of places: right in the middle of a Charles Gwathmey project. Gwathmey had invited his friend to design one of his famous murals, just as Michael had done for so many of his own clients, for the Manhattan offices of the petrochemical firm Transammonia Inc. The interior by Gwathmey Siegel (the firm Gwathmey had founded with his friend Robert Siegel—effectively the sixth of the Five) was pure Charlie, a rippling landscape of contoured white walls broken up by courses of glass blocks. Michael's trio of murals, their watery palette similar to Snyderman's, seemed at first like pure Michael, the typical mélange of fragmented geometries and faintly suggestive figures.[21]

Only now, as if they had only been waiting to congeal into some more solid state of matter, the geometries no longer looked so fragmented, and not all the figuration was merely suggestive. A new and unmistakable motif intruded into the composition, not once or twice, but over and over. It was a molding, pictured in various formations—clearly a response to the crowns of the Beaux Arts office buildings visible through the office window [PLATE 19].

Seemingly out of nowhere, moldings—those humble details derived from the classical cornice but as commonplace as any baseboard in any middle-class living room—were everywhere in Michael's work. The same year as Transammonia, he designed another one of his Princeton additions for another local client, the Wageman family; here the moldings multiplied, creating a lower datum at the height of the windows and another, almost a true cornice, toward the top. The house was put on hold (indefinitely, as it turned out), but Michael stuck with the theme, and it cropped up in his next built work, the Claghorn House.

Yet another extension to yet another Princeton residence, this one a Queen Anne–style home from the 1890s, Claghorn discarded the more free-flowing interiors of Michael's previous additions in favor of discrete functional spaces for kitchen, breakfast room, bar, and pantry, as well as an outdoor terrace. Fragments of molding appeared in the interior, both on the countertop and on a wall in the existing dining room, as well as outside, tracing a false pediment on the extension volume—a classical allusion more blatant by far than the Athenian and Italian echoes of Hanselmann. The deck was topped by a white frame structure, but its Benacerraf-like abstraction was subverted by something more conspicuous: a lattice, applied to the northern wall, reminiscent of the skirting screens found below old American houses [PLATE 20].

The first time Steven Harris saw the house and that stuck-on' latticework, he recalled, "I thought it was hysterical—like my grandmother's back porch at the beach."[22] Then a student at the Rhode Island School of Design, Harris met Michael in 1975 as he was preparing to apply to graduate school at Princeton, and despite some familiarity with Michael's work (or, rather, because of it) he didn't "get" Claghorn right away. He would in time.

Appearances to the contrary, the project was only a half step away from Michael's *Five Architects* houses. Its chief innovation was to couple his customary Cubist grammar with a new glossary of architectonic images, images derived less from Le Corbusier and more from the traditional building next door. (And from further afield as well: the lattice was inspired in part by a trip Michael took to Newport, Rhode Island, in search of the old shingle-style houses that Vincent Scully had chronicled.)[23] The same narrative content present in Michael's older projects—the house telling of its own coming into being—was now expanded by its interleaved quotations—the lattice, the moldings, the pediment—to tell a bigger story, one about the suburban good life and the persistence of the past.

All the extrusions and whirling forms that had borne the weight of Snyderman's visual plot making were compressed, in Claghorn, into the walls themselves—a strategy that had the ancillary benefit of reducing building costs and making the addition more structurally sound. Its departure from the Whites' Corbusian minimalism may have raised eyebrows (Harris's among them), but at least the kitchen worked better qua kitchen. "I don't know what they say about Michael," Marge Claghorn was known to have said. "I just know it feels like a million bucks to do dishes here."[24]

LEAKING ROOFS ASIDE, what precipitated Michael's movement away from his earlier, more Modernist work was the growing suspicion that he had been speaking above his audience's heads, a suspicion reinforced by the criticism of *Five Architects*. The book was reissued in 1975 by Oxford University Press in a far larger printing, drawing still more attention and with it still more criticism, much of it directed at Michael and his supposedly hermetic, overheated stylistics. Looking back, Michael told an interviewer in 1980, "I thought it was going to be a lonely world out there for me if I continued to speak in what seemed to be a more or less private language."[25] The statement seems a poignant reflection of the speaker's psychological complexion.

In his architecture as in his teaching, the reasons behind Michael's changing attitude were only tangentially related to those that underwrote the Grays' critique of Modernism. For them, the problem of Modernist design—be it the towers in a park of Le Corbusier or the icy monumentality of Mies or the repetitious and car-centric planning schemes of Mies and Corb's American heirs—was the damage that it had done to the physical and social coherence of the American city. For them, the crisis was a civic one; for Michael, in the 1970s, the crisis was rather more personal.

Almost all of his completed projects to date had won prizes, many from the New Jersey chapter of the American Institute of Architects (Oyster Bay Town Plan in 1967, Hanselmann in 1973, even the mangled Union County Nature and Science Museum in 1974). Yet none of these accolades, nor the copious media coverage surrounding the New York Five, registered with Michael as the kind of recognition he longed for. Or at least it was not *all* the recognition he longed for. His proposal for the Rockefeller house had garnered him a Progressive Architecture Design Award citation, a high honor that came with guaranteed publication in the eponymous magazine; but when the *Progressive Architecture* issue featuring the project hit newsstands ("a brilliant tour de force," juror Thomas Vreeland declared the house, from an architect "deeply immersed in the heroic period of modern architecture"), Michael remembered that he "sent the magazine to my parents and waited for a response."[26] He heard nothing. "They didn't realize what a big deal that was for a very young architect to win."

Whatever Erma and Bud made of Michael's divorce (and they would have done well to hold their tongues, given Bud's secret first marriage), their son's work was still completely impenetrable to them. His brother, Tom, was now a major executive at the Union Pacific Railroad, living with his family in comfort in the Midwest; Michael was living in Princeton Community Village with children who weren't even his own. What good were his buildings, his talk of abstraction and figuration, if this was all it got him? And his parents were only a proximate barometer of the larger problem: they didn't care for his early houses, and neither did Charles Moore. Neither perhaps did the average Princetonian, ambling through the village and wondering: What *were* these baffling white excrescences, sprouting incongruously from the sides of otherwise normal houses?

From a strictly practical angle, too, Michael recognized that it would avail him nothing to stump his hoped-for clientele. Paul Benacerraf, a philosopher of mathematics and no slouch on matters intellectual, lived in the Princeton house that Michael had designed for him for forty-two years, without ever once having understood it in the least. "No clue," said Professor Benacerraf. "I have no idea what he was trying to do."[27]

It had all seemed so simple to Michael. The exhilarating imago of a technological form in a natural setting—"the machine in the garden," as the literary critic Leo Marx termed it—was part of what had drawn him to Le Corbusier's work since his Harvard days. All the machine wanted, Michael inferred, was a pictorial schema, like Cubism, that could make its operations intelligible to everyone. Not so, he now concluded. He began to turn to other sources, some of them new, some very old indeed, in hopes they might succeed where Corb had failed.

Though confounded by this sudden volte-face ("For whatever reason," Meier said, "he wanted to go in a different direction"), Michael's friends could at least take heart that he was inserting these new forms into the same Cubist framework, in the same collage-like way he always had.[28] So long as he did that, he was still doing nominal obeisance to Modernism; so long as he did that, he was still a White, albeit one straying further and further into heterodoxy.

EMBOLDENED BY CLAGHORN, Michael continued to elaborate his new language in two more projects, one realized and the other not, for a pair of clients in Princeton and Fort Wayne, respectively.

In New Jersey, he and his associates designed and executed the Schulman House, an appendage enfolding two sides of a very plain two-story colonial. It included a new living room, a new street facade, and a new backyard enclosure, and, like Claghorn, it sported a trellis-like lattice on the garden front, this time blown up in scale to match the gridded wall beside it [PLATE 21]. But that wasn't the only one of its allusive flourishes.

The grid formed around a network of windows that incorporated glass blocks, a material common enough at the time—Gwathmey loved it—but here calling to mind its more common application in Art Deco buildings of the 1920s and '30s. To the street, the renovated house now presented a color scheme that again flattened the visual narrative to the depth of the wall: bands of dark and light blue connected a portion of the existing structure to the new one, creating the illusion of a triad of related forms that read as a kind of primitive village. What was more, a pair of towering columns, their classical origins only slightly obscured, now stood to the left and right of the front door, one segmented into a lower and upper portion and the other rising unbroken into the chimney of the new fireplace.

Then there was the fireplace. The interior of the new dining and living room, festooned in colorful sconces and moldings, played an ongoing game of alternating scale and perspective that culminated above the firebox in a false-ziggurat "mantel." It was an arresting image: like the fragments of molding that appeared in the walls and in the recessed living-room soffit above, the fire hood receded into the surrounding pattern of windows and decorative elements when viewed at an angle. Yet when seen from the living room, it was a commanding presence, imparting a neat symmetry to the space [**PLATE 22**].

This dual character is all the more interesting because this was not Michael's sole proposal for the fireplace. In sketches made in late 1976 or early '77, he imagined a

The alternative Schulman fireplace (at bottom), alongside other sketches

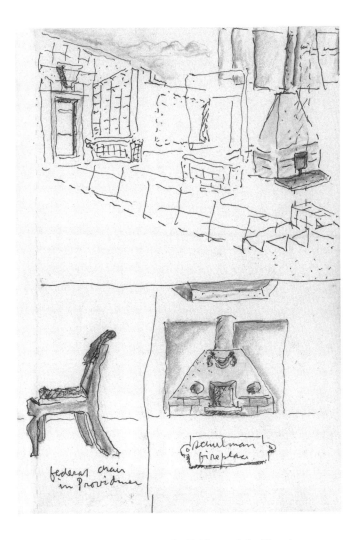

much larger, much grander hood, one that could be read properly only from within the living room itself. With a lower course of rusticated masonry blocks, it was decked out in pendant dials and a large, decorative swag—very much in the mode of the Villa Snellman—at the top. The sketch may have been only a passing thought, but it shows how quickly history was encroaching into Michael's design process.

A fireplace for the Fort Wayne house of the Crooks family, begun in 1976, also became the repository of Michael's historical fascination. Drawings for the Crooks inglenook, from slightly later in the design process, show it as even more decorative, and figurative in the most literal sense: in bas-relief on the lower trapezoid of the hood, an actual figure in classical dress and another, possibly statuary form stand on either side of a column of rising smoke. Above them, on projecting wings beside the flue, two sets of peplos-clad women bearing what appear to be ritual offerings gesture toward the central axis of the chimney [**PLATE 23**]. The depiction is obviously that of a ceremonial rite—a hecatomb being burned to some pagan god—and while the narrative rationale for putting this Grecian scene over a fireplace seems clear enough, putting it in this particular house seemed almost like heresy.

The never-executed Crooks House might be judged Michael's collagist achievement par excellence, his adroit use of layered montage reaching its most sophisticated and varied articulation yet. In plan it carried the germ of his early projects, comprising two discrete structures connected by a slender ligature, in this instance a decorative wall that carried the visual themes of the buildings' facades. These themes

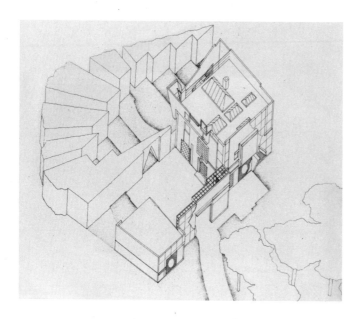

Axonometric
drawing of the
Crooks House,
1976

alternated among grids, lattices, pediments, glass blocks, French windows, and keystones (their first appearance to date), and they were variously isolated, chipped, separated into discrete squares, or slipped one over the other. In the garden elevation, the house met the viewer with a strikingly human aspect, its symmetry punctuated by a triangular "nose." Arriving vehicles would have passed through an opening in the connecting wall that matched inscribed square "openings" beside it. Drivers might have been unsure, if only for an instant, whether they were entering a real opening or a fake one [**PLATE 24**].

Steven Harris worked on the house's design, and, as he put it, Crooks marked "a transition": the project found Michael midshift between "all these ideas of diptychs, flips, references to Juan Gris" on the one hand and on the other, his "more figurative work." The grandiose fireplace, conceived in 1978, shows the extraordinary speed with which Michael's practice was changing during the project's rather lengthy lifespan.[29] Running, as many of Michael's schemes did, more than slightly over budget, Crooks was subject to constant changes, though in the end it was doomed not by cost but by a local property ordinance that made the area less attractive to development.

Development, in fact, was slowing all across America, as the economic downturn of the 1970s dragged on. What had been a general uptick in the volume of work coming into the office turned into another dry spell, and Crooks remained for some time one of Michael's few still-active commissions. He produced countless sketches and resketches of it, imagining different configurations of the exterior patina and different perspectives of its interior spaces, where the approaches to its tomblike fireplace, set in the middle of the living room, terminated all the multifaceted confusion of the design in a single, monumental vision.

DAYS AFTER ARRIVING in Princeton from MIT in 1977, newly minted firm associate Karen Nichols (then Karen Wheeler) went with Michael to see the just-finished Claghorn House as it was being set for a shoot by the architectural photographer Yukio Futagawa. As they walked through the house, Michael showed Nichols how the design had come together—how it functioned as a Cubist assemblage, how its quotidian materials resonated with ideas of place and entry, of the private and the public spheres.

Nichols, like Harris before her, didn't get it.

Finally, Michael took her by the shoulders and stood her square in front of the terrace, aiming her directly at the latticed facade of the terrace wall. "Can't you see it?" he said.

"See what?"

"There's a picture plane!"

He then proceeded to show her how the puzzle fit together: how the diagonal cutaway of the lattice shaped the space before it; how the lattice blended with the big post-and-beam structure to create the appearance of a trellis; how the trellis, the horizontal courses, and the doorjamb all framed the kitchen, pointing the way toward the entrance. It was all perfectly clear, Michael insisted, once you looked at it the right way, as a frontal tableau.

All at once, it clicked. "Before that," recalled Nichols, "I had understood it in three dimensions."[30]

Consonant with the vertical focus of the Asplund Problem, Michael's design process during these years began to place more and more emphasis on elevations. In good Corbusian fashion, he had usually begun with the plan—a more than adequate template for his painterly skills, Corb himself having proved their compositional potential.[31] But as Michael wrote at the time:

> Plan is seen as a conceptual tool, a two-dimensional diagram or notational device with limited capacity to express the perceptual elements....Plans are experienced only in perspective as opposed to the vertical surfaces of a building which are perceived in a frontal manner.[32]

No one, in other words, can appreciate the artistic merit of a plan except insofar as the elevation bears it out. Floors are mute. Walls can speak.

With elevations taking center stage, Michael began to rely heavily on large-format yellow tracing paper to render them. Painting, which he continued to do off and on, was never used as a medium for developing specific designs, though his artistic work always took place in parallel with his architectural activity. ("I use the same formal ensemble of objects in my paintings that I use in my architecture," he put it.)[33] Likewise his habit of creating what he termed "referential sketches": scribbled in small notebooks, sometimes on loose pieces of paper, often in the margins of larger drawings or even next to student work, these were strictly mental musings, intended as his visual "diary," as he described it.[34] They would serve as background material for "preparatory" and finally "definitive" drawings, where facade treatments could be worked out at length in the open space of the large yellow sheets, to be handed off later to his associates for detailing and coloring and then returned to him.

Such would remain the standard procedure at Michael Graves Architect for decades. But during this pivotal stage in his career—the moment, it might be said, when Michael Graves became Michael Graves—there was a special importance to his private sketching and painting.

A set of maroon-bound sketchbooks, kept by Michael over an approximately seven-year time frame starting in 1975, affords a unique glimpse into his design

Erma Sanderson
Lowe Graves,
sketched by
Michael just
prior to his
mother's death

approach as it was then evolving. Different versions and views of both the Schulman and Crooks fireplaces turn up in these pages, alongside countless other "referential" caprices floating through his architectural subconscious: churches and landscapes, some recalled from his time in Europe; drawings of John Hejduk's "Wall House" proposals; images culled from books of architectural history, including a phantasmagorical temple by the eighteenth-century Frenchman Jean-Jacques Lequeu [**PLATE 25**]; and a remarkable quantity of interior fixtures, sconces, chairs, and other details, some of them ones he was considering for purchase whenever (or if ever) he had the money. Of his day-to-day life he sketched nothing, except once—a tiny, exquisite portrait, marked "ESLG," which he dashed off on a visit to Indianapolis. It is the only known picture he ever drew of his mother, Erma, and one of very few images he ever created of any family member.[35]

While many of these casual sketches show their subjects in conventional perspective, the more finished, inked-in drawings in the notebooks show that frontality and elevation were still foremost in Michael's mind. The more artistic his intent, the flatter the object became: one compositional trope is the imposition of disjointed figurative elements upon what are presumably pieces of landscape, at times pictured on an upright frame as though projected on a human body. In some cases the landscapes appear to be inscribed with snaking structural forms, forms reflected back again in the figuration—a compounding of elevation and plan, implying that the two might be interchangeable. This he had already begun to demonstrate in architectural form with Crooks, "a built chunk of landscape," as his Princeton colleague Alan Chimacoff called it.[36] A building's relation to its site, its spatial development, its whole *parti* could be performed, Michael was suggesting, by a single wall.

Or by several walls, of several buildings, standing together. Michael was always interested in a building's appearance in context, the way it played off against either existing structures or others of his own design. But this was part and parcel of the same pictorial logic. One need only look at Giorgio Morandi's bottles and jars or the arrangements of tables and chairs in Henri Matisse's interior scenes to see the artists who were then most important in Michael's imagination. Matisse and the ever-present Pablo Picasso were standard fare in his Princeton classes, and both painters informed his compositional investigations: the illusion of depth in their work often collapsed into the patterning on the picture plane. Writing of Picasso, the historian Rosalind Krauss—whom Michael knew and admired greatly—noted: "A sense of the flat and opaque plane was made to qualify every other experience the painting might offer."[37]

This artistic insight had been acting on Michael's mind for some time, and his architectural production had always had a compressive quality, even in more spatially dense works like Hanselmann and the dizzying Snyderman.[38] But what he had discovered at Claghorn was that basic functional accommodations were better handled by a plain box. That left him free to make his exteriors more like two-dimensional projections: a convenient solution, since that was more or less how he'd always seen buildings to begin with.

Here the matter of Michael's ocular defect is impossible to ignore. "I thought for years that he didn't see the way other people did," said Karen Nichols, who went on to spend the next four decades (and counting) with the firm.[39] As she witnessed at Claghorn in the very beginning, Michael could discern continuities—between, for example, a structure that sat in front of a wall and the wall itself—that were all but invisible even to trained architects. Frustrated, and more eager than ever to make himself understood, Michael's response was to make his work even flatter, eliminating the likelihood of misinterpretation by doing in two dimensions what he had nominally done in three. To his mind and, more importantly, to his eye, nothing would be lost in this translation. Just as his strabismus collapsed spatial arrangements into planar ones, he could sense a dynamism in planar surfaces that most viewers would experience only in perceiving and moving through space. Of course, what made Michael able to see things other people couldn't also made him unable to see things other people could.

Observing Michael that day at Claghorn, Nichols was getting a closer look at a man whom she'd first met a year earlier during a trip down from Cambridge. In the intervening months, she noticed that an alarming change had come over her new employer. "I never saw such a transformation," she recalled.

After eight years together, Lucy and Michael had separated, their relationship succumbing to the passions and volatility that had birthed it. It had been, all in all, an unconventional marriage, and both parties had some cause for resentment, though the balance of bitterness seems to have held them both to a tenuous entente that made the divorce at least as civil as Michael and Gail's had been. Still, in its immediate aftermath, Michael was gutted: "a basket case," Nichols called him.[40] He had embarked on one of his periodic crash diets, and he looked drawn and tired.

His troubles continued. Bud had died in October 1975; given the distance between father and son, his passing had not much affected Michael, at least outwardly. But two years later, and only months after Michael had sketched the touching portrait of her in his notebook, Erma died as well. The anguish of losing the individual who had always been the one constant in his life could only have been redoubled by his feeling that he, for all his accomplishments, had not yet proved himself to his mother—had not yet shown that his work had real meaning to real people, the end to which all his present efforts were being directed.

To be nearer their father, Gail had brought the children back to Princeton, and he now saw them every other weekend; he also remained close to his stepchildren, making for a mixed but merry brood that he would sometimes load into his car for architectural tours to places like Thomas Jefferson's Monticello. (On the way to Virginia, the four kids held up a sign in the rear windshield: HELP WE'RE BEING KIDNAPPED.)[41] Nonetheless, at forty-three, Michael was now an orphan, twice divorced, with little architectural work to sustain him or his office.

Pigeonholed, as he described it, into the role of the "Cubist Kitchen King," he felt himself stuck doing different versions of the same small, less-than-remunerative home-improvement project.[42] When Nichols came on board, she was informed by Michael and Caroline Constant that, for the time being, the firm could not afford to pay her. The year 1977 looks, in retrospect, like Michael's *annus horribilis*. Yet it was also, paradoxically, an *annus mirabilis*.

Its sewers flowing freely once more, the municipality of Princeton had lifted its building moratorium in 1974, allowing Michael to move ahead with renovations to the Warehouse. Three years later he moved out of Princeton Community Village and into the small central portion of the 1926 structure that had been cleared of debris and improved according to Michael's plan. The delay had been, as he put it, "a reprieve," allowing him time to work up a thorough, integrated scheme for turning the rotting hulk into the home of an architect, the way Ray Roush's home had been to him.[43]

As Roush's house had been a proving ground for his architectural ideas, Michael wanted the Warehouse to show what was possible in the new language he was then inventing. It wasn't going to be easy: the Warehouse was shaped like an L, with a thick northern wing and a longer western addition jutting southward toward the street. Michael first set up house in the latter section, where the previous owner —"the guy sat there and drank all day long," Michael recalled—had kept his office; the rest of the conversion would have to wait until funds were available to fix it.[44] For the next decade-plus, this meant he would share a roof with an empty, rather creepy bunker. "It looked very tattered and everything was peeling and damp," he said later. "But I didn't let it worry me."[45]

Dashing gleefully through the house on their first visit there, Sarah and Adam and their stepsisters had divvied up the rooms, deciding who would sleep where. In reality there was scarcely room for anyone save for Michael: when he moved in, the rehabilitated section consisted of a space with a secondhand stove that he used as a kitchen, a modest sitting room, and an upstairs bath and bedroom with a television and some of his books. "I was living like a student," he recalled. His colleague Alan Chimacoff, who had given him the stove, recalled the place as being so dusty that after his first visit he was seized with an asthma attack.[46]

Michael's master plan, however, was already in motion. The door in front of the kitchen served as the main entrance, but he proposed to remove it to the northern wing, just off the corner of the L, leading into a small foyer with a dining room to the left and living room to the right. On the second floor, accessed via the living-room staircase, he would situate the master bedroom, along with a private studio and a photographic darkroom. The interior scheme for all this was astonishing: a constantly metamorphosing grid, shaped from windows and tiles and glass blocks and punctuated by rounded columnar supports, was to give the rooms and connecting hallways a sense of continuity and rhythm [**PLATE 27**]. (The early renderings also show neoclassical statuary, antique furniture, and much else that Michael couldn't possibly afford at the time.)

In the first version of the house's renovation, a portion of this grid system was realized, the downstairs and upstairs bath (as well as the early solarium next to the kitchen) taking up the theme and giving the house a splash of Art Deco flair, accentuated by Michael's then-unfashionable 1930s furniture. Shifting gridded apertures were also added to the exterior: the Warehouse's stucco surface, covering a structure of bricks backed by hollow clay tile, was cut with glass-block openings on the eastern flank and to either side of the kitchen door. The house even had a whiff of the scalar and historical vertigo that Crooks might have had, a few windows being blocked with blind squares, and a patch of painted-on masonry—like that found on the rusticated lower floors of Renaissance palaces—gracing the front of the south-facing wall.

Soon the upstairs guest rooms were ready for the kids, and Michael was able to welcome a few select visitors. He was now a bachelor, and there are perhaps less enviable situations for an unmarried man than to be living in a large, very romantic former industrial building, refashioned after his own design, surrounded by charming odds and ends of furniture gathered from rural flea markets around New Jersey. He had a twenty-dollar cupboard and a half-wrecked Biedermeier breakfast table, the first piece of what would become a substantial collection. He would hear of a rug for sale in a nearby town and drive over to see if it would work in the narrow hallways—shades again of Villa Snellman—that ran between the upstairs rooms. "When you're doing your own house," he said, "you don't know what you want. I didn't know if I wanted a Persian rug or a Modern rug."[47] As his tastes continued to change, the Warehouse would be Michael's personal design laboratory.

ESSENTIALLY CAMPING OUT in his own home for the first several years, Michael didn't often entertain large groups. But on one memorable occasion in late 1977 he assembled a gaggle of students and a few academic heavyweights—among them Alan Colquhoun, Kenneth Frampton, and Colin Rowe—for an after-hours get-together. That evening, the newly renovated Warehouse became the scene of a minor architectural scandal.[48]

Rowe had always been known as a heavy drinker, and on the night in question he had been running off to the kitchen in regular spurts to pour together ad hoc cocktails from whatever bottles were sitting out. He fell into a belligerent, goading sort of mood, which took as its object the usually mannerly Colquhoun. "Rowe was punching his arm in a semifriendly way," recalled Frampton. "He had this game of calling people 'buddy boy.'"[49] There is some disagreement about what followed, but one way or the other it ended with someone—Rowe most likely—being pushed back into Michael's fireguard. Michael very discreetly buttonholed Frampton and asked him to escort Rowe back to his hotel. The two Englishmen got no farther than the sidewalk before Rowe executed a clumsy somersault and landed on the asphalt.

"God," he said to Frampton. "Isn't this a *bore*?"

"The row with Rowe," as Michael described it, was "half personal," mostly the result of mixing dissimilar characters and dissimilar alcohols. But it was also, Michael noted, "half architectural," a view bolstered by Frampton; in the latter's account, the argument had begun over Colquhoun's critiques of student work, which often revolved around the political and social intent of their projects. This was what had raised Rowe's hackles, leading to the fireplace fiasco.[50]

It was symptomatic of Rowe's position at the time. The doubts about the political agency of architecture that Rowe had expressed at CASE 1 had only grown deeper over the preceding decade, and in his newest book, *Collage City* (portions of the manuscript were already in circulation, though it was not published until 1978), Rowe deliberately set fire to a few of his Modernist boats. Setting aside the presumed moral authority of the Modern movement, he was now advancing a new role for the architect in shaping urban space—a more liberal, eclectic one that made room for history and diversity in both form and spirit. In particular he was sympathetic toward the "residue of classical decorum," as the book labeled it, taking it as an emblem of tradition still plastic enough to be applicable in the twentieth century.[51]

The Grays had long drawn strength from Rowe; they could now claim him almost as one of their own. But more so than previous expressions of their ideas, Rowe's appeal in *Collage City* chimed with Michael's emerging views. Art historical in its frame of reference, its very title alluding to one of Michael's preferred artistic techniques, the book seemed to grant personal benison to everything Michael had been trying to do for the last five years and more. Rowe had long had Michael's admiration. Now he had his ear.

Michael's eye, meanwhile, was still up for grabs—and in short order, that sensitive organ was captured by another thinker who passed through Princeton in 1977, the man who had first espied Michael sitting on a floor in Milan: Léon Krier, who came to the university that fall at Michael's invitation to fill in for Anthony Vidler, then on sabbatical.

Unlike Rowe—a key figure in the United States for more than a decade, the disputed idol of both the White and the Gray factions—Krier was an outsider, a wild-haired visionary who blew in from the London office of the architect James Stirling. Rowe's thinking had been integral to Michael's own since the early 1960s, changing as he changed; by contrast, Krier struck in a flash, his friendship with Michael lasting only a few short years but its effects long outliving their personal and professional association.

Krier had not yet emerged as the scorched-earth sloganeer he would become in the early 1980s, renowned for such fiery declarations as "I am an architect because I don't build" and "Forward, comrades, we must go back" (the latter commandeered from the novelist Wolfgang Parth). But already he had begun to stake out a reputation as a daring iconoclast, one who would proclaim himself in opposition not just to Modernist architecture but to the entire mechanism of modern consumer culture. Possessed, as the scholar Joseph Rykwert would write, of "a political innocence verging on insensibility," Krier's critique of the Western city as rebuilt by Modernism was so unyielding that he would even suggest a reappraisal of Albert Speer's Hitlerian classicism.[52] Although he had not yet reached that conclusion in 1977, it was well in

Léon Krier,
Blundell's Corner
proposal for
Hull, England,
early 1977

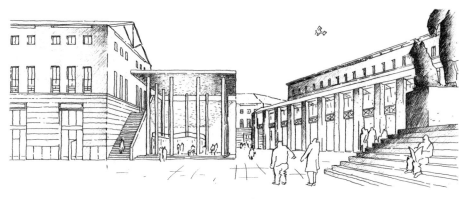

THE NEW BLUNBELL SQUARE

LOOKING TOWARDS THE PUBLIC LOGGIA FROM THE STEPS OF
THE SOCIAL CLUB

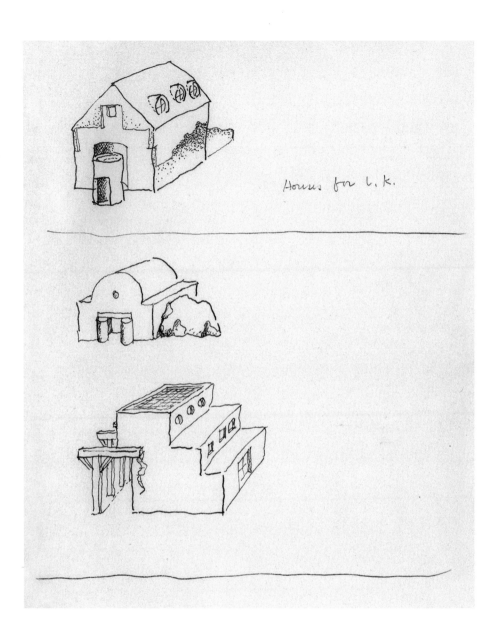

Houses for L.K.

From the
Year of Krier:
Michael's house
sketches for
then-friend Leo

train, evident in his drawn work like his echt-classical Blundell's Corner proposal for the English town of Hull. If Rowe had become a Gray, Krier was edging ever closer to being something like a Black.[53]

Initially reluctant (despite a few visits) to take up a longer lectureship at Princeton, Krier at last had relented to Michael's entreaties, and on the drive from the train station to the Warehouse Michael waxed enthusiastic about the fun they were about to have.

"Leo," he said, "we're going to teach together!"

Krier answered with a dark joke: "Why not rather stay friends?"[54]

His pessimism turned out to be prescient. "In the end it was a disaster for our relationship," Krier recalled.[55] Michael's prestige at the school was now nearing its height, and he was unaccustomed to having a presence in the classroom as large as Krier's. The two attempted to coteach a studio, but immediately gave up, clashing over the treatment of students, the content of the course, and even over the direction of Michael's work, with Krier confessing a preference for the early Corbusian houses as opposed to the more muddled stylistic wanderings of the middle 1970s. By the time the semester was out, they were barely speaking.

The falling-out made little difference, for Krier had already cast his spell. It may be wondered why Michael—unencumbered as he was of almost any politics more profound than the platform of the Democratic Party—would gravitate toward a zealot like Krier. The answer lies not in his doctrine but in his drawings. "I know drawing better than any of my colleagues," Michael once said. "I'm better at it. But I'm not better at it than Leo Krier."[56]

Like his (somewhat more worldly) architect brother, Rob, Krier was a draftsman of unsurpassed delicacy, his superb sketches and diagrams conjuring a misty past of simple town squares and column-lined public buildings, often portrayed in didactic contrast to the faceless towers of Modernism. The temples and the dwellings and the civic basilicas that filled his sketches were symmetrical, with the classical tripartite division of foot, body, and head, and they radiated a mesmeric aura, redolent as much of memory or dream as of history. More than Krier's incisive rhetoric, it was his drawings that persuaded Michael of his genius, and Michael began to recapitulate some of their qualities in his own work. On one page of the 1977 maroon sketchbook there is a group of drawings labeled "Houses for L.K." A triad of archetypical, quasi-Tuscan vernacular buildings, they are plainly by Michael's hand, though they could almost as easily be by Krier's.

Not just Michael but a whole generation of critics and practitioners heard the siren call of Krier; among them was Colin Rowe, who had long had his own classical fixations. But Rowe's native circumspection inoculated him against Krier's polemics—an immunity Rowe passed to Michael, for whom the Englishman always remained *the* design intellectual. What Krier gave Michael was not a new philosophy but a new visual order, less labored and convoluted than Cubism, in which to set the images that made up Michael's new architectural dialect. This order would favor symmetry over asymmetry, and it would expand the use of recognizable figures from bits and pieces to the whole of the building. In Eisenman's opinion, "After Krier, Michael's life changed."

"Krier was the Great Destroyer," Eisenman added, "the destroyer of the Whites."[57]

OTHER CLASSICALLY INFORMED SOURCES had begun to seep into Michael's teaching and drawings by the late 1970s; these included the work of the nineteenth-century German architect Karl Friedrich Schinkel, as well as that of Claude-Nicolas Ledoux, whose *architecture parlante* (speaking architecture) attempted to rationalize classical forms to spell out the precise function of his buildings. But nothing served to reawaken Michael's long-held infatuation with the architecture of Rome and Greece quite like the Year of Krier.

The impact was not felt all at once but began to percolate steadily into Michael's work during and after his sometime-friend's Princeton residency. That same year Michael and his associates were commissioned to design an office expansion for Chem-Fleur, a Newark-based manufacturer and materials laboratory. The uncompleted proposal deployed the grid-like cladding that Michael had favored in previous projects, only regularized and reduced, turned into something more like masonry blocks. The reference became even more explicit in the Kalko House a year later, which furthered Chem-Fleur's modulation toward symmetry with a central entryway under a broad, pedimental curve. Neither was built.

The most outstanding realized project begun in 1977 was the Plocek House, located in Warren, New Jersey [**PLATE 26**]. Originally envisioned as a sprawling compound incorporating a central house, walled terrace, and backyard pavilion, it crouched on its cliffside site like a Florentine palazzo in the hills above the Arno. Almost totally symmetrical on its main southern facade, the four-thousand-square-foot central structure (the only portion to be completed) initially appeared in Michael's drawings and sketches as the "Keystone House," a reference to its signature feature: a volume in the rear garden, which the owner intended to use as a study, was shaped as a large trapezoidal wedge, while a void of nearly identical proportions was to be located above the house's columned south front. The narrative sequence is fairly glaring in its clarity—the front keystone is missing, and one must go looking through the house before finding it hidden in the back.[58]

So far as the office was concerned, however, private commissions vanished in importance next to its biggest project of 1977. In that banner year, Michael Graves

Architect unveiled its proposal for a new and altogether novel public structure: the Fargo-Moorhead Bridge.

Straddling the Red River of the North between the towns of Fargo, North Dakota, and Moorhead, Minnesota, the bridge had been the brainchild of a fifth-year architecture student at North Dakota State University named Clyde Schroeder. To commemorate the cities' joint centennial in 1975, the young designer put forward an idea for a new project that could be as much a cultural attraction as a piece of infrastructure. Combining a symphony hall, radio and television stations, and an interpretive center on the natural and human history of the region, the bridge would be the centerpiece of a complex occupying both the eastern and the western banks of the river. To find a designer, a local task force was formed and immediately began to aim high, cooking up a far-fetched list of prospective architects that included Le Corbusier, then twelve years dead.

Five (living) architecture firms were ultimately selected to present before the task force: Hardy Holzman Pfeiffer, Moore Lyndon Turnbull Whitaker, Stanley Tigerman and Associates, Malcolm Wells Architect, and Michael Graves Architect. As a group, the selected designers suggested something of the task force's architectural leanings, with most of its members—Tigerman and Hardy Holzman Pfeiffer especially—having lately drifted toward the Grayer end of the spectrum. Whatever emerged, it was not going to be a glass box, and Michael and his team took that as their cue.

As Karen Nichols put it, Fargo became "a mystical project" for Michael.[59] His design began to take shape in mid-1976, but the final version would not be unveiled until nearly eighteen months later, showing his Cubist grammar as it was tempered more and more by a Krierian sense of classical organization. The bridge declared

A model
of the Fargo-
Moorhead
Bridge proposal

its presence with a pair of broken pediments facing north and south, set off from each other in line with the bend in the waterway so as to appear symmetrical both upstream and down. These twin arches were to be flanked by columns whose flaring "capitals" emulated the form of an empty keystone at the center of the bridge—not unlike Plocek's but faced in glass and issuing forth a constant stream of water from an opening at the base. Adorned in comparable regalia of columns and keystones, the adjoining structures housed the broadcasting facilities and other functions, while the museum exhibitions would have continued into the enclosed margins of the vehicular span.

As evidenced in Michael's "reference sketches," the design finds its historical basis in a sculptural jug that can be seen atop the Medici Fountain in Paris's Luxembourg Gardens. That image, made flush with the bridge facade, served for Michael as the unifying impetus of the whole scheme. It tied together the separate wings of the complex as well the river—imagined as the foundational floor of the building—and the sky—the top of the keystone symbolically opening into it and then drawing upon it to produce the water that gushed below. The poetic valence of this organizing metaphor is conveyed, in the final elevations, in light pastel washes of terra-cotta, delicate red trim, and long strips of pale blue, their gauzy translucency making the monumental bridge seem practically weightless [PLATE 28].[60]

Michael's office had scrambled to get the commission, and his team scrambled to build momentum behind the design when it made its public debut in December 1977. With no experience to speak of in designing an auditorium, they had brought in an auditorium specialist; with no real knowledge of the local landscape, Michael had made repeated trips there to take photos and make drawings. On one trip he brought Karen Nichols, who ventured outside briefly to see the site. The temperature that winter was approaching thirty below. "I walked halfway around it and decided I had to come back," she recalled.[61]

Despite the firm's best efforts, fortune once again was fickle. To raise funds for its half of the project, the city of Fargo staged a referendum in November 1978, which failed by just 3 percent. The firm continued to produce designs for a less ambitious project on the Moorhead side, but without the cooperation of its sister city the enterprise was sunk. The unachieved, "mystical" bridge remained only that; indeed, even had it been built, much of the otherworldliness of the elevations would have belonged forever to the page: as the architect Peggy Deamer has written, no head-on view of the bridge, fountain, and river would have been possible, since the concert hall would have stood in the way.[62] Still, the mystique of the drawings wasn't felt by Michael alone. In a cruel twist, the proposal snagged the firm another Progressive Architecture Design Award only two months after the bond issue was denied. It even elicited interest from outside the parochial limits of the architecture world.

"I was interviewed by ABC, CBS, NBC," Michael recalled—mostly local affiliates, perhaps, but there was national recognition as well, with the *New York Times*'s redoubtable Ada Louise Huxtable calling the rendering "probably one of the most beautiful architectural drawings of recent times" and "the sort of work that sends the viewer away with the sense that some kind of breakthrough is being made."[63] There was international attention too. According to Michael, his local collaborators in Fargo reported that for years afterward, the flat, unlovely slab of a bridge that crosses the Red was regularly frequented by Japanese tour buses. They were still coming to look for Michael's bridge, unaware that it had never been built.[64]

TWO FINAL GRACE NOTES sounded the end of Michael's long and tumultuous 1977. The first came from Italy: following a conversation with the Italian architect Piero Sartogo, Michael helped conceive *Roma Interrotta* (Rome Interrupted), an exhibition featuring himself and eleven other architects and critics to be held the following year in Rome.[65] Using the 1748 Nolli map of the city, which Michael had known since his American Academy days and had used in his classes, the selected participants were assigned separate slices of the city, which they were to reimagine in drawings and sketches, creating fantasias on Rome's history and future [**PLATE 29**]. True to his recent idée fixe, Michael pictured keystones blown up to the level of city blocks and parkway corridors and then inserted into the landscape—another demonstration of his equation of elevation and plan. His submission sat side by side with others from some of Michael's closet allies, not the least being Colin Rowe.

Returning to Rome for the opening the following spring, Michael came back to where it all began, where he'd first discovered what he felt was the real purpose and power of architecture. "Rome was always a welcome place for me," he said, and he was only too glad to have reason to stay: he was made a visiting fellow that year at the Academy, resuming the same pleasant course of evenings around the dinner table that he'd enjoyed night after night with Gail all those years ago.[66] He'd come to the table then as a supplicant, cowed into silence by those he felt to be his betters in knowledge and understanding; two decades later, he was back as a possessor of understanding, a new understanding for a transformed field in which he and his work now towered.

For by now Michael had been, in a sense, canonized. Early in 1977 his firm's work was included in a new book, *The Language of Post-Modern Architecture*, by the American-born, British-based historian Charles Jencks. The critic and author had met Michael in the early 1970s, and the two had been in periodic contact since, many of their conversations revolving around the problem of whether architects should favor an "implicit" or "explicit" approach to symbol making.[67] Jencks inclined toward the latter, and while Michael was not yet sold on the critic's robust, literal approach to signification, he was moving closer to that position by the day.

It was further proof for Jencks that what Venturi and the Grays had begun was fast reaching maturity, as more and more architects branched off from the Modernist family tree to form a discrete and original genus. In Jencks's estimate, the designers' common tactics—exterior ornament, historical quotation, visual wit—qualified them as members of a new movement, a subversive counterassault on Modernism that might restore to the American city some of the color and character that had been steadily leached out of it after three decades of featureless International Style curtain walls. To describe this coalescing anti-Modernist mutiny, Jencks had first coined the term *post-modernist architecture* in a magazine article in 1975, and in his book he named Michael as one of its protagonists.[68] After 1977 the names "Michael Graves" and "Post-modernism" would be forever conjoined, their fortunes rising and falling together.

APOSTASY, SUCH AS MICHAEL'S WAS, was bound to draw condemnation, and the fiercest came from those who had always held his talent in the highest regard—especially Peter Eisenman. His friendship with Michael had weathered the Princeton tenure debacle, and it would weather this too. But Eisenman always detected a venal motive in Michael's PoMo switch. "He had a sense," Eisenman said later, "that Modernism wasn't selling."[69]

True, Modernism had fallen on hard times, and jumping ship might have seemed the prudent move. The degraded state of cities both in the United States and abroad had been widely blamed on the deadening monotony visited upon them by Modernists who'd anointed themselves, Prometheus-like, as the sole bearers of the light in architecture. This conceit had been methodically skewered by the theorist Jane Jacobs in her much-lauded 1961 study, *The Death and Life of Great American Cities;* championing small-scale, traditional city streets over the megablocks and highways of Modern planning, the book had been an early rallying cry for the Grays, and in the ensuing years it had become the popularly accepted verdict on the urban prospect in America. Modernism, the story went, had failed, and though Michael had held out long enough, he now voted with the majority.

Modernism may have been reeling, but Postmodernism was still (as Jencks meant it to be) an avant-garde. It had no large buildings to support the claims of its boosters, no proof of its therapeutic benefits, and its only recognized products were a few small commissions from Venturi, Moore, and a couple of others. Michael's Fargo-Moorhead Bridge seemed to augur great things to come, but it was no more than a pretty picture. In the halls of the professional establishment, Postmodernism seemed much ado about nothing.

In 1980 Michael was set to receive the Arnold W. Brunner Memorial Prize from the American Academy of Arts and Letters in New York. During the ceremony, he was to be called to the podium by the renowned Gordon Bunshaft, the SOM principal whose Pepsi-Cola Building had been the site of Michael's Rome interview. But just as the elder architect was dispensing the envelopes, he paused.

"A lot of things have changed," Bunshaft told the crowd. "We used to give prizes to architects for doing buildings. Now we give prizes to architects for drawing."[70]

Stunned as Michael was (to say nothing of the audience), Bunshaft's barb hit close to home: Postmodernism wasn't much more than yet another 1970s paper architecture. It had, however, scored one major victory. It had won the heart of Philip Johnson.

"The dean of American architecture," as he was invariably called, Johnson had been omnipresent in the field for more than forty years. It was Johnson who helped coin the term *International Style*, the title of the groundbreaking 1932 exhibition he curated with the historian Henry-Russell Hitchcock at MoMA; it was Johnson who, in his decades-long association with the museum—interrupted only by an infamous fascist interlude in the late 1930s—had done as much as anyone to advance the Modernist cause in America.[71] All this he was able to do thanks to a lucky confluence of extraordinary wealth (he was an heir to an aluminum fortune), excellent taste (he owned everything from Poussins to Warhols), and a genius for friendship backed up by immense personal charm. Already he had shown an adaptability that had seen his buildings change with the times, shifting gears more than once since the Mies-inflected elegance of his first and most famous project, the Glass House in New Canaan, Connecticut. The transparent pavilion that Johnson used as his country getaway had entered legend, along with its owner's wit: a lady visitor was reported to have said that she thought it very beautiful, but she could never live there. "Madame," Johnson replied, "I haven't asked you to."[72]

By the mid-1970s, Johnson had begun to feel that his work had grown unpalatably stale. He had been intrigued, in a noncommittal way, by Eisenman's abstruse theoretics and had penned an approving afterword to the second edition of *Five Architects*. But he needed something more pungent, more optically stimulating. He had always been a history buff with a penchant for classicism, and in 1978 he emerged as a fully formed Postmodernist, with the first serious commission for a large-scale building in the new style, the AT&T Building on Manhattan's Madison Avenue.

His overcoat thrown, Frank Lloyd Wright–like, over his shoulders, Johnson would appear on the cover of *Time* magazine, clutching a model of the masonry-clad tower with its distinctive, grandfather-clock broken pediment. But the building would take almost five years to complete, and in the meantime Johnson wanted to use his considerable clout to advance the cause of Postmodernism. He found his chance when he was approached to chair the selection committee for the Portland Public Service Building, a planned government office building in Portland, Oregon.

The project had already appeared on Michael's radar after a brief visit to the city to speak at Portland's local chapter of the American Institute of Architects. During a celebratory dinner following the talk, Michael found himself seated beside a local architect, Edward Wundram, who'd been agitating for Mayor Neil Goldschmidt to look beyond the Pacific Northwest and consider a national architect who could bring the planned municipal building to national attention. Turning to Michael, Wundram put it bluntly.

"What can we do to encourage somebody like you to do a competition for a city hall here in Portland?" he queried.[73]

"Ask," answered Michael.[74]

Johnson and Michael were friendly but not quite friends, sympathetic by architectural happenstance, though unalike in almost every other particular. "My feeling about Philip is he was a marvelous cheerleader for architecture," Michael said, though one "without any beliefs": flippancy was the flip side of the Johnson charisma, and at the regular summits he convened at Manhattan's Century Club, the privileged architect-invitees were expected to keep up a certain level of jousting repartee. Michael could dish as well as anyone, though with his sensitive nature he could rarely take, and at the black-tie soirees his host rarely seated him close to exchange barbed bon mots.[75] But Johnson had Peter Eisenman for that, and others; what he appreciated in Michael was his talent. When John DaSilva, Michael's future student, cold-called his illustrious New Canaan neighbor to ask him where he should go to school, Johnson replied with a question of his own: "Who is that young fellow at Princeton that is changing architecture right now?" That was all the advice Johnson felt the young man needed.[76]

With Johnson heading up the search, Michael had an ace in the hole, but the commission was far from clinched. The limited competition would see Michael pitted against a pair of major firms: Arthur Erickson Associates and Mitchell/Giurgola Architects. Mitchell/Giurgola's scheme, a large concrete donut, was significantly over budget, though that didn't appear to faze Romaldo Giurgola: over breakfast one morning, he told Michael that if the city couldn't pay, they didn't have to hire him. The one Michael worried about was Erickson. His proposal was stridently Modernist, a glass box on stilts with a plaza slipped under the elevated mass. Despite his recent PoMo conversion, Johnson had referred to the Canadian designer as "by far the greatest architect in Canada, and maybe the greatest on this continent"—high praise, indeed.[77] ("I didn't know if he meant it," Michael added.)[78]

Staking their bid on a bold statement, the Graves team sought to answer Mayor Goldschmidt's call for something that would bring a little Jane Jacobs–style street life

Philip Johnson and his circle, in Dallas for Johnson's AIA Gold Medal ceremony, 1978. Back row, left to right: Michael, Cesar Pelli, Charles Gwathmey, Peter Eisenman; front row: Frank Gehry, Charles Moore, Johnson, Stanley Tigerman, Robert A. M. Stern

back to downtown. The forty-thousand-square-foot site on Portland's Pioneer Square was a prime location, one that seemed to beg for a monument, but the Portland city government was famed for its fiscal conservatism and would be sticklers about the skimpy budget of $22,420,000: "Not a penny more nor a penny less was the mantra," recalled Karen Nichols.[79] Michael and his associates would have to thread the needle, finding a sweet spot between the audacious and the down-to-earth.

How they did it is laid bare in referential sketches and preparatory drawings as remarkable as anything the firm ever produced, bearing the traces of everything—from Cubism to Krierism—that shaped Michael in the 1970s. Portland would be the first instance of his mature Postmodernist work, but the process behind it testified to all the potential yet latent in his practice.

Keeping the facade as its subject, the design began with the assumption of vertical symmetry and of a corporeal hierarchy, with a thick base, a regular shaft, and a roof crowned by a decorative border. But this was no Krierian archetype: punctuated by round, square, and rectangular windows, rigged out with oriels and corbels and recesses, Michael's iterative drawings cast the elevation as a playground of forms, each motioning in a different direction, toward a different reading. Though freighted with classical elements, the appeal to anthropomorphism was so strong that the building might have had no easy typological classification. Seen together in the sketchbooks, the different versions of Portland appear to scuttle across the page like a swarm of mechanical insects [PLATE 30].

Reduced, for the purposes of the competition, to a more temperate outline, the scheme still preserved much of the madcap creativity that went into it. On the flanks,

Michael imagined billowing garlands atop oversize pilasters; on the northwestern face, a statue of "Lady Commerce" would swing dramatically; and high above, a team of little *aediculae*—shrines or huts, each one different—would dot the roof, as though the top of the building had been colonized by a tiny *trulli* village. Historical allusion, civic character, and human scale would all be present, a fulfillment of the Postmodernist ideal more picturesque than Venturi's "decorated sheds" and less facetious than Johnson's corporate clock case for AT&T.

With Johnson's sage counsel, the citizen jury opted for Michael Graves Architect's proposal by a vote of four to one. They had been given further encouragement by their technical advisers, who assured them that Graves's was the cheapest and the easiest to construct. He had kept most of his windows very small—a bonus during the 1970s energy crisis—and for all the exuberance of its exterior, the floor plan was reassuringly conventional. Johnson hailed the decision, announcing that the new Portland Building "would be a landmark from inception, watched and studied by the public as well as architects around the world."[80] All Portland had to do was build it.

VII

THE TOWER

THE DAY AFTER Michael Graves Architect's winning bid for the Portland Building was announced, the public began to weigh in—heavily. Newspaper writers called the design "a fortress," "ominous and inhumane"; letter writers lambasted it as "an experiment in architectural fad" and "an affront."[1]

That was just for starters. All through the spring of 1980, architecture's Battle of Portland raged on, a spat that would pit architect against architect, Portlander against Portlander. The citizen jury would have to be seconded by a city council vote, and the debate that ensued drew in two mayors, the national media, and the architecture community on both coasts, becoming a referendum on Michael's design philosophy and Postmodernism as a whole.

Leading the charge was the elder statesman of Portland architecture, the man who had all but single-handedly established the Modernist tradition in the Pacific Northwest: Pietro Belluschi. The eighty-one-year-old Belluschi took dead aim at the Graves scheme in a case made directly to the city council, savaging the design as "a large jukebox or beribboned Christmas gift," rife with "visual chaos."[2] Belluschi and Johnson had a long-running enmity dating back several decades, and in Michael's proposal Belluschi saw an incursion onto his home turf by the dastardly easterner.

He wasn't far wrong: Johnson had tipped the scales for Michael from the outset, bowling over the citizen jurors during an elegant luncheon in his Manhattan offices, where he'd praised the Postmodernist scheme as a radical break that could put Portland on the design-world map. (He took no payment for his advisory post, requesting only a couple of the Northwest's famous Chinook salmon.) The Johnson name had carried the project thus far, but in the chambers of Portland's government, Michael had only one real friend—his old Cincinnati acquaintance Robert Frasca, then practicing in Oregon. The Graves proposal was innovative and fresh, Frasca told the council, and such flaws as it had were the inevitable outgrowth of a flawed brief. "If the materials aren't the best," he averred, "neither is the budget."[3]

Final perspectival
of the Portland
Building as
originally sub-
mitted for the
competition,
1980

Portland's
incommodious
lobby, the
source of much
complaint
from visitors
and employees

The financial lid that had been placed on the project had been an issue from the start. Edward Wundram—also pulling for the Graves side—had cautioned Michael early to stay within the budget, and while the tip had been essential to the firm's success, it was also the cause of much of the public outcry; in the eyes of many, the only thing recommending Michael's scheme was its lowball estimate. For all the furor over the design's aesthetic merit, the root problem was understood to be the penny-ante price tag insisted upon, with miserly resolve, by City Commissioner Frank Ivancie. Former mayor Neil Goldschmidt was no longer in a position to inveigle on the side of quality, having left Portland to join the Carter administration, and his replacement, Connie McCready, was struggling just to keep up with the byzantine process.

Muddying things further, the city council proceeded to make demands that would increase the cost of Michael's proposal while attempting to offset these by corralling its more outré accessories. The garlands would have to come off, but the windows could be (slightly) larger; the exterior walls would have to be built of sturdy concrete instead of the cheaper stucco Michael had specified, and the lobby's grand staircase would have to go. Greater provisions would have to be made for disabled access. The rooftop *aediculae* were nixed. In an additional twist, as Graves and company rushed to make these changes for a second-round review, they found they would not be alone. Arthur Erickson's firm would have another shot as well, retooling its high-Modernist box so that the city of Portland could continue mulling its stylistic options.

"Threats of a suit and countersuits" followed, reports the historian Meredith Clausen.[4] Michael's contractor complained that Erickson's plan had fallen short of the brief, while Erickson's contractor said the same of the Graves submission. The standoff culminated in a second presentation before the city council, and while Michael entered the room with a definite advantage, he needed to make the case for a design that, notwithstanding Postmodernism's notional populism, didn't seem terribly popular. Warming to his theme, Michael explained that American architecture was embroiled in an argument—

an argument…about the direction of architecture. You find yourselves very interestingly in the middle of it. You find yourselves having to choose between schemes that represent on the one hand the human attitude, the way we see ourselves represented in our buildings, or on the other hand, the craft or traditions of making the building. It's your choice. We feel, however, that to give the city its legibility, to give comprehension to the park and understanding of this particular and rather glorious site…we have an enormous opportunity here to not only say something about city government, but to say something about any building in the city.

His address, wrote Clausen, "was met by stunned silence."[5] The local politicos still didn't understand it, but they were evidently impressed by the strength of Michael's conviction. Moreover, they had an impatient Ivancie standing over them, eager to start work as soon as possible in order to lock in a favorable interest rate. After winning the original contest by the near-unanimous vote of the citizen jury, the commission was awarded to Michael effectively by default: construction on the Graves design started in Pioneer Square in July 1980, without the city council having ever bothered to declare an official winner.

SHORTLY AFTER PORTLAND was completed, Michael recalled attending the AIA national convention in New Orleans. The event organizers had printed up festive buttons with a picture of his building on them, and as a form of protest some of the membership had printed up buttons of their own that read "I DON'T DIG GRAVES."[6]

Rarely in the history of American architecture has a building been met simultaneously with such cacophonous opprobrium and acclaim. An in-flight magazine on a major airline put it on the cover: "It's the Building of the Future," the headline read.[7] Frank Ivancie—now Mayor Ivancie, having bested McCready in the 1980 election—reportedly declared that the building would be "Portland's Eiffel Tower."[8] All three national networks descended upon the city for the building's opening in 1982, and Michael appeared on all of them, surrounded by baton-twirling majorettes and a festive balloon launch. "Finally," he declared from the podium, "architecture has come home."[9]

For the Postmodernists and their sympathizers, the building's debut was a vindication. Charles Jencks hailed it as "the first major monument of Postmodernism," conclusive evidence that "one can build with art, ornament, and symbolism on a grand scale, and in a language the inhabitants understand."[10] The scholars Marvin Trachtenberg and Isabelle Hyman would laud it—"a truly civic building, permeated with dignity, scale, color, vitality."[11] And the *New York Times*'s Paul Goldberger, who had cottoned to the urbanist aspirations of the Postmodernist camp, greeted it with applause, calling it "a beacon, illuminating the distance we have come from the moment when the steel-and-glass vocabulary of orthodox modern architecture seemed the only way in which to make a large, public building."[12] Even before its unveiling, Goldberger had already baptized Michael as "the most original voice that American architecture has produced in some time."[13]

The doubters were equally outspoken. "Why is this better than a Glass Box?" asked *Architectural Record*'s Douglas Brenner. "For all the messages it was meant to convey, the Portland Building remains eerily mute."[14] The distinguished architectural publication *Skyline* ran a special issue on the project, lifted mostly from an IAUS symposium during which Portland came in for abuse from Alan Colquhoun, Kurt Forster, and, stunningly, Philip Johnson, who pronounced himself "disappointed."[15] Figures from the mainstream press were even less restrained: "a rather condescending exercise performed by a sophisticated academic on a culturally average community," wrote *Newsweek*'s Carter Wiseman; *Time*'s Wolf von Eckardt ripped the project as "dangerous Pop surrealism."[16]

More damning were the reviews from the projects' users, the municipal employees of Portland. From day one, they complained that the low-ceilinged interiors and small windows made for a substandard office environment. Workers reported getting headaches and feeling distracted by the drone from the building mechanicals, and they groused about the narrow and dimly lit ground-floor lobby, which had to be renovated only a couple of years after the building opened. Ivancie finally relented on the garlands, which were added to the exterior in a flattened appliqué of glass and concrete, and in 1985 the statue over the door—created by the artist Raymond Kaskey, its title changed by Michael from the prosaic *Lady Commerce* to the more poetic *Portlandia* (whence the popular television show)—was finally hoisted into place [**PLATE 31**]. But while local Portlanders have long appreciated the building's attempt to stand out in the streetscape, they've never quite made it their own. Over the past three decades, with the building increasingly suffering from structural failures and general decay, the city has continually vacillated between restoring it and demolishing it.

Looking back, Michael said, "The negativity was greater than I thought it would be."[17] His skin always had been somewhat permeable, and the vociferousness of the project's detractors did not go unnoticed. Until the end of his life Michael voiced understandable ambivalence toward his most famous built work, wishing that the windows had been larger, the swags more detailed. Yet there were so many other parties to blame: the client; the brief; Emery Roth & Sons, the venerable New York firm that partnered with the Graves office as architects of record to counterbalance the Princetonians' perceived lack of experience. Michael felt a good measure of pride in what he believed to be Portland's successes, but with so many other chefs in the kitchen, he could ascribe its obvious failures to other people's mistakes—and this, the building's alibi, was to be decisive in what followed.

Because this time, the criticism did not send Michael back to the drawing board. In his preparatory drawings for Portland, he had rolled together his love of the classical, his belief in the empathic power of anthropomorphic forms, and his artistic infatuation with pictorial surface. If the result had fallen short, he would get it right next time, and his subsequent work would be a matter of fine-tuning, not abandoning, the rhetoric of Portland. And he could now afford to do that on a grander scale than he'd ever imagined: he now had a foot in the door as a designer of large-scale buildings, and for all its critics the Portland project had won him at least as many admirers, not a few of them quite influential.

Whatever people thought about Michael Graves, they were definitely thinking about him. He recalled reading an unscientific poll in 1982 that asked average Americans which three architects they knew by name. First place went, predictably, to Frank Lloyd Wright; third went to I. M. Pei, the Chinese American architect who had recently completed an extension to the National Gallery in Washington, DC. In between them was Michael Graves.[18]

ARCHITECTURE WAGS WOULD begin to joke about "the Gravesy train."[19]

Michael's sudden celebrity touched off a flood of commissions that stunned seasoned architecture watchers. In part it was a happy coincidence: in 1983, after nearly a decade of episodic recessions, the national economy roared back to life, most especially (thanks to the regulatory and tax rollbacks of the Reagan administration) the real estate sector, which swiftly went into overdrive. Michael had chosen a good time to become famous, and in a decade that loved to buy, there were more things for an architect to sell than ever before.

That said, the seeds of Michael's commercial success had been planted earlier. Hustling to keep the roof over his associates' heads back in Princeton (sometimes for reasons unrelated to finance: they were booted out of one office for playing loud music), Michael had learned early how to package his architectural enthusiasms for public consumption.[20] In 1979 his architectural drawings had been the subject of a major exhibition at Max Protetch Gallery in Manhattan, the first solo show at what would become the design world's primary beachhead in the surging 1980s art market. Protetch had seized on an emerging vogue for architectural drawings then taking hold in New York, a by-product of MoMA's spectacular *The Architecture of the École des Beaux Arts* exhibition in 1975, as well as a 1977 show on architectural renderings at the Architectural League of New York, which featured Michael's own work. His colorful drawings, on his hallmark yellow paper, had more than a whiff of Beaux Arts glamour about them, and the Protetch show was a smashing success, stirring up some much-needed media buzz for Michael's practice (and a little cash in the bargain). The lesson—that there were more ways to reach his audience than just building buildings—was one Michael had not failed to learn.

Nor was that his only early foray into the popular marketplace. Among Fargo-Moorhead's most ardent admirers was the critic Martin Filler, who was on the staff of *Progressive Architecture* at the time the bridge proposal won the magazine's self-titled award. In his role as the publication's interior design editor, Filler was contacted in 1978 by the former CEO of the Knoll furniture company, Bobby

Cadwallader, who was planning to launch a new high-end interiors firm. Cadwallader was looking for an architect to create the showrooms for his incipient contract furniture brand, and with his swashbuckling if abrasive attitude (Filler remembered him once hurling a choice epithet at Julian Niccolini, the Italian co-owner of Manhattan's Four Seasons restaurant), the businessman, Filler thought, might be amenable to trying his luck on an untested young designer with a daring new aesthetic. "I just said, 'Michael,'" recalled Filler.[21]

An amalgam of Cleveland-based Hauserman Inc. and a recently acquired Canadian subsidiary, Cadwallader's new venture would be called Sunar-Hauserman Inc., and it had set its sights on besting the major manufacturers such as Knoll that had been dominating the furniture trade for years.[22] Sunar-Hauserman's business plan called for a quick rollout, with as many as five locations (originally titled either Sunar or Hauserman) to open across the country in the space of about three years. When Cadwallader approached Michael regarding the showroom commission, he jumped at the chance, recognizing it as an opportunity to expand his office's reach.

"We've never had so much fun devising plans," said Michael.[23] Solidifying their axial, symmetrical approach to space making, the firm designed interiors—beginning in 1979, with a temporary space in Manhattan—that were a snapshot of Postmodernism in its infancy [PLATE 32]. In the several installations that followed, each room was a brightly lit, chamber-like theater. The hallways were devised as long colonnaded enfilades ending in trompe l'oeil murals; the original New York space featured the company's fabrics slung like wisteria over makeshift pergolas made from large paper tubes painted pale terracotta. The budget was small, but Michael and his associates were accustomed to working on a shoestring, and they understood quickly that the showrooms had struck a chord. On first seeing them, the company's marketing director exclaimed to Michael, "Finally I have something to write about! Not just black, white, and gray."[24]

Most of the articles on display in the showrooms were by recognized figures with years of experience designing furniture. But in his negotiations with Cadwallader, Michael had consented to design the showrooms on the condition that Sunar would allow him to create furniture as well. Cadwallader consented, and, pleased by the showrooms' reception, he commissioned Michael to create a small line of seating for the brand: maple-clad, thickly upholstered chairs, boxier renditions of the lounges that Michael had been collecting of late. The Graves team had designed a few small fixtures for private projects, including a series of rugs, lamps, and tables for the Plocek House, as well as rugs for the V'soske brand in 1979. The Sunar chairs, however, represented the team's first outing in the rough-and-tumble arena of commercial furniture design.

It was something Michael had long dreamed of. Among the unintentional side effects of the Modernist hegemony in architecture was that furniture design had been

Michael Graves
Architect's
contribution
to the "Strada
Novissima" at
the 1980 Venice
Biennale of
Architecture

partially deleted from the remit of architects. With large corporate firms like Gordon Bunshaft's SOM busily peopling the landscape with glass towers, the furniture that filled those towers was left to companies such as Knoll, working with designers specializing in Modernist interiors—such as George Nelson, Michael's former boss. This ran counter to the model of practice advanced by the founders of Modernism itself: as Michael noted, "Corb, Eames, Saarinen, Wright—all of them did furniture, and their own interiors for their buildings."[25] The Bauhaus in particular had posited the objective of "total architecture," in Gropius's phrase, whereby design and industry would work hand in hand to create the ideal environment for modern life.[26] Postmodernist though he now was, Michael was drawn to that Modernist model, and he used Sunar as his entrée.

The chair sold poorly, but the showrooms touched off a minor media bonanza. In 1981 Michael was named Designer of the Year by *Interiors* magazine, which devoted a two-page spread to his proposal for a "prototypical PoMo apartment," replete with rugs and tables and chairs along the same lines as his Sunar work. None of the pictured products went into production, but the story provided further evidence that Postmodernism was speedily gaining the heights of the American design scene.

In Europe, meanwhile, its ascent was no less vertiginous—or controversial. Practitioners like O. M. Ungers in Germany and James Stirling in the United Kingdom had helped it proliferate across the Continent, against steady political and architectural headwinds. In particular in Italy, which had clawed its way back from postwar ruin by remaking itself as a producer of ultramodern consumer products, the break with Modernist principles represented a nervy and possibly risky disruption.

That wasn't stopping Italian designers. *La presenza del passato* (The Presence of the Past) was the theme of the 1980 International Architecture Exhibition at the Venice Architecture Biennale, the first and still most celebrated edition of what has since become the most important architecture show in the world. Curated by Paolo Portoghesi, its highlight was the Strada Novissima, an imaginary street composed of fake fronts, each designed by a different architect. Portoghesi, an architect and historian known for mixing his métiers, worked alongside an advisory board that included Michael's critical champion Charles Jencks, and together they assembled a who's who of Postmodernism's leading figures, among them Robert Venturi, Stanley Tigerman, Léon Krier, Aldo Rossi—and Michael, who put together a minimal ensemble from his new kit of parts: twin columns supporting a curved pediment with a Roman lattice window above.

Also present at the fair was the innovative design collective Alchimia and its most outstanding figure, Ettore Sottsass. His name had already become synonymous with the flamboyant Postmodernist style in Italy, and before the year was out Sottsass broke with Alchimia to establish a new collaborative outfit, Memphis, with the goal of making furniture that could harness the burgeoning PoMo zeitgeist—and, he hoped, cash in on it. In Michael's work, he saw a way to do just that.

The Milan-based Sottsass and his Memphis Group invited the Graves team to join their new stable of designers; in 1981 their first collection would debut during Milan's gargantuan Salone del Mobile, and the line for the opening-night party stretched around the block.[27] Michael's main contribution, along with a bed of comparable character, was a dressing table [**PLATE 33**]. Faced in bird's-eye maple, studded with Christmas-style bulbs, and offset with globe lamps and chrome details, it combined Art Deco glam with an elegance that recalled the work of the Viennese designer Josef Hoffmann (a Graves favorite, one whose influence would become more and more essential).

The vanity was everything Michael's buildings were, only more so—a vertical hodgepodge of mixed geometries, completely frontal in attitude, reflecting the symmetry and order of the human body. It was even more effective, in some senses, than his buildings, since its smaller size made it easier to understand in a picture. At a time when garish music videos, colorful advertisements, and glossy magazine covers were shaping public taste as never before, Michael's pictorial mastery helped make his Postmodernist products the image of the movement.

SIMILARLY SMITTEN WITH what he'd seen of Michael's work in Venice was Sottsass's former Alchimia partner, Alessandro Mendini, who had recently been engaged on a unique commercial project. Mendini had been drafted by Italian kitchenware magnate Alberto Alessi to assemble a list of architects for a pilot program imagined as an irreverent mash-up—in true Postmodernist fashion—of urbanism and consumerism. A product line to be called Tea and Coffee Piazza, the project would challenge architects to use the space of a simple coffee tray to create a sort of idealized town in miniature, with creamer, sugar bowl, coffeepot, and teapot standing in for city buildings. From the Venice Biennale, Venturi, Rossi, Tigerman, and Graves were all brought on board, and their limited-edition services were brought to market over the next three years. Mendini felt that Michael would bring "a little oxygenation," recalled Alessi, "new inspiration, new ways of expression." Keen to add some pizzazz to his august family brand, Alessi never intended these "oxygenating" designs for mass production, seeing them only as promotional objets d'art for the serious collector and setting a price point of around $12,000.[28]

Little surprise, then, that many of the sets remain unsold even thirty-plus years later. But Michael's Piazza did relatively well, with forty of them doing actual duty at buyers' breakfast tables (or at least sitting behind vitrines in museums). Four roughly cubic volumes, identically clad in faintly columnar metal fluting and accented with festive turquoise balls, the traytop village is a stylistic mix of Josef Hoffmann and Deco, with a little anthropomorphism thrown in for good measure. Alessi liked what he saw, and at Mendini's and Sottsass's urging, he decided to bring Michael back— alone, save for Rossi, among the Piazza collaborators—for a bigger commission.

In the spring of 1984, the product maker gave him a short, seemingly undemanding brief. The company then had one teakettle in its catalog, an industrial-looking bronze and chrome model by the German designer Richard Sapper. Alessi wanted to see what Michael could do, given the same parameters—namely, his design would have to be reasonably cheap to produce, boil water as fast or faster than anything on the market, and make a distinctive whistle when it steamed, just as Sapper's did.

And then, Michael remembered, Alessi added one more stipulation.

"Make it *American*," he said.[29]

"I remember," said Alessi years later, "when I opened the first pack sent by Michael's office with the rough prototype of his kettle. We were very surprised by what we were handling in our hands."[30]

What Alessi beheld was a rounded pyramid in stainless steel, with a handle projecting in a three-quarters circle from one side and a conical spout popping jauntily from the other. These three basic geometries were complemented by three decorative details: a blue polyamide handle cover, a black knob atop the lid, and a red bird over the spout, attached by a hinge. The initial impression was more than a little absurd. The geometries were so broad, the handle cover so fat, the bird so cartoonish, that it seemed as though each element had been fashioned independently of the others.

Which, in a sense, they were—except that they combined to make a series of cogent statements about what a teakettle is meant to do. "If I make a handle blue," Michael said, "I'm suggesting subliminally that it's cool, not hot. If I make the bird red, I'm also saying it's hot: don't touch it."[31] In architectural terms, the Alessi 9093 kettle was an instance of Ledoux's *architecture parlante* applied to a commercially available household item [PLATES 34 AND 35].

Setting eyes on it for the first time, Ettore Sottsass was astounded. "You must have a great courage as a designer to design something like this," he told Alessi. It was not, perhaps, meant as a compliment.[32]

But Alessi believed the design was salable, and his faith was not misplaced. The 9093 teakettle by Michael Graves landed in stores in Europe and the United States in 1985 and was expected to be on the shelf for two to three years. The team behind it realized they had a phenomenon on their hands when it was still selling briskly five years later; shortly after 1990 it passed the one million sales mark. Originally pegged at $65—at a time when teakettles were sold for less than half that—demand nonetheless held up even as the Alessi company incrementally raised the price. Today, retailing at $190, the 9093 is still in production and well on its way to two million total units, selling about seventy thousand a year. Alberto Alessi's only regret was asking Michael to make the bird spout removable. "It's the most stolen part," he said. "People pass by the shelves, and they grab it."[33]

NEW FIRM ASSOCIATE (later partner) Donald Strum joined the Graves office in 1983, and he watched as the Alessi commission progressed from Michael's early sketches, originally with a squared-off handle, through rough models hacked out of wood, until the day the first complete prototype arrived at the office. "Michael was circling around the room looking at the teakettle from all different angles and vantage points," Strum recalled. One of Michael's Biedermeier pieces, a large wall mirror, was hung nearby, and Strum watched as Michael looked at the kettle's reflection, seeing it pictured in the ornate, tarnished frame.

The moment felt charged, and the room was silent. At last Strum turned to Michael. "The office is getting commission after commission," he said, "and here you are, staring at your first industrialized product. What are you thinking at this very moment?"

Michael's response said it all. In a hoarse whisper, he exclaimed: "*Motherfucker.*"[34]

A little fist pumping was warranted. The firm was riding high, as Postmodernism continued to make headlines. In 1981 the muckraker-novelist Tom Wolfe published *From Bauhaus to Our House*, a windy jeremiad on what the white-suited Southerner deemed the baleful blandness of Modernism. Why, he wondered, had the American people wished upon themselves an architecture that spoke of nothing? "They look up at the barefaced buildings they have bought," he wrote, "and they can't figure it out themselves."[35] It was the very case the Grays had been making for more than a decade, but coming from the great tribune of America's counter-counterculture, it galvanized public sentiment. The book did not, notably, offer much endorsement for the Postmodernist alternative, but then Michael, who knew Wolfe from Philip Johnson's tony club evenings, didn't much endorse him, either. "I have a problem with people who dress—like *that*," he once said.[36]

Michael often had a problem with how people dressed and was known to offer unsolicited advice on the subject. (Robert A. M. Stern remembered him once casting a jaundiced eye over a Polo tweed suit being worn by Charles Gwathmey, declaring simply, "Too much Ralph.")[37] Now, with the wind at his back professionally, Michael could at last afford to live up to his sartorial standards. In his Armani jackets, patterned silk scarves, and lightly colored shirts open as far as a seemly second button, he was a dedicated follower of fashion, with a trim figure maintained not through exercise—even if he'd been disposed, his work schedule wouldn't have allowed it— but through his occasionally severe dieting, a regimen made easier by a deathly aversion to garlic, onions, and spices of any kind. On a visit to London to meet his Postmodernist compatriot Charles Jencks, Michael was greeted by his hosts with a traditional English meal of onion-packed steak and kidney pie. "He was going to die," recalled Karen Nichols.[38]

Not just his stomach (better adapted, it might be said, to Indy than to Italy), but Michael's constitution in general was always finicky. In particular he was prey to sinus infections, minor but persistent. None of this would slow him down, however, as he barreled headlong into the prime of his life.

SINCE THE EARLY 1970s, Michael had been an occasional visitor to Los Angeles. The UCLA School of Architecture and Urban Design had been the venue for the onstage matchup between the Whites and the Grays in 1974, and Michael had been coming back to lecture ever since. He had not made many connections in the local architecture community—had failed, really, to take stock among the architects of the

West Coast of an emerging third tendency—and though he had enjoyed teaching at UCLA, he spurned an offer to succeed Charles Moore as head of the school, reportedly saying that he "couldn't teach at a school whose library is smaller than mine."[39]

The most meaningful relationship he developed in California was a personal one. Kitty Hawks was the daughter of Howard Hawks—the acclaimed Hollywood director of such films as *Scarface* and *The Big Sleep*—and his second wife, the glamorous socialite Slim Keith, known (with Babe Paley) as one of the thinly veiled subjects of Truman Capote's unfinished novel *Answered Prayers*. Michael and Kitty met in or around 1980, while she was enrolled in the UCLA program, their introduction effected during a lunch that was, as Charles Jencks recalled, a "setup" orchestrated by him.[40] They swiftly became seriously involved, and she agreed to come back East with Michael and take up residence in the Warehouse. "It was more of an intellectual exercise than a place of physical comfort," she remarked. "Which sort of sums up Michael."[41]

Spanning some five years, Michael and Kitty's relationship was founded on their shared passion for architecture and culture. Kitty subsequently launched a successful interior design practice, and in their time together, the two traveled frequently to attend building openings and lectures, becoming, in a discreet way, an early-1980s power couple. Kitty was quickly integrated into Michael's professional set, making friends with Meier and Eisenman; she, in turn, insinuated Michael into the Los Angeles design scene, introducing him to Eric Owen Moss and another architect a few years older than Michael, Frank O. Gehry, in those days still favoring his middle initial.

Courtesy of Kitty, Michael also came into contact with a few people outside his usual social ken, among them the actress Candice Bergen and her good friend the writer and satirist Fran Lebowitz. For reasons that neither of them could quite account for, Michael and Lebowitz—the mild-mannered midwestern aesthete and the chain-smoking Jewish wit—hit it off, and soon they and Kitty had formed a small clique, spending weekends together at the Shelter Island house that Bergen shared with her husband, the film director Louis Malle. An unlikely admixture of Hollywood, Manhattan, and the Ivy League, Michael's new milieu was typical of a decade that saw him moving in very rarefied circles indeed.

He designed stage sets for the Joffrey Ballet [**PLATE 36**], a trophy for *GQ* magazine's annual award, a shopping bag for Bloomingdale's. He designed the Clos Pegase Winery in California's Napa Valley, a carriage house renovation in Manhattan for a Vanderbilt heir, and a sweeping master plan (unrealized) for a resort complex in Galveston, Texas, comprising twelve towers and dozens of smaller condominiums arrayed in a terrace like the eighteenth-century Royal Crescent in Bath, England.

He was invited to the Ronald Reagan White House on the occasion of a royal visit from Queen Elizabeth II, and he and Kitty—who was acquainted with the Reagans

Michael by the
kitchen door of
the Warehouse,
1981

through her mother—were conducted into the Blue Room after dinner for a private interview with the First Lady. Welcoming them in, Nancy Reagan showed them the official presidential collection of china, stemware, and flatware, and told Michael she thought that one of the Alessi Piazza services would make a beautiful addition. Since the Reagans couldn't accept the gift personally, it would have to be donated by Alessi through official diplomatic channels, and Michael said he would ask Alberto Alessi himself. When he did so, however, his client made his feelings on the subject very plain. "Tell Mrs. Reagan," he said in Italian, "fuck you."[42]

Michael related this story at lectures for several years (usually capping it off with the traditional Italian arm gesture) until he began receiving angry letters from Republican audience members. One person who didn't object, when she heard the anecdote years later, was Nancy Reagan. "She had a sense of humor," Michael remembered, though he still voted against her husband twice.[43]

He created original drawings for a special illustrated edition of F. Scott Fitzgerald's *The Great Gatsby*—spare vignettes in pencil of Gatsby's mansion and motorcars—and a special installation for the gallerist Leo Castelli—a pair of archaic follies—and he took on a commission from the fashion designer Diane von Furstenberg [**PLATE 39**], whose career was then caught in a temporary trough.[44] Von Furstenberg was looking to relaunch her collection with a new storefront diagonal to Manhattan's Plaza Hotel. Her instructions to Michael, written out on a single three-by-five note card, were among Michael's all-time favorite briefs, less a programmatic laundry list than an emotional wish list.

"Make it a little shrine to Venus," she told him. "Make it a place where a woman can walk in and dream and fantasize, and for a man who wants to indulge her."[45]

The firm obliged with a gracious, muted interior and a facade topped by the figure of a gold-leaf-covered loving cup, still visible from the street long after the designer (whose career shortly picked up again) moved to larger quarters.

Riding the lecture circuit, Michael made regular hops over to England—where he created a room for Charles Jencks's private home [**PLATE 40**]—as well as to France and Italy. He also began a years-long string of visits to Japan, whose real estate market was then, like America's, in full boom. While there he befriended the fashion designer Issey Miyake, known for his loose-fitting but meticulously crafted garb for men and women.

Miyake invited Michael to one of his Paris fashion shows, an over-the-top spectacle featuring enormous swimming pools into which the wedding dress–clad models jumped following their stroll down the catwalk. Later, the architect attended a dinner—small, colorful plates of nouvelle cuisine—as Miyake's guest and was delighted to find himself seated beside a lovely young woman who turned out to be his host's fabric specialist.

In the middle of the dinner, Miyake walked over to Michael's dinner companion and presented her with a small box: "A thank-you present," he said. Inside was a model car, a red Mercedes convertible.

"Why is he giving me a toy car?" asked the fabric specialist.

"He's isn't," Michael explained. "He's giving you a *car*."[46]

There were moments like these when the spirit of the times seemed to coalesce around him, and Michael savored them. But there were other moments—and they accounted for the majority—when Michael was all but inured to everything save for his work.

Looking back, he said, "The '60s, the '70s, the '80s, they all bleed into each other. I'm not a good one to say, 'The '80s were like this.'"[47] The same years that witnessed the rise of Michael's "figurative architecture," as he called it in his first full monograph, also witnessed a return to figuration in contemporary art (as in the portraiture of Robert Longo and Julian Schnabel) and a renewed interest in classical counter-point in music (as in the compositions of Philip Glass) and in formal traditions in poetry (as in the historical gamesmanship of Kenneth Koch and John Ashbery).[48] Yet none of this much interested Michael, who continued to practice a Postmodernism of one. "The people who interested me," he would say, "were the people who could say, 'Build a building for me.'"[49]

SUCH PEOPLE WERE now beating a path to his door. One week in the summer of 1981, Michael's staff was told to drop everything and spruce up the office in prepara-tion for a most important meeting. Steven Harris, Karen Nichols, and Julie Hansel-mann—the Hanselmanns' youngest daughter, who had come to work and study with Michael in Princeton—repainted all the floors, put in new millwork, and even installed a temporary fountain in the office lobby. "Everything had to be spick-and-span," recalled Hanselmann.[50] The Whitney Museum of American Art was coming to call.

The venerable storehouse for American art had long outgrown its home, the clunky yet endearing stack of granite-faced concrete on Madison Avenue designed by Marcel Breuer in 1966. Circulation problems were rife in the aging structure; only a small percentage of the permanent collection could be displayed; and the Whitney was losing ground to its Midtown competitor, MoMA, which was undertaking a bold new capital improvement under the direction of Cesar Pelli. Searching to build their way out (or up), the Whitney trustees and Director Thomas N. Armstrong III were conducting interviews with a handful of firms over the course of six months, and Michael Graves Architect (as well as Gwathmey Siegel and Robert Venturi and Denise Scott Brown) had made the short list.

The preliminary sit-down with the Whitney group had taken place at the Ware-house; Nichols had thrown together a lunch of pasta primavera (no garlic, of course), and the whole affair had come off without a hitch. Now the would-be clients were returning for seconds. The museum's most illustrious, most influential board mem-ber, the billionaire shopping-mall developer A. Alfred Taubman, flew in to the meet-ing from Detroit via Princeton's municipal airport. The scrappy Graves team greeted him and his colleagues with homemade muffins.[51]

"Michael understood how important it was," recalled Hanselmann.[52] To date Michael's only executed museum work was the less-than-satisfactory Union County Nature and Science Museum, and though he still had a relationship with the Newark Museum, his successive proposals had led to only one realized project, a small installation for the children's art workshop. Newark would turn to the firm for more substantive work in the following years—but Newark was not the Whitney.

This was a chance for Michael to leave his imprimatur on the New York streetscape and on one of the city's and the country's most venerated cultural institutions.

No specific scheme had to be put before the Whitney board, no definite plan sketched out. The trustees simply wanted to test the waters with their prospective designer. Michael was his usual, expansive self, zeroing in on the museum's dilemma —its addition had to show deference both to the Modernist Breuer and to the older buildings surrounding it, and while it had acquired the neighboring row houses, it would still be difficult to accommodate the museum's spatial needs on-site. As he considered the problem, his associates put on a brave show of professionalism: when the Whitney asked who could negotiate a contract, Nichols confidently declared that she would take it in hand, despite having no idea whatsoever how to do it.[53]

In October the Whitney made its decision. As Armstrong told the press,

> We didn't go to an architect of Breuer's generation, nor to one who had done building designs in New York. We wanted an architect who would try to make the building as important a contribution to architecture as Breuer made with the old. It's very exciting, because we don't know what the solution will be."[54]

Their architects didn't know what the solution would be, either. Michael and the team had won the commission, but it would be nearly four years before they had something to present to the public. That was according to schedule, of course, as the Whitney understood it would take them at least that long to come up with a plan that worked. It would, in fact, take them much longer than that.

INSTITUTIONAL COMMISSIONS OFTEN move slowly; private ones, however, can race forward at a bracing clip, provided the client is properly motivated. Michael had had very few such clients, and even when he did (the Snydermans, the Crooks, himself at the Warehouse), his projects seemed to run up against unforeseen obstacles with a frequency that made him feel snakebit. Somewhere, there had to be people with both the will and the wallet to make a building that lived up to the promise of his drawings.

It was perhaps only a matter of time before Michael, aswim in the much larger client pool of 1980s, met people like Wendell Cherry and David A. Jones, a pair of businessmen from Louisville, Kentucky.

"Wendell," recalled Jones, "was more like a brother." Cherry and Jones had gone into business together as Extendicare Inc. in 1961, opening a single Louisville nursing home. Within a decade they were the largest operators of such facilities in the nation, and by the late 1970s they had moved forcefully into the hospital marketplace while taking on a new name: Humana. Growing at the pace of a hospital a month, the company was a juggernaut, and in need of a new Louisville corporate headquarters commensurate with its growing stature in the industry.[55]

The two executives decided with characteristic brio to get the very best to build it for them, requesting proposals from a few select designers—starting with Philip Johnson. They wanted "a symbol for the company," Jones told Johnson. The architect was tempted, but his workload, to say nothing of his self-esteem, made him disinclined to compete with other designers. Instead, Johnson told them, "There's a young architect named Graves." He suggested they bring Michael into the fold.[56]

Intending to stay close to home, Humana had bought a site at the corner of West Main Street just across South Fifth from its existing offices in the First National Bank Tower, a forty-story skyscraper designed by Wallace K. Harrison and his partner, Max Abramovitz (Michael's onetime dinner companion in Bologna). The design saw the famously adaptable duo working in a Miesian vein, their building a solid black shaft whose debt to the German *Baumeister* was underscored by another structure on the other side of Main: the American Life Building, an actual Mies project completed just after his death in 1969. The mid-rise pavilion, set back from the street on a plaza-decked plinth, was not Mies's finest work, and the two standoffish structures had done nothing to reverse—and might possibly have exacerbated—a long decline in the area that made Humana's decision to stay a fairly courageous one. Whiskey Row, as the strip was called, was then a corridor of mostly semidefunct bourbon distilleries, and many of its stately brick buildings either were unoccupied or had been demolished.

The latter fate had befallen the previous occupant of Humana's new lot, which abutted a still-standing specimen and a Beaux Arts–ish former bank. Accordingly, Michael's design for the $60 million project began by examining this mixed-up contextual combination—flush with two historical structures to the south and west, diagonal to a Mies building, and directly opposite a Mies knockoff. Given his long-standing antipathy for the severe, hard-edged Modernism he'd learned at Cincinnati, it would have been easy enough for Michael to have simply made his Humana design an exuberant riposte to Mies, an affirmation of the old against the new. Instead, he sought a way to mediate among all of the competing architectural forces at hand: a tower serious enough to stand shoulder to shoulder with Harrison and Abramovitz's, as open to the public as Mies's plaza, and with the texture and classical touches of the historical cast-iron mercantile buildings.

He was facing off against a mixed bag of different solutions. Chicago's Helmut Jahn proposed a glittering, multifaceted ensemble of triangular glass; London-based Norman Foster suggested a round turret with a diamond-grid facade, set off by a slender steel spire. The two other competitors, Ulrich Franzen and Cesar Pelli, put forward a kind of PoMo Lite, one design horseshoe-shaped with a circular oculus at the top, and the other octagonal and capped by a reflective roof. "Wendell and I sat down and wrote out a list of four of the five," recalled Jones. Out of the other's view, each partner jotted down their preferred proposals from most to least favored and then compared lists. Some of their selections were different, but not the first. "We both agreed on Michael," said Jones.[57]

"They had the money," Michael recalled, "and it wasn't fifty dollars per square foot."[58] Michael knew his clients would see the $60 million project through. After the competition had been won, he altered the building's facade arrangements, changing the south front to give it a curved central bay so that it would not appear to turn its back on the city; the change would also allow for a series of employee break rooms located behind the elevator core. But for the next two and a half years he largely kept his distance from goings-on in Louisville, wrapped up as he was in the firm's other doings.

His associate Peter Hague Neilson, who joined the firm just as Humana was getting underway, recalled that "Michael was never interested in construction," although his Kentucky clients were never far from his mind.[59] One afternoon, on a visit to the Whitney for talks with the trustees, Michael sprinted across the street to an antiques shop and spotted a Josef Hoffmann fruit bowl. Knowing Cherry was a collector, Michael recommended he buy it; Cherry said he'd consider it.[60]

Later, Michael would make his presence felt in the selection of the stone—thirty-two thousand pieces in all—that covered the facade and the street-level loggia—pink granite from Finland, red from India, gray from Spain.[61] When the cladding had been applied, Michael at last came to Louisville and took a look at the contractor's work. He told Cherry and Jones they weren't getting their money's worth. "They took a lot of stone down," Michael said, "and did it again."[62]

Opening night in 1985 was kicked off with a gala dinner, and Michael and Kitty were there at a table with Fran Lebowitz and Candice Bergen, whom they'd invited down as their guests. It was a glittering event, with the mayor and the governor in attendance, and toward the end of the evening Cherry motioned to Michael, saying he had something he wanted to give him. Michael knew what it was—the Hoffmann fruit bowl. "You couldn't have done a better building for us," his client told him.

Wendell Cherry died in 1991, but David A. Jones still recalls his partner's philosophy when it came to business. "It was the confidence of total ignorance," said Jones. "We learned early that when you don't know anything about something, hire someone who does."[63] By letting their architect take the lead, the partners helped bring about what was arguably the most accomplished project of Michael's career [PLATE 42].

Rather than just a corrective to Miesian Modernism, Humana was Michael's attempt to answer for the failings of Portland. Absent the restrictions of a government budget and government stakeholders, he had free rein to create a building that came much closer to his original concept, perhaps closer than anything else he ever designed. Portland had shown that Postmodernist buildings could be built, but Humana proved that they could be built well.

Whether it was the more influential of the two is less certain. In elevation, the twenty-seven-story Humana was more irregular, more active than almost any of the countless Postmodernist towers that followed it: its contextual gestures included an eighth-story projecting cornice (a nod to the scale of the old distilleries), a glass central bay in the northern facade (a reference to the glassy tower across the street), and a lofty loggia at sidewalk level, backed up by a cascading water feature (a public amenity like Mies's plaza, though more spectacular by far). More than that, it had the *aediculae* that had been excised from Portland, not grouped together but separately dangling from each facade. On the northern front, holding up the bowed exedra of the upper-level terrace, it sported a red steel truss similar in appearance to the box frame of the Fourteenth Street Bridge just up the Ohio River. Standing on the windswept twenty-fifth-floor balcony, one could look through the multi-framed window of the terrace's projecting glass pavilion and see the real bridge in the distance.

Philip Johnson had warned Michael early and often that he should "stop drawing and start building."[64] Humana showed that Michael had taken those words to heart: its rich materials gave it a heft and a presence none of his previous projects had had, while its interior sequencing, moving from a low-ceilinged foyer to a high-vaulted lobby to a central rotunda, suggested that Michael's elevation mania hadn't sapped his ability to shape interior spaces [**PLATE 41**]. The project won plaudits from the architectural press, with Paul Goldberger proclaiming it "in every way Mr. Graves's finest building, a tower that proves his ability not only to work at large scale, but to create interior and exterior details as well wrought as those of any architect now practicing."[65] After its excoriation of Portland, *Time* would name Humana one of the ten best buildings of the 1980s.[66]

Not everyone was convinced. "Probably no other contemporary office high-rise in the United States presents a more strangely disorganized collection of elements," wrote the *Chicago Tribune's* Paul Gapp.[67] In an informal poll conducted by the *Louisville Courier-Journal*, local readers were split almost exactly in half between admirers and detractors.[68] Academic opinion ran slightly in Michael's favor (the architectural theorist Karsten Harries said the project "strengthened [Graves's] claim to being our most interesting architect," while Vincent Scully endorsed its "visually rich, solid, sculptural" design).[69] But mostly what Humana received from the academic community was silence. Neither the high-minded exegeses that had followed the houses of the 1970s nor the clamor that attended Portland were anywhere to be found.

That Michael's largest, most expensive project to date should attract so little scholarly interest may seem surprising. Then again, this was a corporate project, not a private home or a public building, and by the time of its completion there were many such towers on the rise as PoMo fever swept over the American development community. Postmodernism was no longer a philosophical exercise, but big business.

AT HOME MICHAEL'S RELATIVE AFFLUENCE at last allowed him to press forward with renovations to the Warehouse, which were carried out over four years beginning in the middle 1980s.[70] The exterior was covered in fresh stucco, and the north wing transformed according to his earlier scheme, minus the proposed darkroom and with a door to the garden covered by a trellis and topped by a semi-elliptical Diocletian window. The main entrance, now formed into a rotunda, was topped with a light well; from the second floor, the well was cordoned off by a columned, open-topped *tempietto*, with a skylight in the ceiling above. The revised plan now put a far stronger focus on poche—the walls made thicker and indented with niches and recesses, such that each room had a different spatial character and a different quality of light. It was an atmosphere that owed much, by Michael's own admission, to the London home of the Regency-era architect Sir John Soane.

Like Soane's, Michael's house was now almost a small museum of art and antiquities, larded with curios and baubles picked up in New York and abroad. His collection, begun with a five-dollar Etruscan vase he'd bought in Rome in 1960, swelled to include classical pottery and inkwells shaped like the Roman Temple of Vesta ("I could never resist buying one when I saw it," he said), as well as baroque candlesticks and engravings by Gunnar Asplund and ever more pieces of nineteenth-century German Biedermeier: "On one trip to Munich, I went to six Biedermeier antique shops," he recalled.[71] It was an expensive habit that nonetheless would have been more costly a mere decade later, as Biedermeier came back into fashion and prices soared.

All this luxury Michael now had to himself, as he and Kitty Hawks had parted ways, and she had moved out of the Warehouse. The split was even more cordial than either of Michael's divorces—a welcome circumstance, since it meant that he could continue his love affair with Kitty's best friend: her blue merle Australian Shepherd, Earl, whom she'd brought from California and who had become a fixture in the house as well as in Michael's office. Now relocated to the eastern end of Nassau Street, Michael Graves Architect was converted into a high-class kennel, with Michael bringing first Earl and then his own dog. His employees followed suit en masse.

Another relationship that survived Hawks's departure was Michael and Fran Lebowitz's, whose friendship ultimately outlasted the one between Lebowitz and Hawks; the latter imploded during a party at Kitty's Westchester house when the hostess asked Lebowitz to step outside to smoke. ("They were inviting *me*," said Lebowitz, the shock of it still fresh despite the passage of years. "Besides," she added, "I hate going to parties out of town.")[72] The ensuing "knock-down, drag-out fight," as Michael described it, did nothing to diminish his affection for the lovable if curmudgeonly writer, and the only cloud that ever hung over their amity was the presence of Michael's pets. "Fran," recalled Hawks, "would rather leave the country than spend time with a dog."[73]

Dogs were to be Michael's constant companions for many years, the only—or almost only—regular cohabitants of the Warehouse compound. Girlfriends there would occasionally be, "François" having returned to action, but for the moment, at least, no family or close friends were part of Michael's ménage. His and Gail's children were getting to be young adults, Sarah a student at Colby College in Maine, Adam a boarder at the Landmark School in Beverly, Massachusetts.[74] The program there was geared toward students with learning disabilities, and Adam's enrollment was acknowledgment of a condition that had been evident to his parents for several years. Even when Adam was still small, Michael had noticed that his son was different. "I wanted to play ball with him," he recalled, "but he had his own agenda."[75]

The more crowded agenda, however, was Michael's, and ball-playing with Adam would never quite be at the top of it. Fatherhood had always hung awkwardly on Michael's shoulders, and his son's social anxiety made the role that much more difficult to fill. With Sarah, at least he had been able to do things like teach her to paint; together the two had created a Morandi still life so convincing that Michael's associate Peter Waldman mistook it for the real thing.[76] With Adam, such attempts to bridge the distance between father and son would be sporadic at best, a function not just of his son's condition but of Michael's own well-documented tendency toward isolation. As his fame grew, he fell out of touch with many old friends, including his former mentor Ray Roush, to whom he rarely spoke during the several decades leading up to Roush's death in 2002 from complications of Alzheimer's disease.[77]

Meanwhile, as Humana opened in Louisville and the Alessi teakettle hit stores worldwide, Michael and his associates were rushing to finalize their Whitney design. "We met all the time with the building committee," Michael said. "Trips to get to know the trustees. Tom Armstrong put me out there."[78]

In May 1985 Michael presented his proposal to the board and to the public [**PLATE 43**]. To meet the client's implicit mandate to preserve Breuer's iconic museum while incorporating it into a larger complex, Michael used one of his go-to artistic devices: the diptych. A second volume, comparable in breadth and similarly jagged and telescoping along one edge, would be situated on the south corner of the same

Madison Avenue block, its facade inscribed with a triangle that would mimic the Cyclops-like aperture on the Breuer building. Between the two would be a third, cylindrical structure, housing a new staircase and acting as a visual pivot between the old building and the new, while an enormous crown, receding tier by tier to end in a rooftop stoa, would unite the assemblage into a single mass.

The plan managed to do what had seemed almost impossible, shoehorning 31,600 feet of additional exhibition and office space (plus a 250-seat theater, a library, and a study center) into a sliver of street frontage while leaving the Breuer almost entirely intact. But "intact" was not quite "untouched." Breuer's southern stairwell was to be demolished to make way for the central hinge structure, while the symmetrized facade and setback forms above undid the deliberately top-heavy, off-kilter character of Breuer's creation. Worse, the scheme did nothing to allay the concerns of those who'd always objected that Breuer's building was out of place—concerns exacerbated by the new scheme's proposed demolition of the neighboring brownstones.

Attacks from both Modernist and non-Modernist factions commenced almost instantly. Within months of the plan's debut, an Ad Hoc Committee to Save the Whitney had filed a petition—cosigned by the architects I. M. Pei and Edward Larrabee Barnes—complaining that the Graves addition would "totally destroy the architectural integrity" of Breuer's design. Local groups were determined to fight the proposal tooth and nail before the city's Landmarks Commission, claiming that the loss of the brownstones would do lasting damage to the Upper East Side Historic District. In a rare concurrence of opinion, critics of every stripe, from the right-wing Hilton Kramer ("combines an appalling poverty of architectural thought with a maximum of ornamental ostentation") to the left-wing Michael Sorkin ("Hands off the Whitney, Graves!") turned out to protest the proposal.[79] The uproar, Michael told a reporter, made "Portland seem like a picnic."[80]

Not that the plan was totally friendless: Philip Johnson got behind the proposal, blasting the signatories of the petition as "modern-architecture holdouts who still yearn for the days of old."[81] No less a figure than Vincent Scully—who had overcome an early dislike for Michael and had even written an essay for his first full-length monograph—insisted that the addition would finally weave Breuer's building "into the larger pattern of urban order."[82] Approving letters were penned by both Ulrich Franzen, Michael's Humana competitor, and Alex Cooper, Jaquelin Robertson's sometime partner, while in the press Paul Goldberger declared himself (provisionally, at least) a supporter.[83] Martin Filler did the same, though he qualified his endorsement by noting a fundamental incongruity in the project's DNA. "It would be hard," he wrote, "to name a contemporary architect whose aesthetic is more opposed to Breuer's than Michael Graves."[84]

That much Michael had understood from the first. Trying to integrate the stubbornly noncommunicative Breuer into his own architectural vocabulary posed, as he said at the time, "a particular challenge." To do so he had used forms that were more abstract and less overtly classical than most of his projects of the period. But by dint of sheer size, the addition still reduced the original building to a bit player in a new and very different ensemble. A change so extreme was bound to ruffle a large number of very prominent feathers, especially given the endemic fussiness of the museum's assorted stakeholders—Modern architects, Upper East Siders, and art lovers, to name but a few.

The last two of those groups were represented in force on the museum's board, and several trustees voiced their anxiety about the scheme. "Everyone agrees an expansion is necessary," said the billionaire trustee Leonard A. Lauder, "but does it have to be that large?"[85] Facing a lukewarm client and a rising volume of red tape, Michael was stuck once again in the same fix he had finally escaped with Humana—the expansion, as he put it later, "just wasn't going to be anybody's child."[86] Before it could reach the Landmarks Commission review, and unbeknownst to the various parties baying for the proposal's blood, the building committee elected to remand the scheme to Princeton, charging the designers with making it more palatable to the museum's competing constituencies.

During l'affaire Whitney and through all the very public travails and triumphs of the 1980s, Michael concocted a curious game plan for managing his office and its public profile. By contemporary standards it seems almost unthinkable, and even for its time it surprised many of his friends and colleagues, who looked on with envy at what appeared to be the well-oiled machine of Michael Graves Architect.

"How big is your marketing department?" other architects would ask.

"I don't have one," he would reply.

The Gravesy train, such as it was, ran primarily on elbow grease—and fame. Michael had learned how to delegate authority to trusted deputies, especially on the fine points of construction that had always bored him, and from twenty-five employees in 1983 the firm ballooned to more than fifty in just three short years, squeezed together in every corner of the new office on Nassau and Harrison.[87] Such para-architectural matters as public relations and the writing of proposals were mostly carried on in-house by trusted associates such as Karen Nichols, who could rely on a steady stream of magazine editors and prospective clients panting for the attention of America's hottest architect. Michael, in turn, grabbed at every opportunity: though his cash crunch of the '70s was over, Michael "never felt we had enough money," Nichols recalled.[88] His acquisitive streak might not have helped matters, but the compulsion to do everything and be everywhere at once was simply part of his makeup. Projects for private clients, for a music center back in Cincinnati, more plans for the Newark Museum...Michael designed, and Michael taught, and when he was doing neither he pushed the firm toward every prize and project competition he could. His notoriety took care of the rest.

This strategy, or lack of it, was not without hazard. The firm now found itself surrounded by larger offices that could produce architecture superficially like its own but at much greater speed and with far greater technical proficiency. In 1985 Michael entered a competition for another high-profile commission in Manhattan, a huge commercial development to replace the outdated New York Coliseum on Columbus Circle. In the run-up to Humana, he had come up against other practices pushing a Postmodern agenda, but this time around there were even more of them: Kevin Roche John Dinkeloo submitted a Rockefeller Center–esque skyscraper; a Futurist-Deco pastiche was drawn up by Cesar Pelli; and a straight-up 1920s tower group, just like the twinned Deco spires that spike Central Park West, was submitted by none other than the great behemoth of American Modernism, Skidmore Owings & Merrill.[89]

SOM had gone Postmodern, and along with them had gone other Modernists of formerly sterling reputation such as Kevin Roche, Helmut Jahn, and I. M. Pei. Also in the mix were newer, larger offices in New York such as Kohn Pedersen Fox (KPF) and Polshek Partnership, and all of them were gunning for the same projects Michael was—and often winning them, as SOM did the Columbus Circle commission.[90] The maddening thing for Michael was that he had brought this on himself: in 1980 he had participated in a roundtable at Manhattan's Harvard Club alongside Robert A. M. Stern and others, where he had stood before SOM's principals and attempted to educate his International Style–loving peers about Postmodernism.[91] His listeners had learned all too well, and taking a page from the chameleon-like Philip Johnson, they had now changed their stripes. Johnson himself was a major competitor for Michael, the only Postmodernist of equal or greater standing and a seemingly magnetic force for well-to-do clients. He still played godfather to his Postmodern progeny, but he was careful to reserve the choicest commissions for his own delectation and that of his then-partner, John Burgee, with whom he was designing buildings at a torrid pace.

Considering Michael's catch-as-catch-can take on job getting, it was only by chance that Johnson failed to gain the upper hand when a plush prospect came their way one evening at Lincoln Center in early 1985. Michael was still dating Kitty Hawks at the time, and the two flagged down Johnson and his companion, David Whitney, after a concert. As they stood talking, another man joined them: Michael Eisner, the recently appointed CEO of the Walt Disney Corporation. So long as he was in New York and standing in front of two of the country's foremost designers, Eisner availed himself of the opportunity to tell them about a new office center, the Team Disney Headquarters, that he was planning to build in Burbank, California.

Describing the project in depth, Eisner was clearly paying court to the senior architect. But Johnson, newly turned eighty, was not quite certain who Eisner was, and could not hear the Disney executive over the postconcert din. To all of Eisner's remarks, the much-feted "dean of American architecture" could muster no response more compelling than *"What?"*[92]

At last Johnson and Whitney gave up and politely withdrew, wandering off to get a Perrier—"a lucky break for me, I guess," said Michael. Months later Michael Graves Architect entered talks with Disney to draft a master plan for the entertainment leviathan's new corporate campus.

WHEN IT WAS, he could never remember. The mid-1980s, perhaps, or later. Possibly earlier…

Speeding along the autostrada in northern Italy, Michael was en route to join the architect Aldo Rossi for dinner at a restaurant in Milan. Somewhere in the flatlands outside the city, he saw something so arresting at an intersection of two country roads that he peeled off and stopped the car. It was a small building, an electrical station, not more than fifteen feet on a side and about four stories high, with a "funny little roof," as he remembered it, and openings for a window and a door. Alone in the rustic landscape of Lombardy, the building was neither imposing nor prepossessing, but it nonetheless had, in Michael's judgment, "the most exquisite proportions you can imagine."[93]

At dinner that night, as Rossi munched on a steak-size serving of portobello mushroom, Michael told him about the crude, shack-like pile he'd seen in the countryside. The words were barely out of his mouth before Rossi smiled gently.

"Isn't it great?" he said. He knew exactly the building Michael meant, and he too had often lingered there at the crossroads.

In a by-now-familiar pattern, Rossi was another figure with whom Michael was on personable but not personal terms, their careers running in parallel in the wake of their introduction at the 1973 Triennale. (If anything, Rossi was the more strident anti-Modernist; he once declared, "I cannot be Postmodern, as I have never been Modern.")[94] It is hard to say whose influence predominated over whom. Michael's Postmodernist language was much indebted to Rossi's, while Rossi's subsequent success—he would also work for Disney—saw him mining a vein of Gravesian populism. "They influenced each other. Or ruined each other, you could say," quipped Mary McLeod.[95]

Aldo Rossi's
San Cataldo
Cemetery
in Modena,
Italy, 1971

Even at his most commercial, however, Rossi always sought in his work an elusive quality encapsulated in some ways by that little power station in the country. Whether one chooses, following Le Corbusier, to call it the "masterly play" of masses in light; or "frozen music," as Goethe once described architecture; or by any other name—the uncanny, the ineffable—it is, simply put, the magnetic affective sway upon the mind of abstract forms in space. In Rossi's masterwork, the San Cataldo Cemetery at Modena (that "island-like city of the dead," as the scholar Reinhold Martin once called it), the looming geometries of his ossuary and its surrounding pavilions exude a pervasive melancholy that makes the whole ensemble somehow more than the sum of its parts.[96] For the Postmodernists, always yearning for a past beyond recall, Rossi's project had been an early touchstone. But as their movement gained traction, the surrealism and mystery of Modena were falling by the wayside in favor of other values: values like communicability or (as Peter Eisenman had termed it) accessibility.

The lightning-fast spread of Postmodernism seemed proof enough that the style *was* accessible to people—and that, for Michael, was enough. Drawing on the classical tradition he'd absorbed in Rome, imbuing it with his own artistic sensibility, he felt he'd finally found a design language that had the meaning and the empathic capacity he'd been looking for. In 1980, just starting out on his PoMo path, he told an interviewer:

> I felt, reading reactions to my buildings in the '60s, that I was not just losing readers; I felt they were not reading into my abstractions what I expected.... The problem to overcome, if one is willing, is to play into an abstract language, necessary in any art form—to have some purposeful ambiguity—but to not run the risk of being so abstract as to lose the reader. There has to be some balance.[97]

Michael's fully gelled Postmodern style was far more figurative, more literal in its ornamentation and flatter in its pictorial facade-ism, than any of his transitional work of the 1970s. Yet he had not lost purchase on that "purposeful ambiguity," or on the emotional content it portended. The sensation he felt on beholding that small building in Italy—not so different, perhaps, from the one that had overtaken him as a boy at the Indianapolis stockyards—was evident everywhere in his drawings and paintings, those "seductive presences," as Paul Goldberger once described them.[98] Where Michael differed from Rossi was in his faith that only figuration could weave those feelings into narratives that would make them palpable—make them understandable, the way he'd wanted to understand his father's old office building—with the language of classicism acting as the prime figurative agent. Portland, with its garlanded tale of civic pride and public spirit, had opened the door; Humana, with its *aediculae* and cornices telling a story of the city and the river, the past and the present, had brought him closer. Now, with so many products and buildings in the offing, the possibilities seemed limitless.

As for that other architect, Léon Krier, whose classical images were so close but whose radical ideas were so far from his own—Michael did have one fateful encounter with him in the early 1980s. At Jaquelin Robertson's invitation, Michael participated in a series of conversations at the University of Virginia School of Architecture (of which Robertson was now dean), taking place in November 1982 and published three years later under the title *The Charlottesville Tapes*. During a presentation by the architect Tadao Ando, Krier called on his deep reserves of moral outrage, thundering against the windowless, bare-bones concrete house that the Japanese designer had put before his colleagues. As the transcript records it, the minimal-Modernist project then received a spirited defense from an unlikely quarter: Michael.

LÉON KRIER: This has nothing to do with architecture. It is a miserable hole.

MICHAEL GRAVES: [Ando] obviously doesn't think it is a miserable hole.

LÉON KRIER: It is not a matter of what he thinks. Architecture has a tradition of thousands of years, and we are the inheritors of it.

MICHAEL GRAVES: Well, he is just an architect, as you are, and we are all members of this society; we do not separate ourselves from that society...[99]

In Krier's view, Michael was simply admonishing him to give up his vaunted principles for the sake of professional expediency. "He was saying, 'Leo, you have to get into the real world! You have to get into the real world and build shit,'" recalled Krier. "It was like he said you have to degrade yourself...and if I didn't, in that way I will not be 'in the real.'"[100]

An exaggeration, perhaps, but not a total mischaracterization of Michael's argument. Seldom cynical, Michael was nonetheless entirely unmoved by Krier's idealism. So far as he was concerned, pragmatism and accessibility went hand in hand, and one couldn't very well claim to care about "the masses" while hiding from them in the groves of academe.

So BOUNDLESS WAS his scope of action in the 1980s that although Michael knew there were more things in design's heaven and earth than PoMo, there was little reason for him to give them much thought. Among the attendees at the Charlottesville meeting was one of Eisenman's IAUS associates, the Dutch architect Rem Koolhaas. In 1978 he had published a hilariously seditious book called *Delirious New York*, but he had yet only one real project to his name and seemed to Michael tangled in theoretical coils he might never undo. Another Charlottesville attendee, Frank Gehry, had built more, but his only major public commission—the Loyola Law School in downtown Los Angeles—seemed to be a tip of the hat to Michael himself, all primitive forms and collapsed columns. His more adventurous work, like his own house in Santa Monica, was considered beyond the popular pale. "Gehry was terrific," recalled the critic Martin Filler. "But we all thought, 'We like it, but the public won't.'"[101]

Perhaps the only inkling that there might be something transcending the White-Gray dichotomy came in 1983, when Michael lost a promising commission for a new arts center on the campus of Ohio State University. The one who'd bested him: Peter Eisenman, in what would become his first (and one of his very few) institutional projects. Eisenman had turned away from the linguistics of Noam Chomsky and toward the even more recondite conjectures of Jacques Derrida, and his design for what would come to be called the Wexner Center for the Arts was a web of unresolved structural matrices and purposely conflicting plans. No longer just thumping his Corbusian bible, Eisenman was using the voguish deconstructionist branch of literary theory to strike out into terra incognita, while proving that he and others like him could succeed in the worldly sphere of the building business. After winning Wexner he told an interviewer, "There are two or three reasons we're excited about this. One of course is that it was nice to beat Michael Graves."[102] A flicker of a smile played across his face.

Still, the balance of professional power remained tilted decisively in Michael's favor. When a major New York department store wanted to know what "next year's colors" would be, it was Michael they called; when *People* magazine wanted someone to weigh in on "the race to challenge 'glass boxes,'" Michael was the architect they trusted to explain it all to millions of Americans idling in supermarket lines.[103] Between Disney, Whitney, and Alessi, Michael Graves Architect had momentum to spare, and the whole world was watching.

VIII

THE HOUSE, THE TOMB,
AND THE TEAKETTLE

A PICTURE OF MICHAEL GRAVES in his office on Nassau Street, one hand atop a stack of drawings, the other resting casually on his hip.

> For me, the things that endure are those that blend the traditions we all know with the spirit of new invention. The familiarity of the past at ease with the freshness of the present.
>
> When the people at Dexter showed me their shoes, I said "Perfect, this is just what I mean about combining the classic and the contemporary...."
>
> Which just goes to prove what I've been saying for years. There is nothing more important than starting with a good foundation.

The Maine-based Dexter Shoes had been running an ad campaign featuring eminent Americans—the ballplayer Ted Williams, the yacht designer David Tedrick—and when the company asked Michael to join its stable of prominent pitchmen, he signed up without hesitation. When the advertisement ran in the *New York Times* in late 1987, "there was a lot of grief from my peers," he said.[1] It was the first such promotional gimmick he had ever appeared in. It would not be the last.

He would go on to plump for Absolut Vodka, for Millstone Coffee, for the digital design company Autodesk. His own clients loved to put him front and center: for Alessi he donned an ankle-length overcoat and opened it, flasher-like, to reveal the teakettle as well as the flatware and ceramics he had also designed for the brand. For his 1993 project in Miami Beach, the developers had him appear on a giant billboard by the side of the highway, lying flat with the beach behind.

Michael was good for business, and business was good for Michael. Subsequent exhibitions at Max Protech Gallery fared well [**PLATE 37**]; at one point Neiman Marcus sold prints of the Fargo-Moorhead Bridge. Prices for Michael's drawings had grown so high that some of his students, it was rumored, were squirreling away his doodles from their deskside crits, hoping to make a tidy sum off their illustrious prof.[2]

The 1993 highway billboard for 1500 Ocean Drive, the Graves condominium project in Miami Beach

STATUS AND SALES FIGURES, however, would be of no help to Michael in the ongoing Whitney Museum fight, now stretching into its third year.

In 1987 Michael Graves Architect revealed its new and improved scheme for the Whitney, its outward appearance only slightly altered from the first [PLATE 44]. Somewhat less decorative, but with a quarter the square footage and with a shorter crown, it actually had more exhibition space than the first proposal, having slashed auxiliary functions like office and retail spaces. The revised version still used the diptych to carry its narrative water, setting the Marcel Breuer building and its new counterpart into a dialectical frame that emphasized both their differences and their similarities. The correlation was even more explicit this time, as the pyramidal fenestration on the new wing turned into a trapezoid of identical dimensions to Breuer's, only upright instead of sideways, as though it had been helped to its feet.

Michael had defended the diptych in expressly artistic terms, comparing it to Botticelli's *Annunciation*, in which the Virgin Mary and Archangel Gabriel face each other on either side of a column. The project's critics, however, detected a different painterly strategy at work, and not a welcome one. The composition, wrote Victoria Geibel in *Metropolis*, "registers as much discord as Picasso's fragmented female in the 1939 painting *Woman with a Blue Hat*."[3] Michael's Cubist affinities had been muffled in his later Postmodern work, which tended to favor classical resolution over modern tension. Deprived by the presence of the Breuer of the chance to make a perfectly symmetrical whole, his collagist impulses returned, and no matter how toned down the new building might be, the overall crazy-quilt effect was distressing to lovers of the older building's muscular unity.

While the pile-on continued from Breuer partisans, the Whitney did eke out a small victory over the historical preservationists, as Community Board 8 sided with the museum on the question of demolishing the five adjacent brownstones. It was a good omen for how the Landmarks Commission might rule. Yet once again, the museum's building committee got cold feet, yanking Michael's second scheme and requesting a third, still more unobtrusive proposal. Under what must have been horrendous pressure, he agreed and took up his axe one final time.

Be they ever so prickly, the Whitney trustees were still Michael's prize clients, and he held on to the project for dear life. "It was such a great opportunity," he said. "Such an important institution, given its mandate on American art."[4]

Exasperating though the museum project was, Michael Graves Architect did not want for consolations: a high-rise in Atlanta, commissions from Steuben Glass, an academic building for the University of Virginia. As the 1980s roared on, the firm expanded from twenty-five, to sixty-five, then one hundred and twenty employees, drawn as usual from promising Princeton grads. "I had a greater ear with the students because I had a practice," Michael said. His divided loyalties to both working and teaching could be taxing at times, but his runaway success also reinforced his standing at Princeton.[5]

School ties had been frayed only slightly by the 1983 completion of Gordon Wu Hall, a dining facility in the very heart of the university campus designed by Robert Venturi and Denise Scott Brown. The Pennsylvanian had at least equal claim to being a Princetonian (he'd studied there under Jean Labatut), and the university had a long-standing prohibition against hiring its own professors to design buildings. Yet Michael's pride was bruised.

Unsurprisingly, the two most outstanding contemporaries in American Postmodernism (setting aside the elder Johnson) were not exactly simpatico. Half-hearted attempts at interoffice comity had been attempted, with mingled results: in 1980 the Philadelphians had been invited to Princeton for a day of cookouts, croquet, and softball, and though the younger associates got on well enough, Venturi and Scott Brown remained stationed with bemused indifference in the middle of the field for the duration, reading the newspaper. "Venturi thought he was the real thing, and everyone else was cosmetics," as Peter Eisenman put it.[6] For his part, Michael ranked Colin Rowe far above the author of *Complexity and Contradiction*—though even Michael was prepared to concede that his Postmodernism had been partly predicated on an aesthetic-minded construal of Venturi's thinking. "Bob Venturi makes you understand you can flatten these kind of symbols, and sometimes they're more powerful," Michael once said. "So that's what I did."[7]

When the two faced off for a much bigger commission, however, it was Michael's aestheticism that carried the day. Michael Eisner's still-unfinished Burbank project was no one-off: Disney was on a building spree, and the wheels were in motion to erect a rambling hospitality complex at their Walt Disney World Resort in Orlando, Florida. In 1986 Eisner approached the Graves and Venturi offices and suggested that they tackle the eighty-seven-acre complex as a team—a suggestion that struck Michael as implausible.

"Isn't that like putting Steven Spielberg and George Lucas together?" he asked.

"Remember," answered Eisner, "I did that." The result had been the *Indiana Jones* franchise.[8]

Venturi, however, was having none of it and insisted on a competition. Thanks to Michael's prior relationship with Eisner, the Graves team had the edge going in and beat out Venturi's plan after a few changes to the structures to "lighten up them up," per Eisner's request.[9] The Disney exec kept a close watch over the high-stakes project throughout its development. "Every move," as Michael put it, "was packed full with dollars," and Eisner "knew he'd get called on the carpet whatever we did."[10] The project was no less critical for Michael Graves Architect: the urban-scale design could show what the firm could do when given room to run.

Eisner had already inked a deal with construction giant Tishman, but when the Graves team showed its initial proposal to CEO John Tishman, the builder balked. The design, he claimed, was "outrageous and impossible," the buildings making "no sense practically or economically." Tishman demanded to use his preferred architect, Alan Lapidus, a Florida-based designer who had also participated in the initial competition with Venturi—and also lost. But Lapidus (the son of Morris Lapidus, famed for his Miami Beach resorts) had extensive experience building hotels, and both Michaels concurred that a little expertise might come in handy. The Lapidus and Graves teams agreed to collaborate.[11]

Tempered by his colleague's emendations, Michael's final design was still almost as dumbfounding as the one that had stymied Tishman. Opened in 1990, the Swan and Dolphin Hotels [PLATES 46 AND 47] featured nearly 2,500 guest rooms, multiple conference and business spaces, ballrooms, themed restaurants, and a convention center of 1.4 million square feet. Staggering in scale, the Graves solution opted not to break down the whole into digestible pieces, relying instead on two simple envelopes: a 257-foot pyramid for the Dolphin, and for the Swan a single vault-like arch. As easily legible as these formal outlines were, they were not half as eye-catching as the decorative fixtures applied to each, with statues of 47-foot-high swans and 56-foot-high dolphins affixed to the roofs of the corresponding structures. (It was whispered that they were actually fixed to the *wrong* structures, and that the names of the hotels had to be changed accordingly. The architects have always denied this.)

The entire complex was alive with visual narrative. The swan statues "floated" on the waves painted on the facade; the dolphins, in Michael's telling, were cast there during an imagined volcanic eruption that produced the "island" of the curved hotel volume, its tropical character attested by the images of banana leaves sprouting across the surface.[12] Many of the figurative forms pointed to historical precedents—the triangular peak of the Dolphin a tribute to the visionary cenotaphs of the eighteenth-century draftsman Étienne-Louis Boullée, the hotel's fishy statues recalling the ones at the base of Gian Lorenzo Bernini's Fontana del Tritone in Rome. There were less-lofty sources as well: Lapidus claimed that the wallpaper of the Beverly Hills Hotel in Los Angeles, where the two architects stayed frequently during the design process, provided the inspiration for the banana leaves.[13] All these motifs and more, right down to the patterns on the plates in the restaurants, were plotted with agonizing attention to detail. Even the sand in the hotel ashtrays was printed with the applicable animal.

Flights of fancy were, of course, appropriate to the client—these being the people who brought America singing dandelions, affectionate Volkswagens, and Flower the talking skunk. But there was something incontrovertibly weird about a major American architect, an Ivy League professor no less, having a hand in such a breathtaking shrine to the unreal. "More big than beautiful," as Paul Goldberger described it, the design's artificiality combined jarringly with its extravagance, and its prodigious bulk lent a sinister cast to its wholesome whimsy.[14] One local architect was reported to have described the experience of an overnight stay in the resort as "rather like spending the night with a friendly Venus flytrap."[15]

At least the narratives of the Swan and Dolphin were Michael's own; for the Team Disney Building, completed in 1991, he was compelled (albeit willingly) to adopt the narrative of his client. The main building in his campus master plan was an unfussy classical pavilion in the style of Claude-Nicolas Ledoux, another of Michael's eighteenth-century heroes, topped by intersecting barrel vaults and fronted by a monumental arbor-sheltered approach. But when Eisner first viewed the scheme, it left him cold, and immediately he called his architect.

"It looks like a bank!" he told Michael.

"Let me give it some Disney flavor," Michael answered.[16]

The flavor, as it turned out, involved replacing the conventional pilasters in the second level and attic story with Disney characters—first Donald, Mickey, and the brand's core characters, and then, at Eisner's prompting, the titular gnomes from the 1937 classic *Snow White and the Seven Dwarfs*. This was a bridge too far for some. "One wonders," asked Ada Louise Huxtable, "who is having whom." Disney, she contended, had folded Postmodernism back on itself, turning its accessible historicism into a corporate prop.[17]

Michael was not the only one implicated in this Disneyfication of PoMo. In 1991 Eisner assembled an architectural dream team that included Graves, Robert A. M. Stern, Robert Venturi, and Stanley Tigerman, tasking them with carrying out Disney's most sweeping development project to date: the Euro Disney park and resort outside Paris. Likening themselves to the combine of designer-planners who created the World's Columbian Exposition in 1893, the Disney group's individual and collective schemes steered well clear of Swan- and Dolphin-level quirk. (Michael's Hotel New York, opened in 1992, was actually quite restrained.) But unlike the Chicago fairgrounds of old, Euro Disney did not spark a new wave of similarly fantastical architecture—if anything, it signaled that Postmodernism had breached a certain horizon. Only one architect involved with the park ever explicitly distanced himself from it, but significantly he was also the only one not classed among the Postmodernists. Looking back, Frank Gehry said, "I lost control."[18]

"THERE WAS A LINE in the sand, as far as we were concerned," said Charles Jencks.[19] Alongside James Stirling, Jencks decried the Disney work of Michael and others as a betrayal of Postmodernism's promise, a dumbing down for the grade-school set—though if Michael's Disney work seems childish, at least it can be said it was meant to be. As Eisner said to Michael, "I have two young sons, and when I'm looking at your designs, I'm thinking of them."[20]

"Appropriateness" was a central topos of Michael's Postmodernism—related to, and part of the same continuum as, his dedication to accessibility, empathy, and communication. "Colin Rowe would see [appropriateness] as too flabby a concept," Michael observed. "But I say, some solutions are appropriate, some are not."[21] This conviction had served him well at the very dawn of his Postmodernist phase, in 1983, when his office completed a library for the town of San Juan Capistrano [PLATE 38]. Practically no major public works had been built in the tiny mission town in Southern California since its late eighteenth-century founding, and the community had been understandably anxious at the introduction of a large new structure by a controversial East Coast architect. But Michael and the firm managed to strike just the right chord: adopting and adapting the region's familiar Spanish Colonial style to their own Postmodernist language, they created a building that was both original and suitable to its context, and one that's since become a much-loved local landmark.

To Michael's mind, an architecture of meaning would have to be a malleable architecture, one that could play on all stylistic and affective keys, from the supercilious to the silly. When critics mocked the Alessi 9093 as "kitschy," he would counter (with questionable etymological accuracy) that "kitsch comes from the kitchen."[22] A teakettle with pretensions of intellectualism would be as inapposite as, say, a building for Mickey Mouse that aspired to seriousness.

The limits of appropriateness, however, were being tested daily in the fight over the Whitney. Just before the turn of the new year of 1989, Michael's office produced its third proposal for the museum expansion [PLATE 45]. This one extended an even bigger olive branch to the project's assorted enemies, slicing away at the decorative details to leave only a blank, colonnaded facade (remarkably similar, as Robert A. M. Stern would note, to the work of Aldo Rossi), with the rooftop volume pared down to an oblong block and no interstitial cylinder intruding on Breuer's south stairwell.[23] Though the brownstones would still have to go, this was as far as the Graves team could possibly bend to accommodate both Breuer lovers and NIMBY-ish local residents. It was not enough.

Three more years would go by before the Whitney, under a new director, would officially declare the project dead. In the end, it fell victim to the hue and cry of its opponents as well as to the winds of economic chance: the soaring American economy went into a brief nosedive in late 1989, and the already hesitant board members were now even less inclined to front the necessary funds. Michael had tried, with each proposal, to make his addition everything to everyone, and perhaps no other architect could have done more. "We should have done one scheme with the building behind the brownstones," Michael would say later, but two other architects, Rem Koolhaas and Renzo Piano, would try just that in later years, with identical results.[24] In 2015 the Whitney at last gave up altogether and moved downtown into a new, somewhat less obtuse box by Piano, leaving the Breuer building to be used as an annex by the Metropolitan Museum of Art.

From the day the building committee came for lunch in Princeton to the day Tom Armstrong's successor called a halt to the Graves addition in March 1992, the Whitney development had consumed more than a decade of Michael's professional life. The letdown was immense, though how much so depends on one's point of view. In Peter Eisenman's opinion, "losing [the Whitney] hurt him psychologically," throwing Michael off balance for years; to Karen Nichols, while she admitted that Michael "was rocked" by the experience, it seemed he moved on with relative ease.[25] "Michael got interested in other things," she said—a defense mechanism he'd employed before, and one facilitated by a design methodology that saw him most engaged in working out the initial *parti*, then moving on to the next project as quickly as possible.

And there were still so many next ones for Michael to move on to. The Whitney hadn't been merely wasted effort: the relationship with trustee A. Alfred Taubman forged during the expansion fight would yield commissions later on, including a major one for the Detroit Institute of Arts. But what seemed to nag Michael about the loss of the museum expansion was the suspicion that he had been undone not by the particular failings of his design but by the fickleness of a few powerful figures in and around the institution who had decided they "wanted somebody more hip" and felt that Michael, and the architecture he represented, had lost their luster.[26]

The Michael Graves of 1979 would have found it all but impossible to believe, but the greatest problem for the Michael Graves of 1989 was not too little work but too much. To his mind, at least, he had climbed to the pinnacle of the profession only to be brought low on the Upper East Side by the perception that he was too successful, too mainstream. This was an oversimplification: the failure of the other architects who followed him to devise an acceptable plan for the original Whitney is proof that the coolness factor was not decisive. But Michael's status had slipped, and it had happened by his own hand. In an otherwise approving 1990 profile in the *New York Times*, Paul Goldberger would say of Michael that he often appeared "less like a man eager to broaden the arena of serious design than one willing to put his name on anything that could be sold."[27]

Shortly after the debut of the teakettle, Michael remembered turning to Linda Kinsey, a recent hire and now partner, telling her that the firm would "do this [product design] for five years, and if it doesn't work, we're done."[28] Those five years turned into many more, and by 1994 Michael had opened a shop in Princeton on Nassau Street, the Graves Design Studio Store, which featured homewares of the firm's own creation, made on his firm's behalf by dozens of fabricators: china sets for ceramics maker Swid Powell, numerous products from Alessi, a mantel clock, watches, jewelry, scarves…The list of products grew and grew, but the more it did, the more Michael and the practice were exposed to charges of being mercenaries, of turning their backs on the high seriousness of Modernist architecture in order to hawk PoMo tchotchkes to yuppie suburbanites.

This was an unforeseen turnabout, and a cruel one in certain respects. Michael's firm little suspected that its first faltering steps into the world of products would lead to an industrial design practice operating at nearly industrial scale. Until the 1980s almost every effort of "serious" design to appeal to Americans consumers had collapsed under its own weight, either due to price (not many Americans could *afford* a George Nelson sofa) or because popular taste was so widely divergent from that of the very Modernists so eager to cater to it (many Americans never *wanted* a George Nelson sofa). Indeed, in its latest incarnation—the one to which Michael had belonged prior to the late 1970s—the Modernist avant-garde had given up any pretense of catering to the people at all, or to their needs. "The transcendence of accommodation," Charles Gwathmey had written, "is the difference between the art of architecture and building."[29]

Of course, Postmodernism had been reared from the cradle to have broader appeal. Beginning with Rowe's anti-elitist rumblings—or further back, to the mass-media enthusiasms of England's Independent Group—the critics of Modernist design had always prescribed a rapprochement with popular tastes. This only made Michael an even less likely vector for PoMo's ascent in the marketplace: he had never shared Robert Venturi's interest in Pop Art, or in the cynical, Warholian cheek that came with it. He had arrived at Postmodernism by a different channel, and his allegiances always remained to the communicative and to the classical. In spite of Postmodernism's much-ballyhooed irony, its joyful celebration of the kitschy and the middlebrow, the man most responsible for commercializing it was nothing if not ingenuous. And now, for all the earnestness of his intent, and for all the risks he'd taken (the store on Nassau never really made money and closed after a few years), Michael felt he was being pilloried for trying to do what so many Modernists had tried and failed to do themselves.

Not just the product work but the countless commercial building projects proceeding from the Graves office provided bait for the critics. From the Aventine—a gigantesque hotel and office complex in La Jolla, California—to a mixed-use office building a few blocks from the White House—destined to be the home of the International Finance Corporation—to master plans, mostly unexecuted, for commercial centers in Los Angeles, Brussels, Israel, and elsewhere, Michael continued to chase down every opportunity as though it would be his last. Steven Harris, who left the office in 1982, was not the last associate to depart exhausted by a boss who regularly "kept everyone up night after night for an AIA submission, redoing models, redoing everything," as he recalled.[30] The pace in the Princeton office did not slacken in the years that followed, as Michael was determined to keep ahead of the larger Postmodernist practices, no matter the cost.

Not just commercial but institutional clients beckoned, and Michael was only too glad to have them. In 1989 the Newark Museum finally made good on its decades-old pledge, completing a 175,000-square-foot renovation based on a completely revised Graves scheme that included a new Postmodernist side entry: a somber, tomblike facade with a greenhouse roof. A year later the firm designed an elaborate sequel to its small 1982 addition to Emory University's museum of art and archaeology, the stately, marble-clad Michael C. Carlos Museum. Most gratifying for Michael personally, he was asked to return to his undergraduate alma mater to design the Engineering Research Center for the College of Engineering at the University of Cincinnati; in another bid for appropriateness, the office's design resembles a giant piston engine, with towering vent stacks breaking the roofline [**PLATE 48**]. Though lightened by ground-floor arches and the firm's telltale polychromy, the building's overall lugubriousness seems coincident with Michael's life-long abhorrence of engineering, dating back to when Erma Graves first laid down the law on his career prospects.

Greater than all this, however, was the volume of work Michael Graves Architect was taking on in Japan. Beginning in the mid-1980s and accelerating rapidly over the next decade, the firm completed some fifteen office buildings and interiors, residential high-rises and mid-rises, a hotel [**PLATE 49**], a design school, and a municipal building, establishing a presence in the East Asian market well ahead of the twenty-first-century invasion of continental China by big-name Western architects. Informed once again by Rossi, the projects there—such as the Kasumi Research and Training Center in Tsukuba City—derived most of their visual interest from their dynamic massing, with discrete volumes in solid colors grouped into semiurban arrangements. Given a cultural climate where columns, cornices, and the other *disjecta membra* of the European tradition were largely irrelevant, Japan was a proving ground for a more universal Gravesian idiom, one that downplayed ornamental detail while leaning still more heavily on anthropomorphism and typological simplicity.

Convenient vehicles for new design ideas and a valuable shelter from the early 1990s US recession, the office's projects abroad (in addition to Japan, there were contemporaneous ones in northern Europe and Egypt) took shape largely out of the eye of the American design scene. Like a well-known American actor appearing in foreign television advertisements, they tended—especially given how little work many architects then had—to lend credence to the accusations of commercialism leveled by Goldberger and others. Still, Michael did include them in his three monographs published in the 1990s and early 2000s, and he presented them from time to time during stateside lectures. On one occasion in the mid-1990s, a number of architects were invited to Harvard to show work they'd done abroad; Michael presented his designs, then sat down next to Rem Koolhaas, the Rotterdam-based architect whose hyperactive rereading of the Modernist tradition had already won him a few major commissions as well as legions of fans. Koolhaas presented his work, and as he came back to his seat, he leaned over to Michael.

"The number of projects you have in Japan," Koolhaas said, in a heavy Dutch accent, "is *nauseating*."

"I didn't know whether to thank him, tell him off, or point him to the bathroom," Michael recalled.[31]

Compliment or critique? With Koolhaas, the remark could easily have been both. The acerbic Dutchman was, and is still, a deft hand at paradox, a talent that had helped elevate him in the 1990s to cultlike status in a field looking for a more piquant architecture for a more fractious age. Years later, when the Whitney picked Koolhaas to carry forward its doomed expansion plan, it came as confirmation that he was one of those "hip" architects who had set Michael back on his heels.

By then, the 1988 *Deconstructivist Architecture* show at MoMA—featuring Koolhaas, among others; shepherded by Philip Johnson and co-curator Mark Wigley; helped along by Peter Eisenman—had come and gone. The exhibition "made it remorselessly clear," wrote the scholar Nancy Levinson, "that the spotlight had swerved, leaving in the dark the decorated bulk of the Portland building."[32] The SOMs, the KPFs, and the other megafirms that had jumped onto the PoMo bandwagon would continue to build their jazzed-up skyscrapers for years yet; they only dug PoMo's critical hole even deeper.

Animadversions against Postmodernism from the academic side had reached an all-time high. In 1989 Mary McLeod wrote that the phrase "Postmodernism is the architecture of Reaganism" had already become a cliché in academic circles, albeit one with some merit.[33] Without validating Decon's accelerated strain of Modernism, McLeod traced a thread of reactionary politics in Postmodernism that ran straight from Colin Rowe through the building boom of the 1980s. "Collectively, Postmodern architects have exhibited a marked indifference to economic and social policy," she pointed out: in its rejection of Modernist aesthetics, the movement had thrown out the socially progressive baby with the formal bathwater, allowing Postmodernism to be appropriated by a conservative political order and evacuated of its urbanist and pluralist values.[34] As the 1980s turned to the '90s, this left Postmodernism looking banal, co-opted, and passé.

Upon Michael in particular, the hammer fell with devastating force. McLeod herself had been a student of Michael's; Peggy Deamer, also a product of Princeton, would say of his later work that it was "not nostalgia," but "hallucination."[35] Alan Colquhoun, one of Michael's earliest academic allies, would go on to denounce the "Mickey Mouse style he later adopted."[36] The pervasive sense that Michael's work was all too congruent with the ideological climate of the 1980s had taken hold early: just after the opening of Portland, a television interviewer had sounded Frank Gehry on the building. "One might speculate that that kind of imagery is politically related to the Reagan Administration," Gehry said, with a laugh. "I can imagine that. That we're looking at a kind of a return to imperial architecture."[37]

On formal grounds alone, the door was open for another architecture to reclaim the progressive mantle, and Gehry, Koolhaas, Daniel Libeskind, and the rest eventually walked through it. Their work, as McLeod understood from the start, was no more politically potent than Michael's, but its lack of Greco-Roman pomp made it appear comparatively forward-looking, even if the future it foresaw was one of frenzied technological confusion. That vision, in fact, was part of what gave the new brace of anti-Postmodernists their verve—and unlike Michael's work, the irregular geometries of Gehry, the swooping curves of Zaha Hadid, and the slashes and gashes of Libeskind could not be so easily vulgarized by bigger, more corporate practices. Their noisy novelty shouted down Michael's Apollonian quietism, and their resistance to duplication made them seem (for the nonce, anyway) durably cool.

By the end of the Clinton years, Herbert Muschamp, who succeeded Paul Goldberger at the *New York Times* in 1992, would say of Michael:

> Few architects today are less trendy than Mr. Graves. In the early 1980s, he was a trend beyond compare.... Today he is regarded by many as a stale trend: yesterday's bag. And in these fast-paced times a stale trend is virtually ancient history.[38]

"I will never do anything that will please him," Michael said of Muschamp.[39] It was Muschamp, above all, who beat the drum in the popular press against Postmodernism, and it was Muschamp, above all, who led the swelling chorus of praise that greeted Frank Gehry's Guggenheim Museum Bilbao in northern Spain when it opened in 1997. Dubbed "the Miracle in Bilbao," Gehry's warped, sinuous creation was a masterful marriage of technology and expressionism, and it would be the watershed for everything that followed in the digital age. The "starchitect" was born.

THAT MICHAEL STAYED COMMITTED to his vision of an architecture of meaning, long after its meaning had shifted so dramatically, is the great puzzle of his later career.

Philip Johnson, never one to be caught in last season's clothes, had already shifted away from his Postmodernist work; by the early 2000s, SOM would do the same. Michael, had he followed suit, could have done so without the semblance of cynicism, given the depth of his practice: his work in the 1970s had been teeming in latencies, in unexplored potential. Why didn't he mine it for something else?

There are any number of possible explanations, but key to them all is that Michael, correctly or not, came to believe that he *had* escaped Postmodernism—or that he was never part of it to begin with. Looking back in 1994, he said of his work, "I didn't call it postmodern—none of us thought much of it as a name."[40] True, he had been happy enough to accept the label when Charles Jencks was feting him alongside Frank Lloyd Wright as one of America's "Kings of Infinite Space" in a television documentary the critic produced in 1983.[41] But after less than a decade, even Jencks no longer recognized his erstwhile hero as a proper Postmodernist; by then, wrote Jencks, the work "was the reverse of Postmodernism."[42] Far from being complex and contradictory, Michael's later projects had become perfectly harmonious, their accessibility so absolute as to foreclose alternate readings.

The architect had not done this unthinkingly. By the 1990s Postmodernist disunity had ceased holding the same allure for Michael it once did. Instead, he preferred to speak of a parallel, non-Modernist unity, one that had been neglected by Modernists and Postmodernists alike. As the scholar (and later Princeton dean) Stan Allen wrote, Michael "mapped out an alternative genealogy for Modernism,"[43] cobbled together from sources he'd been assimilating for years and constituting what the critic Reyner Banham might have called *une architecture autre*: an "other" architecture.

This "other" property Michael found in the stripped classicism of Gunnar Asplund and in the decorative daintiness of Josef Hoffmann and the Vienna Secession. He saw it in the work of C. F. Hansen, a nineteenth-century Danish classicist whom he'd begun to include in his lectures, and in the buildings of Jože Plečnik, a Slovenian architect whose buildings throughout Central Europe Michael had tracked down over the years. These "extraordinary architects...who the world doesn't know," as Michael called them, were complemented by the work of an artist the world (and Aldo Rossi) knew very well: the painter Giorgio de Chirico, whose haunting landscapes often included vaguely Renaissance structures adrift in unplaceable settings.[44] The Italian Surrealist would be a major touchstone for Michael's own paintings from the late 1980s onward.

Combining these several strands, Michael's architectural language became more succinct and ascetic, a revolving wheel of hazily familiar typologies with reduced decorative touches. His buildings, as a consequence, also became more repetitive—but hidden in the repetitions, Michael's late style sometimes afforded a glimpse at his dreamed-of otherness, nowhere more so than in the design for the Denver Public Library, the most exceptional project from Michael Graves Architect of the mid-1990s.

Completed just eighteen months before Gehry's Bilbao museum, the library project emerged from a 1990 competition in which Michael's office squared off against Robert A. M. Stern and the Denver architects Hoover Berg Desmond. The terms of the commission called for the out-of-town contestants to be paired with a local firm, and Michael teamed up with the Colorado-based studio of the designer Brian Klipp, meeting him for the first time only the night before their initial interview with the library commission. "He was always flying in from someplace," recalled Klipp.[45]

As with Lapidus in Florida, Michael carried on an amiable and productive partnership with Klipp, relying on the Denverite's knowledge of the city's history and character. Occupying a downtown block on Broadway adjacent to Civic Center Park, the new library would be a 405,000-square-foot extension to an existing midcentury structure, a comely if commonplace Modernist volume that would receive an extensive interior renovation and become part of Michael's overall massing scheme. The site of the addition had formerly been home to a dry-cleaning plant, and the construction team had to perform extensive soil remediation after solvent deposits were discovered during excavation. The area in general was considered rather unsavory, and for the municipal government the project involved some "soul searching," as Klipp put it, a moment for Denver "to figure out what it was as a city."[46] The library would be the first in what has since become a suite of new institutional buildings in the district (including a new Denver Art Museum addition by Daniel Libeskind from 2006), and Michael's proposal won over a local jury trying to find a cornerstone for this new cultural acropolis.

It's not hard to see why. The completed library creates an urban scene *ex novo*, a cluster of volumes arrayed, like some of the Japanese projects, into a family group, but with its members crowded closer together and more dynamically interrelated in plan [PLATES 50 AND 51]. Seen from the south on West Thirteenth Avenue, a russet mass, "the Bar" as the architects called it, passes through the ensemble from the eastern and western fronts; it is braced by a blue block, which steps down to a symmetrical beige porch. Surrounding these volumes are a number of semi-engaged dependencies, most dramatically a green, gable-topped tower—nicknamed by the designers "the Pencil"—and a central cylinder—nicknamed "the Drum." Capped by a flat plane in shining copper, the Drum sprouts sets of brachiated piers, also in copper, suggestive of the woodwork trabeation of rustic barn lofts.

The piers were a form that was appearing more and more in Michael's paintings at the time, and in some buildings as well, such as the porch of his 1996 Indianapolis Art Center for his hometown of Broad Ripple Village. All the elements of the library, in fact, were well-worn standards of the Graves repertoire: the insertion of the Drum into a rectilinear mass was a main feature of Team Disney, while the well-sharpened point of the Pencil turned up in several Japanese projects. But Denver was not just another spin through Michael's patented album of forms.

The design excelled, thanks to a nervy act of insolence during its initial development. The original brief circulated by the clients stipulated that the building was to be limited to a single entrance facing Broadway. This made perfect sense: libraries are jealous protectors of their own books; the less porous they are, the safer their collections are likely to be. But at Michael's insistence, the Graves-Klipp scheme included a second entrance on the western side, facing a pedestrian walkway that cuts through the block between the library and one of the older galleries of the Denver Art Museum. "We broke the rules," noted Klipp, and the change might easily have lost them the commission. Instead, it became a rare moment in which Michael's formal intention to project a communal, village-like image is borne out by the program, with the double entryways turning the high-ceilinged public lobby that connects them into a bustling indoor street.

The library had another quality as well, one even harder to come by in the firm's work. Clad in cast and natural stone quarried in Germany, the building has an alternating patina of lighter and darker masonry, granting it a depth and tactility that stiffens the spine of its soft, pastel palette. Everywhere one looks, in the timbered rotunda in the Western History Room and in the copper strips on the Pencil pyramid exterior, unusual care was taken with materials, presenting them with fewer encumbrances of decorative detailing, allowing them, at last, to speak for themselves.

Though he mocked its toylike classicism as "Mr. Rogers meets McKim, Meade and White," even Herbert Muschamp owned up to a certain regard for the Denver Library.[47] The project was special for Michael: he made it the cover of his third monograph, an honor held in the previous two by Portland and Humana, and it helped snag him *GQ's* Man of the Year for design in 1997. Michael was increasingly leaving the firm's larger architectural projects to his retinue of partners—especially Karen Nichols, Tom Rowe, and Patrick Burke, all three of whom were elevated to the title of "principal" in 1998 when the firm changed its name to Michael Graves & Associates. But the founder stayed close to the library project during the design process, making minute changes to it throughout (as he was known to do). One of these nearly sabotaged the pleasing solidity of the Drum by doing it up in ornamental bands, a plot foiled by the objections of the client.[48]

The library's popularity with locals and its reasonably warm critical reception confirmed for Michael that his modified Postmodernist language was still a viable medium for public architecture. And around the same time that he began work on Denver, he had finally completed another project that showed his late style's potential to create a rich, sensuous environment for private life. After thirty years and countless thousands of dollars, he had finished the Warehouse.

Having polished off a few final tweaks to the kitchen wing, Michael could now entertain in style, celebrating the renovation by hosting a garden party for the National Governors Association in 1992. During the festivities, the wife of one of the governors approached the homeowner to compliment him on the building.

"How long has the house been finished?" she asked.

"About twenty minutes," Michael said: the gravel in the driveway had been laid down just before the guests' arrival.[49]

In its final state, the house represented the fullest flowering of Michael's alternate-historical vision. Enclosing the graveled court on two sides to form a de Chirico–esque piazza, the exterior was a perfectly serene composition in burnt umber, the facade sparingly ornamented and interrupted only by a few projecting volumes, including the south-facing chimney breast. Inside, every detail had been fully regularized and classicized: the original exposed ductwork (representative of his style at the time of the Gunwyn Ventures office) had been obscured, marked now by black iron grilles, and the library fronting the eastern garden was made into a narrow forest of columns, painted to resemble Michael's cherished bird's-eye maple but in fact made of humble PVC pipes and MDF board. As in Sir John Soane's Museum, many of the house's adornments were fake—Michael's Pierre-Paul Prud'hon painting was real, but his Nicolas Poussin was a convincing replica. All the Corots were actually by Michael Graves.[50]

He had bought the neighboring houses to the east and west of his own entry allée, using them as rental properties and occasionally lending them out to friends. Among the latter was Fran Lebowitz, who holed up in one of the homes for a year and a half starting around 1993, during an excruciatingly long renovation of her Manhattan apartment building. "My writing room faced Michael's house," she recalled, and looking into his in-home studio, she could see him at work "about twenty-one hours a day."[51] In one of her fitful efforts to shake off her epic case of writer's block ("writer's blockade," as she once called it), Lebowitz had agreed to produce a children's book and was working on it during her stay in Princeton. Considering Michael's obviously packed schedule, it came as some surprise when Michael's girlfriend at the time approached Lebowitz and told her that he was "very hurt" he hadn't been asked to illustrate her book. She did ask, and he accepted.[52] The result, 1994's *Mr. Chas and Lisa Sue Meet the Pandas*, is the largest body of realist paintings Michael ever produced, as well as the only new book by Fran Lebowitz in more than three decades.

Several years later, her apartment building still being overhauled, Lebowitz asked if she could stay in the house again but found that it already had another tenant. Michael had installed his son there. Adam stayed on in Princeton for several years while working in a peripheral capacity at his father's firm, the lengthiest period of personal contact between Michael and his second child. Sadly, this tentative rapprochement was no more effectual than previous ones. When Gail, after another lengthy stint in Cambridge, decided to move back to Indianapolis, it was thought best by all concerned that Adam go with her.

AFTER THAT, MICHAEL WAS once again alone, though rarely lonely. Besides friends and lovers, he had found a new passion: golf, which he took up in the mid-1990s and for which he demonstrated an ability not quite coequal to his enthusiasm, taking off early from work many days to hit the Springdale Golf Club in the company of one of his dogs. His associate Patrick Burke recalled him attending a client meeting on the range, and when the rest of the group headed to the clubhouse for drinks, Michael stayed behind to get in a few more swings. Hours passed before his clients and associates emerged to find him still slicing away, hitting balls into the twilight until it was too dark to see.[53]

Michael's singleness of purpose was unquestionably another factor governing his choice not to alter the basic character of his practice in the 1990s. Stubbornness was his specialty, not merely a facet of his psyche but its basic substrate.

Peter Eisenman, who was in psychotherapy for several decades, related that at some point in the mid-1970s he encouraged Michael to have a preliminary session with his own analyst. Subsequently, Eisenman asked his doctor whether Michael would be continuing with treatment. The doctor indicated vaguely that he did not think it would be useful for Michael to do so.[54] It was not, one infers, that the depths of the Gravesian mind were so impossible to plumb: rather, what would make Michael a hard nut to crack for even the most seasoned psychologist was his marked distaste for self-examination, a quality remarked upon by many people who knew him over the years: "There was a mystery to him," as Mary McLeod put it; he didn't "come out of his shell," said Caroline Constant; "never introspective," in Steven Harris's view.[55]

And yet Michael's inner drives were but poorly hidden, floating to the surface again and again in his work. The need to communicate, the desire to give his buildings and products a human aspect, the compulsion to always do more, make more, build bigger…It is not mere armchair pathologizing to connect these things to the boy with the cockeyed stare who felt himself so out of place no matter where he went, from the playing fields of Indianapolis to the halls of Harvard. Nor is it hard to see how architecture may have furnished a form of wish fulfillment for some of the ongoing struggles of his later life. It was Paul Goldberger who once observed (unaware, he later realized, of his own perspicacity) that Breuer's Whitney, in its stone-faced obscurantism, was an "autistic" building.[56] Michael's pitched battle to speak to it was more than strictly architectural.

The cumulative disappointments of the post-Whitney years, as Michael's critical standing took a heavy hit, did not sit well with his sensitivity, or with his stubbornness. Despite having won almost every major award the architecture world had to offer (the AIA Gold Medal, the Richard Driehaus Award, the Topaz Medallion, a pile of Progressive Architecture Awards), in later life Michael grumbled loudly about his failure to win architecture's highest honor, the Pritzker Prize, which had gone to friends and competitors such as Richard Meier, Aldo Rossi, and Robert Venturi. His critiques of his contemporaries became increasingly pointed and ad hominem: Rem Koolhaas struck him as "a complete narcissist," Daniel Libeskind as "angry."[57] Michael's persistent social angst—the legacy of Bud Graves, Broad Ripple Village, and all the psychic cargo of his background—made his relative loss of status all the more upsetting, and his lifelong unease on matters of class found expression in his ever more resolute classicism.

This reflexive turn to the classical past as the locus of legitimacy was an acquired trait of his time in Rome, and this was the mixed blessing of those years. As the critic Joan Ockman has written, Michael and other architectural pilgrims had found, in the city's timeworn streets, "the shock of the real," its glorious history somehow more substantial than the flimsy present. Impressing itself upon a young man so hungry for authenticity, the architecture of classicism had wound itself around Michael's belief in an architecture of meaning, until the two had become almost inextricable.[58] And so, threatened and bewildered by a changing world, it was in this double dream that Michael now sought asylum.

Nowhere was this more obvious than in the Warehouse, the gorgeous, building-size totem to Michael's image of the good life and his image of himself. Away from the world's welter, immured in an ambience of antique splendor, he made his home an elaborately contrived containment device, a place where he could live, as the critic Kenneth Frampton put it, like "the mythic aristocrat he thought himself to be."[59]

BUT WAS EVER AN ELITIST such an irrepressible populist? Michael, as Patrick Burke put it, "never wanted his designs to be challenging."[60] From the same springs as Michael's anxieties and jealousies there also came his overwhelming desire to be *liked*, and this, above all, is what drove his continued devotion to an architecture of bright colors and recognizable forms, where meaning was never hard to find. Whenever his team was working on a design, the surest sign that they were onto something was when Michael would turn up his chin slightly and utter one of his best-known catchphrases:

"That'll put a smile on their faces."

"I'm not making designs for a new gravestone," he would say, and while his work was not so jokey as sometimes believed, there was never anything too grave about Graves.[61] This made him, from a certain perspective, an odd choice to take on a commission for what was effectively a large hunk of funerary architecture.

In 1997 the United States National Park Service announced that Michael Graves Architect had been selected to design the scaffolding for the planned two-year restoration of the Washington Monument. Target, the nationwide chain of discount retailers, was planning to expand into Washington, DC, and under the advisement of Vice President of Marketing Bob Thacker they had hammered out a high-profile promotional opportunity by subscribing as official sponsors to the monument project.[62] For a $1 million contribution (plus $4 million drummed up from other corporations), Target had the privilege of helping to choose the architect, and Thacker thought to approach Michael.

With the firm aboard, Thacker flew to Princeton to meet his architect for the first time. An Amtrak train bringing representatives from the National Park Service was late in arriving, and while Michael and Thacker waited, they took a quick walk, during which Michael broached the idea of collaborating with Target on some kind of commercial initiative. Thacker's interest was piqued, and within a matter of weeks the company's vice president of merchandising, Ron Johnson, proposed a Graves-branded product line to be sold in Target stores nationwide.

In one of their first meetings, Michael explained to Johnson that a large, low-cost product collection was exactly what he'd been wanting to do for years. "Ron," Michael said, "my whole problem is that everything I create is out of the price range of my students at Princeton." Proud though he was of the firm's Swid Powell dinner plates, Alessi salt and pepper shakers, and all the rest, Michael thought the firm could get still closer to the dream of bringing real design to real people. He said he'd be thrilled to work with Target.[63]

The next eighteen months were among the busiest in the history of Michael's office. The steady stream of residential building projects continued apace—an apartment building in Midtown Manhattan, an embassy in Korea, luxury residences in Europe. All the while, the firm was hurriedly readying the design for the monument scaffold and simultaneously scaling up its products division in time to make a rollout planned for only eighteen months after the Target contract was signed. One hundred and sixty products were to be part of the initial launch, and to ready them the firm devised a system that would ensure that all of the work had a consistent but flexible identity: they developed "a new language," as associate Donald Strum put it, a matrix of forms that were rooted in Michael's drawings and sketches but that could be applied to any product by any designer sufficiently fluent in Graves-ese.[64]

Central to this new formal language was an egg-like shape, deployed first as a handle for cleaning and kitchen utensils and then later as the inspiration for whole products. "I just fell in love from the moment we held the egg," said Johnson.[65] The executive and his designer quickly "got to be pals," recalled Michael, but while they were on the same aesthetic wavelength, Michael's graphic approach didn't quite suit Johnson, who preferred not to pass judgment on drawings alone.[66] Instead, Michael's studio produced models, prototype after prototype flowing out of the Princeton office toward Target HQ in Minneapolis, all of them styled with their own distinctive personalities: a streamlined toaster with peaked shoulders, a comical-futurist teakettle, like the 9093 dressed up for an episode of *The Jetsons*, a coffee maker with the silhouette of a short, bald sparrow [**PLATES 52–54**].

By early 1999 the scaffold was up in Washington, DC, and public opinion came down solidly in favor. The glowing, reticulated fabric sheath that covered the metal grid carried its Graves-ism lightly: its azure hue faintly recalled the one Michael had used in his drawings, on the Alessi teakettle, and in other projects, while the boxy patterning on the surface was a subtle historicist gesture, referencing the cyclopean masonry blocks beneath it [**PLATE 55**]. Intentionally or not, the structure was also open to alternate interpretations, with some viewers reading it as a purely artistic wrapping—reminiscent of the work of the installationists Christo and Jean-Claude—and others seeing it as a boldly industrial overlay—"a splashy, high-tech hairnet," as one critic wrote.[67] Opening as it did during the public campaign against AIDS, still others couldn't help but read it as a giant prophylactic, fitted snugly over the nation's most famous phallic symbol.[68]

Synchronized with the scaffold's completion, and just in time for the opening of a local DC Target outlet, the Graves "Design for All" collection went on sale all across America, and it became an instant best seller. Over the next thirteen years, the line would expand to more than two thousand products—spatulas, brooms, dog toys, all in the telltale bright blue boxes and labeling. While Target has declined to release precise sales figures, there's little doubt they ran into the millions of units and into the billions of dollars. The first in a series of designer collaborations that would go on to include Thomas O'Brien and others, Michael's collection helped recast the brand as the more urbane alternative to Kmart and Walmart. "Tar-*zhay*" the public was calling it now, the name pronounced à la française.

Using inexpensive materials, value-engineered to ensure efficient production and to stand up to wear and tear, the products made real Michael's dream—and the dream of generations of Modern designers, from Walter Gropius on down—of bringing sophisticated architectural thinking to everyday household items affordable to nearly everyone. In exchange Michael received the anticipated hoots from formerly supportive critics who said he'd been "consumed by consumerism," in the words of

Charles Jencks—the popularity of the products further justifying their portrayal of Michael as an irredeemable sellout.[69] Michael recalled being asked to speak at the AIA shortly after the collection's debut, and as he approached the podium, the emcee for the evening introduced him by saying, "It's a wonder Michael Graves has taken time from drawing teakettles to grace us with his presence."[70] Gordon Bunshaft had died, but his spirit lived on.

Would the reaction have been so hostile if the products had exhibited less of Michael's cheery anthropomorphism and more of the Bauhaus's undemonstrative functionalism? Perhaps, perhaps not. If they had, there's no telling whether they would have been half so popular—or half so functional, with many buyers holding onto their twist-mops and toilet cleaners long after they'd gone out of production, only to call up the designers in Princeton and beg for replacements.[71] And not all the critics turned up their noses at the Target line's alleged frippery. In a pleasing bookend to the Battle of Portland, coming directly from the halls of Michael's yet-unforgiven grad school, *Harvard Design Magazine* published an appreciative article in 2000 on the Target homewares, written by the midwestern designer and academic Daniel Naegele. "We Dig Graves," the author declared.[72]

HAD THE PRODUCTS NOT SOLD as well as they did, Michael might have had good reason to question his choices, indisposed though he was to second-guessing. As it was, the 1990s had seen him take his lumps and come up smiling—ever his favorite expression, the adolescent joker in him alive and well despite his advancing years. Michael Graves & Associates greeted the new millennium with a staff of more than eighty and dozens of commissions in the pipeline.

Bedimming his contentment somewhat was the end of his Princeton seminar, which was removed from the course list at the School of Architecture in 1999.[73] The popularity of both the renamed "Thematic Studies in Architecture" and his graduate studio course had dipped over the decade in tandem with Michael's critical reputation. What exactly precipitated the termination of his undergraduate teaching is in dispute. Michael felt that the director of graduate studies at the time, the architect Elizabeth Diller, had been instrumental in removing 402 from the bulletin; Diller contends that this was not so.[74] Certainly Michael felt a rather extraordinary animus toward Diller, having once (while talking to former dean Bob Geddes) dismissed her work and that of her well-known office, Diller + Scofidio, as "performance art."[75] Whatever the case, the outcome was clear enough. "That's when I lost my clout," Michael would say later. "I kept going for a while afterward, but it wasn't much fun without the seminar."[76] Soon he stopped teaching the studio course as well, remaining on the faculty in an emeritus capacity but scarcely ever returning to campus.[77]

Next to the elusive Pritzker, this was Michael's greatest sore spot. However market-friendly his practice had become, he had never ceased craving academic approval. In the mid-1990s he was coteaching a Princeton studio with Peter Eisenman—who had long since patched things up with the university that had formerly rejected him—and the two invited Colin Rowe to attend as a critic. Another visitor, the Columbia University historian (and later MoMA architecture curator) Barry Bergdoll, recalled watching Michael and his old friend jockeying for the august critic's attention, still trying to curry favor with the man whom both claimed as an intellectual forefather.[78]

Not having coursework had its advantages, however, leaving Michael more time for other pursuits. As part of the contract for his 1998 condo project in Miami Beach, he got an apartment in the waterfront building for his own use and stayed there frequently to visit his new girlfriend, Lynn Min. South Florida was an ideal climate for golf, and the building was an ideal climate for Michael—a total Graves environment inside and out, including one of his murals in the lobby. Michael would fly down for a few days, fly back up, fly down again. Min told him of her pregnancy while driving him to the airport, and even though their relationship formally ended, Michael looked forward to flying down even more to visit her and his soon-to-be-born son. "We stayed more than just friends," said Min. "We were family."[79]

Michael flew and flew. "He saw flights as the only downtime he had," recalled Patrick Burke.[80] Michael and Burke flew back and forth to Egypt many times, designing a series of resorts there; Michael flew with firm partner Tom Rowe to Houston to design a branch of the Federal Reserve Bank and then a master plan for the campus of Rice University. For all his success, the architect still felt he needed the work ("I can't afford to retire," he'd say), but in some ways it might be said that he did not, after so many years, know how to stop.[81] Michael flew to Shanghai, where the firm was involved with the restoration of one of the Beaux Arts beauties on the Bund, and he flew to Nashville, and to Pittsburgh, and then back to his childhood turf in Indianapolis to design the NCAA Hall of Fame. He flew and he flew, and one day he flew to Germany, feeling a touch under the weather and carrying in his bag a bottle, possibly half-empty, of what may or may not have been antibiotics.

IX

THE SKY AND THE FRAME

EVERY MORNING FOR the last decade of his life, Michael Graves awoke between five thirty and six thirty. "I get up," as he put it, "not in the sense of 'getting up'": his nurse would enter his room, roll him onto his side, and then go through a ritual process of washing his body, face, and back.[1] Immobile during the night, he often sweat heavily in his sleep, despite an automated air mattress that puffed up and down at regular intervals to reduce his discomfort and fend off bedsores.

After washing, his nurse would lay out his breakfast—oatmeal two mornings out of the week, cereal the rest, and toast on weekends, though the gluten and carbohydrates of white bread had to be avoided to try to keep his weight down and his digestion good. After breakfast, his nurse would dress him, his attire less formal than in the old days but not without a certain panache, often with a colorful sweater thrown around his neck. He had learned, while in rehabilitation, how to dress himself and could even wash himself if need be with the aid of a mirror on a long stick. Naturally he preferred to have his nurse do both, though even with her help the business of tooth brushing, fingernail trimming, and pill taking could take several hours, and he usually did not arrive in the office until close to ten-thirty.

"But I don't leave for lunch," he noted.[2] With his wheelchair in a standing position to improve his circulation, Michael would draw and take meetings until midafternoon, when he would enjoy a small snack of crackers and cheese. (If a visitor was present, he might permit himself a sandwich and a cookie.) He would then resume working and keep on going until at least five, or later still if he was reviewing his associates' designs during a project charrette, before being loaded once again into his customized van and taken back to the Warehouse.

There, his trusted nurse (or one of her associates; his primary nurse also worked two half-days a week at the local hospital) would place Michael on his exercise bike for a brief spell, then serve him dinner in bed, which he would eat while watching television. He had developed a special fondness for MSNBC's Rachel Maddow and would watch all the network's programming straight through her talk show before drifting off to sleep.

That was Michael's day, day after day, barring travel or other special occasions. Even when these intervened, his illness and the struggle to overcome it were the logic of his life. His condition did, at times, provide a useful pretext: to avoid the dreaded pressure ulcers—a bedsore had ultimately killed his fellow paralytic Christopher Reeve—Michael could not be allowed to remain in any one position for too long. With a still-packed schedule of sometimes tedious cocktails and gala functions, the architect now had the perfect excuse to give his gracious hosts. "If I'm at a dinner party and I don't want to stay," he explained, "I just tell them I've got to get out of the chair. And I leave."

BY THE TIME of his paralysis, Michael had all but lost touch with his second wife, Lucy, who had long ago remarried. His daughter, Sarah, was in Calgary with her husband and children, and though he spoke to Gail on occasion, she had her own life, and Adam, in Indianapolis. Even if any of his current or former family members had been available to do so, none of them could have been expected to take on the level of responsibility necessary to help him in the wake of his illness. He required the commitment and expertise of a trained professional, but one with a personal touch.

Michael was slow to accept that his condition would not improve. "He was stubborn," recalled his surgeon, Dr. Barth Green, but as Michael began to reckon with the long-term nature of his illness, he started to search for a permanent home health aide, hoping for the right match.[3] Several came and went, and none quite seemed to fit—until he met a forty-three-year-old woman from Hangzhou, China, a nurse at the local University Medical Center of Princeton, where Michael stayed briefly in late 2003 while the Warehouse was being retrofitted to accommodate his wheelchair. The nurse's name, in a cosmic coincidence, was Min Lin, closely matching that of Lynn Min, Michael's last girlfriend and the mother of his infant son, Michael Sebastian.

"He needed help," said Min Lin.[4] When the two met, Michael's condition had stabilized, but he was gaining weight and in poor spirits. After being hired at the suggestion of Michael's lawyer, Susan Howard, Lin quickly put Michael on a new workout and dietary regimen. Schedule allowing, she accompanied him everywhere, to black-tie galas and client meetings, lectures and dinners. Her presence in the last decade of Michael's life was vital: totally unable to fend for himself, he needed assistance with nearly everything, and he and Min shared an intimacy more intense, in some ways, than that of any other relationship in his life. "Except for the romantic thing, we're warmer and closer to each other than ninety percent of couples," Michael would say. He called her "Minnie."[5]

With Minnie's help, everything in Michael's world was reconfigured and reordered around his health and his limited mobility. Hotels were vetted in advance to ensure they could cater to his needs; medicines were refilled and monitored to make sure he took them in the right amounts and at the right time. The costs were sometimes astronomical—and not just in terms of dollars. Some of his medications caused Michael's hands to shake uncontrollably. He would need Minnie's help to hold a fork and draw it to his mouth, and he chafed at the feeling of infantilization.

The third and final phase of Warehouse renovations [**PLATES 61 AND 62**] included the installation of an elevator to the south of the old kitchen door and the removal of the miniature *tempietto* in the second-floor hallway so that his wheelchair could pass through. (Conveniently, the open oculus in the floor had already been covered with a glass top after one of the dogs fell through it into the foyer.) Every university and institute to which Michael was invited as a guest panelist or presenter had to be fully accessible, with means of getting him from van to greenroom to auditorium stage, wheelchair and all.

Or wheelchairs, plural. For everyday use, Michael favored a Permobil c500, a standard utility model equipped with a built-in table for eating or perusing documents. But on weekends, or when painting and drawing, he switched to something called an iBOT—a technological marvel created by Dean Kamen, the inventor responsible for the battery-powered Segway transportation device. The iBOT featured multiple sets of wheels, six in all, and was equipped with an ingenious system of gyroscopes and gears that allowed Michael to mount and descend stairs, as well as "stand" to a height of nearly six feet. A fellow paraplegic and acquaintance of Michael's, the artist Chuck Close, is also a proud iBOT owner, and while the device went out of production in 2009 (at $25,000, it was beyond the reach of most prospective buyers), it was still possible to have it serviced. Michael became adept at maneuvering the contraption and in midconversation could often be seen making subtle adjustments using the joystick control, shifting in place to avoid feeling cramped or uncomfortable.

The wheelchairs, along with Minnie's vigilant care, helped put Michael back in control of much of his professional life. But some things would never return to normal. He had forgotten the physical demands of the act of creating architecture: instead of being able to draw on the big rolled-out sheets of yellow trace, he was confined to smaller templates. "You've got to see it the way Morandi did," he'd say, "not the way de Kooning did," though he could make slightly larger drawings by stitching miniature ones together via digital scans.[6] When clients requested one of his murals, he would do the cartoon and then have an associate complete the painting. He was never displeased with the result, but he sorely missed the satisfaction of completing a big piece himself.

The operations of the office had changed, and although his associates continued to keep Michael engaged as much as possible, many of the larger architectural projects were handled almost exclusively by designated associates working autonomously with limited input from the chief. No renovations were undertaken to the labyrinthine rooms in the south building of Michael Graves & Associates, discouraging random drop-ins by the boss. This kind of devolution of power is not uncommon as firm principals grow older and move into semiretirement—Carl Strauss's dependence on Ray Roush was a perfect example—but in Michael's case it took a sharper turn owing to his disability.

The tale was different at the Michael Graves Design Group, the products division established as a separate entity in 2003, where Michael's influence was paramount. First at a temporary space down Nassau, later in the house that formerly held the retail space across the street from the architecture studio, ramps and adequate circulation space gave Michael room to maneuver and allowed him to keep up with all the goings-on. He had decided, while still recuperating at Kessler Institute in New Jersey, to point the industrial design department toward the health-care market, and the firm now began a pitched effort to remake the entire patient environment, from bedpans to hospitals. With the man whose name was on the door himself in a wheelchair, the firm could draw on his unique insights into the challenges of the physically impaired. Improving their lot became the cause of Michael's life.

"The more places I went, the worse they were," Michael said.[7] Early in his illness, he recalled sitting in a restaurant and watching as an older customer walked in with a pronounced limp. The maître d' showed the guest to his table and then left him there, and as the gentleman stood motionless, it became evident that he had no way of settling himself into the armless chair in front of him. Scooting it as close as he dared to the table, he remained standing there for several minutes trying to think of a way of lowering himself safely onto the cushion without leaning so hard on the back as to tip it over.

"I wanted to get out and go help him," recalled Michael, "to say, 'Here, the chair is behind your knees, I got my hand behind your back, let yourself down slowly, if you can.'" Confined to his wheelchair, he could only look on helplessly.[8] He resolved then and there to create a chair that could help people like his fellow diner regain a bit of their autonomy, and a bit of their dignity.

Moving into the health-care sphere was like starting all over again, going back to the days when he first tried (and frequently failed) to cultivate clients and create work for his fledgling studio. Hanging out a shingle and hiring some new staff would not suffice; the firm would need to aggressively court major manufacturers and forge new industry contacts. The investment of time and money would be steep, but Michael felt he had no choice. "I had to do it," he said. "I had the empathy, and I wanted to get involved."[9]

Rob Van Varick, a graduate of the Rhode Island School of Design, joined the Michael Graves Design Group in March 2003, just a couple of weeks after Michael had taken ill. His first meeting with Michael was at Kessler: "He was just talking about how terrible everything there was," recalled Van Varick. "The sponges on a stick!"[10] In time, under the guidance of firm principal for product design Donald Strum, Van Varick began—along with a growing complement of his colleagues—to transition into research and development for health-care products that could relieve some of the vicissitudes of the patient experience.

A clamp-on adjustable tub rail, a bath seat, a showerhead [PLATE 57], a cane that folded neatly into a carrier bag—the firm's first creations for the brand Drive Medical in 2005 signaled the comprehensiveness of its approach, as well as the sensibility it brought to the field. Most medical product design, noted Strum, "didn't conjure any thought except for the thought of how sick you are"; the Gravesian flair for color and contour made the products a welcome change of pace.[11] In a convenient coincidence, the bulbous, egg-like geometries that had given the Target products their goofy charm had an added advantage when applied to accessibility design: for cramped fingers unable to grasp narrow handles and for bodies prone to bump against sharp edges, the fattened volumes of the Graves health-care line were far easier and safer to use.

The Drive Medical relationship was short-lived, the economic realities of the marketplace making it difficult to achieve production at the scale and with the quality the design team had hoped for. It was followed, however, by a more gratifying partnership, launched in 2009 with medical device maker Stryker [PLATES 58–60]. An over-bed table, a bedside table, a hospital transport wheelchair, and a stand-assist chair have been its main results to date, and they've shown how far the firm is willing to go in adapting its long-established design formulas to meet the demands of its new customer base. The stand-assist chair in particular, born of Michael's restaurant revelation, is notable for its unprepossessing profile and practicality: "It's just a chair," said Michael, "not a [Mies] Barcelona chair. It's not going to grab you in terms of its looks, though it's not medicinal-looking."[12] Its arms made of a flexible composite that gives just enough resistance to spring off or settle into, the stand-assist chair is miles away from the decorative excesses of Michael's Memphis days, while still somehow remaining recognizably Graves.

Perhaps the most remarkable product in the Stryker line is the firm's hospital wheelchair, which has quickly become the most sought-after model on the market. The design process behind the device delved into the fine grain of how such products are really used in the health-care space. "We went into hospital rooms," said Van Varick, "interviewing cleaning staff, watching them clean the furniture, documenting that, making models, trying them out."[13] The numberless contingencies of the user experience for an in-patient transport wheelchair (how long the average user sits in it, how likely the chairs are to be stolen, the danger of getting extremities caught in the works) required a more data-driven, trial-and-error approach than Michael's firm had ever attempted. And for his young associates, the final testing stage was the most intimidating of all: the team had to bring each product to Michael, who would make sure that the wheelchair's seat cushion was comfortable enough, that its foot-rests didn't get in his way when getting in or out of it.

Gradually, the transition from a more aesthetically minded to a more research-oriented design process began to affect every aspect of the firm's product practice, which also continued to grow outside of the health-care realm. After Ron Johnson stepped aside at Target, the Graves design team found itself passed off to a succession of executives, most of them supportive, though the bond between client and designer began to fray as Target moved on to other brand collaborations (Marimekko, Isaac Mizrahi) inspired by its initial success with Graves. When Johnson landed at JCPenney in 2011, he called his old friend Michael and asked if he'd be interested in jumping ship from Target; he said yes, and the new Michael Graves Design Collection for JCPenney was launched in 2013. Unfortunately, Johnson did not enjoy the same success at JCPenney that he had Target, and within months of the new collaboration's debut he was ousted as CEO. The new Graves product line was orphaned at birth and gradually went out of production.

Products, however, were not Michael's only line of attack in transforming his office. Hospitals, wellness centers, and large-scale medical facilities of every kind have become central, over the last decade, to the firm's portfolio. Designed mostly by firm associates, the half-dozen projects to date nonetheless preserve much of the spirit of Michael's own thinking. In Lincoln, Nebraska, the firm completed the Madonna Rehabilitation Hospital in 2016, a modest but thoughtfully designed facility of some 240,000 square feet, specializing in exactly the kind of treatment Michael had received at Kessler. In Washington, DC, the firm's St. Coletta of Greater Washington, a school for the disabled, resembles nothing so much as a small, multi-colored *trulli* village [**PLATE 56**]. The warm, welcoming gaggle of forms is a perfect solution given the emotional sensitivities of its occupants: the facility specializes in children with serious intellectual disabilities, another instance of Michael achieving in his work some of the things left undone in his life.

ILLNESS BROUGHT MICHAEL full circle in countless ways. With Minnie, he was once again entrusted to the care of a nurse, just as he had been as a child, when Erma was his sole protector. Grappling with immobility, he was facing down a challenge not so different from his mother's. Disability had been the leitmotif of his existence—"I think my family is cursed," he once told Minnie—and in his final disability he triumphed over some of the older ones: gone was the needling guilt, a disability of its own that had driven him so hard for so many years.[14] With his health-care work, Michael could dispel any questions about having made himself "of use."

There was still one last disability left unreckoned with: Adam's. Yet even there, Michael decided it was time to seek again, if not reconciliation, at least normalization. After trying telephone and video chats without success, Michael and his elder son discovered that they could keep up an email correspondence. It wasn't much, but it was an improvement, and Michael helped secure his son a job working at a Target store in Indianapolis, checking in by email to see how he was faring.

Michael's other personal relationships remained more or less as they'd always been. With his older brother, Michael kept in regular if not frequent contact, though before Tom died in 2008 Michael had the opportunity to repay him for his early financial support. Of Michael's peers, John Hejduk had died in 2002 and Charles Gwathmey nine years later, leaving only three of the Five. Michael and Eisenman, after all they'd been through, were still as close as ever: they attended their last football game together in the fall of 2014, an Indiana versus Rutgers matchup on the latter's home turf in New Brunswick, New Jersey.[15] Long content to sit in the nosebleeds, they now enjoyed Eisenman's private box seats, a better perch by far and a necessity given Michael's wheelchair.

Both Michael and Eisenman remained in frequent contact with the other surviving Fiver, Richard Meier: all three participated in awards juries together, though Michael's thoughts on design were so at odds with those of his friends, and of the field in general, that Meier recalled he mostly said nothing except occasionally, "Oh! This is *terrible*."[16] Fran Lebowitz was still close, too (paraplegia had spelled the end of Michael's years of dog ownership, much to her relief), and she continued to prank him constantly. She spread a rumor that Michael's favorite food was Peeps, the ubiquitous yellow marshmallow treats found in stores around Easter, and once persuaded the marketing director for the candy maker to send Michael a truckload of Peeps and Peepsiana—strawberry and chocolate Peeps, Peeps coloring books, Peeps toys. Michael hated Peeps and gave most of the stuff away.[17]

One last personal relationship took on special importance in Michael's later life: the one with his preadolescent son, Michael Sebastian. Michael's youngest only ever knew his father in a wheelchair—his head grown bald, his voice lower, and his speech slightly slurred. Yet Michael's role in his namesake's early life was more active and involved than it had been with his older children, back when he had his strength. Though separated by hundreds of miles, the two were constantly in touch, and Michael continued to keep his apartment—retrofitted, like the Warehouse, for his wheelchair—in the South Beach apartment building he had designed, with regular stays there to visit Michael Sebastian and his mother. Embittered as Michael was by his condition, fatherhood turned out to be the great consolation of his final years, a late reminder that empathy mattered not just in design but in life.

WHAT REMAINED OF Michael's time and energy, after his work and the day-to-day aggravations of his illness, was largely absorbed by painting—which he did regularly despite the difficulty involved—and by advocacy—to which he now devoted his still-considerable celebrity.

Of the paintings, there was really only one: The Painting [PLATES 65 AND 66], as his partners called it. A continuation of the genre he had begun working in starting in the late 1990s, The Painting appeared in hundreds of iterations, the canvases varying in size and dimensions but generally small and square, featuring a dusty, indeterminately Tuscan setting populated by vaguely architectural forms. The colors were soft and Corot-like, their composition bringing to mind Giorgio Morandi, but the mood was closer to Giorgio de Chirico, dreamy and elegiac. In Michael's at-home studio, the canvases eventually covered every inch of available wall space, reminding the visitor of the clipping-covered hovel of a conspiracy-minded shut-in in a Hollywood thriller—which, in a sense, it was. "He always said, 'I can't play golf, so I just draw and paint," recalled Minnie.[18] Painting was the last outlet for Michael's compulsive bent.

Keeping Michael from becoming a true shut-in was his advocacy work. Once he'd found Minnie and the iBOT, the architect hit the circuit, giving a TED talk on accessibility, lecturing in cities large and small, bending the ear of anyone he could on the subject. Even before his firm began producing health-care products, he'd attempted to persuade Target to move into the field; when he heard that Jackson Memorial, the Miami hospital where Dr. Green had operated on him, was planning a rehabilitation center, he wanted to be involved and donated lavishly to its construction. (Naturally he had originally hoped to design it himself.) He formed friendships with other disabled celebrities, including the radio and print journalist John Hockenberry, who has been wheelchair-bound since the age of twenty. The title of Hockenberry's 2006 interview for Metropolis magazine summed up Michael's experience in the foregoing three years: "The Re-education of Michael Graves."[19]

Equipped with his new understanding, Michael gained prominence as an accessibility advocate. In 2011 the Graves firm was selected by fair-housing specialists

Clark Realty Capital for a pilot initiative of the Wounded Warrior Project to design small private homes optimized for returning veterans with special needs. Two of the houses have been built to date [**PLATE 63**], typical suburban residences but fine-tuned for the disabled, with adjustable-height countertops and one-floor plans that obviate the need for ramps (or for an iBOT). Ideally Michael's firm wanted to stock them full of its own health-care products, creating the health-care equivalent of the Swan and Dolphin Hotels: wall-to-wall Graves environments, only this time for life, not just for pleasure. The logistics proved too complicated, much to Michael's displeasure.

Hope, however, came from a higher office. Two years after Michael took on the Wounded Warrior Project, President Barack Obama named him to a position on the Architectural and Transportation Barriers Compliance Board, a federal sub-agency dealing with accessibility in public accommodations. Mostly ceremonial, the appointment nonetheless afforded Michael a still bigger platform to speak out on the issues that mattered to him most, and he took the posting seriously. "We would go to Washington for meetings every other month," recalled Minnie, and although Obama and he never met personally (the only president since Reagan of whom that can be said), Michael felt that his administration was poised to do real and lasting good.[20] Michael had been in Washington for one such meeting the day before he died, and his presence on the panel was so forceful that those who were there could hardly believe the news of his passing.

WHO COULD HAVE FORESEEN that Michael Graves—epicure, soft-voiced academic, lukewarm liberal—would turn into a fiery spokesman on behalf of some of America's most vulnerable citizens? Much less one whose output, in the last decade of his life, put such a strong emphasis on function over form?

For this was the great reversal in Michael's last decade as a designer. Meaning—and the language of classicism, absorbed in Rome, that he used to convey it—had taken such primacy in Michael's work for so long that it had crowded out the fundamental principle of utility. To Michael's way of thinking, functionalism had been raised to a fetish by the Modernists, in a way that had made the built environment hostile to any human needs beyond the merely mechanical. Now, at the end of his life, Michael pulled off a surprise rapprochement with functionality: without losing its anthropoid profiles or its symbolism (or even, in the case of the hospital projects, its pastiche historicism), the firm's work for the health-care market was as robustly functionalist as anything from the fever dreams of the early Modernists.

Indeed, the poetics of Le Corbusier and the stern rigor of Mies had often given more the appearance than the substance of function. Not so the health-care designs from Michael Graves Design Group, which, if they failed at their functions, could cause serious harm. The work was not formalism-free, of course. Michael wouldn't hear of that, and invariably his critiques of prototypes from the products workshop would take aim at the color of a finish, at the shape of a cabinet knob. Of the prevailing hideousness of the health-care environment ("Most of what exists now," Michael would always say, "is just too depressing to even die in"), the designer remained an unwavering foe.[21] But the dewy color schemes and the rounded contours had become part of a more comprehensive objective. "Accessibility" had taken on a whole new meaning.

Closing the loop, in a sense, on Michael's career-long commitment to connecting with ordinary people, the turn to health-care design advocacy, albeit precipitated by his personal crisis, was almost a natural one. His disability forced him to see things through different eyes. Dealing with objects at close range, his perceptive powers were now trained on details rather than facades and envelopes. His products still communicated, but their meaning now rang closer to how the critic Reyner Banham once defined beauty: "the promise of Function, made sensuously pleasing."[22] Far from blunting his critique of other design strategies, Michael's new insights into functionality sharpened it.

As often as not, that critique was aimed at his contemporaries. "Our nail clippers and tweezers"—created for the cosmetics brand Slice—"are for arthritic users, for octogenarians, for anybody that would have trouble with a more abstracted handle," Michael noted. He contrasted this approach with that of well-known designers like Philippe Starck, with his ungainly, spiderlike orange squeezer for Alessi, or Frank Gehry, with his chairs made from flimsy cardboard or hard, rolled steel.[23] The work of these figures and others evinced what Michael deemed "egotism," an unseemly disregard for human service that stoked his already appreciable resentment. Characteristically, Michael's empathy and Michael's anger were two sides of the same coin.

His feisty vitality made Michael's death feel far more abrupt than one would expect an eighty-year-old paraplegic's to be. In the last year of his life, he traveled to China; only a year before that, he had returned one last time for a special Notre Dame and University of Miami–sponsored trip to Rome, wheeling gamely through the hilly, bumpy streets he had come to know on that first night with Gail and Ted Musho. The visit was an occasion to toss aside his nurse's usual dietary strictures, and Michael plowed into the hearty Italian fare. "It was so hard to say no when he wanted something," recalled Minnie.[24]

On the morning of March 12, 2015, Michael died of heart failure—not a direct consequence of either his illness or his appetite, though no doubt abetted by twelve years without proper exercise save for his stationary bike. His death took friends and family by surprise and left many hanging threads, in particular the Warehouse: Michael had intended to endow his home to Princeton as a perpetual trust, but it was declined by the university because of fears about maintenance costs. His archives, too, remained unconsolidated, though the majority of his original drawings and drafts are in safekeeping with the firm.

Michael's legacy, however, did not die intestate. The machinery of fame, its interlocking gears of public caprice and modern media, had made Michael a public figure in the 1980s and then later diminished his standing as the nature of celebrity changed and settled on other designers. A cautionary tale, one might say. But before his death, Michael could already see that his name would long outlive him.

In 2014, on the fiftieth anniversary of his firm's founding, the New Jersey art and design venue Grounds for Sculpture staged a full retrospective of Michael's work, showcasing the exceptional breadth of his output as a maker of both buildings and products. The show dovetailed both with the thirtieth anniversary of the Alessi 9093 teakettle in 2015—relaunched with a special edition "Tea Rex" model, with a dragon in place of the conventional bird—as well as the announcement of a new initiative aimed at institutionalizing Michael's legacy: the Michael Graves College at New Jersey's Kean University, a program devoted to preserving Michael's commitment to drawing and his belief in design as civic engagement. The school, where classes are now underway, is slated to have a satellite location in Wenzhou, China [**PLATE 64**], a five-hundred-acre campus whose master plan Michael Graves & Associates helped develop. Dean David Mohney, a former student of Michael's, has described the school's mission as "not at all a kind of stylistic question" of emulating Michael's buildings but a question of honoring his "intellectual approach."[25] Stepping up where Princeton did not, Kean has also recently assumed ownership of the Warehouse and will preserve it as a center for study, meetings, and scholarly residencies.

The debuts of both retrospective and school were extraordinarily timely. Ambivalent as Michael's feelings had become toward the movement, Postmodernism returned in the second decade of the twenty-first century as a subject of serious academic research and professional interest. At a two-day symposium at New York's CUNY Graduate Center in 2011, Michael found himself on stage with a coterie of his PoMo compatriots: his former students Andrés Duany and Elizabeth Plater-Zyberk—whose Congress for the New Urbanism had championed a return to traditional town planning—as well as Tom Wolfe, Charles Jencks, and Robert A. M. Stern. The event was packed, the conversation lively, and the issues discussed were not long confined to the lecture hall. In the years that followed, the preservationist community has begun to consider not whether but which Postmodernist monuments might deserve the legal protections of official landmark status, the same protections that have been accorded so many Modernist buildings over the last two decades. Among the structures at the heart of this debate has been Michael's own Portland Building, whose fate is still undecided, but which appears likely to escape the scrap heap.[26]

Beyond mere historical interest, Postmodernism survives in altered form long after its supposed expiration date. Though most of the firms behind today's highest-profile projects would bristle at any suggestion of PoMo-era stylemongering, the past is always with us. In a bid for appropriateness, Jean Nouvel's upcoming Louvre Abu Dhabi incorporates traditional Muslim motifs; for a splash of populist romance, SHoP Architects' new Fifty-Seventh Street tower in Manhattan is an obvious nod to the beloved Gothic skyscrapers of old. (Robert A. M. Stern, it should be added, has never ceased practicing in a historically minded fashion and currently heads a massive office producing residential high-rises sometimes indistinguishable from their early twentieth-century counterparts.) This is to say nothing of the transparently historicist shopping centers and condominium towers that one can see in cities and towns all across the country—and if the city in question happens to be Austin, Tokyo, or any of dozens of others, some of the buildings one sees are by Michael Graves & Associates, still one of the foremost exponents of the PoMo vernacular.

Michael's firm, and in particular its ongoing health-care work, is still another of his durable achievements. Combining its two separate wings, the rebranded Michael Graves Architecture & Design continues to build, from Singapore to Lower Manhattan, and remains without question the biggest designer name in the medical sphere. In a conversation after his paralysis, the critic Paul Goldberger told him that his "greatest contribution" was his office and its drive to improve health-care design.[27] Creating easy-to-use wheelchairs and tweezers was never likely to earn Michael a Pritzker. But that is the moral bequest he has left to his firm, and to the world.

Together for the last time on stage, Michael and Peter Eisenman at the Architectural League of New York's symposium "Michael Graves: Past as Prologue," held at the New School in November 2014

If none of this were enough to secure Michael's place in the canon, his voice would still linger. Onstage with Peter Eisenman at an event at the New School in New York only four months before his death, he was at his most pithy and passionate, lighting into his competitors, and his old friend, with undiminished relish:

MICHAEL: Nouvel, Zaha, Rem. They have their phones ringing all the time, people asking them, "Would you do this for us?"

EISENMAN: Why?

MICHAEL: To keep ahead of Frank! [Audience bursts into laughter] You and I are in a different parade....Rem made a building. It has a tower, a horizontal tower, and then another on its side, comes back down to the ground, and there's a tower on the ground. And nobody said, *Why*? What the fuck is that about? Where's the door? What are you doing, man? Are you *high*? And the magazines publish it like it was heaven on earth....I like my buildings to have a foot, a discernible door or more, and windows to look out of, thank you very much. And you, Peter, call it a populist architecture! Because I like the *people*....Years ago I went to [Mies's IIT] with a friend who taught me a lot. People get so excited about the floating steps at the school of architecture. Somebody will fall down them because they're so treacherous. And somebody else will put up a railing on them someday, and they'll be called *populist*....We sit here talking about architecture, without the will to get on with it and to make life better for all of you [looking at audience]. All of you will be in walkers and canes and contraptions one day, in the next ten or twenty years.[28]

It was an astounding performance. Nowadays, whenever certain architects congregate, the mood of mutual appreciation can be almost smothering. Michael's diatribe was nettling, unsettling, and strangely refreshing.

Over a career spanning five decades, Michael had seen how design had moved from the utopian aspirations of Modernism toward the corporatization of the International Style; how it evolved, through the intellectual crises of the 1960s, into the Postmodernist reaction; and then, charging ahead undaunted, how it had embarked into the post-Bilbao millennium, giddy with its own technological wizardry and big-budget glitz. At a crucial juncture in the 1980s, Michael himself had been a central figure in shepherding design into the hypermediated age of big-name branding—and now, in the unlikeliest turn of all, he had returned, like Charles Dickens's Jacob Marley, shaking his chains and moaning with righteous indignation at a profession that he felt had lost its social soul.

Marley, of course was trying to atone for his sins. Perhaps Michael was too. But the apparent contradiction of a PoMo pop icon railing about architecture as human service was not evidence of some near-deathbed conversion on his part. A contradiction, yes—but one that had always been intrinsic to the Postmodernism that Michael had practiced, with its simultaneous strivings toward accessibility and abstraction, monumental grandeur and everyday appropriateness, mass-market appeal and high-minded humanism. Forty years on, Michael was still wrestling with those issues, loudly and publicly.

So is contemporary architecture, though rarely with half so much candor. The unreconciled impulses that drove Postmodernism have been inherited lock, stock, and anxiety-inducing barrel by contemporary design, which is even now navigating them anew—struggling, in our media-addled age, to move beyond the era of celebrity starchitects and toward an architecture that both connects and serves. Of Postmodernism's many lessons for today's architecture, the movement's attempt, however flawed, to deal frankly with these problems must be reckoned the most pertinent of all. Once again, Michael Graves had simply seen what was right before everyone's eyes.

FEW HAD BETTER REASON to mourn Michael than the man who had labored so diligently to give him his twelve-year lease on life, Dr. Barth Green. He and Michael had grown close; one of Green's colleagues in Miami sponsored yachting trips for victims of paralysis, and when Michael recovered from his surgery, Green had taken him sailing on Biscayne Bay. Sprayed with water, whipped by the wind, the incorrigible landlubber at last got a taste of the sea.

Green gave Michael something else as well, though it's unclear how well his patient understood it, or its implications. In the hours-long operation that Green had performed on Michael's spinal column, he had seen, as no CAT scan ever could, precisely what Michael's disease really looked like. From his lengthy observations, Green developed a theory—a couple, in fact, but one in particular that he favored. "It could have been optic myelitis," he said. The degenerative nerve disorder tracks very closely with Michael's pathology, and it begins, as the name implies, with an inflammation in one of the two main optical nerves.[29]

The diagnosis is not official, and the coincidence would seem almost too cosmic—given the course of Michael's life and career—to think that his eye might have been his undoing. Then again, Michael's illness never did undo him, not completely. He had spent his last years doing pretty much as he'd done, for better or worse, for most of his life. Which was...whatever he felt like doing.

The memorial service for Michael, held in spring of 2015 in Princeton's Richardson Auditorium, was beautiful and moving, and went on far too long. "It was awful!" said Eisenman, with characteristic overstatement.[30] (His own eulogy was not necessarily notable for its brevity.) It seemed that everyone had something to say about Michael—his son Michael Sebastian; his daughter, Sarah Stelfox; Karen Nichols; Patrick Burke; Richard Meier. Fran Lebowitz did not attend, though Michael would have understood. Grand emotional gatherings are not her bailiwick, and in any case this one qualified as an "out of town party." Robert A. M. Stern was in the audience, along with Steven Harris, Caroline Constant, Mary McLeod, and Peter Waldman; Lucy and her children were there too. During the reception afterward, everyone milled around with Princetonians of assorted vintage, and when it was over, the crowd emerged to find that it was a fine April afternoon, the sky above a suitable shade of blue.

Acknowledgments

FOLLOWING MICHAEL GRAVES'S death, three parties ensured that the project we had begun in the last two years of his life saw the light of day.

One was Michael's family—above all his daughter, Sarah Stelfox, whose assistance and whose memories of her father have been invaluable.

Another was Michael's eponymous firm, in particular his longtime partner Karen Nichols and communication manager Sal Forgione. The former has been instrumental at every stage, from proposal to interviews to fact checking, and the latter saw to it that all the images and archival material I needed were put at my disposal.

Last but certainly not least is the team at Princeton Architectural Press, where publisher Kevin Lippert and editors Jennifer Lippert, Nolan Boomer, and especially Sara Stemen have helped usher the manuscript into something at least halfway worthy of its subject.

For my part, my commitment to seeing the project through—while never in doubt—has been constantly bolstered by my wonderful agent and dear friend Nicole Tourtelot. Along with fellow agent David Kuhn, it was she who first fixed on a Graves book as a promising idea, one very cold and miserable January day back in 2013.

As per the footnotes, nearly sixty individuals consented to be interviewed by phone, email, or in person about Michael Graves, all of them essential but too many to be listed here. I do, however, feel compelled to thank those who went the extra mile to help track down other interviewees or documents on my behalf: Peter Eisenman, Dean Bob Geddes, Mike Graves (genealogist, of Texas), Léon Krier, Mary McLeod, Jayne Merkel, Lois Rothert (formerly Hanselmann), and Robert A. M. Stern.

In a similar vein, although the bibliography on the succeeding pages gives credit to most sources, four names that appear there merit special mention: the neurobiologist Margaret Livingstone; Nancy Nall, longtime chronicler of Fort Wayne history for the *News-Sentinel*; the architecture scholar Meredith Clausen of the University of Washington; and the Disney-ologist Chuck Mirarchi. Each of their respective studies —of lazy eye; the Snyderman House; the Portland Building; and the Swan and

Dolphin Hotels—proved so definitive as to render almost every other written account practically superfluous.

On a personal note, this book was a part of my life for nearly four years, with many lulls, detours, and cliffhangers along the way. I am eternally grateful to all those who have lent so much support—practical, emotional, often both—during this time, including but by no means limited to Éva Calon; Mr. and Mrs. Christopher Cox; Charles Curkin and the editors of *Surface*; Rachel Geller; Katie Gerfen and the staff at *Architect*; Rachel Gracey; Mr. and Mrs. Justin Jamail; Chris Knutsen and the editors of *WSJ: The Wall Street Journal Magazine*; Susan Grant Lewin and the staff of SGLA Public Relations; Michael Scott Paulson; Sophie Pinkham; Julian Rose and the staff at *Artforum*; Jenna Sauers; Abigail Shaw; Brian Spinks; Oli Stratford and the editors of *Disegno*; Mr. and Mrs. Jim Turner; Mr. and Mrs. Ian Volner Sr.; Matthew Volner; Mildred Weisz; Daniel Wenger and the editors of the *New Yorker* online; and Jennifer Wright.

Finally, it bears repeating that none of this would have been possible without the candor and kindness of Michael Graves. He is much missed.

Selected Bibliography

BY MICHAEL GRAVES

"The Amenable Shelter." Accompanying texts for undergraduate thesis at University of Cincinnati, 1958.

"Architect's Statement." In *Piranesi as Designer*, edited by Sarah E. Lawrence, 339. New York: Assouline, 2008.

"A Case for Figurative Architecture." In *Michael Graves: Buildings and Projects 2, 1966–1981*, edited by Karen Nichols, Peter Arnell, and Ted Bickford, 11–14. New York: Rizzoli, 1982.

"Foreword." In *Michael Graves: Images of a Grand Tour*, edited by Brian Ambroziak, ix. New York: Princeton Architectural Press, 2005.

"A Grand Tour," lecture.

"Has Postmodernism Reached Its Limit?" *Architectural Digest* 45 (April 1989): 6, 8, 10.

"Introduction." In *Le Corbusier, Selected Drawings*, 8–25. London: Academy Editions, 1981.

"The Necessity for Drawing: Tangible Speculation." *Architectural Design* 47 (June 1977): 384–94.

"Referential Drawings." *Journal of Architectural Education* 32 (September 1978): 24–27.

"Roman Interventions." *Architectural Design* 49 (1979): 3–4.

With Caroline Constant. "The Swedish Connection." *Journal of Architectural Education* 29 (September 1975): 12–13.

"What Is the Status of Work on Form Today?" *ANY: Architecture New York*, nos. 7–8 (1994): 61.

ON MICHAEL GRAVES

"American Architecture Now: Michael Graves." Taped interview with Barbaralee Diamonstein-Spielvogel, 1980.

Bletter, Rosemarie Haag, Alan Colquhoun, and Anthony Vidler. "About Graves." *Skyline* 3 (Summer 1979): 2–3.

Buck, Alex, and Matthias Vogt. *Michael Graves: Designer Monographs 3*. Berlin: Ernst and Sohn, 1994.

Carl, Peter. "Peter Carl on Michael Graves." *PSOA Rumor* 1, no. 2 (Spring 2010): 6, 8.

CBS *Sunday Morning*. "Passage: Postmodern Architect Michael Graves." Aired March 15, 2015.

CBS *Sunday Morning*. "Sunday Profile: Michael Graves." Aired April 2, 2006.

Colquhoun, Alan. "Michael Graves." In *Michael Graves: Architectural Monographs 5*. New York: Rizzoli/Academy Editions, 1979.

Davies, Paul. "Reputations: Michael Graves (1934–)." *Architectural Review*, April 25, 2014, accessed January 10, 2017, https://www.architectural-review.com/rethink/reputations/michael-graves-1934-/8661699.article.

Deamer, Peggy. "Michael Graves: Bodybuilder?" In *Thinking the Present: Recent American Architecture*, edited by K. Michael Hays and Carol Burns, 6–22. New York: Princeton Architectural Press, 1990.

Eisenman, Peter. "The Graves of Modernism." *Oppositions* 12 (Spring 1978): 21–27.

Filler, Martin. "Michael Graves: Before and After." *Art in America* 68 (September 1980): 99–105.

Goldberger, Paul. "Architecture of a Different Color." *New York Times*, October 10, 1982.

Iovine, Julie, Marisa Bartolucci, and Raul Cabra. *Michael Graves: Compact Design Portfolio*. New York: Chronicle Books, 2002.

Jencks, Charles. "Michael Graves (1934–2015)." *Architectural Review*, March 21, 2015, accessed January 10, 2017, https://www.architectural-review.com/rethink/viewpoints/michael-graves-1934-2015/8680204.article.

Jordy, William H. "Aedicular Modern: The Architecture of Michael Graves." *New Criterion* 2 (October 1983): 43–50.

Patton, Phil. *Michael Graves Designs: The Art of the Everyday Object*. London: DK Publishing, 2004.

Scully, Vincent. "Michael Graves's Allusive Architecture: The Problem of Mass." In *Michael Graves: Buildings and Projects, 1966–1981*, edited by Karen Nichols, Peter Arnell, and Ted Bickford, 289–98. New York: Rizzoli, 1982.

ON MICHAEL GRAVES PROJECTS

Arnell, Peter, and Ted Bickford. *A Tower for Louisville: The Humana Competition*. New York: Rizzoli, 1982.

Brenner, Douglas. "Portland." *Architectural Record* 170 (November 1982): 90–99.

Clausen, Meredith L. "Michael Graves's Portland Building: Power, Politics, and Postmodernism." *Journal of the Society of Architectural Historians* 73 (June 2014): 248–69.

Davies, Julie Hanselmann. *Michael Graves: Hanselmann House, Snyderman House: Residential Masterpieces 4*. Edited by Yukio Futagawa. Tokyo: ADA Edita, 2013.

Doubilet, Susan. "Conversation with Graves: The Portland Building." *Progressive Architecture* 64 (February 1983): 108–15.

Forster, Kurt W., et al. "Portland." *Skyline* 2 (January 1983): 16–21.

Goldberger, Paul. "An Appraisal: The Humana Building in Louisville: Compelling Work by Michael Graves." *New York Times*, June 10, 1985.

———. "The Whitney Paradox—To Add Is to Subtract." *New York Times*, January 8, 1989.

Hockenberry, John. "The Re-education of Michael Graves." *Metropolis*, October 2006, 123–27.

Jencks, Charles. "Plocek House." *Architectural Design* 5–6 (1980): 130.

Knight, Carlton. "Michael Graves Shakes Up Manhattan with His Museum Add-On." *Christian Science Monitor*, November 12, 1985.

Kramer, Hilton. "The Whitney's New Graves." *New Criterion* 4 (September 1985): 1–3.

Merkel, Jayne. *Michael Graves and the Riverbend Music Center*. Cincinnati: Contemporary Arts Center, 1987.

Mirarchi, Chuck. "A Look Back: Walt Disney World's Swan and Dolphin Hotels." http://blog.wdwinfo.com/2015/05/05/a-look-back-walt-disney-worlds-swan-and-dolphin-hotels/.

Muschamp, Herbert. "A Wonder World in the Mile High City." *New York Times*, May 7, 1995.

Nall, Nancy. "The Snyderman House." http://nancynall.com/2011/08/15/the-snyderman-house/.

Powell, Kenneth. *Graves Residence*. New York: Phaidon, 1995.

Robinson, Gaile. "Michael Graves' Designs Are Right on Target." *St. Louis Post-Dispatch*, December 21, 2000.

Sorkin, Michael. "Save the Whitney." *Village Voice*, June 25, 1985.

Stephens, Suzanne. "Living in a Work of Art." *Progressive Architecture* 59 (March 1978): 80–87.

Trescott, Jacqueline. "Washington Monument to Be under Wraps." *Washington Post*, October 17, 1997.

Volner, Ian. "A Much-Watched Kettle." *Disegno*, no. 9 (Autumn–Winter 2015).

Vreeland, Thomas. "Citation: Michael Graves." *Progressive Architecture* 51 (January 1970): 86.

Whiteson, Leon. "A New Hotel Reflects Company's Ambitious Plan to Tap Some of the World's Most Innovative Designers." *Los Angeles Times*, January 25, 1990.

ON MODERNISM

Banham, Reyner. *Theory and Design in the First Machine Age*. Cambridge, MA: MIT Press, 1980.

Cohen, Jean-Louis. "The Man with a Hundred Faces." In *Le Corbusier Le Grand*, edited by Tim Benton, 7–17. New York: Phaidon, 2008.

Giedion, Sigfried. *Space, Time, and Architecture: The Growth of a New Tradition*. Cambridge, MA: Harvard University Press, 1941.

Gropius, Walter. *Scope of Total Architecture*. New York: Collier, 1962.

Hitchcock, Henry-Russell, and Philip Johnson. *The International Style: Architecture since 1922*. New York: W. W. Norton, 1932.

Le Corbusier. *Towards an Architecture*. Translated by John Goodman. Los Angeles: Getty Publications, 2007.

Merkel, Jayne. *In Its Place: The Architecture of Carl Strauss and Ray Roush*. Cincinnati: Contemporary Arts Center, 1985.

Nelson, George. *Problems of Design*. New York: Whitney Library of Design, 1965.

Pevsner, Nikolaus. *Pioneers of the Modern Movement*. London: Faber and Faber, 1936.

Puente, Moisés, ed. *Conversations with Mies van der Rohe*. New York: Princeton Architectural Press, 2008.

ON CASE, THE WHITES, AND THE NEW YORK FIVE

Anderson, Stanford O. "CASE and MIT: Engagement." In *A Second Modernism: MIT, Architecture, and the "Techno-Social" Moment*, edited by Arindam Dutta, 578–651. Cambridge, MA: MIT Press, 2013.

Colomina, Beatriz. "Interview with Peter Eisenman, *Oppositions* Editor." In *Clip, Stamp, Fold: The Radical Architecture of Little Magazines 196X–197X*, edited by Beatriz Colomina and Craig Buckley, 261–80. New York: Actar, 2010.

Deamer, Peggy. "Structuring Surfaces: The Legacy of the Whites." *Perspecta* 32 (2001): 90–99.

Five Architects. New York: Oxford University Press, 1975.

Frank, Suzanne. *IAUS, the Institute for Architecture and Urban Studies: An Insider's Memoir*. Bloomington, IN: AuthorsHouse, 2011.

Gandelsonas, Mario. "On Reading Architecture: Eisenman and Graves: An Analysis." *Progressive Architecture* 53 (March 1972): 68–87.

Goldberger, Paul. "Architecture's '5' Make Their Ideas Felt." *New York Times*, November 26, 1973, 33, 52.

———. "Should Anyone Care about the 'New York Five'?…or about Their Critics, the 'Five on Five'?" *Architectural Record* 155 (February 1974): 113–16.

Malgrave, Harry Francis, and David J. Goodman. *An Introduction to Architectural Theory: 1968 to the Present*. Oxford: Wiley-Blackwell, 2011.

Tafuri, Manfredo. "L'architecture dans le boudoir: The Language of Criticism and the Criticism of Language." *Oppositions* 3 (May 1974): 37–62.

———. "Five × Five = Twenty-Five." *Oppositions* 5 (Summer 1976): 35–74.

Stern, Robert A. M., et al. "Five on Five." *Architectural Forum* 138 (May 1973): 46–57.

"White and Gray: Eleven Modern American Architects." Guest edited by Peter Eisenman and Robert A. M. Stern. *A+U* 52 (April 1975): 25–180.

ON POSTMODERNISM

Blackwood, Michael, dir. *Beyond Utopia*. Michael Blackwood Productions, 1984.

The Charlottesville Tapes. New York: Rizzoli, 1985.

Colquhoun, Alan. "From Bricolage to Myth, or How to Put Humpty-Dumpty Together Again." In *Architecture Theory since 1968*, edited by Michael Hayes. Cambridge, MA: MIT Press, 1998.

Gotkin, Michael, and Paul Makovsky. "The Post-modern Watchlist." *Metropolis*, November 2014, 74–94.

Huxtable, Ada Louise. "Inventing American Reality." *New York Review of Books*, September 3, 1992, 24–29.

Jencks, Charles. "The Rise of Postmodern Architecture." *Architectural Association Quarterly* 7 (October–December 1975): 3–14.

——— . *Free-Style Classicism*. New York: Architectural Digest, 1982.

——— . *The Language of Postmodern Architecture*. New York: Rizzoli, 1984.

Larson, Margali Sarfatti. *Behind the Postmodern Façade: Architectural Change in Late Twentieth-Century America*. Berkeley: University of California Press, 1993.

Martin, Reinhold. *Utopia's Ghost: Architecture and Postmodernism, Again*. Minneapolis: University of Minnesota Press, 2010.

McLeod, Mary. "Architecture and Politics in the Reagan Era: From Postmodernism to Deconstructivism." *Assemblage* 8 (February 1989): 22–59.

Rowe, Colin, and Fred Koetter. *Collage City*. Cambridge, MA: MIT Press, 1983.

Rykwert, Joseph. "Reputations: Leon Krier." *Architectural Review*, June 3, 2013, https://www.architectural-review.com/rethink/reputations/leon-krier-1946-/8648311.article.

Smith, C. Ray. *Supermannerism: New Attitudes in Post-Modern Architecture*. New York: Dutton, 1977.

Stamp, Jimmy. "Reconsidering Postmodernism." *Journal of Architectural Education* 66 (2012): 28–30.

Stern, Robert A. M. "Gray Architecture as Post-Modernism, or, Up and Down from Orthodoxy." *L'architecture d'Aujourd'hui* 186 (August–September 1976): 83–98.

Venturi, Robert. *Complexity and Contradiction in Architecture*. New York: Museum of Modern Art, 2002.

Venturi, Robert, Denise Scott Brown, and Steven Izenour. *Learning from Las Vegas*. Cambridge, MA: MIT Press, 1972.

Watkin, David. *Morality and Architecture Revisited*. Chicago: University of Chicago Press, 2001.

Wolfe, Tom. *From Bauhaus to Our House*. New York: Picador, 1981.

OTHER TOPICS

Granger, Alfred Hoyt. *Charles Follen McKim: A Study of His Life and Work*. Boston: Houghton Mifflin, 1913.

Huxtable, Ada Louise. *On Architecture: Collected Reflections on a Century of Change*. New York: Walker and Company, 2008.

Latour, Bruno. *We Have Never Been Modern*. Translated by Catherine Porter. Cambridge, MA: Harvard University Press, 1993.

Levinson, Nancy. "Notes on Fame." *Perspecta* 37 (2005): 18–23.

Livingstone, Margaret. *Vision and Art: The Biology of Seeing*. New York: Abrams, 2008.

Mohney, Brian G., et al. "Mental Illness in Young Adults Who Had Strabismus as Children." *Pediatrics* 122, no. 5 (November 2008): 1033–38.

Ockman, Joan. "Bestride the World like a Colossus: The Architect as Tourist." In *Architourism: Authentic, Escapist, Exotic, Spectacular*, edited by Joan Ockman and Solomon Frausto, 158–85. New York: Prestel, 2005.

Rowe, Colin. *The Mathematics of the Ideal Villa and Other Essays*. Cambridge, MA: MIT Press, 1987.

Scully, Vincent. *Modern Architecture and Other Essays*. Princeton, NJ: Princeton University Press, 2003.

Stern, Robert A. M., David Fishman, and Jacob Tishlove. *New York 2000*. New York: Monacelli, 2008.

Vitruvius. *The Ten Books on Architecture*. Translated by Morris Hicky Morgan. Cambridge, MA: Harvard University Press, 1914.

Notes

Initials followed by dates indicate an interview conducted by the author, in person or via telephone. Email correspondences, written notes, and taped lectures are labeled as such.

AA	Alberto Alessi	MF	Martin Filler
AC	Alan Chimacoff	MG	Michael Graves
BG	Bob Geddes	MGGTL	Michael Graves Grand Tour lectures
BK	Brian Klipp		
CC	Caroline Constant	MGMD	Michael Graves monograph documents
CJ	Charles Jencks		
DAJ	David A. Jones	MM	Mary McLeod
DBG	Dr. Barth Green	ML	Min Lin
DS	Donald Strum	PC	Peter Carl
FL	Fran Lebowitz	PE	Peter Eisenman
GG	Gail Graves	PG	Paul Goldberger
JHD	Julie Hanselmann Davies	PW	Peter Waldman
		RAMS	Robert A. M. Stern
JM	Jayne Merkel	RJ	Ron Johnson
KF	Kenneth Frampton	RM	Richard Meier
KH	Kitty Hawks	RVV	Rob Van Varick
KN	Karen Nichols	SH	Steven Harris
LK	Léon Krier	SS	Sarah Stelfox
LR	Lois Rothert		

p. *vi*, top From "The Double Dream of Spring," originally published in *The Double Dream of Spring*, © 1970, 1997, 2008 by John Ashbery. All rights reserved. Used by arrangement with Georges Borchardt, Inc., for the author.

***vi*, bottom** Vitruvius, *The Ten Books on Architecture*, trans. Morris Hicky Morgan (Cambridge, MA: Harvard University Press, 1914), 13.

1 Le Corbusier, "Three Reminders to Architects," *L'esprit nouveau*, no. 1 (October 1920): 61.

2 Bruno Latour, *We Have Never Been Modern*, trans. Catherine Porter (Cambridge, MA: Harvard University Press, 1993).

3 The word *Postmodernism* as applied to architecture has been contentious from the start. In almost every other field, literature especially, the phrase is generally taken to mean a state of *accelerated* modernity, following (roughly) Jean-François Lyotard's 1979 elucidation in *The Postmodern Condition: A Report on Knowledge*. In the realm of design, while a recidivist *anti*-modernity is usually implied, the title has also lived a number of different lives, thanks in part to its nominal inventor, Charles Jencks, who has been known to group multiple formal trends under the label. Further confusing matters is Fredric Jameson's well-known 1991 book *Postmodernism, or The Cultural Logic of Late Capitalism*, which deals at length with an entirely different set of phenomenological qualities. And, just to make things more interesting, different authors and publishers have taken to using different capitalization and hyphenation conventions at different times, including *Post-modernism, Post-Modernism, postmodernism*, etc. (Jencks has tried to popularize the diminutive *PM*. His efforts have mostly been in vain.)

For all the confusion, there remains a baseline consensus within architectural discourse as to what Postmodernism is, at least in retrospect: an architecture of historical bricolage that succeeded the midcentury International Style as the default mode of urban development in America and that reached its crescendo in the 1980s. There are plenty of holes to be punched in this received understanding as well, especially given the historicist wave that struck American architecture as early as the 1960s (evident in projects like the Italianate Lincoln Center), to say nothing of the unexpurgated traces of Karl Friedrich Schinkel in such a staunch Modernist as Mies van der Rohe. But that way madness lies.

Modernism can be recognized, in the American context, as a movement consistent in its effect, if not its origins; so can Postmodernism. Modernism is what the Postmodernist architects fled from, and Postmodernism is what architects have been fleeing from ever since. For consistency's sake, both will be capitalized, and the latter will be written as one word.

4 Alastair Gordon, "Of D-Con and Doorways," *East Hampton Star*, November 10, 1988. Jencks's original line was "Modern Architecture died in St. Louis, Missouri on July 15, 1972 at 3:32 PM (or thereabouts) when the infamous Pruitt-Igoe scheme, or rather several of its slab blocks, were given the final coup de grace by dynamite." Jencks did not, it should be said, hang all of the Modernist project's failures on its formal limitations alone, but saw them as betokening an overly conformist social ideology. Charles Jencks, *The Language of Post-Modern Architecture* (New York: Rizzoli, 1984), 9.

5 Jean-Louis Cohen, email correspondence.

6 Jimmy Stamp, "Reconsidering Postmodernism," *Journal of Architectural Education* 66 (2012): 30.

7 Reyner Banham, "1960–4: History under Revision," *Architectural Review*, May 1960, 327.

8 "Although employment grew by nearly 19 million jobs, its strength was uneven: three-fourths of the increase was in services and retail trade." Lois M. Plunkert, "The 1980's: A Decade of Job Growth and Industry Shifts," *Monthly Labor Review* 113 (September 1990): 3.

I · THE SEA

1 Hospital admission records being confidential, the exact date of Michael's initial health crisis has been triangulated based on the date of that year's Ambiente fair (which he attended) as well as the recollections of his associates. MGMD; KN notes; DS notes.

2 MG 4/29/13.

3 PE 2/25/16.

4 See Franz Schulze, *Philip Johnson: Life and Work* (New York: Alfred A. Knopf, 1994), 397. The show was co-curated by Mark Wigley.

5 PG 1/18/17.

6 Herbert Muschamp, "Who's That Peering out of the Grid?," *New York Times*, March 18, 2001.

7 MG 8/22/13.

8 For instance, Minnesota Public Radio, "Michael Graves: A Household Name," January 19, 2007; Kristin Hohenadel, "From Teakettles to Libraries, the Wide-Ranging Career of Michael Graves," Slate.com, March 13, 2015; etc., ad nauseam. The phrase even appears in Michael's *Encyclopaedia Britannica* entry, as well as in his *New York Times* obituary.

9 KN notes.

10 MG 8/22/13; PE 2/25/16; SS 1/21/16; MGMD; Julie Iovine, "An Architect's World Turned Upside Down," *New York Times*, June 12, 2003.

11 MG 8/22/13.

12 MGMD.

13 PE 2/25/16; RM 2/29/16.

14 SS 1/21/16.

15 FL 3/4/16.

16 Iovine, "An Architect's World Turned Upside Down."

17 KH 6/25/16.

18 MG 8/22/13.

19 Elizabeth Plater-Zyberk interview 11/9/16.

20 Interviewed on CBS *Sunday Morning*, "Sunday Profile: Michael Graves," aired April 2, 2006.

21 Joan Chiross, "Spinal Surgery at Miami Project Stopped Michael Graves' Paralysis from Advancing," *Miami Herald*, March 16, 2015.

22 FL 3/4/16.

23 MG 8/22/13.

24 Iovine, "An Architect's World Turned Upside Down."

25 CC 5/16/16.

26 MG 5/16/13.

27 MF 5/4/16.

II · THE RIVER AND THE COMPASS

1 To his daughter and first wife, Gail, Michael never spoke of any other home in his early adolescence save for the one on Indianola. Yet the 1940 census clearly states that the Bud Graves family was not then living in Broad Ripple. No date certain for the family's move can be ascertained via city directories or other contemporary sources, but since Michael either did not remember living in Forest Hills or did not think it worth mentioning, it is presumed that they moved shortly after the census year.

2 "New Residence Completed," *Indianapolis Star*, February 17, 1924.

3 SS 3/8/16.

4 Robert Bodenhamer and Robert G. Barrows, *The Encyclopedia of Indiana* (Bloomington: Indiana University Press, 1994), 1202.

5 Paul Donald Brown, *Indianapolis Men of Affairs* (Indianapolis: American Bibliographical Society, 1923), 240.

6 As attested by family genealogist Mike Graves of Austin, a distant cousin of the architect.

7 "Review of Securities for the Week," *Indianapolis Star*, March 16, 1913, 52.

8 "Burned by Gasoline," *Indianapolis News*, March 13, 1894; "Mrs. Emma Sells Graves Dead," *Indianapolis News*, March 14, 1894.

9 "Society," *Indianapolis Star*, December 25, 1904.

10 "E. M. Graves Services Will Be Held Here," *Indianapolis Star*, September 25, 1932.

11 "Charges Livestock Exchange Is Trust," *Indianapolis Star*, September 26, 1922.

12 Imminent federal action (see note 14) evidences how easily the industry had thus far evaded the 1890 Sherman Antitrust Act; consider, for example, Upton Sinclair's novel *The Jungle* (1906).

13 "Want Exchange Dissolved: Livestock Dealers Ask Department of Justice to Investigate," *New Philadelphia Daily Times*, November 16, 1910.

14 The two main federal initiatives were the Packers and Stockyards Act of 1921 and Capper-Volstead Act of 1922.

15 "Weddings and Engagements," *Indianapolis Star*, December 3, 1922.

16 A long and insidiously complex paper trail—including marriage records, property listings, and census documents—tells the tale of Max and Bessie's divorce and improbable remarriages. This, as with much else in the Graves family backstory, was unearthed with the help of the genealogist Mike Graves. The land transfer is reported in "Real Estate Transfers," *Indianapolis News*, February 15, 1922, 23; Margaret's marriage to William I.

Coons Jr. appears in the Marion County Index to Marriage Records for January of the same year; and Bessie's marriage to William I. Coons Sr. is documented in census records and city directories as early as 1929. In all likelihood Bessie was remarried to her in-law by the early 1920s, shortly after Max's land transfer, which was settled for her—via her future husband—while she was still using the name Graves.

17 Regarding the pony, see Ted Newmarket, "Along Hoosier Saddle Trails," *Indianapolis Star*, April 27, 1941.

18 MG 5/6/13.

19 MG 8/22/13.

20 Ibid.

21 "Marriage Licenses," *Greenfield Hancock Democrat*, August 11, 1927; Lois Leeds, "August Bride," *Indianapolis Star*, August 16, 1927. Given Michael's relative candor concerning Bud's abusive behavior, his failure to mention anything about his father's earlier marriage—either to his daughter, his first wife, his firm partners, or his biographer—has led to the general consensus that he did not know anything about it. It was only by happenstance, following Michael's death, that the author and the Graves family historian discovered the issuance of the older marriage license. It is not known what became of Bud's first wife, Ethel Duncan.

22 "Mrs. Thomas B. Graves," *Indianapolis News*, March 2, 1931.

23 MGMD.

24 Michael claimed at various times to have studied the piano and the violin as child. He was never known to play either as an adult.

25 MG 8/22/13. The doctor was also a family friend, making litigation still less appealing. SS notes.

26 MG 8/22/13.

27 MG 5/6/13.

28 MGMD.

29 MG 4/29/13.

30 Ada Louis Huxtable, "Architecture View," *New York Times*, May 27, 1979.

31 MGMD.

32 MG 8/22/13.

33 Michael suggested to some (Karen Nichols and his daughter, Sarah) that his condition may in fact have been brought on by a *previous* eye surgery—intended to remedy the fact that he was born cross-eyed—which had overcorrected for the condition and caused his lazy eye. No baby photos

show him to be visibly cross-eyed. KN 9/2/16; SS emails.

34 Margaret Livingstone interview 12/8/16. Dr. Livingstone of Harvard Medical School has written extensively on the complex links between strabismus and artistic ability; see, for example, Margaret Livingstone, *Vision and Art: The Biology of Seeing* (New York: Abrams, 2008).

35 MGMD.

36 Karen Nichols would recall that even as an adult, Michael preferred photographs that didn't catch both eyes head-on—and even edited at least one portrait to make it appear as though his eyes were both straight. KN notes.

37 See Brian G. Mohney, Jeff A. McKenzie, et al., "Mental Illness in Young Adults Who Had Strabismus as Children," *Pediatrics* 122, no. 5 (November 2008): 1033–38.

38 MGMD.

39 Witold Rybcyznski, "The Late, Great Paul Cret," *New York Times*, October 21, 2014.

40 MG 4/29/13.

41 MG 8/22/13.

42 Ibid.

43 PW 11/16/16.

44 MGMD.

45 MG 8/22/13.

46 Mike Graves (genealogist) email correspondence.

47 "A Society Ripple," *Indianapolis News*, June 19, 1900. Edward caused a minor scandal when his engagement to a local girl in Ithaca, New York, was abruptly called off after he and T. S. were detained by a local officer of the law for an unpaid bill.

48 MGMD.

49 MG 8/22/13.

50 LR 3/22/16.

51 Ibid.

52 MG 8/22/13.

53 Ibid.

54 Ibid.

55 Ibid.

56 MGMD.

57 J. K. Birksted, *Le Corbusier and the Occult* (Cambridge, MA: MIT Press, 2009), 10.

58 Charles and Berdeana Aguar, *Wrightscapes: Frank Lloyd Wright's Landscape Designs* (New York: McGraw Hill Professional, 2002), 1.

59 Vincent Scully, *Modern Architecture and Other Essays* (Princeton, NJ: Princeton University Press, 2003), 184.

60 PE 2/25/16.

1 M. H. Trytten, *Student Deferment in Selective Service: A Vital Factor in National Security* (Minneapolis: University of Minnesota Press, 1952). A useful summing up with tables is available online at the Korean War Educator, http://www.thekwe.org/topics/homefront/p_selective_service.htm.

2 MGMD; GG email.

3 MG 4/29/13.

4 GG email.

5 Mike Pulfer, "Strauss Built a Name for Himself," *Cincinnati Enquirer*, November 13, 1999.

6 MG 4/29/13. In Michael's application for the Rome fellowship several years later, he stated that he in fact spent the first year of his UC co-op in a different office, that of Garber, Tweddell & Wheeler Architects. The experience was apparently not a memorable one, and Michael never spoke of it.

7 Quoted in Vincent Canizaro, *Architectural Regionalism: Collected Writings on Place, Identity, and Modernity* (New York: Princeton Architectural Press, 2008), 304.

8 Rebecca Billman, "Obituary: Raymond Roush," *Cincinnati Enquirer*, July 20, 2002.

9 MG 4/29/13.

10 The house was lately available for sale, and enterprising local design enthusiasts posted a series of interior photographs, available online at http://www.visualtour.com/show.asp?t=1159509&prt=10003.

11 JM 7/8/16.

12 Decades later, Reed would be a key patron for a project by the Graves firm in Cincinnati, the Riverbend Music Center (1983). JM 7/18/16.

13 JM 7/8/16.

14 MG 4/29/13.

15 Ibid.

16 GG email.

17 MG 4/29/13.

18 GG email.

19 MGMD.

20 MG 4/29/13.

21 Peter and Alison Smithson, "The Heroic Period of Modern Architecture," *Architectural Design* 12 (December 1965).

22 Moisés Puente, ed., *Conversations with Mies van der Rohe* (New York: Princeton Architectural Press, 2008), 16.

23 David Watkin, *Morality and Architecture Revisited* (Chicago: University of Chicago Press, 2001), 146.

24 MG 4/29/13.

25 Kathryn E. Pickett, "Weddings, Engagements Crowd Spring, Summer Social Docket," *Indianapolis Star*, March 27, 1955.

26 Gregory Korte, "Complex Was Troubled from the Beginning," *Cincinnati Enquirer*, September 1, 2002.

27 MG 5/6/13.

28 MG 8/22/13.

29 Jayne Merkel, *Michael Graves and the Riverbend Music Center* (Cincinnati: Contemporary Arts Center, 1987), 22–23.

30 Dr. Donald Jacobs (son) interview 12/23/16.

31 GG email and other sources. One need only look at the scale of Michael's library and the well-worn, sticky-noted pages of books on Pablo Picasso, Juan Gris, etc.

32 GG email. Besides the *trulli*, Michael's housing scheme bears an eerie resemblance to the Trenton Bath House, completed in 1955, by the Philadelphia architect Louis Kahn. While it seems highly unlikely that Michael knew of either the architect or the design at this early date, Kahn's project cannot be ruled out as an unacknowledged source.

33 Archival documents found on Warehouse property.

34 MG 8/22/13.

35 MG 4/29/13.

36 GG email.

37 MG 4/29/13.

38 GSD's formation was accompanied by not a little discord, Gropius being the larger "name" but Hudnut the dean. The two did not get along. Robert A. M. Stern, *The Philip Johnson Tapes* (New York: Monacelli, 2008), 87–88.

39 MGGTL, Indianapolis Museum of Art 4/14/13 and Harvard GSD 8/14/13.

40 MG 4/29/13.

41 Le Corbusier, *Towards an Architecture*, trans. John Goodman (Los Angeles: Getty Publications, 2007), 102.

42 Le Corbusier, "Five Points on Architecture," in *Programs and Manifestoes on Twentieth Century Architecture*, ed. Ulrich Conrads (Cambridge, MA: MIT Press, 1971), 99.

43 Le Corbusier, *The Radiant City* (New York: Orion, 1967).

44 Le Corbusier, *Towards an Architecture*, 291.

45 Quoted in Caroline Zalseki, *Long Island Modernism: 1930–1980* (New York: W. W. Norton, 2012), 104–5.

46 To say nothing of Corb's own wartime

transgressions; his brief flirtation with Vichy is well documented. See Jean-Louis Cohen, "The Man with a Hundred Faces," in *Le Corbusier Le Grand*, ed. Tim Benton (New York: Phaidon, 2008), 16.

47 MG 4/29/13.

48 MGMD.

49 Lo-Yi Chan interview 11/8/16. Because Harvard University does not release student records until eighty years after enrollment has ceased, Michael's exact course list cannot be ascertained. Chan does not recall seeing Michael in Giedion's class, nor in the class of Eduard F. Sekler, a longtime Harvard fixture then at the beginning of his career. Since history had been reinstated as a requirement, however, it seems likely that Michael took at least one such course. See Eduard F. Sekler, "Sigfried Giedion at Harvard University," *Studies in the History of Art* 35 (1990): 265–73.

50 MG 4/29/13.

51 Le Corbusier, *Towards an Architecture*, 86.

52 Ibid., 151.

53 Christopher Klemeck, *The Transatlantic Collapse of Urban Renewal* (Chicago: University of Chicago Press), 100.

54 PW 11/16/16. Soltan would become a more "official" member in 1962, when he was included in the group's publication *Team Ten Primer*. See Stephen Sennot, *Encyclopedia of Twentieth Century Architecture* (New York: Fitzroy Dearborn, 2004), 1311.

55 MG 4/29/13.

56 Michael's brief employment at Carl Koch's office, though not remembered by Gail Graves, is attested in his application for the American Academy in Rome fellowship the following year.

57 PE 2/25/16.

58 Ibid.

59 MG 4/29/13.

60 Lo-Yi Chan interview 11/8/16.

61 MG 8/22/13.

62 MG 4/29/13.

63 Regarding the rainstorm anecdote, see Robert A. M. Stern and Jimmy Stamp, *Pedagogy and Place* (New Haven, CT: Yale University Press, 2016), 43.

64 George Nelson, *Problems of Design* (New York: Whitney Library of Design, 1965), 13.

65 MG 4/29/13.

66 MG 8/29/13.

67 MGMD.

68 MG 8/29/13.

69 RM 2/29/16.

70 Ibid.

71 Jane Allison, "Big Future Awaits Two Indiana-Born Artists," *Indianapolis Star*, August 14, 1960.

72 RM 2/2/16.

73 MG 4/29/13.

74 MGMD. Meier has no recollection of saying this, though this may be attributable to the passage of years and his condition on the evening in question.

75 GG email.

76 Stern and Stamp, *Pedagogy and Place*, 46.

77 Michael Graves American Academy in Rome fellowship application, December 28, 1959, courtesy of American Academy in Rome archives, New York.

78 List of jurors courtesy of ibid.

79 Paul Goldberger, "House Proud," *New Yorker*, July 2, 2001.

80 MG 4/29/13. The girl, he later discovered, was Astra Zarina, who went on to become a successful architect.

81 Letter from Michael Graves to Dean Sert, April 11, 1960, courtesy Sarah Stelfox.

IV · THE LIGHT

1 The date September 30, 1960, is an educated guess, Gail Graves not having recorded their arrival in her diary. Their departure date, however, is attested in a letter from the Academy (courtesy of Sarah Stelfox), and an itinerary for the *Colombo* from 1965 lists an eight-day travel time: http://www.timetableimages.com/maritime/images/colombo.htm.

2 MG 4/29/13.

3 See Paolo Scrivano, "Signs of Americanization in Italian Domestic Life: Italy's Postwar Conversion to Consumerism," *Journal of Contemporary History* 40 (2005): 317–40.

4 Their route through the city is conjectural, based on Michael and Gail's recollections. MG 4/29/13; GG email.

5 MG 4/29/13.

6 Alfred Hoyt Granger, *Charles Follen McKim: A Study of His Life and Work* (Boston: Houghton Mifflin, 1913), 90.

7 GG email.

8 MGGTL.

9 A full list of departmental theses is available at http://artandarchaeology.princeton.edu/research/dissertations/completed.

10 MGGTL.

11 Ibid.

12 GG email.

13 Michael had already seen, at least once, how much Piranesian verve was possible in ink alone, thanks to a postcard Ted Musho had sent him from Rome the previous March, congratulating Michael on winning the fellowship. Musho's rendering of the roof of Saint Peter's clearly presages the mode that Michael would deploy when he too reached Italy. GG email.

14 MGGTL.

15 Thomas Coryat, *Coryat's Crudities* (Glasgow: Robert MacLehose and Company, 1905), 1–2.

16 See Geoffrey Trease, *The Grand Tour: A History of the Golden Age of Travel* (New York: Holt, Rinehart and Winston, 1967).

17 MGGTL.

18 GG email.

19 Ibid.

20 Ibid.

21 Ibid.

22 Ibid.

23 SS notes.

24 KN notes.

25 MGGTL.

26 RM 2/29/16.

27 LH 3/22/16.

28 SS 3/8/16.

29 Peter Eisenman, "The Graves of Modernism," *Oppositions* 12 (Spring 1978): 26.

30 GG email.

31 MG 4/29/13.

32 Brian Ambroziak, *Michael Graves: Images of a Grand Tour* (New York: Princeton Architectural Press, 2005), 2.

33 MG 8/29/13.

34 MG 4/29/13.

35 PE 2/25/16.

36 MG 4/29/13.

V · THE GARDEN AND THE MACHINES

1 SS email.

2 F. Scott Fitzgerald, *This Side of Paradise* (Cambridge: Cambridge University Press, 1995), 41.

3 Sabra Follet Meservey began her studies in April 1961. *Princeton Alumni News*, April 29, 1961, 8.

4 PE 2/25/16.

5 Robert Hillier interview 9/13/16.

6 PE 2/25/16.

7 Ibid.

8 Rowe was Eisenman's mentor—though his official thesis adviser was Leslie Martin.

9 Colin Rowe, *The Mathematics of the Ideal Villa and Other Essays* (Cambridge, MA: MIT Press, 1987), 122, 123.

10 Peter Smithson, *Conversations with Students* (New York: Princeton Architectural Press, 2005), 19.

11 MG 8/22/13.

12 PW 11/16/16; MG 4/29/13. The official record does not list a name for the course Michael taught that semester, and he is not formally recognized as the instructor for his 204 studio until

the fall of 1963. Seeley Mudd Manuscript Library archivist emails.

13 MG 4/29/13.

14 JHD 6/15/16.

15 PE 2/25/16.

16 PW 11/16/16. Among Waldman's colleagues in that first Graves class was Tod Williams, now the architect—in partnership with his wife, Billie Tsien—of many prominent buildings, including the upcoming Obama presidential library.

17 SH 5/20/16.

18 MG 2/17/15.

19 Michael Graves, "What Is the Status of Work on Form Today?" NY: *Architecture New York*, nos. 7–8 (1994): 61.

20 MG 4/29/13.

21 Ibid.

22 Quoted in Beth Dunlop, *A House for My Mother: Architects Build for Their Families* (New York: Princeton Architectural Press, 1999), 31.

23 MG 4/29/13.

24 SH 5/20/16; MG 8/22/13.

25 MG 8/22/13.

26 Letter to Michael Graves from University

Secretary Alexander Leitch, April 19, 1963, courtesy of Sarah Stelfox.

27 MG 8/22/13.

28 PE 2/25/16. In a bizarre coincidence, Professor Szathmary's brother wrote the original theme music to *Get Smart*, Michael's scholarly anthem back in Rome.

29 Ibid.

30 Suzanne Frank, *IAUS, the Institute for Architecture and Urban Studies: An Insider's Memoir* (Bloomington, IN: AuthorsHouse, 2011), 19.

31 Quoted in Stanford O. Anderson, "CASE and MIT: Engagement," in *A Second Modernism: MIT, Architecture, and the "Techno-Social" Moment*, ed. Arindam Dutta (Cambridge, MA: MIT Press, 2013), 648.

32 Karrie Jacobs, "Linear City," *Dwell*, June 10, 2010, 112.

33 CC 5/16/16.

34 PE 2/25/16.

35 *LIFE*, "The U.S. City: Its Greatness Is at Stake," December 24, 1965.

36 CC 5/16/16.

37 Anderson, "CASE and MIT: Engagement," 588.

38 Ibid.

39 Ibid., 587.

40 SS email.

41 AC 11/18/16. Chimacoff first met Michael briefly during a Cornell jury in this period; contemporary photos confirm that he had grown bulky.

42 Muriel Emanuel, *Contemporary Architects* (London: Macmillan, 1980), 304. Michael typically excluded his early competition proposals from his own monographs.

43 PE 2/25/16.

44 BG 11/11/16.

45 Quoted in Frank, *IAUS, the Institute for Architecture and Urban Studies*, 4.

46 PC 12/27/16.

47 LR 3/22/16.

48 JHD 6/15/16.

49 LR 3/22/16. This was not the end of the "village" solution. As Lois explained, "He just stacked the two small buildings, and added a third 'building' between the first two." Bumping the parents' bedroom to the upper story of the main volume, Michael removed Lois's studio to an adjacent unit, connecting the two by way of a raised viaduct accessed via a stairway that acted as the main entry.

50 Ibid.

51 JHD 6/15/16.

52 LR 3/22/16.

53 Julie Hanselmann Davies, *Michael Graves: Hanselmann House, Snyderman House: Residential Masterpieces 4*, ed. Yukio Futagawa (Tokyo: ADA Edita, 2013), 6.

54 Barbara Klinkhammer, "After Purism: Le Corbusier and Color," *Preservation Education and Research* 4 (2011): 115.

55 Hanselmann Davies, *Michael Graves: Hanselmann House, Snyderman House*, 7.

56 LR 3/22/16.

57 MG 4/29/13.

58 CC 5/16/16.

59 "Calendar," *Princeton Alumni Weekly* 68, October 10, 1967, 17.

60 KF 6/16/16.

61 BG 11/11/16; PW 11/16/16. Johnson and Michael had almost certainly been introduced by this point, though it's not clear whether Michael had yet been invited—as Robert A. M. Stern and other young architects often were—to call on Johnson at his Glass House compound in Connecticut.

62 PW 11/16/16.

63 Peggy Deamer, "Michael Graves: Bodybuilder?," in *Thinking the Present: Recent American Architecture*, ed. K. Michael Hays and Carol Burns (New York: Princeton Architectural Press, 1990), 7.

64 MG 8/22/13.

65 MG 5/16/13.

66 SS 1/21/16.

67 Ibid.

68 MG 8/22/13.

69 Ibid.

70 JHD 6/15/16.

71 LR 3/22/16.

72 These quotes come from Nancy Nall (full name Nancy Nall Derringer), "The Snyderman House" (2002), archived on her website at http://nancynall.com/2011/08/15/the-snyderman-house/. Nall is a former *Fort Wayne News-Sentinel* columnist.

73 Alan Colquhoun, "From Bricolage to Myth, or How to Put Humpty-Dumpty Together Again," in *Architecture Theory since 1968*, ed. Michael Hayes (Cambridge, MA: MIT Press, 1998), 342.

74 Suzanne Stephens, "Living in a Work of Art," *Progressive Architecture* 59 (March 1978): 84.

75 Martin Filler, "Michael Graves: Before and After," *Art in America* 68 (September 1980): 104.

76 JHD 6/15/16.

77 Quoted in Nall, "The Snyderman House."

78 Ibid.

79 PE 2/25/16.

80 Frank, *IAUS, the Institute for Architecture and Urban Studies*, 51.

81 MG 4/29/13.

82 Ibid.

83 PE 2/25/16.

84 Eisenman recalls that the production quality of the first edition was so poor that a second, paperback one was shortly released, with as many as five hundred copies printed.

85 Colin Rowe, "Introduction," in *Five Architects* (New York: Oxford University Press, 1975), n.p.

86 Paul Davies, "Reputations: Michael Graves (1934–)," *Architectural Review*, April 25, 2014, https://www.architectural-review.com/rethink/reputations/michael-graves-1934-/8661699.article.

87 MG 8/29/13.

88 LK 12/28/15.

89 RAMS 3/2/16; Robert A. M. Stern et al., "Five on Five," *Architectural Forum* 138 (May 1973): 46–57.

90 PE 2/25/16.

91 The conference "Four Days in May," also known as "White and Gray Meets Silver," is typically accepted as the inception date for the White versus Gray nomenclature. The Silvers were a more loosely affiliated faction of Los Angeles–based high-tech architects, including Craig Hodgetts, Cesar Pelli, and others. See Harry Francis Malgrave and David J. Goodman, *An Introduction to Architectural Theory: 1968 to the Present* (Oxford: Wiley-Blackwell, 2011), 45.

92 Vincent Scully, "Introduction," in Robert Venturi, *Complexity and Contradiction in Architecture* (New York: Museum of Modern Art, 2002), 10.

93 Venturi, *Complexity and Contradiction in Architecture*, 16.

94 Stern et al., "Five on Five," 49, 47, 49.

95 Ibid., 56.

96 Ibid., 47.

97 Ibid., 54.

98 Ibid., 51.

99 MM 6/8/16.

100 PW 11/16/16.

101 MG 4/29/13.

102 PE 2/25/16.

103 Paul Goldberger, "Architecture's '5' Make Their Ideas Felt," *New York Times*, November 26, 1973.

104 As with the Grays and the Whites, the exact timing of and responsibility for the "New York Five" coinage is slightly obscure. Goldberger is generally credited, though in the original *New York Times* article (ibid.), he prefers the term deployed by Arthur Drexler in his prologue, referring to a "New York School." Only later would Goldberger publish an article entitled "Should Anyone Care about the 'New York Five'?...or about Their Critics, the 'Five on Five'?," *Architectural Record* 155 (February 1974): 113–16. Whatever the case, the formula of city name followed by number was a trope of the time, an inheritance of the late 1960s, when radical groups, notably the Chicago Seven, often assumed such monikers. The very name "Chicago Seven" would be adopted by a group of architects led by Stanley Tigerman; their ranks actually varied between six and ten, but the title lent them, as it did the Five, a soupçon of subversion.

VI · THE BRIDGE AND THE HEARTH

1 Eric Owen Moss interview 1/27/16.

2 MG 5/16/13.

3 Quoted in Kenneth Powell, *Graves Residence* (New York: Phaidon, 1995), 9.

4 Ibid., 10.

5 MG 5/16/13.

6 RAMS 3/2/16.

7 JHD 6/15/16.

8 "Newsletter 8 (1973–1974)," Princeton School of Architecture, courtesy of Dean Bob Geddes. This is the first mention of the Asplund Problem in PSOA newsletter, confirming Mary McLeod's conviction that her fall 1973 studio was the first to receive it. MM 6/8/16.

9 MG 5/16/13.

10 Michael Graves and Caroline Constant, "The Swedish Connection," *Journal of Architectural Education* 29 (September 1975): 13.

11 Peter Carl, "Peter Carl on Michael Graves," *PSOA Rumor* 1, no. 2 (2010): 6, 8.

12 Graves and Constant, "The Swedish Connection," 12.

13 "Newsletter 8 (1973–1974)," Princeton School of Architecture. In 1982 Michael would change the title to "Thematic Studies in Architecture." Seeley Mudd Manuscript Library archivist emails, courtesy of Dean Bob Geddes.

14 "Thematic Studies in Architecture" curriculum, Spring 1991.

15 Ibid.

16 MG 4/29/13.

17 John R. DaSilva, "Recollections for a Celebration of the Career of Professor Michael Graves, May 26, 2010," *Princeton Alumni Weekly*, April 17, 2015, https://paw.princeton.edu/article/essay-john-r-dasilva-85.

18 MG 5/6/13.

19 RAMS 3/2/16.

20 MG 4/29/13.

21 The Fort Wayne medical offices' mural features one extremely compacted fragment of a cornice; without real shading, it is barely recognizable as such. Interestingly, the Transammonia mural (along with the Triennale mural) was excised from Michael's first full-length monograph, despite having featured in his first book from Academy Editions/Rizzoli.

22 SH 5/20/16.

23 Deamer, "Michael Graves: Bodybuilder?," 13.

24 CC 5/16/16. The project has since been demolished.

25 Barbaralee Diamonstein-Spielvogel, "American Architecture Now: Michael Graves," taped interview, 1980.

26 Thomas Vreeland, "Citation: Michael Graves," *Progressive Architecture* 51 (January 1970): 86; MG 8/22/13.

27 Paul Benacerraf interview 11/14/16.

28 RM 2/29/16.

29 SH 5/20/16.

30 KN 9/2/16.

31 PC email correspondence.

32 Graves and Constant, "The Swedish Connection," 12.

33 MG 8/22/13.

34 See Michael Graves, "The Necessity for Drawing: Tangible Speculation," *Architectural Design* 47 (June 1977): 384–94.

35 Toward the end of his life Michael would produce a number of sketches of his young son, Michael Sebastian. KN notes.

36 AC 11/18/16.

37 Rosalind E. Krauss, *Terminal Iron Works: The Sculpture of David Smith* (Cambridge, MA: MIT Press, 1971), 33. Michael and Krauss had regular contact through Eisenman's IAUS, where she was a frequent participant.

38 A similar quality of "spatial collapse" was noted by Peggy Deamer in the Gunwyn Ventures office. Deamer, "Michael Graves: Bodybuilder?," 10.

39 KN 9/2/16.

40 Ibid.

41 SS 1/21/16.

42 KN notes.

43 Powell, *Graves Residence*, 13; MG 5/16/13.

44 MG 5/6/13.

45 Ibid.

46 AC 11/18/16.

47 MG 5/6/13.

48 KF 6/16/16; MG 4/29/13.

49 According to Frampton, Rowe's drinking had likely been a factor in his not being offered a position at Princeton, despite extensive lobbying by Eisenman in the mid-1960s. Bob Geddes disputes this, saying he simply felt he'd already stacked the department with enough (mostly younger) British scholars. KF 6/16/16; BG 11/11/16.

50 KF 6/16/16.

51 Colin Rowe and Fred Koetter, *Collage City* (Cambridge, MA: MIT Press, 1983), 128.

52 Joseph Rykwert, "Reputations: Leon Krier," *Architectural Review*, June 3, 2013, accessed January 10, 2017, https://www.architectural-review.com/rethink/reputations/leon-krier-1946-/8648311.article.

53 The author here plagiarizes himself, repackaging a phrase he used to describe the later work of Robert A. M. Stern. Ian Volner, "Architecture's King of Tradition," NewYorker.com, August 21, 2015, http://www.newyorker.com/culture/culture-desk/architectures-king-of-tradition.

54 LK 12/28/15.

55 Ibid.

56 MG 2/17/15.

57 PE 2/25/16.

58 In the house as built, these features are not really in evidence: the rear studio, for example, was never constructed. Alan Chimacoff would also note the debt that both the Plocek and Crooks landscapes owed to Asplund's Royal Chancellery. Deamer, "Michael Graves: Bodybuilder?," 21 note 6.

59 KN 9/2/16.

60 Other key sources included a proposed bridge between France and Italy by the French nineteenth-century architect Henri Labrouste, as well as Ledoux's Salt Works at Chaux, which Anthony Vidler helped bring to Michael's attention. Deamer, "Michael Graves: Bodybuilder?," 18.

61 KN 9/2/16.

62 Deamer, "Michael Graves: Bodybuilder?," 19.

63 MG 4/29/13; Ada Louise Huxtable, *On Architecture: Collected Reflections on a Century of Change* (New York: Walker and Company, 2008), 250.

64 Moorhead did ultimately build an interpretive museum, the Hjemkomst Center, opened in 1985 and designed by the local architects who had teamed with Michael Graves Architect on the original bridge proposal.

65 Geoffrey Broadbent, *Emerging Concepts in Urban Space Design* (New York: Van Nostrand Reinhold, 1990), 333.

66 MGGTL.

67 CJ 11/11/16.

68 Charles Jencks, "The Rise of Postmodern Architecture," *Architectural Association Quarterly* 7 (October–December 1975): 3–14.

69 PE 2/25/16.

70 Tom Wolfe, *From Bauhaus to Our House* (New York: Picador, 1981), 101. The late Mr. Brunner, who had died in 1925, was surely the greatest accidental patron of Michael's early career: the fellowship that had helped send Michael to Rome was *that* Academy's Brunner Prize.

71 Johnson's Nazi period has been well chronicled. See Franz Schulze, *Philip Johnson: Life and Work* (New York: Alfred A. Knopf, 1994), 102–68.

72 Paul Goldberger, *Why Architecture Matters* (New Haven, CT: Yale University Press, 2009), 51.

73 Margali Sarfatti Larson, *Behind the Postmodern Façade: Architectural Change in Late Twentieth-Century America* (Berkeley: University of California Press, 1993), 111.

74 Michael suggested at one point that he, in fact, had recommended Johnson to Wundram— somewhat scandalous if true, since it would have meant he'd effectively stacked the deck for himself. Karen Nichols doubts that this was so; Mr. Wundram declined to comment. MG 4/29/13; KN notes.

75 MG 8/29/13.

76 DaSilva, "Recollections for a Celebration of the Career of Professor Michael Graves"; MG 4/29/13.

77 Edith Iglauer, "Seven Stones," *New Yorker*, June 4, 1979, 42.

78 MG 4/29/13.

79 KN notes.

80 Quoted in Meredith L. Clausen, "Michael Graves's Portland Building: Power, Politics, and Postmodernism," *Journal of the Society of Architectural Historians* 73 (June 2014): 256.

VII · THE TOWER

1 These and other reactions and developments are reported in Clausen, "Michael Graves's Portland Building: Power, Politics and Postmodernism," 256–58.

2 Ibid.

3 Ibid.

4 Ibid., 259.

5 Ibid., 261.

6 MG 5/6/13; KN 9/2/16.

7 As reported in Lance Knobel, "It's the Building of the Future," *Architectural Review*, November 1983.

8 The comparison is frequently attributed to Ivancie, though the source of the quote cannot be identified. See Brian Libby, "Reevaluating Postmodernism," *Architecture Week*, June 5, 2002, C1 1.

9 Michael Blackwood (dir.). *Beyond Utopia*, Michael Blackwood Productions, 1984.

10 Charles Jencks, *The Language of Postmodern Architecture* (New York: Rizzoli, 1984), 7. This is in the introduction to the revised edition.

11 Marvin Trachtenberg and Isabelle Hyman, *Architecture from Prehistory to Post-Modernism: The Western Tradition* (New York: Abrams, 1986), 573.

12 Paul Goldberger, "The Modern Cityscape Now Finds Room for the Picturesque," *New York Times*, December 26, 1982.

13 Paul Goldberger, "Architecture of a Different Color," *New York Times*, October 10, 1982.

14 Douglas Brenner, "Portland," *Architectural Record* 170 (1982): 90.

15 Kurt W. Forster et al., "Portland," *Skyline* 2 (January 1983): 19.

16 Quoted in Joe Stecker, "A Hollow Icon," *Portland Mercury*, November 19, 2014; Wolf von

Eckardt, "A Pied Piper of Hobbit Land," *Time*, August 23, 1982.

17 MG 5/16/13.

18 MGMD; MG 8/29/13. The origin of this poll has not been identified.

19 In all candor, this pun is a bit of rank gossip. The author recalls hearing it bandied about the lunch room at Columbia's Avery Library as far back as the early 2000s, and was given to understand that it had been in circulation for decades. No interviewee, however, would claim responsibility or go on record to substantiate it. Scholarship must, on occasion, give way to *jouissance du texte*.

20 KN 9/2/16.

21 MF 5/4/16.

22 The name change would take place later, in 1983. Linda Kinsey notes.

23 MG 5/6/13.

24 MGMD.

25 MG 4/29/13.

26 See Walter Gropius, *Scope of Total Architecture* (New York: Collier, 1962).

27 As recounted by the designer Matteo Thun in Katrina Israel, "Memphis Revival: The 1980s Design Movement Gains Fresh Momentum with New Shows and Fashion Collections," *Wallpaper**, May 19, 2014.

28 AA 8/27/15. The interview was conducted for my article "A Much-Watched Kettle," *Disegno*, no. 9 (Autumn–Winter 2015), from which much of this material is taken.

29 MG 4/29/13.

30 AA 8/27/15.

31 MG 5/6/13.

32 AA 8/27/15.

33 Ibid.

34 Donald Strum interview 11/18/16.

35 Tom Wolfe, *From Bauhaus to Our House* (New York: Picador, 1981), 5.

36 MG 8/29/13.

37 RAMS 3/2/16.

38 KN 9/2/16.

39 Charles Jencks, "Michael Graves (1934–2015)," *Architectural Review*, March 21, 2015.

40 CJ 11/10/16.

41 KH 6/25/16.

42 MG 2/17/15.

43 Ibid.

44 Featuring ninety-seven original drawings by Michael, the *Gatsby* book appeared in a limited edition of only three hundred fifty copies. F. Scott Fitzgerald, *The Great Gatsby* (San Francisco: Arion Press, 1984).

45 Diane von Furstenberg, *Diane: A Signature Life* (New York: Simon and Schuster, 1998), 178.

46 MGMD; MG 8/29/13.

47 MG 8/29/13.

48 See David Lehman, *The Last Avant-Garde* (New York: Anchor Press, 1999). The parallels between Graves and Koch (pronounced *coke*), with whom the author studied as an undergraduate, are extraordinary. Both favored free-form abstraction in the 1960s, but moved toward an explicitly narrative formalism in the mid-1970s; both used historical quotation to semicomical effect; and both were esteemed as much for their commitment to undergraduate education as for their creative output. Although ten years Michael's senior, Koch lived in Cincinnati as a young man, was educated at Harvard, moved to the West Village after graduating, spent key years with his first wife in Italy (an experience he too fetishized in his work), and upon his return to the United States took a post at an Ivy League college, becoming affiliated with a group known as the New York School—an appellation sometimes applied to the Five. Capping off the list of remarkable similarities, the poet suffered from a disability that was almost a perfect analogue to the architect's lazy eye, affecting the faculty most essential to his craft: Koch had an incurable stutter. Koch died in 2002, and according to Michael, the two men never met.

49 MG 8/29/13.

50 JHD 6/15/16.

51 KN 9/2/16.

52 JHD 6/15/16.

53 KN 9/2/16.

54 Grace Glueck, "Graves Named to Design Addition on the Whitney," *New York Times*, October 18, 1981.

55 David A. Jones interview 8/11/16. The company did not go into health insurance, for which it is best known today, until the building was nearly complete.

56 Ibid.

57 Ibid.

58 MG 5/6/13.

59 Peter Hague Neilson interview 9/2/16.

60 MG 8/29/13.

61 "The Humana Building," promotional pamphlet from Humana Inc., Department of Public Affairs, 1985, 5.

62 MG 5/6/13.

63 DAJ 8/11/16.

64 Blackwood, *Beyond Utopia*.

65 Paul Goldberger, "An Appraisal: The Humana Building in Louisville: Compelling Work by Michael Graves," *New York Times*, June 10, 1985.

66 Julie Iovine, Marisa Bartolucci, and Raul Cabra, *Michael Graves: Compact Design Portfolio* (New York: Chronicle Books, 2002), 11.

67 Paul Gapp, "Humana's New Tower in Louisville Done In by Silly, Pointless Façade," *Chicago Tribune*, August 4, 1985.

68 Glenn Rutherford, "Readers' Reactions to New Humana Edifice," *Louisville Courier-Journal*, February 17, 1985, 3.

69 Karsten Harries, "Modernity's Bad Conscience," *AA Files* 10 (Autumn 1985): 55; Vincent Scully quoted in "The Humana Building" pamphlet, 4.

70 Kenneth Powell, *Graves Residence* (New York: Phaidon, 1995), 13.

71 MG 5/6/13.

72 FL 3/4/16.

73 MG 8/29/13; FL 3/4/16; KH 6/25/16.

74 SS email.

75 MG 8/29/13.

76 PW 11/16/16; SS email.

77 GG email; Rebecca Billman, "Obituary: Ray R. Roush, Leading Architect," *Cincinnati Inquirer*, July 20, 2002.

78 MG 8/29/13.

79 Hilton Kramer, "The Whitney's New Graves," *New Criterion* 4 (September 1985): 1; Michael Sorkin, "Save the Whitney," *Village Voice*, June 25, 1985.

80 Quoted in Carlton Knight, "Michael Graves Shakes Up Manhattan with His Museum Add-On," *Christian Science Monitor*, November 12, 1985.

81 Ibid.

82 Quoted in Albena Yaneva, *The Making of a Building: A Pragmatist Approach to Architecture* (Oxford: Peter Lang, 2009), 94; Paul Goldberger, "An Appraisal; A Daring and Sensitive Design," *New York Times*, May 22, 1985.

83 Yaneva, *The Making of a Building*, 93.

84 Martin Filler, "The Sum of Its Arts," *House & Garden* 157 (August 1985): 80–81.

85 Quoted in Douglas McGill, "Expansion at Whitney: The Debate Broadens," *New York Times*, November 26, 1985.

86 MG 8/29/13.

87 Paul Goldberger, "Architecture of a Different Color," *New York Times*, October 10, 1982; KN notes.

88 KN notes.

89 Robert A. M. Stern, David Fishman, and Jacob Tishlove, *New York 2000* (New York: Monacelli, 2008), 757.

90 The Time Warner Center took so long to build that the firm had actually reverted to a Modernist mode by the time it was completed in 2004.

91 Paul Goldberger, "Architects Meet to Note Failures of Modernism," *New York Times*, December 11, 1980.

92 MGMD.

93 MG 8/22/13.

94 "Non posso essere post-moderno perché mi vanto di non essere mai stato moderno." Quoted in Alberto Stabile, "Quell'Architetto—Poeta Che Incanta L'America," *La Repubblica*, June 10, 1987.

95 MM 6/8/16.

96 Reinhold Martin, *Utopia's Ghost: Architecture and Postmodernism, Again* (Minneapolis: University of Minnesota Press, 2010), 171.

97 Diamonstein-Spielvogel, "American Architecture Now: Michael Graves." On this subject of figurative versus abstract "balance," Michael was given to citing the poet Wallace Stevens, though his paraphrasing was sufficiently liberal as to leave the exact source unidentifiable.

98 Goldberger, "Architecture of a Different Color."

99 *The Charlottesville Tapes* (New York: Rizzoli, 1985), 127.

100 LK 12/28/15.

101 MF 5/4/16.

102 Blackwood, *Beyond Utopia*.

103 Ibid.; Richard Klein, "In the Race to Challenge Glass Boxes, Michael Graves Is Building a Solid Lead," *People*, February 8, 1982.

1 Suzanne Slesin, "Architect Tries on New Shoes," *New York Times*, November 26, 1987.

2 Nancy Levinson, "Notes on Fame," *Perspecta* 37 (2005): 20.

3 Quoted in Stern, Fishman, and Tishlove, *New York 2000*, 958.

4 MG 8/29/13.

5 MG 2/17/15.

6 PE 2/25/16.

7 MG 5/16/13.

8 James B. Stewart, *Disneywar: The Battle for the Magic Kingdom* (New York: Simon and Schuster, 2005), 67.

9 Chuck Mirarchi, "A Look Back: Walt Disney World's Swan and Dolphin Hotels," http://blog.wdwinfo.com/2015/05/05/a-look-back-walt-disney-worlds-swan-and-dolphin-hotels/.

10 MG 8/29/13.

11 Stewart, *Disneywar*, 67.

12 Related by fellow Disney historian Jim Korkis in Mirarchi, "A Look Back."

13 Alan Lapidus, *Everything by Design* (New York: St. Martin's, 2007), 188.

14 Paul Goldberger, "Disney Deco; and Now, an Architectural Kingdom," *New York Times*, April 8, 1990.

15 Leon Whiteson, "A New Hotel Reflects Company's Ambitious Plan to Tap Some of the World's Most Innovative Designers," *Los Angeles Times*, January 25, 1990.

16 Michael Eisner interview 5/17/16.

17 Ada Louise Huxtable, "Inventing American Reality," *New York Review of Books*, September 3, 1992.

18 Ibid.

19 CJ 11/10/16.

20 MG 8/29/13.

21 Ibid.

22 MG 5/6/13.

23 Stern, Fishman, and Tishlove, *New York 2000*, 959.

24 MG 8/29/13. The architect Richard Gluckman did succeed in carrying out a limited renovation of the uppermost floor.

25 PE 2/25/16; KN 9/2/16.

26 MG 8/29/13.

27 Paul Goldberger, "Raising the Architectural Ante in California," *New York Times*, October 14, 1990.

28 MG 5/6/13.

29 Quoted in Muriel Emanuel, *Contemporary Architects* (London: Macmillan, 1980), 331.

30 SH 5/20/16.

31 MGMD; MG 8/29/13.

32 Levinson, "Notes on Fame," 20.

33 Mary McLeod, "Architecture and Politics in the Reagan Era: From Postmodernism to Deconstructivism," *Assemblage* 8 (February 1989): 23.

34 Ibid., 30.

35 Deamer, "Michael Graves: Bodybuilder?," 19.

36 Pierre Chabard, "Alan Colquhoun in Conversation with Pierre Chabard," *AA Files* 67 (2013): 143.

37 Blackwood, *Beyond Utopia*.

38 Herbert Muschamp, "Graves's Progress from Paper Visions to Giant Teakettles," *New York Times*, January 14, 1999.

39 Quoted in Gaile Robinson, "Michael Graves' Designs Are Right on Target," *St. Louis Post-Dispatch*, December 21, 2000, 95.

40 Quoted in Jo Ann Lewis, "It's Postmodern," *Washington Post*, March 27, 1994.

41 The feature was accompanied by a book, Charles Jencks, *Kings of Infinite Space: Frank Lloyd Wright and Michael Graves* (London: Academy Editions, 1985).

42 Jencks, "Michael Graves (1934–2015)," *Architectural Review*.

43 Stan Allen, "Michael Graves (1934–2015)," *Art Forum*, May 1, 2015, www.artforum.com/passages/id=51897.

44 MG 8/29/13.

45 Brian Klipp interview 7/14/16.

46 Ibid.

47 Herbert Muschamp, "A Wonder World in the Mile High City," *New York Times*, May 7, 1995.

48 Brian Klipp interview 7/14/16.

49 Kenneth Powell, *Graves Residence* (New York: Phaidon, 1995), 13–14.

50 MG 5/6/13.

51 FL 3/4/16.

52 Ibid.

53 Patrick Burke eulogy 4/12/15.

54 PE 2/25/16.

55 MM 6/8/16; CC 5/16/16; SH 5/20/16.

56 Paul Goldberger, "The Whitney Paradox—To Add Is to Subtract," *New York Times*, January 8, 1989; Paul Goldberger interview 1/18/17.

57 MG 8/29/13.

58 Joan Ockman, "Bestride the World like a Colossus: The Architect as Tourist," in *Architourism: Authentic, Escapist, Exotic, Spectacular*, ed. Joan Ockman and Solomon Frausto (New York: Prestel, 2005), 161.

59 KF 6/16/16.

60 Patrick Burke eulogy 4/12/15.

61 MG 5/16/13.

62 Thacker's technical title was "vice president of cause marketing," a post created by the company to identify opportunities like the Washington Monument initiative that could elevate Target's brand profile. Linda Kinsey notes.

63 RJ 4/29/16.

64 DS 11/18/16.

65 RJ 4/29/16.

66 MG 8/29/13.

67 Jacqueline Trescott, "Washington Monument to Be under Wraps," *Washington Post*, October 17, 1997, A1.

68 The author was attending high school in the capital at the time and can attest that this was the view universally held by seventeen-year-old boys.

69 Jencks, "Michael Graves (1934–2015)."

70 MG 5/6/13.

71 Rob Van Varick interview 9/2/16.

72 Daniel Naegele, "We Dig Graves—All Sizes," *Harvard Design Magazine* 12 (Fall 2000): 100.

73 Seeley G. Mudd Manuscript Library archivist emails.

74 MG 2/17/15; Elizabeth Diller interview 1/10/16. Ralph Lerner, the dean at the time, died in 2011.

75 BG 11/11/16. The office is now known as Diller Scofidio + Renfro.

76 MG 2/17/15.

77 KN notes. With Michael's retirement from the faculty, his firm was eligible to design campus buildings for the university and was selected for a pair of projects in the mid-2000s—including the Wu-Wilcox Halls renovation and addition, an expansion of Robert Venturi's Gordon Wu Hall.

78 Barry Bergdoll interview 12/14/16. Rowe died in 1999.

79 Lynn Min interview 12/5/15.

80 Patrick Burke eulogy 4/12/15.

81 Quoted in Ilene Dube, "Michael Graves—Drawn to Design," *Princeton* magazine, April 2015, 17.

IX · THE SKY AND THE FRAME

1 MG 8/22/13.

2 Ibid.

3 DBG 12/2/16.

4 ML 11/18/16.

5 MG 5/6/13.

6 MG 8/22/13.

7 MG 8/29/13.

8 Ibid.

9 Ibid.

10 RVV 9/2/16.

11 DS 11/18/16.

12 MG 8/29/13.

13 RVV 9/2/16.

14 ML 11/18/16.

15 PE 2/25/16.

16 RM 2/29/16.

17 MG 8/29/13.

18 ML 11/18/16.

19 John Hockenberry, "The Re-education of Michael Graves," *Metropolis*, October 2006, 123–27.

20 ML 11/18/16.

21 Quoted in Barbara Sadick, "Famed Architect Michael Graves, in a Wheelchair, Widens His Design Focus," *Washington Post*, July 14, 2015.

22 Quoted in Bryan Appleyard, *Richard Rogers: A Biography* (Boston: Faber and Faber, 1986), 328. Banham is paraphrasing the sculptor Horatio Greenough.

23 MG 5/6/13.

24 ML 11/18/16.

25 Amelia Taylor-Hochberg, "Deans List: David Mohney of the Kean University's Michael Graves School of Architecture," Archinect.com, December 16, 2014, http://archinect.com/features/article/116056065/deans-list-david-mohney-of-the-kean-university-s-michael-graves-school-of-architecture.

26 See especially Michael Gotkin and Paul Makovsky, "The Postmodernist Watchlist," *Metropolis*, November 2014, 74–94.

27 Recalling the conversation years later, Goldberger qualified the remark, calling the health-care work "a key part of [Graves's] oeuvre." PG 1/18/17.

28 "Michael Graves: The Past as Prologue," event sponsored by the Architectural League of New York, November 22, 2015.

29 DBG 12/2/16.

30 PE 2/25/16.

Index

Italic page numbers refer to illustrations within the text; those in the color plate section are labeled accordingly.

Abbey, Bruce 100

Abramovitz, Max *plate 42,* 74–75, 160

Absolut Vodka 173

Abstract Expressionism 50, 58, 79, 94

Acropolis 75, 95, 109

Ad Hoc Committee to Save the Whitney 165

Agrest, Diana 113

Alberobello 51–52, 75, 95

Alberti, Leon Battista 73

Alchimia 152

Alessi, Alberto 156
growing product line of, 181
salt and pepper shakers of, 191
teakettle of, *plate 34, plate 35,* 3, 14, 152–53, 164, 173, 180, 192–93, 205

Alexander House *plate 16,* 103

Allen, Stan 185

"Amenable Shelter, The" (Graves) *plate 1,* 51

American Academy, Rome 64, 66–71, 74, 91, 101, 116, 137

American Academy of Arts and Letters, New York 139

American Institute of Architects (AIA) 119, 141, 146, 182, 190, 193

American Life Building *plate 42,* 160

Amsterdam 77

Anderson, Lennart 79

Anderson, Stanford 91–92

Ando, Tadao 170–71

Annunciation (Botticelli) 175

Answered Prayers (Capote) 155

Architectura, De (Vitruvius) vi

Architectural and Transportation Barriers Compliance Board 203

Architectural Digest magazine *plate 29*

Architectural Forum magazine 59, 62, 108

Architectural League of New York 91, 148

Architectural Record magazine 146

Architecture of the École des Beaux Arts, The (MoMA exhibition) 148

Architecture without Architects (Rudofsky) 52

Arcibasilica di San Giovanni 72, 78

Armstrong, Thomas N., III 158–59, 164, 180

Art Deco xi, 120, 128, 151–52, 167

Arthur Erickson Associates 140

Ashbery, John vi, 158

Asplund, Gunnar 113, 163, 185, 226 note 58

Asplund Problem 113–16, 124, 225 note 8

AT&T Building 139, 142

Athens 37, 75, 95, 109

Austria 77

Autodesk 173

Aventine 181

Avery Library 228 note 19

Bachelard, Gaston 101

Balkans 74, 76

Banham, Reyner xi, 185, 204

Barcelona Pavilion 44

Barnes, Edward Larrabee 65, 88, 165

baroque 57, 163

Barozzi da Vignola, Giacomo 73

Barthes, Roland 116

Basel 77

Basilica of Maxentius *plate 5, 72*

Baths of Caracalla 67

Bauhaus 44, 54, 56, 80, 84, 150, 154, 193

Beaux Arts xi, 29, 43, 56, 68–69, 85, 117, 148, 160, 194

Belluschi, Pietro 143

Benacerraf House *plate 15,* 99–100, 103, 106, 110, 118, 120

Bergamo 75

Bergdoll, Barry 194

Bergen, Candice 161

Bernini, Gian Lorenzo 177

Biedermeier furniture 129, 153, 163

Big Sleep, The (film) 155

Birksted J. K. 39

Bloomingdales 155

Boone, Daniel 18

Botticelli, Sandro 116, 175

Boullée, Étienne-Louis 177

Bramante, Donato 72

Braque, Georges 79

Brenner, Douglas 146

Breuer, Marcel
European Modernism and, 54
lack of communication by, 166
Meier and, 64
Mies and, 54
Nelson and, 63–64
Modernism and, 159
Roush and, *43, 44, 47,* 54
Stern and, 179
Whitney Museum and, 158–59, 164–65, 175, 179–80, 189–90

Brilliant, Richard 70–71, 78

Broad Ripple High School 32–34, 37, 40–41

Broad Ripple Village 77, 93–94, 101–2, 186, 190
annexation of to Indianapolis, 15
Gail and, 101
Graves's early years in, 16, 20–21, 24, 29, 32, 36, 40, 44, 71
Indianapolis Art Center porch and, 186
influence of, 101, 186, 190
wedding in, 48
world outside of, 77, 94

Brown, Walter David x

Brussels 77

Brutalism xi

Bryan, William Jennings 18

Bunshaft, Gordon 65, 139, 150, 193

Burgee, John 167

Burke, Patrick 187, 189–90, 209

Burnham, Daniel 47, 69

Bush, George W. 13

Cadwallader, Bobby 148–49

Caesar, Julius 73

Cafe Wha? 62

Calder, Alexander 26, 57

Campus Martius 68

Capitoline Hill 68

Capote, Truman 155

Carl, Peter 100–1, 108, 114–15

Carl A. Strauss & Associates 44

Carter, Jimmy 145

Casa Batlló 76–77

CASE (Conference of Architects for the Study of the Environment) 89–92, 94, 99, 105–8, 130

Cassirer, Ernst 116

Castelli, Leo 157

Castel Sant'Angelo 68

Catalonia 77

Central Park West 167

Chadwick, Gordon 62, 80

Chagall, Marc 26

Chan, Lo-Yi 60–61, 222 note 49

Charlottesville Tapes, The (Robertson) 170

Chem-Fleur 134

Cherry, Wendell 159–61

Chicago School 47

Chicago Seven x, 225 note 104

Chicago Tribune newspaper 162

Chimacoff, Alan 113, 126, 128, 224 note 41, 226 note 58

Chomsky, Noam 107, 171

Christo 192

CIAM (Congrès

internationaux d'architecture moderne) 55–59, 90
Cincinnati Enquirer 42, 44
civil rights 52
Claghorn House *plate 20*, 102, 118, 120, 123, 126–27
Clark Realty Capital 203
Clausen, Meredith 145–46
Clay, Cassius 67
Clinton, Bill 184
Clinton, Hillary 2
Clockwork Orange, A (film) 116
Close, Chuck 197
Clos Pegase Winery 155
Cohen, Jean-Louis x
Collage City (Rowe) 130
Colmar 77
Cologne 77
Colosseum 67, 72
Colquhoun, Alan 103, 129, 147, 184
Columbia University 69, 194
Columbus Circle 167
Complexity and Contradiction in Architecture (Venturi) 108, 115, 176
Constant, Caroline 13, 90–91, 98, 100, 113, 115, 127, 189, 209
Constantine 72
consumerism 152, 192
Cooper, Alex 165
Cooper Union 106
Corinthian style 73
Corot, Jean-Baptiste-Camille 71, 104, 188, 202
Coryat, Thomas 73–74
Cret, Paul Philippe 29
Croatia 76
Crooks House *plate 23, plate 24*, 122–23, 125–26, 129, 159, 226 note 58
Cubism 97
   Claghorn House and, 123
   Corbusian style and, 97–98, 100, 104, 118, 120
   Five Architects and, 118
   Hanselmann House and, 97–98, 100
   Krier and, 134–35, 141
   Picasso and, 24, 26, 58, 79, 94–95, 126, 175
   Snyderman House and, 104
   strabismus and, 26–27
"Cubist Kitchen King" 127
CUNY Graduate Center 205

Dahl-Wolfe, Louise 52
Da Silva, John 116, 140
Davies, Julie Hanselmann 85, 95–98
Davies, Paul 107
Deamer, Peggy 136, 184
Dean, Laura *plate 36*
Death and Life of Great American Cities, The (Jacobs) 138

de Chirico, Giorgio 185, 202
Deconstructivist Architecture exhibition x, xii, 2, 183
de Kooning, Willem 50, 62, 77, 94, 197
Delirious New York (Koolhaas) 171
Democratic Party 9, 18, 52, 133
Denver Art Museum 186
Denver Public Library *plate 50, plate 51*, 186–88
Derrida, Jacques 171
Designer of the Year award 150–51
design tourism 127, 157
   Fargo-Moorhead Bridge and, 137
   Grand Tour and, 67, 73–77, 80, 95
   Roush and, 44–46, 53
Detroit Institute of Arts 180
Dewey, Thomas 29
Dexter Shoes 173
Dickens, Charles 207
Diller, Elizabeth 193
Diller+Scofidio 193
diptychs 94, 116, 123, 164–65, 175
Disney 50, 172
   building spree of, 176
   Eisner and, 9, 167–68, 176–79
   Euro Disney and, 178
   Jencks and, 178–79
   Lapidus and, 177
   Postmodernism and, 177–79
   Swan and Dolphin Resort and, *plate 46, plate 47*, 177–78, 203, 211–12
   Team Disney Headquarters and, 168, 178, 187
   Venturi and, 176–78
Doric style 73
Double Dream of Spring, The (Ashbery) vi
drawing
   Alessi teakettle and, *plate 34*
   Basilica of Maxentius and, *plate 5, 72*
   Bunshaft on, 139
   Carl and, *114, 115*
   classical influences and, 134
   Crooks inglenook and, 122
   Davies and, 85
   Eisenman and, 59, 63
   Graves and, *plate 3, plate 4, plate 5, plate 8, plate 30, 2, 5, 24, 34, 37–38, 49, 56–57, 66, 71–79, 86, 88, 108, 122, 124–25, 133–37, 173, 191–93, 197, 205*
   The Great Gatsby and, 157
   iBOT and, 197
   Jersey Corridor proposal and, *plate 9*
   Krier and, 133
   mechanical, 37, 66

Parthenon and, 38
Piranesi and, 30
Portland Building and, *plate 30*, 147
Protetch and, 148
   referential sketches and, *plate 25*, 124, 141
   Rome and, *plate 3, plate 4, 72, 74, 78–79*, 170
   schematic, 24, 37
   Sert and, 56–57
   Unité d'habitation and, *plate 8*
   Vidler and, 90
   working, 59, 86
Drexler, Arthur 90–91, 93, 105, 225 note 104
Drive Medical *plate 57*, 199
Duany, Andrés 205
Dylan, Bob 2

Eames, Charles 62, 150
Eaton, John C. 70
Egypt 182, 194
Einsiedeln 77
Eisenman, Elizabeth 92
Eisenman, Peter *vii–viii*, 40, 141
   accessibility and, 79, 169
   as architect of the idea, 1–2
   on awards juries, 201
   CASE and, 89–92, 94, 99, 105–8, 130
   competition proposals and, 100
   CUNY symposium and, 206
   deconstructionist literary theory and, 172
   Deconstructivist Architecture show and, 183
   divorce of, 106
   drawing and, 59, 63
   Five Architects and, 106–10
   Graves memorial and, 208
   Hawks and, 155
   Hejduk and, 106
   IAUS and, 94, 105, 146–47, 171, 226 note 37
   Johnson and, 139–40
   Koch and, 61
   Krier and, 134
   Le Corbusier and, 172
   Meier and, 60, 63
   Modernism and, 138
   New School event and, 206, 207
   New York Five and, 2–3, 106–11, 115, 117, 119, 201
   Princeton and, 81–86, 89–94, 98, 138, 194
   psychotherapy of, 189
   Robertson and, 109
   Rowe and, 80, 83–84
   TAC and, 59–60, 63
   theoretics of, 139
   Venturi and, 176
   Wexner Center for the Arts and, 172–73

White faction and, 108
   on Whitney, 180
   Wigley and, 183
Eisner, Michael 9, 167–68, 176–79
Ekberg, Anita 68
"Elder Turtles of Aegina, The" (Holloway) 71
elevation 34, 72, 115, 123–25, 136–37, 141, 162
Elizabeth II, Queen of England 155–56
Emery Roth & Sons 142, 147
Emory University 182
Engineering Research Center, University of Cincinnati *plate 48*, 182
Episcopalians 32–34, 44, 60
estrangement 27
Euro Disney 178

Fargo-Moorhead Bridge *plate 28*, 135–38, 148, 173
Fascism 55, 139
Federal Reserve Bank 194
Filler, Martin 14, 104, 148–49, 165, 171
First National Bank Tower 160
Fisher, Nes, Campbell and Partners 82
Fitzgerald, F. Scott 81, 157
Five Architects 106–11, 115, 118–19, 139
"Five Points of Architecture" (Le Corbusier) 55
Fontana dell'Acqua Paola 72
Fontana del Tritone 177
Forster, Kurt 147
Foster, Norman 160
Frampton, Kenneth 89, 99, 107, 113, 129, 190, 226 note 49
Franco, Francisco 55
Frank, Suzanne 89
Franklin Delano Roosevelt Memorial 64–65
Franzen, Ulrich 160–61, 165
Frasca, Robert 52, 143
French Academy 69–70
frescoes 75
Freud, Sigmund 39
From Bauhaus to Our House (Wolfe) 154
Fukuoka Hyatt Regency Hotel and Office Building *plate 49*
Fundació Joan Miró 57
furniture 16, 112, 200
   Ambiente fair and, 5
   Biedermeier and, 129, 153, 163
   Cadwallader and, 148–49
   Graves and, *plate 33, 48, 53, 88, 128, 151*
   Knoll and, 148–50
   Le Corbusier and, 62
   Mies and, 62, 199
   Modernism and, 149–50

showrooms and, 149–51
Strauss and, 42
Wright and, 62, 150
Futagawa, Yukio 123
Futurist-Deco 167

Galilei, Alessandro 72
Galveston, Texas 155
Garber, Tweddell & Wheeler Architects 221
Garnier, Charles 56
Gaudí, Antoni 76–77
Geddes, Robert 93, 98–99, 193, 226 note 49
Gehry, Frank x, xii, 1, *141*, 155, 171, 178, 184, 186, 204
Geibel, Victoria 175
Germany 77
Getty Square x
Giedion, Sigfried 55–57, 222 note 49
Gilded Age 17
Giotto's frescoes 75
Giurgola, Romaldo 108–9, 140
Glass, Philip 158
Glass, Steuben 175
Glass House 139, 224 note 61
Goethe 169
Goheen, Robert F. 89, 93
Goldberger, Paul 2, 146, 165, 170, 178, 180, 183–84, 189, 206, 225 note 104
Goldschmidt, Neil 140, 145
Gombrich, Ernst 85, 116
Gordon, Alastair x
Gordon Wu Hall 176, 231 note 76
GQ magazine 155, 187
Grand Tour 73–77, 80, 95
Graves, Adam 3, 92, 101, 112, 128, 164, 188–89, 196, 201
Graves, Bessie 20, 219 note 16
Graves, Edward 18, 33, 220 note 47
Graves, Erma Lowe Sanderson 119, 201
   Bud's drinking and, 21
   dancing school and, 30–32
   drawing of, 125, 127
   fortitude of, 22, 34
   leg amputation of, 22–23, 25
   Michael's youth and, 15, 21–26, 30–38, 40
   views on career choice, 24, 26, 88, 182
Graves, Gail Devine 41, 164, 196
   background of, 36, 38
   city life and, 62–63
   design tourism and, 45–47, 73–77, 80, 95
   divorce of, 101–2, 112, 119, 127
   Europe and, 67, 70, 74, 80, 137, 204
   Grand Tour and, 73–77, 80, 95
   Johnson Wax Headquarters

trip and, 46, 62
   matriculation of, 42
   Princeton and, 81, 84, 86, 88, 92, 94, 101–2, 126–27
   rapprochement attempts and, 189
   Roush and, 44–45, 53
   shyness of, 92
   social changes and, 61
   wedding of, 48, 49
Graves, Lucy James 101–2, 112–13, 127, 196, 209
Graves, Margaret 20, 219 note 16
Graves, Max 15–16, 18–21, 32, 39, 219 note 16
Graves, Michael *vii–viii, 83*
   as accessibility advocate, 202–4
   airline travels of, 194
   Alessi teakettle and, *plate 34*, *plate 35,* 3, 14, 152–53, 164, 173, 180, 192–93, 205
   as architect of the eye, 1–2
   Architecture 204 and, 84
   Asplund Problem and, 113–16, 124, 225 note 8
   on awards juries, 201
   awards of, 2, 119, 150–51, 187, 190
   background of, 15–40
   Basilica of Maxentius and, *plate 5,* 72
   Bunshaft and, 139
   CASE and, 89–92, 94, 99, 105–8, 130
   classicism and, 2
   Clintons and, 2
   clothing tastes of, 88–89, 154
   college grades of, 49
   competition proposals and, 100
   CUNY symposium and, *206*
   death of, xv, 204–5
   as Democrat, 9, 18, 52, 133
   design tourism and, 44–47, 53, 67, 73–77, 80, 95, 157
   desire for Pritzker Prize, 190, 194, 206
   desire to be liked, 189–91
   divorces of, 4, 101, 112, 119, 127, 163
   drawing and, *plate 3, plate 4, plate 5, plate 8, plate 30,* 2, 5, 24, 34, 37–38, 49, 56–57, 66, 71–79, 86, 88, 108, 122, 124–25, 133–37, 173, 191–93, 197, 205
   early commissions of, 94–101
   elevations and, 34, 72, 115, 123–25, 136–37, 141, 162
   figurative architecture and, 122–23, 125, 157–58, 170, 177, 229 note 97
   finding his architectural niche, 86–89
   furniture and, *plate 33,* 48, 53, 88, 128, 151

Graduate School of Design (GSD) and, 53–54, 56, 58–60, 62, 64–65, 84, 115, 221 note 28
Grand Tour and, 73–77, 80, 95
Hawks and, 10, 155, 161, 163, 167
health issues of, 1, 4–14, 26–27, 41, 189, 195–204, 208
Humana Building and, *plate 42,* 160–62, 164–67, 170, 187
increased fame of, 148–59, 173, 174
influence of Rome on, 66–83, 94–95, 101, 116, 134, 137, 139, 163, 170, 177, 190, 203–4, 223 note 13, 227 note 70
Jacobs sculpture and, 49–50
Jencks and, 137–38, 146, 151, 154–55, 157, 178, 185, 193, 205, 218 note 5, 218 note 6
Jersey Corridor and, *plate 9,* 90–91, 113
Johnson Wax Headquarters trip and, 46, 62
lazy eye of, 25–27, 41, 126, 220 note 33, 220 note 36
Le Corbusier and, 98
lectures and, 80, 116, 154–57, 183, 185, 196, 202
legacy of, 205–8
love of dogs, 163–64
masters degree of, 61
medical designs of, 198–200
memorial for, 208–9
Miesian Modernism and, 51
monographs of, 157, 165, 183, 187, 224 note 42, 226 note 21
Nelson and, 61–65, 80, 88, 150, 181
new language of, 118–20, 128, 191
New School event and, *206,* 207
as painter, *plate 65,* 9, 14, 24, 26, 38, 50–51, 66, 71, 94, 97–98, 124, 170, 185–86, 188, 197, 202
as PoMo revanchist, 2
Portland Building and, x–xi, 1, 140–48, 183, 206
postgraduate education of, 52–58
Postmodernism and, ix, 1, 142–48 (*see also* Postmodernism)
Princeton University and, xiii, xv, 4 (*see also* Princeton University)
Roush and, 43–54, 60, 65–66, 93–94, 128, 164, 198
Sert and, 54–61, 65–66, 71, 84–85, 97, 115
showrooms and, 149–51
Target and, *plate 52, plate 53, plate 54,* 3, 5, 9, 11, 191–93, 199–202
teaching style of, 84–85

TED talk of, 202
trulli houses and, 51–52, 56, 75, 95, 142, 200, 221 note 32
undergraduate thesis of, 51
University of Cincinnati and, 38, 41–43, 46, 49, 51–52, 54, 56, 60, 64, 71, 182
the Warehouse and, 4–5, 11, 23, 39, 112, 127–29, 133, 155, *156,* 158–59, 163–64, 188, 190, 195–97, 202, 205
Washington Monument and, *plate 55,* 2, 29, 32, 191–92, 231 note 61
wedding of, 48, 49
White faction and, 108
Whitney Museum and, 158–61, 164–68, 172, 175, 179–80, 183, 189–90
Graves, Michael Sebastian 3, 12, 201–2, 209
Graves, Nave & Company 17, 19
Graves, Sarah *See* Stelfox, Sarah Graves
Graves, Thomas Browning (Bud) 15–16, 20–22, 30, 32–33, 37, 39, 60, 119, 127, 190, 219 note 1, 220 note 21
Graves, Thomas Smith 16–20, 29, 32–33, 220 note 47
Graves, Tom 15, 20–21, 24, 32, 35, 88, 119, 201
Graves Commission Company 32
Graves Design Studio Store 180–81
Grays 116, 225 note 104
Four Days in May and, 225 note 91
Hardy Holzman Pfeiffer and, 135
Le Corbusier and, 119
Modernism and, 119
Rowe and, 130
Tigerman and, 135
UCLA School of Architecture and Design and, 154–55
Venturi and, 108–9, 115, 138
Wolfe and, 154
Great Depression 20
Great Gatsby, The (Fitzgerald) 157
Greece 74–76, 134, 184
Green, Barth 11–13, 196, 202, 208
Greenberg, Allan 106, 108
Greenwich Village 62–63
Gris, Juan 79, 123
Gropius, Walter 47, 54, 56, 59, 65, 80, 150, 192
Grounds for Sculpture 205
Guernica (Picasso) 58
Guggenheim Museum, Bilbao 1, 184
Gunwyn Ventures 103

Gwathmey, Charles 9, *141*
CASE and, 105
clothing choices and, 154
death of, 201
glass blocks and, 120
industrial design and, 181
Le Corbusier and, 88
New York Five and, 2–3,
  106–11, 115, 117, 119, 201
parents' house, *87*, 88
on transcendence of accommodation, 181
White faction and, 108
Whitney Museum and, 158
Gwathmey, Robert 88
Gwathmey Siegel 117, 158

Hackemeyer, Eleanor 35
Hadid, Zaha x, xii, 184
Hanselmann, Jay 35–36, 41,
  94–96, 102
Hanselmann, Jennifer 95
Hanselmann, Julie *See* Davies,
  Julie Hanselmann
Hanselmann, Lois *See* Rothert,
  Lois Hickman Hanselmann
Hanselmann House *plate 11*,
  plate 12, plate 13, plate 14,
  94–99, 102–6, 109, 113,
  118–19, 126
Hansen, C. F. 185
Hardy Holzman Pfeiffer 135
Harper's Bazaar magazine 52
Harries, Karsten 162
Harris, Steven 85, 118, 123, 158,
  181–82, 189, 209
Harrison, Wallace K. 74, 160
Harvard 183, 189
elitism of, 61, 66, 70, 78, 88
Graduate School of Design
  (GSD) and, 53–54, 56, 58–60,
  62, 64–65, 84, 115, 221 note 28
Graves's contempt for, 60
Gropius and, 47
lack of history at, 73
Le Corbusier and, 54, 58–59,
  82, 120
Sert and, 71
Strauss and, 53–54
Harvard Club, Manhattan 167
Harvard Design Magazine 193
Hauserman Inc. 149
Hawks, Howard 155
Hawks, Kitty 10, 155, 161,
  163, 167
Hejduk, John
background of, 106
CASE and, 89, 105
death of, 201
as marginal figure, 106, 117
Modernist box and, 86
New York Five and, 2–3,
  106–11, 115, 117, 119, 201
paper architects and, 105
Wall House and, 125
White faction and, 108

Hillier, Robert 81
Hitchcock, Henry-Russell 139
Hjemkomst Center 227
  note 64
Hockenberry, John 202
Hoffmann, Josef 151–52,
  161, 185
Holloway, R. Ross 71
Holmes, J. L. 16
Hoover Berg Desmond 186
Hopper, Edward 26
Hotel New York 178
Howard, Susan 7
Humana Building *plate 41*,
  plate 42, 170, 187
Johnson and, 162
Mies and, 160–62
Modernism and, 160–67
poor academic response to,
  162–63
Postmodernism and, 160–67
Scully on, 162
Huxtable, Ada Louise 24,
  137, 178
Hyman, Isabelle 146
hypermodernism xii

iBOT 197, 202–3
Illinois Institute of Technol-
  ogy 45–47
Imaginary Prisons (Piranesi)
  30, 31
Independent Group 59, 181
Indiana Livestock Exchange
  19–20
Indianapolis Art Center 186
Institute for Architecture and
  Urban Studies (IAUS) 94,
  105, 146–47, 171, 226 note 37
Interiors magazine 150–51
International Architecture
  Exhibition 151
International Finance Corpo-
  ration 181
International Style xi, 47–48,
  84, 138–39, 167, 207
Ionic style 73
Italian Futurism xi
Ivancie, Frank 145–47, 227
  note 8
Izenour, Steven 115

Jacobs, Donald 49–51
Jacobs, Jane 138, 140
Jacobs, Karrie 90
Jahn, Helmut 160, 167
James, Frank 18
James, Jesse 18
Japan 157, 182–83, 186–87
JCPenney 200
Jean-Claude 192
Jeanneret-Gris, Charles
  Édouard *See* Le Corbusier
Jefferson, Thomas 127
Jencks, Charles x, 218 note 5,
  218 note 6

consumerism and, 193
CUNY symposium and, 205
Disney and, 178–79
Hawks and, 155
home of, *plate 40*, 157
Kings of Infinite Space and,
  184–85
*The Language of Post-Modern
  Architecture* and, 137–38
Portland Building and, 146
Portoghesi and, 151
Postmodernism and, 154
Venice Architecture Biennale
  and, 151
Whitney Museum and, 165
"Winter" fireplace and, *plate 40*
Jersey Corridor Project *plate
  9*, 90–91, 113
Joffrey Ballet *plate 36*, 155
Johnson, Philip x, xii, 2, *141*,
  225 note 104
AT&T Building and, 139, 142
Belluschi and, 143
competition from, 167
as dean of American architec-
  ture and, 139
Deconstructivist Architecture
  show and, 183
Eisenman and, 139–40
Eisner and, 167–68
Glass House and, 139, 224
  note 61
Humana Building and, 160, 162
International Style and, 139
Modernism and, 139
Portland Building and, 140,
  142–43, 147
Postmodernism and, 139–40,
  176, 185
Rockefeller family and, 100
Time cover of, 139
wealth of, 139
Whitney Museum and, 165
Wolfe and, 154
Johnson, Ron 9, 11, 191–92,
  200
Johnson Wax Headquarters
  46, 62
Jones, David A. 159–61

Kahn, Louis 59, 74, 221 note 32
Kamen, Dean 197
Kandinsky, Wassily 54
Kaskey, Raymond 147
Kasumi Research and Train-
  ing Center 182
Katz, Alex 64
Kean University 205
Keeley House 103
Keith, Slim 155
Kelty, Matt 103
Kessler Institute 8–12,
  199–200
Kevin Roche John Dinkeloo
  167
Keystone House 134

Kiley, Dan 45
Kings of Infinite Space
  184–85
Kinsey, Linda 180
kitsch 2, 179, 181
Klee, Paul 54
Klinkhammer, Barbara 97
Klipp, Brian 186–87
Kmart 192
Knoll 148–50
Koch, Carl 60–61, 228 note 48
Koch, Kenneth 158
Kohn Pedersen Fox (KPF)
  167, 183
Koolhaas, Rem *plate 40*, 171,
  180, 183–84, 190
Kramer, Hilton 165
Krauss, Rosalind 126
Krier, Léon
Ando and, 170–71
Blundell's Corner and, *131*
drawing capabilities of, 133
Fargo-Moorhead Bridge
  and, 135
Le Corbusier and, 133
Modernism and, 130–31, 133
as outsider, 130
Postmodernism and, 151
Princeton lectures and, 133
Rowe and, 133–34
teaching and, 133
Whites and, 134
Year of, *132*, 134
Krier, Robert 133

Labatut, Jean 81–82, 117, 176
Lady Commerce (Kaskey
  statue) 142, 147
Lambert House 86, *87*
La Montaine, John 70
Landmarks Commission
  165–66, 175
*Language of Post-Modern
  Architecture, The* (Jencks)
  137–38
Lapidus, Alan 177, 186
Lapidus, Morris 177
La Riche, William 107
Latour, Bruno ix
Lauder, Leonard A. 166
Learning from Las Vegas
  (Venturi, Scott Brown, and
  Izenour) 115
Lebowitz, Fran 9–10, 12, 155,
  161, 163–64, 188, 201, 209
Le Corbusier ix, 37, 39, 65
Asplund Problem and, 124
car-centric planning of, 119
CIAM and, 55–59, 90
color and, 97
Constant and, 90
Cubism and, 97–98, 100, 104,
  118, 120
Eisenman and, 172
"Five Points of Architecture"
  and, 55

flat whites of, 97
furniture and, 62, 150
geometric order and, 78, 95
Giedion and, 56
Grand Tour and, 74
Grays and, 119
Gwathmey and, 88
Hanselmann House and, 95
Harvard and, 54, 58–59, 82, 120
influence of, 57–59, 62, 104, 109, 118–20
Krier and, 133
light and, 98, 169
machine-like forms of, 58
Meier and, 86
minimalism and, 118
Modernism and, 55, 58–59, 62, 84, 105, 115
New York Five and, 107
Notre Dame du Haut and, 59
painting and, 58
plan as generator approach of, 58
plasticity and, 86
poetics of, 203–4
Schroeder and, 135
Sert and, 54–59, 65
style of, 54–55, 57, 103, 203–4
symmetry and, 57
translation of, 90
travels of, 74
Unité d'habitation and, *plate 8*, 76
villas of, 55, 99, 116
Whites and, 118
Ledoux, Claude-Nicolas 29, 134, 153, 178
L'Enfant, Pierre 29
Lequeu, Jean-Jacques *plate 25*
Letterman, David 34
Levinson, Nancy 183
Libera, Adalberto 67
Libeskind, Daniel 184, 186, 190
Life magazine 91
Lincoln Center 167
Lin, Min 196–97, 201–4
"Little of the Old In and Out, A" (Graves) 116
Longo, Robert 158
Louisville Courier-Journal newspaper 162
Louvre Abu Dhabi 206
Loyola Law School 171
Lucas, George 176
Luxembourg Gardens 136

McCready, Connie 145–46
McKim, Charles Follen 69
McKim, Mead & White 69
McLaughlin, Robert 81, 89, 93
McLeod, Mary 109, 113, 168, 183–84, 189, 209, 225 note 8
Maddow, Rachel 195–96
Madonna Rehabilitation Hospital 200
Malcolm Wells Architect 135

Marienkapelle Church 77
Marimekko 200
Martin, Reinhold 169
Marx, Leo 120
Matisse, Henri 126
Max Protetch Gallery *plate 37*, 148, 173
Medici Fountain 136
Meier, Carolyn 86
Meier, Jerome 86
Meier, Richard 66, 71, 107, 113, 120
art enthusiasm of, 63–64
on awards juries, 201
Breuer and, 64
CASE and, 89, 105
as easily influenced, 84
Eisenman and, 60, 63
Essex Fells and, 88
on European influence, 77–78
Five Architects and, 106
glass and, 64
Graves's memorial and, 209
Hawks and, 155
Lambert House and, 86, 87
Le Corbusier and, 86
low teaching interest of, 84–85
New York Five and, 2–3, 106, 111, 115, 117, 119, 201
painting and, 9
parents' home by, 86
Princeton and, 84, 86
Pritzker Prize and, 190
Stella and, 64
White faction and, 108
Wright and, 64
XV Triennale di Milano and, 108
Memphis Group 151
Mendini, Alessandro 152
Merkel, Jayne 44, 49
Mezzo House 103
Miami Beach condominiums 173, 174
Michael C. Carlos Museum 182
Michael Graves & Associates 2, 5, 9, 187, 193, 198, 205–6
Michael Graves Architect *plate 32*, 227 note 64
Denver Public Library and, *plate 50*, *plate 51*, 186–88
Disney and, 168, 172, 176–78
Fargo-Moorhead Bridge and, 135
Japan work of, 182
launching of, 93
marketing department for, 166
office pets and, 163
Portland Building and, 142–43
standard procedure of, 124
Strada Novissima and, 150
Washington Monument and, 191
Whitney Museum and, 158, 175
Michael Graves Architecture

& Design 206
Michael Graves College *plate 64*, 205
Michael Graves Design Group 3, 5, 198–99, 204
Michelangelo 68, 109
Mies van der Rohe, Ludwig
Abramovitz and, 160
American Life Building and, *plate 42*, 160
Barcelona chair and, 199
Barcelona Pavilion and, 44
Breuer and, 54
car-centric planning of, 119
First National Bank Tower and, 160
furniture and, 62, 199
Glass House and, 139
Harrison and, 160
Harvard and, 82
Humana Building and, 160–62
icy monumentality of, 119
Illinois Institute of Technology and, 45, 207
on improvisation, 111
influence of, 47
Meier and, 86
Modernism and, 51, 54, 84, 160–62
Nelson and, 61–62, 65
reductivism and, 47
Robert F. Carr Memorial Chapel and, 45, 47
Roush and, 45–47
SOM and, 65
spatiality of, 78
stern rigor of, 203
symmetry and, 64
transformation of, 39
Wright on, 65
Miller, J. Irwin 45
Miller, Sam 99
Millstone Coffee 173
Min, Lynn 3, 12, 194, 196
Miró, Joan 57–58
MIT 89–91, 123
Mitchell/Giurgola Architects 140
Miyake, Issey 157
Mizrahi, Isaac 200
Modernism
American, 61, 167
apostasy from, 138–42
Asplund Problem and, 113–16, 124, 225 note 8
Bauhaus and, 44, 54, 56, 80, 84, 150, 154, 193
Belluschi and, 143
Breuer and, 54, 159, 165
California, 111
CASE and, 89–92, 94, 99, 105–8, 130
CIAM and, 55–59, 90
CUNY symposium and, 205
Deconstructivist Architecture and, 183

Denver library and, 186
design tourism and, 46
Eisenman and, 138
Erickson and, 145
Europe and, 151
functionalism and, 203
furniture and, 149–51
Giedion and, 55–57, 222 note 49
Giurgola and, 140
good-life, 42
Grays and, 119
heroic, 47
high seriousness of, 181
Humana Building and, 160–67
hypermodernism and, xii
Jencks and, 138
Johnson and, 139–40
Koolhaas and, 183
Krier and, 130, 133
Le Corbusier and, 55, 58–59, 62, 84, 105, 115
Mies and, 51, 54, 84, 160–62
minimalism and, 170
Nelson and, 61–65, 80, 88, 150, 181
New York Five and, 2–3, 106–11, 115, 117, 119, 201
Nordic, 113
Portland and, 141, 143, 145, 206
Princeton and, 81, 83–84, 86, 89–92, 98, 104, 108–9, 185
Rossi and, 168
Roush and, 44, 46–47, 52, 54, 65
Rowe and, 130, 181
Rudofsky and, 52
SOM and, 167
space value and, 78
Swifton Village Apartments and, 48
teaching, 56, 118–20
Team X and, 59, 83–84, 89
utopianism and, 92, 207
Wolfe on, 154
zone of silence and, xi
Mohney, David 205
monographs 157, 165, 183, 187, 224 note 42, 226 note 21
Moore, Charles x, 108–10, 119, 138, 141, 155
Moore, Henry 50
Moore Lyndon Turnbull Whitaker 135
Moore-Rogger-Hofflander condominium x
Morandi, Giorgio 79, 126, 197, 202
Morelli, Giovanni 73
Moretti, Luigi 67
Moss, Eric Owen 111, 155
Mr. Chas and Lisa Sue Meet the Pandas (Lebowitz) 188
Mrs. Gates's Dancing School 31–32
M. Sells & Company 17
Muschamp, Herbert 2, 184, 187

Museum of Modern Art, New York x, 2, 52, 90–94, 99, 105–6, 139, 148, 158, 183, 194
Musho, Ted 64, 67–68, 204, 223 note 13

Naegele, Daniel 193
National City Tower *plate 42*
National Governors Association 188
National Livestock Exchange 17, 19
National Mall 29
Nave, George 19
Nazis 29, 48, 76, 92, 130, 227 note 71
Neilson, Peter Hague 161
Neiman Marcus 173
Nelson, George 61–65, 80, 88, 150, 181
neoclassicism 69, 128
Nervi, Pier Luigi 67
Newark Museum 99, 158, 167, 182
New City show 91, 93
New Urbanism 10, 205
New York Coliseum 167
New York Five 2–3, 106–11, 115, 117, 119, 201, 225 note 104
New York School 50, 225 note 104, 228 note 48
Niccolini, Julian 149
Nichols, Karen Wheeler 7, 154, 220 note 33, 220 note 36, 227 note 74
   Claghorn House and, 123–24, 126–27
   Fargo-Moorhead Bridge and, 135–36
   Graves's memorial and, 209
   increased projects of, 187
   office procedures and, 166
   Portland's fiscal conservatism and, 141
   Whitney Museum and, 158, 180
Noguchi, Isamu 50
Nolli, Giambattista 116
Notre Dame du Haut 59
Nouvel, Jean 206

Obama, Barack 203, 223 note 16
O'Brien, Thomas 192
Ockman, Joan 190
O'Hara, Frank 62
Owings, Nathaniel 65
Oyster Bay, New York 98

Padua 75
painting
   abstract, *plate 2*
   Alessi teakettle and, 14
   Archaic Landscape and, *plate 65*
   Botticelli and, 116
   Brilliant and, 70

Corot and, 104
   Cubism and, 26 (*see also* Cubism)
   de Kooning and, 50, 77, 94, 197
   Graves and, *plate 65*, 9, 14, 24, 26, 38, 50–51, 66, 71, 94, 97–98, 124, 170, 185–86, 188, 197, 202
   Indianapolis Museum of Art and, 24
   Le Corbusier and, 58
   Meier and, 9
   murals and, *plate 19*, 94, 97–98, 103, 108, 113, 117, 149, 194, 197, 226 note 21
   Nelson and, 62
   The Painting and, 202
   Picasso and, 24, 26, 58, 79, 94–95, 126, 175
   Pollock and, 50
   Postmodernism and, 143
   Poussin and, 57–58, 139, 188
   Rome and, 70–71, 79
   Transammonia and, *plate 19*, 117, 226 note 21
   watercolors and, 49, 71
Palais Garnier 56
Paley, Babe 155
Palladio, Andrea 83
Pantheon *plate 6*, 68, 79
Pappagallo's 74–75
Parth, Wolfgang 130
Parthenon 37–38, 75, 95
Peeps 201
Peirce, Charles Sanders 116
Pei, I. M. 148, 165, 167
Pelli, Cesar 46, 158, 160–61, 167
Penn Station 92
People magazine 172
Pepsi-Cola Building 65, 139
Pevsner, Nikolaus 47
Piano, Renzo 180
Piazza Barberini 68
Piazza Navona 68
Piazza Venezia 67
Picasso, Pablo 24, 26, 58, 79, 94–95, 126, 175
Pioneer Square 141, 146
Piranesi, Giovanni Battista 30, 31, 72, 116, 223 note 13
Plater-Zyberk, Elizabeth 10–11, 205
Plaza Hotel, Manhattan 157
Plečnik, Jože 185
Plocek House *plate 26*, 134, 136, 149, 226 note 58
Pollock, Jackson 50–51
Polshek Partnership 167
Pompeii 71, 74, 79
Pop Art 181
pop culture 59, 64, 109, 116
Pope Paul V 72
Popper, Karl 92
Portland Building 187
   Belluschi and, 143
   competition for, 140–43, *144*

completion of, *plate 31*
   controversy over, 141–48
   CUNY symposium and, 206
   Deconstructivist Architecture show and, 183
   fiscal conservatism for, 141–42
   Gehry and, 184
   Goldschmidt and, 140, 145
   Ivancie and, 145–47, 227 note 8
   Jencks and, 146
   Johnson and, 140, 142–43, 147
   limited budget for, 141, 145
   lobby of, *144*
   McCready and, 145–46
   Modernism and, 141, 143, 145, 206
   office environment of, 147
   Postmodernism and, 1, 140–48, 162–63, 183, 206
   reactions to design of, 143
   sketches for, *plate 30*
   Wundram and, 140, 145, 227 note 74
Portlandia statue 142, 147
Portoghesi, Paolo 151
Posner, Donald 78
Postmodernism 182
   appropriateness and, 179
   Arnold W. Brunner Memorial Prize, 139
   Bunshaft and, 139
   Cadwallader and, 149
   Cohen on, x
   contradictions in, 207–8
   CUNY symposium and, 205
   Deconstructivist Architecture and, 183
   decreasing popularity of, 184–85
   Disney and, 177–79
   facade as subject and, 141
   fading favor of, ix–x
   hesitation of, x–xi
   Humana Building and, 160–67, 161
   human scale and, 142
   hypermodernism and, xii
   increasing popularity of, 150–54, 170
   industrial design and, 181
   Jencks and, 137–38, 146, 185
   Johnson and, 139–40, 142–43, 176, 185
   notional populism of, 145
   Plater-Zyberk and, 10
   Portland Building and, 1, 140–48, 162–63, 183, 206
   pseudo-history of, 2
   real estate development and, xii
   remaining viability of, 187, 205–6
   Rossi and, 168
   Rowe and, 179, 181, 183
   SOM and, 167
   Sunar and, 150
   sustained viability of, 207–8

use of term, 218 note 5
   Venturi and, 91, 108–9, 115, 138, 142, 151–52, 158, 176–78, 181, 190
Poussin, Nicolas 57–58, 139, 188
presenza del passato, La (The Presence of the Past) exhibition 151
Princeton Art Museum 82
Princeton Community Village 101, 119, 127
Princeton School of Architecture 80, 90, 93
Princeton University
   Allen and, 185
   Benacerraf House and, *plate 15*, 99, 103, 106, 110, 118, 120
   CASE and, 89–92, 94, 99, 105–8, 130
   Claghorn House and, *plate 20*, 102, 118, 120, 123, 126–27
   conservatism of, 81
   Eisenman and, 194
   Fitzgerald on, 81
   Frampton and, 99
   Goheen and, 89, 93
   Graves's teaching at, 80–95, 103, 108, 113–17, 124, 126, 138, 158, 175–76, 191, 193–94, 205, 225 note 8
   Holloway and, 71
   improving academic culture of, 113, 115
   Kennedy-era America and, 81
   Krier and, 133
   Labatut and, 81–82, 117, 176
   Lebowitz and, 188
   McLaughlin and, 81, 89, 93
   Modernism and, 81, 83–84, 86, 89–92, 98, 104, 108–9, 185
   progressivism of, 113
   Richardson Auditorium and, 208
   stagnant architectural program of, 81–82
   tenure and, 35, 138
   Wageman project and, 117–18
Princeton University Medical Center 6–8, 10, 196
Pritzker Prize 190, 194, 206
Progressive Architecture Design Award 119, 136, 190
Progressive Architecture magazine 103–4, 119, 148
Prud'hon, Pierre-Paul 188
Pruitt-Igoe x
Pulitzer Prize 70
Purdue University 37, 39, 66

Queen Anne style 118

Reagan, Nancy 156
Reagan, Ronald 148, 155–56, 183, 184
reductivism 47, 56

Reed, C. Lawson, Jr. 44, 221 note 12
Reeve, Christopher 8
Rembrandt van Rijn 26
Rhode Island School of Design 118, 199
Rice University 194
Richard Driehaus Award 190
Richardson Auditorium 208
Robert F. Carr Memorial Chapel of St. Savior 45–47
Robertson, Jaquelin x, 108, 165, 170, 225 note 104
Roche, Kevin 167
Rockefeller Center 167
Rockefeller family 70, 74, 100, 103–4, 119
Roma Interrotta exhibition plate 29, 137
Roman Forum 68, 72
Rome
   American Academy in, 64, 66–71, 74, 91, 101, 116, 137
   Basilica of Maxentius and, plate 5, 72
   Campus Martius and, 68
   Capitoline Hill and, 68
   Castel Sant'Angelo and, 68
   Colosseum of, 67, 72
   design tourism in, 66–83, 94–95, 101, 116
   drawing and, plate 3, plate 4, 72, 74, 78–79, 170
   as Eternal City, 69
   Fontana del Tritone and, 177
   Forum and, 68, 72
   Grand Tour and, 73–77, 80, 95
   group dinners in, 70–71
   influence of on Graves, 66–83, 94–95, 101, 116, 134, 137, 139, 163, 170, 177, 190, 203–4, 223 note 13, 227 note 70
   moonlight tour of, 67–68
   Olympics in, 67
   painting and, 70–71, 79
   Pantheon and, plate 6, 68, 79
   Piazza Venezia and, 67
   Saint Peter's Basilica and, 68
   sketches of, 72
   studio number 9 and, 69–70
   Trastevere and, 67
   Trevi Fountain and, 68
Rome Prize 65, 88
Roosevelt, Franklin D. 29
Root, John Wellborn 69
Rossi, Aldo 108, 170
   anti-Modernism of, 168
   de Chirico and, 185
   Japan projects and, 182
   power station and, 168–69
   Postmodernism and, 151
   Pritzker Prize and, 179
   San Cataldo Cemetery and, 169
   Venice Biennale and, 150, 152
   Whitney Museum and, 175, 179
Rothert, Lois Hickman

Hanselmann 35–36, 41, 78, 94–98, 102, 105
Roush, Lucille 44, 53
Roush, Raymond E., Jr.
   architecture trips of, 44–47, 53
   background of, 43–44
   Breuer and, 43, 44, 47, 54
   Cincinnati house of, 43
   creative satisfaction and, 66
   death of, 164
   design tourism and, 45–47
   European architecture and, 43–44
   as hippie, 44, 52
   influence of, 43–47, 49, 54, 60, 65, 93–94, 128, 164
   Jacobs House and, 49–51
   Merkel on, 44
   Mies and, 45–47
   Modernism and, 44, 46–47, 52, 54, 65
   Strauss and, 44, 198
Rowe, Colin 137
   appropriateness concept and, 179
   CASE and, 89–92, 94, 99, 105–8, 130
   Collage City and, 130
   Deconstructivist Architecture and, 183
   drinking of, 129, 226 note 49
   Eisenman and, 80, 83–84
   Five Architects and, 107
   Grays and, 130, 133
   as guest critic, 194
   influence of, 130, 176
   Krier and, 133–34
   Modernism and, 130, 181
   Popper and, 92
   Postmodernism and, 179, 183
   Silow and, 113
   Smithson and, 84
   Team X and, 83–84, 89
   Venturi and, 176
   as visiting Princeton critic, 85
Rowe, Tom 187, 194
Rudofsky, Bernard 52
Rykwert, Joseph 101, 130

Saarinen, Eero xii, 45–46, 150
Saarinen, Eliel 45
Sagrada Familia 76
St. Coletta of Greater Washington plate 56, 200
St. Gallen 77
Saint Peter's Basilica 68
Salisbury Cathedral 77
Salone del Mobile xi, 151
San Cataldo Cemetery 169
San Juan Capistrano Public Library plate 38, 179
San Pietro 72
San Remo 62
Santa Maria del Loreto 72
Sant'Ivo alla Sapienza 72
Sapper, Richard 152

Sartogo, Piero 137
Sartre, Jean-Paul 27
Scarface (film) 155
Schinkel, Karl Friedrich 134, 218 note 5
Schnabel, Julian 158
Schoenberg Church 77
Schroeder, Clyde 135
Schulman House plate 21, plate 22, 120–22, 125
Scott Brown, Denise 115, 158, 176
Scully, Vincent 39, 92, 108, 118, 162, 165
sculpture
   Brilliant and, 70
   categorization of, 73
   Graves's teaching methods and, 116
   Grounds for Sculpture and, 205
   Humana Building and, 162
   Jacobs House and, 49–50
   Le Corbusier and, 57, 76, 88, 116
   Medici Fountain and, 136
   Newark Museum and, 99
   Portland Building and, 142, 147
   Rockefeller House and, 100
   Soldiers and Sailors Monument and, 29
   Unité d'habitation and, 76
Segway transportation device 197
Seinfeld, Jerry 3
Sekler, Eduard F. 222 note 49
Serlio, Sebastiano 73
Sert, Josep Lluís 54–61, 65–66, 71, 84–85, 97, 115
Shannon Graves Commission Company 32
Shklovsky, Viktor 27
SHoP Architects 206
showrooms plate 32, 149–51
Siegel, Robert 107, 117
Silow, Sven 113
Skidmore Owings & Merrill (SOM) 65, 139, 150, 167, 183, 185
Skyline magazine 146–47
Slice 204
Smithson, Alison 47
Smithson, Peter 47, 84
Snow White and the Seven Dwarfs (film) 178
Snyderman, Joy 102
Snyderman, Sanford 102
Snyderman House plate 17, plate 18, 102–5, 117–18, 126, 159
Soane, John 163, 188
Soldiers and Sailors Monument 28, 29, 31, 58
Soltan, Jerzy 58, 59
Sorkin, Michael 165
Sottsass, Ettore 151–52
Space, Time, and Architecture (Giedion) 55–57, 222 note 49

Spain 1, 76–77, 90, 161, 184
Spanish-American War 29
Spanish Colonial style 179
Spanish Pavilion 58
Spanish Steps 68
Speer, Albert 29, 48, 130
Speyer Cathedral 77
Spielberg, Steven 176
Stamp, Jimmy xi
Stanley Tigerman and Associates 135
starchitects xii–xiii, 2, 184, 208
Starck, Philippe 204
statuary 122, 128, 142, 147, 177
Steinberg, Saul 55
Stelfox, Sarah Graves 4, 9, 16, 78, 88, 92, 96, 101–2, 112, 128, 164, 209, 220 note 33
Stella, Frank 26, 64
Stephens, Suzanne 103–4
Stern, Robert A. M. x, 113, 117, 141, 226 note 53
   Architectural League of New York and, 91
   CASE and, 91, 108
   CUNY symposium and, 205–6
   Denver Public Library and, 186
   Eisner and, 178
   Five on Five and, 109
   Graves's memorial and, 209
   Harvard Club and, 167
   high-rises style of, 206
   Johnson and, 224 note 61
   on clothing opinions of Graves, 154
   Rossi and, 179
Stevens, Wallace 229 note 97
Stirling, James 151, 178
Stone, Edward Durell xii, 64–65
Stonehenge 77
strabismus 25–27, 41, 126, 220 note 33, 220 note 36
Strada Novissima 150, 151
Strasbourg 77
Strauss, Carl 42–44, 47, 49, 53–54, 56, 65–66, 198
Strum, Donald plate 35, 153–54, 191, 199
Stryker collection plate 58, plate 59, plate 60, 199–200
Sullivan, Louis 47
Sunar plate 32
Sunar-Hauserman Inc. 149
Surrealism 8, 147, 169, 185
Swan and Dolphin Resort plate 46, plate 47, 177–78, 203, 211–12
Swid Powell 181, 191
symmetry
   Asplund Problem and, 114–15
   Chem-Fleur and, 134
   Claghorn House and, 123
   Denver Public Library and, 186
   Fargo-Moorhead Bridge and, 136

human body and, 151
  Krier and, 133–34, 141
  Le Corbusier and, 54, 57, 97
  Miesian, 64
  Modernism and, 47, 133
  Plocek House and, 134
  Portland Building and, 141
  Schulman House and, 121
  Sert and, 56–57, 66
  showrooms and, 149
  Whitney Museum and, 165, 175
Szathmary, Arthur 89, 224
  note 28

Tanager Gallery 63
Target Corporation *plate 52, plate 53, plate 54*, 3, 5, 9, 11, 191–93, 199–202
Taubman, A. Alfred 158
Tea and Coffee Piazza 152
teakettles *plate 34, plate 35, plate 52, plate 53, plate 54*, 3, 14, 152–53, 164, 173, 180, 192–93, 205
Team Disney Headquarters 168, 178, 187
Team X 59, 83–84, 89
Tedrick, David 173
TED talks 202
Tempietto 72
Ten Books on Architecture (Vitruvius Pollo) 73
Thacker, Bob 191
The Architects' Collaborative (TAC) 59–60, 63, 80, 83
"Thematic Studies in Architecture" seminar 193
Tigerman, Stanley x, 135, 141, 150, 151–52, 178, 225 note 104
Time magazine 64, 147, 162
Time Warner Center 229
  note 90
Tishman, John 177
toasters *plate 53, plate 54*, 3, 192
Topaz Medallion 190
Trachtenberg, Marvin 146
Transammonia murals *plate 19, 117*, 226 note 21
Trenton Bath House 221
  note 32
Trevi Fountain 68
Tripp, Evelyn 52
trulli houses *plate 7, 51*–52, 56, 75, 95, 142, 200, 221 note 32
Trump, Donald 48
Turkey 74–76
Turtles of Aegina 71

UCLA School of Architecture and Urban Design 154–55
Ungers, O. M. 151
Union County Nature and Science Museum 119, 158
Union Station 16–17
Union Stockyards 17
United States National

Park Service 191
University of Cincinnati *plate 48, 38, 41–43*, 46, 49, 51–52, 54, 56, 60, 64, 71, 182
University of Michigan 52
University of Texas 106
University of Virginia 170, 175
urbanism 10, 90, 146, 152, 183, 205
utopianism 92, 207

Vanderbilt family 155, 167
Vanna Venturi House x
Van Varick, Rob 199–200
Venice Biennale of Architecture 150, 151–52
Venturi, Robert x, 231 note 76
  aesthetics of, 176
  background of, 91
  CASE and, 91
  Complexity and Contradiction in Architecture and, 108, 115, 176
  decorated sheds of, 142
  Eisner and, 176–78
  Gordon Wu Hall and, 176, 231 note 76
  Grays and, 108–9, 115, 138
  MoMA and, 158
  Pop Art and, 181
  Postmodernism and, 91, 108–9, 115, 138, 142, 151–52, 158, 176–78, 181, 190
  pride of, 176
  Pritzker Prize and, 190
  Rowe and, 176
  Scott Brown and, 115, 158, 176
  Swan and Dolphin Hotels and, 176–77
  Venice Biennale and, 150, 152
  Whitney Museum and, 158
Verona 75
Via del Corso 68, 79
Vicenza 75
Victoria and Albert Museum xi
Vidler, Anthony *plate 9*, 90–91, 106, 113, 130
Vienna Secession 185
Villa Medici 70
Villa Snellman 113–15, 122, 129
Villa Stein 55, 116
Viterbo 75
Vitruvius vi, 37, 73
Volner, Ian ix–xiii
von Eckardt, Wolf 147
von Furstenberg, Diane *plate 39, 157*
Vreeland, Thomas 119
V'soske 149

Wageman House 117–18
Waldman, Peter 30, 85, 100, 109, 164, 209, 223 note 16
Wall House 125
Walmart 192

Warehouse, the *plate 27, 39*, 133, 155, 159
  Art Deco and, 128
  buying of, 112
  completion of, 188
  dining room of, *plate 62*
  exterior work on, 163
  final phase of, 197
  Graves's new language and, 128
  Graves's death and, 205
  home studio of, *plate 66*
  interior work on, 163
  kitchen entrance of, *156*
  master plan for, 128–29
  as museum, 163
  original purpose of, 4
  pets in, 163–64
  poor condition of, 112–13
  as refuge, 5, 11, 190, 195
  renovations to, 127–29, 163
  retrofitting of, 196, 202
  Rowe incident at, 129–30
  sewer moratorium and, 112, 127
  upstairs study of, *plate 61*
  vertigo of, 128–29
  Whitney group and, 158
Warhol, Andy 139, 181
Washington Monument *plate 55, 2, 29*, 32, 191–92, 231 note 61
Washington Square 62–63
Watchung Mountains 98–99
Watkin, David 48
We Have Never Been Modern (Latour) ix
Wesselmann, Tom 64
Wexner Center for the Arts 172–73
White, Robert Carey 100
White City 68–69
Whites 108, 225 note 104
  Four Days in May and, 225 note 91
  Krier and, 134
  Le Corbusier and, 118
  UCLA School of Architecture and Design and, 154–55
Whitney, David 167–68
Whitney Museum of American Art *plate 45, 172*, 190
  Ad Hoc Committee to Save the Whitney and, 165
  aging structure of, 158
  Community Board and, 175
  Armstrong and, 158–59
  Breuer and, 158–59, 164–65, 175, 179–80, 189
  controversy over, 165–66
  design competition for, 158
  diptychs and, 164–65, 175
  Gwathmey Siegel and, 158
  importance of as client, 158–59, 175
  Koolhaas and, 183
  Landmarks Commission and, 165–66, 175
  long schedule for, 159

as Metropolitan Museum of Art annex, 180
  new scheme for, *plate 44, 175*
  project cancellation of, 179–80
  proposal presentation of, *plate 43, 164–65*
  Scott Brown and, 158
  Scully and, 165
  third proposal for, 175, 179
  Venturi and, 158
Wigley, Mark 183
Williams, Ted 173
Winckelmann, Johann Joachim 73–74
Wiseman, Carter 147
Wittenborn, George 106
Wolfe, Tom 154, 205
Woman with a Blue Hat (Picasso) 175
World's Columbian Exposition 68, 178
World War I 54, 74
World War II 29, 36–37, 43, 47, 74
World War Memorial 29, 37
Wounded Warrior Project *plate 63, 203*
Wright, Frank Lloyd xii, 105, 139
  background of, 39
  furniture and, 62, 150
  horizontal volumes and, 47
  Jencks and, 185
  Johnson Wax Headquarters and, 46, 62
  Meier and, 64
  midwestern roots of, 39
  Mies and, 65
  Modernist interiors and, 105
  original ornament of, 47
  as philosopher-king, 39
  popularity of, 148
  SOM and, 65
Wundram, Edward 140, 145, 227 note 74

XV Triennale di Milano 108

Zurich 77

IMAGES ARE COURTESY OF MICHAEL GRAVES
ARCHITECTURE & DESIGN (MGA&D),
UNLESS OTHERWISE NOTED

Peter Aaron © OTTO Archive: **plates 21, 22, 42**   Steven Brooke
Studios for MGA&D (printed with the permission of the Walt Disney
World Swan and Dolphin Resort): **plate 47**   Steven Brooke Studios
for MGA&D: **plate 48**   Peter Carl: **page 114**   Eisenman Architects:
pages *vii–viii*, 107   © Fondation Le Corbusier / ARS: **page 55**   Scott
Frances © OTTO Archive: **page 87 (bottom)**   Coroson Hirschfeld,
from Jayne Merkel, *In Its Place: The Architecture of Carl Strauss and
Ray Roush* (Cincinnati, OH: The Contemporary Arts Center, 1984):
page 43   Coroson Hirschfeld, from Jayne Merkel, *Michael Graves &
Riverbend: A Summer Pavilion for the Cincinnati Orchestra* (Cincinnati,
OH: The Contemporary Arts Center, 1987): **page 50**   Illinois Institute
of Technology's University Archives: **page 45**   *Indianapolis Star*
(originally published on February 17, 1924): **page 16**   *Indianapolis Star*
(originally published on November 11, 1927): **page 19**   *Indianapolis Star*
(originally published on March 2, 1931): **page 21**   Indiana Historical
Society: **pages 17, 28**   Timothy Hursley: **plate 51**   Scott Hyde for
MGA&D: **plate 33**   T. Kitajima © GA Photographers: **plate 18**   Léon
Krier: **page 131**   Robert Lautman for MGA&D: **plate 55**   Laurin
McCracken © MGA&D: **plate 15**   Norman McGrath: **plate 26**
Metropolitan Home © Meredith Corporation: **page 156**   Richard
Meier & Partners Architects: **page 87 (top)**   MGA&D, printed with
the permission of the Walt Disney World Swan and Dolphin Resort:
plate 46   David Mohney for MGA&D: **page 83**   Douglass Paschall
and William Taylor for MGA&D: **plates 38, 39, 41**   Tim Street-Porter
for MGA&D: **plate 32**   Stryker: **plates 57–59**   Tigerman McCurry
Architects: **page 141**   Leandro Viana: **page 206**   Ian Volner: **page 169**
Tom Yee / *House & Garden*, April 1973 © Condé Nast: **plate 14**